Begin to Code with JavaScript

Rob Miles

BEGIN TO CODE WITH JAVASCRIPT
Published with the authorization of Microsoft Corporation by:
Pearson Education, Inc.

ISBN-13: 978-0-13-687072-2
ISBN-10: 0-13-687072-4

Library of Congress Control Number: 2021941656

1 2021

TRADEMARKS
Microsoft and the trademarks listed at http://www.microsoft.com on the "Trademarks" webpage are trademarks of the Microsoft group of companies. All other marks are property of their respective owners.

WARNING AND DISCLAIMER
Every effort has been made to make this book as complete and as accurate as possible, but no warranty or fitness is implied. The information provided is on an "as is" basis. The author, the publisher, and Microsoft Corporation shall have neither liability nor responsibility to any person or entity with respect to any loss or damages arising from the information contained in this book or from the use of the programs accompanying it.

SPECIAL SALES
For information about buying this title in bulk quantities, or for special sales opportunities (which may include electronic versions; custom cover designs; and content particular to your business, training goals, marketing focus, or branding interests), please contact our corporate sales department at corpsales@pearsoned.com or (800) 382-3419.

For government sales inquiries, please contact governmentsales@pearsoned.com.

For questions about sales outside the U.S., please contact intlcs@pearson.com.

Editor-in-Chief
Brett Bartow

Executive Editor
Loretta Yates

Development Editor
Rick Kughen

Sponsoring Editor
Charvi Arora

Managing Editor
Sandra Schroeder

Senior Project Editor
Tracey Croom

Copy Editor
Rick Kughen

Indexer
James Minken

Proofreader
Scout Festa

Technical Editor
John E. Ray

Editorial Assistant
Cindy Teeters

Cover Designer
Twist Creative, Seattle

Compositor
Danielle Foster

Graphics
Danielle Foster

To Imogen

About the author

Rob Miles spent more than 30 years teaching programming at the University of Hull in the United Kingdom. He now runs a company promoting community uptake of computer technology. He's a Microsoft MVP with a passion for programming and creating new things. If he had any spare time, he'd spend it writing even more code. He loves building devices and then switching them on to see what they do. He reckons that programming is the most creative thing you can learn how to do. He claims to know a lot of really good jokes, but nobody has ever heard him tell one. If you want an insight into the Wacky World™ of Rob Miles, you can read his blog at www.robmiles.com and follow him on Twitter via @RobMiles.

Contents at a glance

Contents

Part 1: The world of JavaScript

Part 2: Coding with JavaScript

5 Making decisions in programs 144

6 Repeating actions in programs 176

Part 3: Useful JavaScript

Introduction

Programming is the most creative thing you can learn how to do. Why? If you learn to paint, you can create pictures. If you learn to play the violin, you can make music, but if you learn to program, you can create entirely new experiences (and you can make pictures and music, too, if you want). Once you've started on the programming path, there's no limit to where you can go. There are always new devices, technologies, and marketplaces where you can use your programming skills.

Think of this book as your first step on a journey to programming enlightenment. The best journeys are undertaken with a destination in mind, and the destination of this journey is "usefulness." By the end of this book, you will have the skills and knowledge to write useful programs and make them available to anyone in the world.

But first, a word of warning: I would not say that learning to write programs is easy. This is for two reasons:

If I tell you that it's easy, and you still can't do it, you might feel bad about this (and rather cross with me).

If I tell you it's easy and you manage to do it, you might think that it isn't worth doing.

Learning to program is not easy. It's a kind of difficult that you might not have seen before. Programming is all about detail and sequencing. You must learn how the computer does things and how to express what you want it to do.

Imagine that you were lucky enough to be able to afford your own personal chef. At the start, you would have to explain things like, "If it is sunny outside, I like orange juice and a grapefruit for breakfast, but if it is raining, I'd like a bowl of porridge and a big mug of coffee." Occasionally, your chef would make mistakes. Perhaps you would get a black coffee rather than the latte that you wanted. However, over time, you would add more detail to your instructions until your chef knew exactly what to do.

A computer is like a chef who doesn't even know how to cook. Rather than saying "make me a coffee," you would have to say, "Take the brown powder from the coffee bag and add it to hot water." Then you would have to explain how to make hot water and how you must be careful with the kettle and so on. This is hard work.

It turns out that the key to success as a programmer is much the same as for many other endeavors. To become a world-renowned violin player, you will have to practice a lot. The same is true for programming. You must spend a lot of time working on your programs to acquire code-writing skills. However, the good news is that just as a violin player really enjoys making the instrument sing, making a computer do exactly what you want turns out to be a very rewarding experience. It gets even more enjoyable when you see other people using programs that you've written and finding them useful and fun to use.

How this book fits together

I've organized this book in three parts. Each part builds on the previous one with the aim of turning you into a successful programmer. We start off discovering the environment in which JavaScript programs run. Then we learn the fundamentals of programming and we finish by making some properly useful (and fun) programs.

Part 1: The world of JavaScript

The first part gets you started. You'll discover the environment in which JavaScript programs run and learn how to create web pages containing JavaScript programs.

Part 2: Coding with JavaScript

Part 2 describes the features of the JavaScript that you use to create programs that work on data. You will pick up some fundamental programming skills that apply to a wide range of other languages and that get you thinking about what it is that programs actually do. You'll find out how to break large programs into smaller elements and how you can create custom data types that reflect the specific problem being solved.

Part 3: Useful JavaScript

Now that you can make JavaScript programs, it's time to have some fun with them. You'll discover how to create good-looking applications, learn how to make programs that are secure and reliable, and finish off with a bit of game development.

How you will learn

In each chapter, I will tell you a bit more about programming. I'll show you how to do something, and then I'll invite you to make something of your own by using what you've learned. You'll never be more than a page or so away from doing something or making something unique and personal. After that, it's up to you to make something amazing!

You can read the book straight through if you like, but you'll learn much more if you slow down and work with the practical parts along the way. Like learning to ride a bicycle, you'll learn by doing. You must put in the time and practice to learn how to do it. But this book will give you the knowledge and confidence to try your hand at programming, and it will also be around to help you if your programming doesn't turn out as you expected. Here are some elements in the book that will help you learn by doing:

MAKE SOMETHING HAPPEN

Yes, the best way to learn things is by doing, so you'll find "Make Something Happen" elements throughout the text. These elements offer ways for you to practice your programming skills. Each starts with an example and then introduces some steps you can try on your own. Everything you create will run on Windows, macOS, or Linux.

CODE ANALYSIS

A great way to learn how to program is by looking at code written by others and working out what it does (and sometimes why it doesn't do what it should). The book contains more than 150 sample programs for you to look at. In this book's "Code Analysis" challenges, you'll use your deductive skills to figure out the behavior of a program, fix bugs, and suggest improvements.

WHAT COULD GO WRONG

If you don't already know that programs can fail, you'll learn this hard lesson soon after you begin writing your first program. To help you deal with this in advance, I've included "What Could Go Wrong" elements, which anticipate problems you might have and provide solutions to those problems. For example, when I introduce something new, I'll sometimes spend some time considering how it can fail and what you need to worry about when you use the new feature.

What you will need

You'll need a computer and some software to work with the programs in this book. I'm afraid I can't provide you with a computer, but in the first chapter, you'll find out how you can get started with nothing more than a computer and a web browser. Later, you'll discover how to use the Visual Studio Code editor to create JavaScript programs.

Using a PC or laptop

You can use Windows, macOS, or Linux to create and run the programs in the text. Your PC doesn't have to be particularly powerful, but these are the minimum specifications I'd recommend:

- A 1 GHz or faster processor, preferably an Intel i5 or better.

- At least 4 gigabytes (GB) of memory (RAM), but preferably 8 GB or more.

- 256 GB hard drive space. (The JavaScript frameworks and Visual Studio Code installations take about 1 GB of hard drive space.)

There are no specific requirements for the graphics display, although a higher-resolution screen will enable you to see more when writing your programs.

Using a mobile device

You can run JavaScript programs on a mobile phone or tablet by visiting the web pages in which the programs are held. There are also some applications that can be used to create and run JavaScript programs, but my experience has been that a laptop or desktop computer is a better place to work.

Using a Raspberry Pi

If you want to get started in the most inexpensive way possible, you can use a Raspberry Pi running the Raspbian operating system. This has a Chromium-compatible browser and is also capable of running Visual Studio Code.

Downloads

In every chapter in this book, I'll demonstrate and explain programs that teach you how to begin to program—and you can then use that code to create programs of your own. I've made a few video walkthroughs for some crucial tasks. The book text will contain screenshots that you can use, but these can go out of date. Follow the links to the walkthroughs to get the latest steps to follow. You can download the book's sample code and video walkthroughs from the following page:

MicrosoftPressStore.com/BeginCodeJavaScript/downloads

Follow the instructions you'll find in Chapter 1 to install the sample programs and code. You'll discover how to use GitHub to make your own copy of the sample programs. You can then use GitHub to publish JavaScript-enabled web pages for anyone in the world to view. You will need to connect to the Internet and create a free GitHub account to do this. You can browse the GitHub site and all the examples here:

www.begintocodewithjavascript.com

Video walkthroughs

You can also find the walkthroughs here:

https://bit.ly/3wEn6zX

Acknowledgments

Thanks to Mary for the cups of tea and Immy for the distraction.

Errata, updates, and book support

We've made every effort to ensure the accuracy of this book and its companion content. You can access updates to this book—in the form of a list of submitted errata and their related corrections—at

MicrosoftPressStore.com/BeginCodeJavaScript/errata

If you discover an error not already listed, please submit it to us at the same page.

For additional book support and information, please visit

http://www.MicrosoftPressStore.com/Support

Please note that product support for Microsoft software and hardware is not offered through the previous addresses. For help with Microsoft software or hardware, go to

http://support.microsoft.com

Stay in touch

Let's keep the conversation going! We're on Twitter:

http://twitter.com/MicrosoftPress

Part 1
The world of JavaScript

We are going to start our journey by looking at the world of JavaScript. We'll begin by considering just what it is that a programming language does. Then we'll investigate the JavaScript programming language and discover how JavaScript programs get to run on your computer. We'll learn how web pages provide an environment for JavaScript and how to use Hypertext Markup Language (HTML) and Cascading Style Sheets (CSS) to create containers for our JavaScript programs. We'll discover just how powerful modern web browsers are as software development tools and how to have a conversation with JavaScript from within a browser. We'll also learn how to manage our software source code and share it with others.

1
Running JavaScript

What you will learn

Programmers have a set of tools and techniques they use when they create programs. In this chapter, you're going to discover how JavaScript programs run on a computer. You'll also have your first of many conversations with the JavaScript command prompt and investigate your first JavaScript program. Finally, you'll download the Git and Visual Studio Code tools and the example programs for this book and do some simple editing.

What is JavaScript?

Before we go off and look at some JavaScript, it's worth considering just what we are running. JavaScript is a *programming language*. In other words, it's a language that you use to write programs. A program is a set of instructions that tells a computer how to do something. We can't use a "proper" language like English because "proper English" is just too confusing for a computer to understand. As an example, I give you the doctor's instructions:

```
"Drink your medicine after a hot bath."
```

We would probably have a hot bath and then drink our medicine. A computer would probably drink the hot bath and then drink its medicine. You can interpret the above instructions either way because the English language allows you to write ambiguous statements. Programming languages must be designed so that instructions written using them are not open to interpretation; they must tell the computer precisely what to do. This usually means breaking actions down into a sequence of simple steps:

```
Step1: Take a hot bath
Step2: Drink your medicine
```

We can get this effect in English (as you can see above), but a programming language forces us to write instructions in this way. JavaScript is one of many programming languages that have been invented to provide humans with a way of telling the computer what to do.

In my programming career, I've learned many different languages over the years, and I confidently expect to have to learn even more in the future. None of them are perfect, and I see each of them as a tool that I would use in a particular situation, just like I would choose a different tool depending on whether I was making a hole in a brick wall, a pane of glass, or a piece of wood.

Some people get very excited when talking about the "best" programming language. I'm quite happy to discuss what makes the best programming languages, just like I'm happy to tell you all about my favorite type of car, but I don't see this as something to get worked up about. I love JavaScript for its power and the ease with which I can distribute my code. I love Python for its expressiveness and how I can create complex solutions with tiny bits of code. I love the C# programming language for the way it pushes me to produce well-structured solutions. I love the C++ programming language for the way that it gives me absolute control of hardware underneath my program. And so on. JavaScript does have things about it that make me want to tear my hair out in frustration. But that's true of the other languages, too. And all programming languages have things about them I love. But most of all, I love JavaScript for the way that I can use it to pay my bills.

PROGRAMMER'S POINT

The best programming language for you is the one that pays you the most

I think it is very fitting that the first programmer's point is one that has a strong commercial focus. Whenever I get asked which is the "best" programming language, I always say that my favorite language is the one that I get paid the most to use. It turns out that I'll write in any programming language if the price is right.

I strongly believe that you can enjoy programming in any language, and that includes JavaScript. Conversely, you can have a horrible time writing bad programs in any language. The language is just the medium which you use to express your ideas.

So, if you tell someone that you're writing JavaScript programs and they tell you that it's not a very good programming language for reasons that you don't understand, just show them how many jobs there are out there for people who can write JavaScript code.

JavaScript origins

You might think that programming languages are a bit like space rockets in that they are designed by white-coated scientists with mega-brains who get everything right the first time and always produce perfect solutions. However, this is not the case. Programming languages have been developed over the years for all kinds of reasons, including ones like, "It seemed a good idea at the time."

JavaScript was invented by Brendan Eich of Netscape Communications Corporation and first appeared in a Netscape web browser that was released at the end of 1995. The language had a variety of names before the company decided on JavaScript. It turned out to be a poor choice of name because it makes it easy to confuse JavaScript with the Java programming language, which is actually quite different from JavaScript.

JavaScript was intended as a simple way of making web pages interactive. Its name reflects the way that it was supposed to be used alongside Java applications (called *applets*) running in a web browser. However, JavaScript was extended beyond all the expectations of its creator and is now one of the most popular programming languages in the world. Whenever you visit a website, it is almost certain that you will be talking to a JavaScript program.

This book will teach you JavaScript, but actually I'm trying to turn you into a programmer. The fundamentals of program creation are the same for JavaScript and pretty much all programming languages. Once you've learned how to write JavaScript, you'll be able to transfer this skill into many other languages, including C++, C#, Visual Basic, and Python. It's a bit like the way that once you have learned to drive, you can drive any vehicle. When you are using a strange car, you just need to find out where the various switches and controls are, and then you can set off on your journey.

JavaScript and the web browser

The inventor of JavaScript intended for it to be used in a web browser, and that is where we are going to start using it. It is possible to create JavaScript programs that run outside the browser, we will consider how to do this in the third part of this text. You can use any modern browser, but the exercises in this text use a browser based on the Chromium framework. I'm using Microsoft Edge, which is available for Windows or macOS. You can use Google Chrome or the Chromium browser for Linux if you prefer.

Our first brush with JavaScript

You've reached a significant point in the process of learning how to program. You're about to begin exploring how programs work. This is a bit like opening the front door of a new apartment or house or getting into a shiny new car you've bought. It's an exciting time, so take a deep breath, find a nice cup (or glass) of something you like to drink, and settle down comfortably.

You are going to start by doing something that you've done thousands of times in the past. You are going to visit a site on the World Wide Web. But then, with a single press of a key, you're going to explore a world behind the web page and get a glimpse of the role that JavaScript plays in making it work.

 MAKE SOMETHING HAPPEN

A web page with secrets

First, you need to open your browser, and then visit the following web page, which is shown in **Figure 1-1**:

http://www.begintocodewithjavascript.com/hello

Figure 1-1 A web page with secrets

This looks like a very ordinary web page, but it holds a secret behavior that you can find by pressing the F12 key on your keyboard. **Figure 1-2** shows the Developer View.

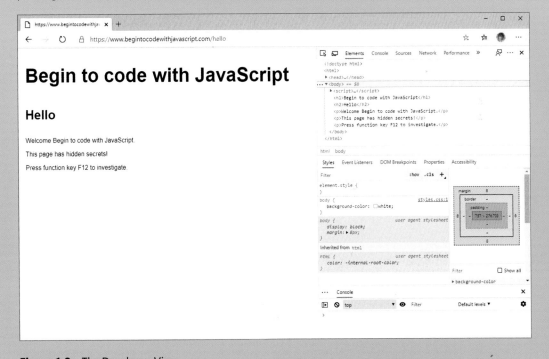

Figure 1-2 The Developer View

This is called *Developer View*. It shows all the elements that make up the web page. A complete description of everything you can do in this view would not fit in this book. Don't be worried about how complicated it all looks, we are only going to use a couple of the features. We are going to start by looking at the elements that make up the text on the page. Make sure that the Elements tab is selected as you can see in **Figure 1-2**. Then look at the text underneath, which is shown in **Figure 1-3**.

```
      Elements    Console    Sources    Network    »
<!doctype html>
<html>
  ▶ <head>…</head>
▼ <body>  == $0
    ▶ <script>…</script>
      <h1>Begin to code with JavaScript</h1>
      <h2>Hello</h2>
      <p>Welcome Begin to code with JavaScript.</p>
      <p>This page has hidden secrets!</p>
      <p>Press function key F12 to investigate.</p>
    </body>
</html>
```

Figure 1-3   Page elements

Figure 1-3 shows the elements on this page. You can see that the text that appears on the page is here. Parts of the text are enclosed in what look like formatting instructions, for example some is marked as <h1> and some as <p>. If you look back at the web page as displayed you will notice that the <h1> text is in a large heading font, whereas the <p> text is in smaller text. This is how pages are formatted. You can see how the page works, but where is the secret? To answer this, click the right-pointing arrowhead at the left of the word *script* to open this part of the view (see **Figure 1-4**).

```
      Elements    Console    Sources    Network    »
<!doctype html>
<html>
  ▶ <head>…</head>
▼ <body>  == $0
    ▼ <script>
          function doAddition(no1Number, no2Number) {
              let result = no1Number + no2Number;
              alert("Result: " + result);
          }

    </script>
      <h1>Begin to code with JavaScript</h1>
      <h2>Hello</h2>
      <p>Welcome Begin to code with JavaScript.</p>
      <p>This page has hidden secrets!</p>
      <p>Press function key F12 to investigate.</p>
    </body>
</html>
```

Figure 1-4   doAddition function

Clicking the arrow opens that part of the listing. The hidden feature is a function called doAddition. This takes two numbers, adds them together, and displays the result using an alert. Later in the text, we will go into detail of how this JavaScript works, but even at this stage, it is quite clear what is going on.

However, this function is never actually used in the web page. We can use it ourselves by entering it into the JavaScript console, which is built into the browser. This performs JavaScript statements that you type in. You can open the console by selecting the **Console** tab at the top of the window (see **Figure 1-5**).

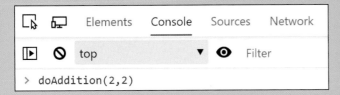

Figure 1-5   JavaScript console

This is the Console window. I've typed in the name of the function and given it two numbers to work on. When the function runs it display an alert with the result it has calculated, as shown in **Figure 1-6**.

Figure 1-6   Result alert

We can use the JavaScript console to type in other JavaScript commands. You can use JavaScript to perform calculations by just entering them. When you press the Enter key, the answer will be displayed. In fact, the console is often keen to give you an answer even before you press Enter. The console will also try to help as you type in by suggesting what you might be typing. You can accept any suggestion by using the cursor key to select the suggestion and then pressing the Tab key.

Talking to JavaScript

We can learn a little about the way JavaScript works by giving the JavaScript console some commands and considering the responses.

```
> 2+3
```

This looks like a sum, and as you might expect, you get a number for an answer

```
<-5
```

We can repeat this with something other than a number:

```
> "Rob"+" Miles"
```

Some text enclosed in double quotes is interpreted by JavaScript as a string of text, and it is perfectly happy to use + to add two strings together. Note that if you want to have a space between the two words in the sum, you have to actually put it into the strings that you add together. (In my example above, there is a space in front of the 'M' in the second word.)

```
<- "Rob Miles"
```

We can do other kinds of sums. For example, we can subtract using minus (–).

```
>  6-5
```

This produces the result that you would expect.

```
<-  1
```

JavaScript seems quite happy when we ask it to do sensible things. Now, let's try asking it to do something stupid. What do you think would happen if we tried to subtract one string from another using the following statement?

```
> "Rob"-" Miles"
```

While it seems sensible to regard + as meaning "add these strings together," there doesn't seem to be a sensible interpretation of minus (–) when you are working with strings. In other words, it is meaningless to try and subtract one string from another. If you enter this into the console, you get a strange response from JavaScript:

```
<-   NaN
```

The JavaScript console is not calling for grandma to come and sort the problem out. The value NaN means "not a number". It is a way that JavaScript indicates that the result of a calculation has no meaning. Some programming languages would display an error message and stop a program if you tried to use them to subtract one string from another. JavaScript does not work like this. It just generates a result value that means "this result is not a number" and keeps going. We will consider how to a program can manage errors like this later in the text.

And because we are talking about errors, how about asking JavaScript to do some silly math:

```
>   1/0
```

When I got my first pocket calculator, the first thing I tried to do with it was calculate one divided by zero. I was richly rewarded by a result that just kept counting upward. What do you think JavaScript will do?

```
<-   Infinity
```

JavaScript says that the result of the calculation is the value Infinity. This is another special value that is generated by JavaScript when it does calculations. Talking of calculations, how about asking JavaScript to do another one for us?

```
>   2/10+1/10
```

This calculation involves real numbers (meaning ones with a fractional part). The calculation is adding 0.2 to 0.1 (a fifth to a tenth). This should produce the result 0.3, but what we get is interesting:

```
<-   0.30000000000000004
```

This number is very, very close to 0.3 (the correct answer), but it is ever-so-slightly larger than it should be. This illustrates an important aspect of the way that computers work. Some values that we can express very easily on paper are not held exactly by the machine. This is only usually a problem if we start performing tests with the values that we calculate, such as a check to see if the calculated result above was equal to the value 0.3 might fail because of the tiny difference. Let's see if we can use JavaScript to do some things for us. How about this?

```
> alert("Danger: Will Robinson")
```

This statement doesn't calculate a result. Instead, it calls a function called `alert`. The function is provided with a string of text. It asks the browser to display the string as a message in an alert box, as shown in **Figure 1-7**.

Figure 1-7 Danger: Will Robinson

This is how the `doAddtion` function displays the result it has calculated. Finally, let's try another function called `print`:

```
> print()
```

What you will see next depends on the computer and the browser that you are using, but you should see a print window appear, which offers you the chance to print the web page. If you've ever wondered what happens when you press the **Print** button on a web page, you know now.

Congratulations. You now know how web pages work. Your browser fetches a file from the server and then follows the instructions in that file to build a page for you to look at. The file contains text that is to be displayed on the page, along with formatting instructions. A page file can also contain JavaScript program code.

The instructions that the browser follows are expressed in a language called Hypertext Markup Language (HTML). In the next chapter, we'll take a detailed look at HTML, but before we do that, we need to get some tools that will let us fetch the sample code for this book onto our computer and work with HTML and JavaScript.

Tools

You will need some software tools to get the best out of the exercises in this book. We are going to start with two, a program called Git that will manage the program files that we work on and a program called Visual Studio Code, which we will use to work on the files. Neither of these will cost you any money, and they are available for Windows, macOS, and Linux. You can follow through the printed instructions below, or you can use one of my video walkthroughs that you can find here:

https://www.begintocodewithjavascript.com/media

PROGRAMMER'S POINTS

Git and Visual Studio Code are professional tools

When you learned to ride a bike, you probably had one with training wheels. And people learning to drive a car usually start in something small and easy to handle. You are learning programming with the tools that professionals work with. This is a bit like learning to drive using a Formula 1 racing car. However, there is nothing to worry about here. A Formula 1 car might look a bit scary, but it still has a steering wheel and the usual set of pedals. And you don't have to drive it fast if you don't want to.

GitHub and Visual Studio code have a huge range of features, but you don't have to use them. Just like there are buttons on my car dashboard that I don't press because I'm not sure what they do, you don't have to know about every feature of these tools to make good use of them.

It is very sensible to start developing with "proper" tools because job recruiters are often as interested in the tools that you are familiar with as they are with the programming languages that you can work with.

Getting Git

The source code of programs that you write is stored on your computer as files of text. These files are called "source code". You work on your programs by changing the contents of these files. When I was starting out programming, I learned very quickly that you can go backward as well as forward when writing software. Sometimes, I would spend a lot of time making changes to my programs that would turn out to be a bad idea, and I would have to go back and undo them all. I solved this problem by making copies of my program code before I did any major edits. That way, if anything went bad, I could go back to my original files.

Lots of other programmers noticed this problem, too. They also noticed that if you release a program to users, it is very useful to have a "snapshot" of that code so that you can keep track of any changes that you make. The best programmers are great at being "intelligently lazy," so they created source code management (SCM) software to manage this. One of the most popular programs is called Git.

Git was created in 2005 by Linus Torvalds who was writing the Linux operating system at the time. He needed at tool that could track what he was doing and make it easy for him to work with other people. So, he created his own. Git is a professional tool and very powerful. It lets large numbers of developers work together on a single project. Different teams can work on their own versions of the code, which can them be merged. There is no need for you to use all of these powerful features, though. You're just going to use Git to keep track of our work and as a way of obtaining the example programs.

 MAKE SOMETHING HAPPEN

Install Git

I'm going to give you instructions for Windows 10. The instructions for macOS are very similar. First, you need to open your browser and visit this web page, which is also shown in **Figure 1-8**:

https://git-scm.com

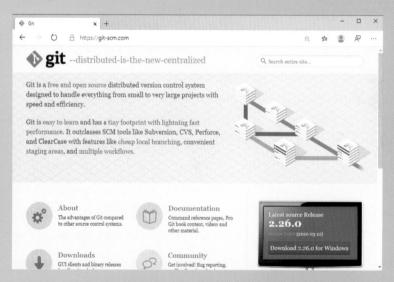

Figure 1-8   Git installation page

Follow the installation process, selecting all the defaults.

Getting Visual Studio Code

If you want to write a letter, you would use a word processor. To perform calculations, you might use a spreadsheet. Visual Studio Code is a tool that you can use to edit your program files. It can do a lot more than this, as we shall see later. But for now, we are going to use it as a super-powerful program editor. Visual Studio Code is free.

 MAKE SOMETHING HAPPEN

Install Visual Studio Code

I'm going to give you instructions for Windows 10. The instructions for macOS are very similar. First, you need to open your browser and visit this web page, which is shown in **Figure 1-9**:

https://code.visualstudio.com/Download

Figure 1-9 Visual Studio Code download page

Click the version of Visual Studio Code that you want and follow the instructions to install it. Once it is installed, you will see the start page shown in **Figure 1-10**.

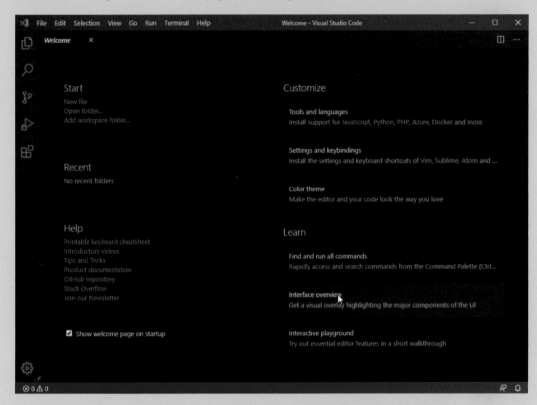

Figure 1-10   Visual Studio Start page

Now that you have Visual Studio installed, the next thing you need to do is fetch the sample files to work on.

Getting the sample files

The sample programs, along with a lot of other stuff, are stored on *GitHub*. GitHub is a service that is underpinned by the Git system. You can store your own files on GitHub (and not just programs). You can also use GitHub to host web pages containing JavaScript programs that you create. For now, we are going to just download the sample repository and edit the hello.html file that we worked with at the start of this chapter.

Clone the sample repository

A *repository* in Git is a collection of files. Whenever I start working on something new, I create a repository to hold all the files I'm going to create. I've got a private repository that contains all the text of this book. And I've made a public repository to hold the sample files. Repositories on GitHub can be accessed directly from the browser. The sample files for this book are at the repository with this URL (uniform resource locator):

https://github.com/begintocodewithjavascript/begintocodewithjavascript.github.io

If you visit this URL with your browser, you will find that you can navigate all the files, including the file `hello.html`, which we investigated earlier, and take a look at what is inside them. See **Figure 1-11**.

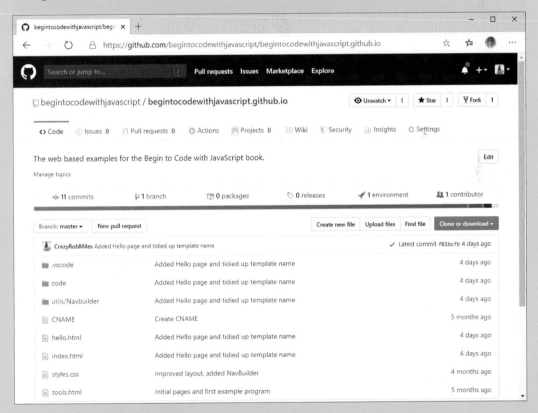

Figure 1-11   Repository home page

You can see that GitHub is keeping track of the changes that I have made to the example programs. We are going to use Visual Studio Code to clone this repository. Start Visual Studio Code and click the **Source Control** button, as shown in **Figure 1-12**.

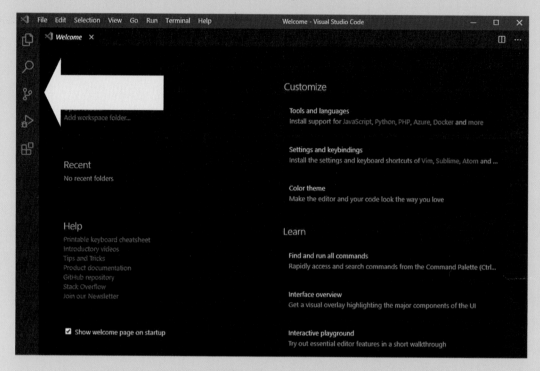

Figure 1-12   Visual Studio Source Control button

This opens the **Source Control** dialog, as shown in **Figure 1-13**. Next, click the **Clone Repository** button to begin the process of fetching a repository from GitHub.

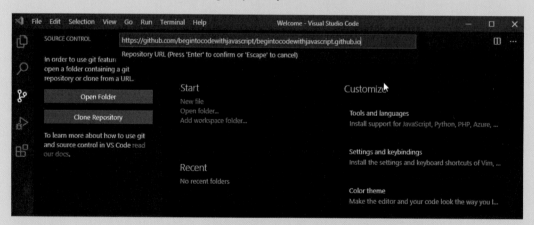

Figure 1-13   Visual Studio Code source clone repository

Visual Studio code will download the contents of the repository and store them on your machine. Enter the URL of the repository in the dialog that appears:

https://github.com/begintocodewithjavascript/begintocodewithjavascript.github.io

When you press Enter at the end of the URL, as shown in **Figure 1-14**, you will be asked where on your computer you want to put the files that are about to be copied. I suggest that you create a folder named **GitHub** in your Documents folder and use that, but you can put the repository anywhere you like. Once you've selected the folder, Visual Studio will copy all the files in the repository from the GitHub site to your computer.

Figure 1-14   Visual Studio Code repository clone complete

When all the files have been copied, Visual Studio Code will ask if you want to open the repository. Click **Open** to open it.

Congratulations, you have cloned you're first repository! Remember that you can use GitHub to store anything that you might want to work on, not just program files. If you have an assignment to write, you could create a repository to hold the documents and images. This would be an even better idea if you were working on the assignment with other people because GitHub is a great collaboration tool.

Working on files with Visual Studio Code

We can round off this chapter by working the JavaScript program that we saw at the very start. The process we are going to follow will look like this:

1. Edit the program in the HTML file.

2. Save the file back to disk.

3. Use a web browser to view the HTML file and see what it does.

This is the process you will be using for a lot of the material covered in the rest of the book.

Edit the secret program

At the end of the last session, you opened the example repository that you'd downloaded from GitHub. Now you get to edit the `hello.html` file that we saw contains the secret program. The Explorer window at the left-hand side of the Visual Studio Code window provides a view of all the files and folders in the repository. There are lots of files here, including ones that contain the source code website at *begintocodewithjavascript.com.* You can click the > in front of folders in the Explorer view to open them and view their contents. See **Figure 1-15**.

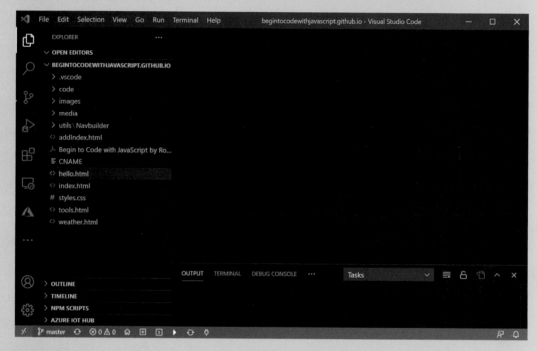

Figure 1-15   Visual Studio Code example repository

For now, you are just going to look in the `hello.html` file, so click the `hello.html` file name in the Explorer to open it (see **Figure 1-16**).

Once the page has opened, you can make some changes to the text in the file. I've changed one heading so that it reads "Hello from Rob." You can save the file by holding down the Control key (Command key on macOS) and pressing S (CTRL+S). Or you could use the **Save** command in the **File** menu. Either way, you now want to view the changed file in a browser to see if the changes have worked.

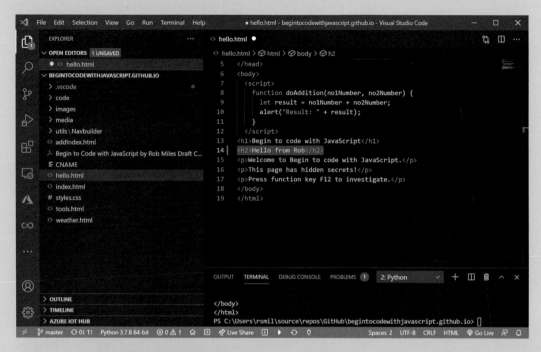

Figure 1-16 Editing the hello.html file

When you cloned the repository, you told Visual Studio Code where to put the files, so now is the time to open File Explorer and navigate to that folder. If you've forgotten where you put the files, you can find out just by hovering your mouse pointer over the file name in Explorer. Visual Studio Code will then show you the path to that file (see **Figure 1-17**).

Figure 1-17 Finding the hello.html file

If we double-click this file, it will be opened by the browser, as shown in **Figure 1-18**.

Figure 1-18   The `hello.html` file open in a browser

Now you will see the file in all its edited glory. Note that the address being browsed is now a file on your local storage, rather than on the web. Note also that you can press F12 if you like and view the contents of the file, just like we did at the start of this chapter.

What you have learned

You might feel that you've spent a lot of this chapter just following instructions, but actually you've learned rather a lot. You've discovered that JavaScript is a programming language that provides a means by which you can tell a computer how to do something. You've had a conversation with JavaScript itself. You've learned that looking after the source files of your programs is important, although great programmers sometimes think of very silly names (for example, Git) for their programs. You've installed the Git system and your program editor, Visual Studio Code. Finally, you've copied all the example code onto your machine by "cloning" the repository held on GitHub and even managed to edit one file and view the effects in your browser.

To reinforce your understanding of this chapter, you might want to consider the following "profound questions" about JavaScript, computers, programs, and programming.

What does the word "script" mean in the name JavaScript?

The word "script" in the JavaScript name refers to the way that JavaScript programs were intended to run. The browser would read each JavaScript statement and then perform it, just like an actor would act out the script of a play. This is not how all programming languages work. Some programming languages are designed to be *compiled*. This means that the source code of the program is converted into the low-level instructions that are run by the computer hardware. These low-level instructions are then directly obeyed by the hardware to make the program run.

Compiled languages run faster than scripts because when the compiled program runs, the computer doesn't have to put any effort into working out what the program source is doing; it can just obey the low-level instructions. However, you need to make a different version of the compiled code for each type of computer. For example, a compiled file for a Windows PC would not run on a Raspberry Pi.

JavaScript was intended to perform simple tasks inside a browser, so it was created as a scripting language. However, it has now become so popular that modern browsers compile JavaScript before running it so that it runs as quickly as possible.

Does my JavaScript program run on the web server?

No. The job of a web server is just to serve up files. The browser (the program running on the user's computer) is responsible for actually creating the display of a web page and running any JavaScript programs in that page.

Do JavaScript programs run at the same speed on all computers?

No. The faster the host computer, the faster the browser (and the JavaScript programs it is hosting) will run.

Do JavaScript programs run faster if I have a faster network connection?

No. A faster network connection will improve the speed at which the JavaScript programs will be loaded into the browser, but the actual speed the JavaScript program runs is determined by the speed of the host computer. Having said that, if the JavaScript program uses the host computer network connection, these actions will, of course, happen more quickly.

Can we view the JavaScript programs in every page we visit?

Yes, you can. The F12 trick (pressing F12 when viewing a web page in a browser) will open the development view of the page. You can use this to view the JavaScript source code in the page. If you are concerned about someone copying the JavaScript code, you can use a tool called an *obfuscator*, which is a piece of software that changes the appearance (but not the behavior) of a program so that it is very hard to understand. Take a look at *https://www.javascriptobfuscator.com/* for more details.

How big can a JavaScript program be?

A JavaScript program can be very large indeed. Modern web browsers are very good at handling large programs, and the speed of modern networks means that the code can be downloaded very quickly. Some people have even created complete computer emulations in JavaScript that you can run in a browser.

Can you run JavaScript outside a web browser?

Yes, you can. Some web pages can be converted into applications, which then run on the local computer. There are also ways in which a computer can be made to host JavaScript applications in the same way that a browser does. We will look at these later in the text when we consider the node.js environment in Chapter 11.

Why is Git called "Git"?

This is probably the hardest question in this book. In the UK, the word "git" is a form of mild abuse. You would call someone a "git" if he or she spilled your drink on purpose. It seems that Linus Torvalds called his first version of the program "His stupid content tracker," and then hit upon the word "git" as a shorter version of this.

Can I do private work on GitHub?

Yes. GitHub is very popular with programmers who are working on open-source projects, but you can also make a GitHub repository private so that only you can see it.

What do I do if I "break" my program?

Some people worry that things they do with a program on the computer might "break" it in some way. I used to worry about this, too, but I've conquered this fear by making sure that whenever I do something, I always have a way back. Git and GitHub are very useful in this respect.

Why does the Visual Studio Code display of the `hello.html` **file appear in different colors?**

This is called *source code highlighting*. Visual Studio Code has a list of words that are "special" as far as JavaScript and HTML are concerned. These special words are called *keywords*. For each keyword, Visual Studio Code has a characteristic color. In the case of Visual Studio Code, keywords are displayed in blue, functions are displayed in yellow, strings of text are orange, and everything else is white. The intention is to make it easier for programmers to understand the structure of the program. Note that there is nothing in the program file that specifies the color of each element; this is something that Visual Studio Code does.

What is the difference between Visual Studio Code and Visual Studio?

Microsoft produces two tools, one called Visual Studio and the other called Visual Studio Code. They can both be used to create programs. We are using Visual Studio Code which, as its name implies, is designed for working with source code. Visual Studio is a much more comprehensive suite of tools that can be used to manage large teams of developers working on huge projects. There is a free version of Visual Studio available that you can download and install if you wish, but how to use it is a bit beyond the scope of this text.

2
Hypertext Markup Language (HTML)

What you will learn

In the previous chapter, you learned that a JavaScript program can live inside a web page. You saw that the file `hello.html` had a secret script inside it. In this chapter, we will find out more about the HTML standard that tells the browser program what a web page should look like. Then we'll discover how to link JavaScript to elements on a web page to allow our programs to interact with the user.

HTML and the World Wide Web

The first version of a *Hypertext Markup Language* (HTML) was created in 1989 by Tim Berners-Lee. He wanted to make it easier for researchers to share information. At the time, research reports were written as individual documents. If a document you were reading contained a reference to another document, you would have to go and find the other one. Tim Berners-Lee designed a system of computer *servers* to share electronic copies of documents. A document could contain *hyperlinks* to other documents. Readers used a *browser* program to read the document from the servers and follow the links from one document to another. These documents are called *hypertext* documents, and the language that described their contents is called the *Hypertext Markup Language*, or HTML.

Tim Berners-Lee also designed a protocol to manage the transfer of HTML-formatted documents from the server into the browser. This standard is called the *Hypertext Transfer Protocol*, or HTTP. Also, now there is a secure version of this protocol called HTTPS, which adds security to the web. HTTPS allows a browser to confirm the identity of a server, and it also protects messages sent between the server and the browser to prevent eavesdropping. The HTTPS protocol is what makes it possible for us to use the World Wide Web for banking and e-commerce.

In 1990, the first system was released as the "World Wide Web." The documents that you could download were called "web pages." The server hosting the web pages was called a "website." In 1993, Marc Andreessen added the ability to display images in web pages, and the web became extremely popular.

The World Wide Web was designed to be extensible, and for many years, different browser manufacturers added their own enhancements to the standards, leading to problems with compatibility where websites would only work with specific browser programs. Recently, the situation has stabilized. The World Wide Web Consortium (W3C) now sets out standards that are implemented by all browser manufacturers. The latest standard, HTML5, is now very stable and is the version used in this book.

Fetching web pages

The location of the page on a server is given using a *uniform resource locator*, or URL. This has three elements:

- **The *protocol***   The protocol is used to talk to the site. This sets out how a browser asks for a web page, and how the server replies. Web pages use HTTP and HTTPS. HTTP stands for "Hypertext Transport Protocol" and HTTPS is the secure version of this protocol.

- **The *host***   This gives the address of the server on the network. The World Wide Web sits on top of a networking protocol called TCP/IP (Transport Control Protocol/Internet Protocol), and this is the address on that network of the system that holds the website you want to connect to.

- **The *path***   This is the host's path to the item that the browser wants to read.

You can see all these elements in the URL that we used to access the `hello.html` page in Chapter 1 (see **Figure 2-1**).

Figure 2-1   URL structure

This URL specifies that the site uses the secure version of the hypertext transfer protocol, that the address of the host server is *begintocodewithjavascript.com*, and that the path to the file containing the web page is *hello.html*. If you leave off the path, the server will deliver the contents of a default file which might be called *index.html* or *Default.htm* or some other name, depending on how the server has been set up.

When the user requests a website, the browser sends a message to the server to request the page. This message is formatted according to the Hypertext Transport Protocol (HTTP) and is often called a "get" request (because it starts with the word GET). The server then sends a response that includes a status code and then, if it is available, the text of the web page itself is sent. If the page cannot be found on the server (perhaps because the URL was not given correctly), the HTTP status code results in the familiar "404 page not found" message. We will learn more about this process later in the book when we write some JavaScript code that gets web pages.

What is HTML?

This is not a guide to HTML. You can buy whole books that do a very thorough job of describing the language and how it is used. But you should finish this section with a good understanding of the fundamentals. HTML is a *markup* language. Markup is what the "M" in HTML stands for. The word "markup" comes from the printing profession. Printers would be given text that had been "marked up" with instructions such as "print this part in large font" and "print this part in italic."

Figure 2-2 shows what happens if you don't use a markup language properly. In this case, the customer wanted a cake with no writing on it. The customer said, "Please Leave Blank" when asked what she wanted written on the cake. Unfortunately, the baker took this instruction literally.

Figure 2-2   Markup taken literally

This kind of misunderstanding is impossible with HTML. The language has a rigid separation between the text that is to be displayed and the formatting instructions. In HTML, if I want something to be *emphasized*, I will use an HTML markup command to request this:

```
<em>This text is emphasized.</em> This text is not.
```

The sequence <em> is recognized by the browser as meaning "make the text that follows this instruction look slightly different from the other text" and is called a *tag*. The browser will display emphasized text until it sees the sequence </em>, which marks the end of the emphasized text. Most browsers emphasize text by displaying it as *italic*. If we viewed the above HTML in a Microsoft Edge, we would see something that looks like this:

```
This text is emphasized. This text is not.
```

Once you understand the fundamentals of HTML, you can use it to format text. The HTML below shows a few more tags.

```
This is <em>emphasized</em><br>
This is <i>italic</i><br>
This is <strong>strong</strong><br>
This is <b>bold</b><br>
This is <small>small</small><br>
This is <del>deleted</del><br>
This is <ins>inserted</ins><br>
This is <u>underlined</u><br>
This is <mark>marked</mark><br>
```

The example HTML above uses a tag, `<br>`, that means "start on a new line." The `<br>` tag does not need to be matched by a `</br>` element to "close it off." This is because it has an immediate effect on the layout; it is not "applied" to any specific items on the page. When I pass this text into a browser, I get the output shown in **Figure 2-3**.

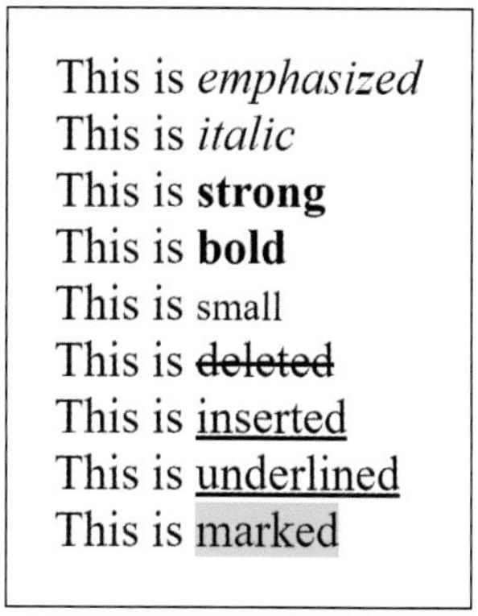

> This is *emphasized*
> This is *italic*
> This is **strong**
> This is **bold**
> This is small
> This is ~~deleted~~
> This is <u>inserted</u>
> This is <u>underlined</u>
> This is marked

Figure 2-3   The <br> tag creates a new line of text.

If you look closely at the text in Figure 2-3, you will notice that some of the requests have similar results. For example, the emphasized (`<em>`) and italic (`<i>`) formats both produced italic output. The bold (`<b>`), italic (`<i>`), and underline (`<u>`) tags are regarded as slightly less useful than the more general ones, such as emphasized (`<em>`) or strong (`<strong>`). The reasoning behind this is that if a display has no way of producing italic characters a request to display something in italic is not going to work.

However, if the display is asked to "emphasize" something, it might be able to do this in a different way, perhaps by changing the color of the text. Output produced by HTML is intended to be displayed in a useful way on a huge range of output devices.

When you use a markup language, you should be thinking about the effect you want to add to a piece of text. You should think "I need to make this stand out, so I'll use the `<strong>` format," rather than just making the text bold.

You can write the commands using uppercase or lowercase or any combination of the two. In other words, the tags `<em>`, `<EM>`, and `<Em>` are all regarded as the same thing by the browser.

Display symbols

By now, you should have a good idea how HTML works. A tag `<blah>` marks the start of something. The sequence `</blah>` marks the end. The tags can be nested (placed inside each other).

```
<em>This is emphasized <strong>This is strong and emphasized</strong></em>
```

This HTML would generate:

```
This is emphsized This is strong and emphasized
```

For every start tag (`<blah>`) that marks a formatted area of text, there should be a matching end tag (`</blah>`). Most browsers are quite tolerant if you get this wrong, but the display that you get might not be what you want.

The question you are probably asking now is, "How I can ever get to display the < (less than) and > (greater than) symbols in my web pages?" The answer is that HTML uses another character to mark the start of a *symbol entity*. The & character marks the start of a symbol. Symbols can be identified by their names:

```
This is a less than: &lt; symbol and this is a greater than &gt; symbol
```

The name of the less than character (<) is `lt`, and the name of the greater than (>) symbol is `gt`. Note that the end of a symbol name is marked by a semicolon (;). If you are now wondering how we display an ampersand (&), the answer is that it has the symbol name `amp`.

```
This is an ampersand: &amp;
```

You can find a handy list of symbols and their names here: *https://dev.w3.org/html5/html-author/charref.* Note that when you give a symbol a name, the case of the names is significant.

```
&Eacute;<br>
&eacute;<br>
```

The HTML above would display the uppercase (É) and lowercase (é) versions of `eacute`. If you like emojis (and who doesn't?), you can add these to your web pages by using a symbol that includes the number of the emoji that you want to use.

```
Happy face: &#128540;<br>
```

This will display a happy face, as shown in **Figure 2-4**.

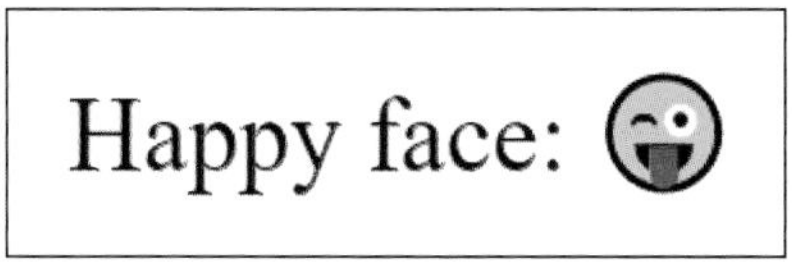

Figure 2-4   Happy face emoji

If you want to discover all the numbers that you can use to put emojis in your web pages, take a look here: *https://emojiguide.org/.*

WHAT COULD GO WRONG

Make sure your emojis mean the right thing

Emojis are a great way to liven up a user interface, but you need to make sure that you know what you are saying with them. Some emoji designs have particular meanings to specific groups of people that are not immediately obvious. Before you send out your emoji-powered pages, you should check a website such as *https://emojipedia.org/* to make sure your page means what you think it does.

Lay out text in paragraphs

We now know how to format text. Next, we must consider how we can lay this text out on the page. When HTML text is displayed, the original layout of the text input is ignored. In other words, consider this text:

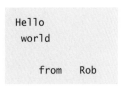

```
Hello
  world

      from    Rob
```

The layout of this text is a bit of a mess. However, when this text is displayed by a browser, you see the following:

```
Hello world from Rob
```

The browser takes in the original text, splits it into words, and then displays the words with single spaces between them. Any layout information in the source text is discarded. This is a good idea because the designer of a web page can't make any assumptions about the display that will be used. The same page needs to work on large and small displays—from smartphones to large LCD panels.

We've seen that the `<br>` sequence asks the browser to create a new line during the display of text. Now we are going to consider some more commands that control how text is laid out when it is displayed. The `<p>` and `</p>` commands enclose text that should appear in a paragraph:

```
<p>This is the first paragraph</p>
<p>This is the second paragraph</p>
```

This HTML will display two paragraphs:

```
This is the first paragraph
This is the second paragraph
```

The `<br>` command is not the same as the `<p>` command; it does not space the lines out like a paragraph would.

Create headings

We can use other tags to markup text as headings at different levels:

```
<h1>Heading 1</h1>
<h2>Heading 2</h2>
<h3>Heading 3</h3>
<h4>Heading 4</h4>
<p>A normal paragraph</p>
```

We can use these in documents to create headings, as shown in **Figure 2-5**.

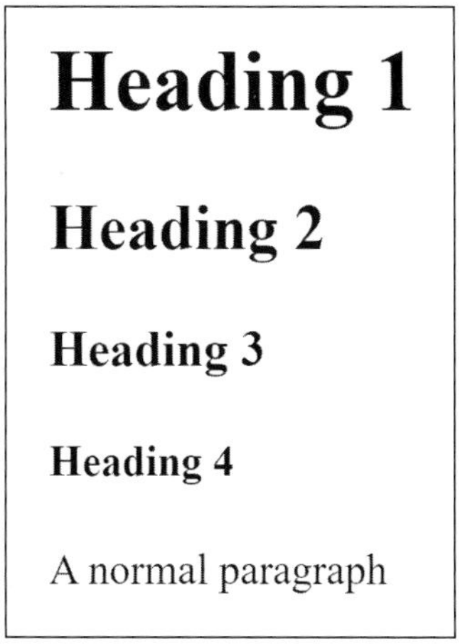

Heading 1

Heading 2

Heading 3

Heading 4

A normal paragraph

Figure 2-5   Headings

You can use headings to create structure in a document.

Use preformatted text

But sometimes, you might have something that you have already formatted. In this case, you can use the `<pre>` tag to tell the browser not to perform any layout:

```
<pre>
This text
  is rendered
    exactly how I wrote it.
</pre>
```

The text enclosed by the `<pre>` tags is displayed by the browser without any changes to the formatting.

```
This text
   is rendered
      exactly how I wrote it.
```

The browser uses a *monospaced* font when displaying preformatted text. In a mono-spaced font all the characters have the same width. Many fonts, including the one used to print this paragraph, are *proportional*. This means that each character has a particular width; for example, the "I" character is much smaller than the "m" character. However, for text such as ASCII art, it is important that all the characters line up. The code for the logo shown in **Figure 2-6** would not look correct if it were not displayed with a monospaced font.

```
<p> My Logo</p>
<pre>
|  _ \ __ | |_   |  \/ ( ) | __  __
| |_) / _ \| '_ \  | |\/| | | |/ _ \/ _ \
|  _ &lt; ( ) | |_) | | |  | | | | |  __/\__  \
|_| \_\___/|_._/  |_|  |_|_|_|\___||__/
</pre>
```

Figure 2-6   A preformatted logo

Note that the ASCII art above contains a < character, which I had to convert to a symbol (`&lt;`) so that it is displayed correctly. This is important. Remember that the browser will not format preformatted text, but it still observes the character con-ventions that you must use to display characters and symbols. You can add tags to the preformatted text to make parts of it emphasized; `<p>` tags inside preformatted blocks of text might work, but this is not advised because it makes your html *badly formed*. The logo appears as shown in **Figure 2-7**.

My Logo

Figure 2-7   My logo

Don't abuse the browser

Browsers are generally very tolerant of badly formatted HTML. The browser will try to display something even if the HTML it receives is badly formatted. This means you can get away with HTML like this:

```
<em>Emphasized <strong>strongly emphazised</em> just strong </strong>
```

The browser will display what you would expect:

> *Emphasized* **strongly emphasized** **just strong**

However, it is *malformed HTML*. You might be wondering why. Let's take a look at the sequence of tags in the text.

```
<em>Emphasized <strong>strongly emphasized</em> just strong </strong>
```

This is an example of what is called *bad nesting*. This is because the `<em>` tag "ends" inside the `<strong>` tag. In properly formed HTML, a tag that is created inside another tag will end before the enclosing tag ends. The complete sequence of a start tag, text, and end tag is called an *element*. While one element can completely contain another, it is not correct for elements to *overlap* like the ones in the above figure. The correct version of this HTML is shown below. Note that each element is complete.

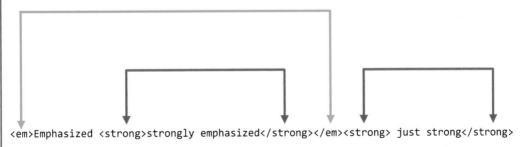

```
<em>Emphasized <strong>strongly emphasized</strong></em><strong> just strong</strong>
```

The above figure shows what correct nesting looks like. Each element ends before its enclosing one. The reason why I'm stressing this is that most browsers can work out the meaning of the badly nested HTML and display it correctly, but some might not. This could lead to your web pages looking wrong to some people. I'm sure you've had the experience of having to switch browsers because a particular website doesn't look right. Now you know how this can happen.

You can identify incorrectly nested HTML when you see an end tag that doesn't match the most recent start tag. If you want to use a program to make sure that your HTML is correct, you can use the official validator site at *https://validator.w3.org/*. You can point the validator at a site you have created or paste HTML text into it for checking.

Add comments to documents

You can add comments to an HTML document by enclosing the comment text in the sequences `<!--` and `-->` as follows:

```
<!-- Document Version 1.0 created by Rob Miles -->
```

The author credit would not be displayed by the browser, but you could view it in the source code by pressing the F12 key to open the developer view. As we go through this text, I'll be telling you regularly how useful it is to add comments to your work, so I think it is a good idea to start doing this now.

Add images to web pages

For the first few years of its life, the World Wide Web didn't have any pictures at all. The image tag was added by Marc Andreessen, one of the authors of Mosaic, the most popular browser in the early days of the web. The image tag contains the name of a file that contains an image:

```
<img src="seaside.JPG">
```

The image tag uses an *attribute* to specify the file that contains the image to be displayed. An attribute is given inside the tag as a name and value pair, separated by the equals character. When the browser finds an `img` tag, it looks for the `src` attribute and then looks for an image file with that name. In the case of the above HTML, the browser would look for an image called `seaside.JPG`. It would look in the same place on the server from which it loaded the web page. We must make sure that file exists on the server; otherwise, the image will not be displayed.

Beware of faulty file names

The `src` attribute in an `img` tag is followed by the name of the file that is to be fetched from the server. While HTML doesn't care about the capitalization of tags (you can write `IMG`, `img`, or `Img` for the tag name), the computer fetching the image file might. Some computers will deliver a file stored as `seaside.jpg` if you ask for one called `seaside.JPG`. Others will complain that the file is not available.

I normally encounter this problem when I take a website off my PC (where it has been working perfectly) and place it on the server (when all the image files suddenly vanish).

You can add another attribute to an `img` tag that provides alternative text that is displayed if the image cannot be found.

```
<img src="seaside1.JPG" alt="Waves crashing on an empty beach">
```

Now the browser will display the text "Waves crashing on an empty beach" if the image can't be located. The alternative text (ALT) is also very useful for visually impaired web users who can't see the image but who would appreciate a text description of what is in it.

The image will be displayed in line with the text on the page. We can use the HTML layout tags to lay an image out sensibly with the surrounding text:

```
<h1>Seaside Picture</h1>
<p><img src="seaside.JPG" alt="Waves crashing on an empty beach"></p>
<p>This picture was taken at Hornsea in the UK.</p>
```

The image shown in **Figure 2-8** is 600 pixels wide. A pixel (short for *picture cell*) is one of the dots that make up the picture. The more pixels that you have, the better looking the picture is.

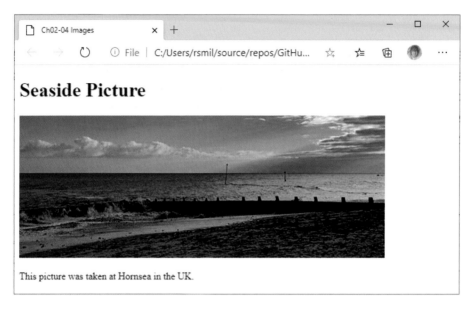

Figure 2-8   An image that is 600 pixels wide

However, this can cause problems if the picture is too large to fit on the device being used to display the image. The `img` tag supports `width` and `height` attributes that can be used to set the displayed size of an image. So, if I want to display the image as 400 pixels wide I can do this:

```
<p><img src="seaside.JPG" alt="Waves crashing on an empty beach" width="400">
```

Note that I didn't specify the height, which means the browser will automatically calculate the height that matches a width of 400 pixels. You can specify both height and width if you like, but you need to be careful not to make the pictures distorted. Setting the absolute width of an image using height and width attributes looks like a good idea at first, but it can be restricting. Remember that an underlying principle of the World Wide Web is that a page should display in a useful way on any device. An image size of 400 pixels might be fine for a small device, but it will appear very small if viewed on a large TV display. In the next chapter, we will discover how we can use style sheets to allow items on a web page to be automatically scaled for the target device.

The HTML document

We now know that we can use tags to mark regions of text as needing to be formatted in a particular way, such as using `<em>` for emphasized text. We can also mark regions of text as being in paragraphs or levels of headings. We can apply several tags to a given piece of text to allow formatting instructions to be layered on top of each other, but we need to make sure that these instructions are properly "nested" inside each other. Now we can consider how to create a properly formatted HTML document. This comprises several sections:

```
<!DOCTYPE HTML>                        Indicates that this is an HTML document
<html lang="en">                       HTML tab with a language attribute
  <head>                               Start of the heading of the web page
      <!-- Heading here --!>
  </head>                              End of the heading
  <body>                               Start of the body text of the web page
      <!-- Body text here --!>
  </body>                              End of the body text
</html>                                End of the HTML text
```

The browser looks for the sequence `<!DOCTYPE HTML>` at the start to make sure that it is reading an HTML file. All the HTML that describes the page is given between `<html>` and `</html>` tags. The `</html>` tag contains a `lang` attribute that specifies the language of the page. The language `"en"` is English. The `<head>` and `</head>` tags mark the start and end of the *heading* of the document. The heading contains information about the content of the page including styling information (which is discussed further in the next chapter). The text between the `<body>` and `</body>` tags is what is to be displayed. In other words, everything we have learned up to now goes into the body part of the web page file.

Linking HTML documents

An HTML document can contain elements that link to another document. The other document can be on the same server, or it can be on a different server entirely. A link is created by using an `<a>` tag, which has an `href` attribute that contains the URL of the destination page:

```
Click on <a href="otherpage.html">this link</a>to open another page.
```

The text in the body of the `<a>` tag is the text that the browser will highlight as the link. In the example HTML above the words "this link" will be the linkable text. This will result in text on the page that looks like this:

```
Click on this link to open another page.
```

If the reader clicks the link, the browser will open a local file—in this case, a file named "`otherpage.html`"—which will be displayed. The destination of the link can refer to a page on a completely different site:

```
<p>Click on <a href="https://www.robmiles.com"> this link</a> to go to my blog.</p>
```

Making active web pages

There are lots of other things that I could tell you about HTML. The language can be used to create numbered and unnumbered lists and tables. However, this is not a book about HTML; it is about programming. What we want is a way of getting JavaScript code to run inside a web page. Then we can start exploring the language.

You already know that a JavaScript program can sit alongside an HTML page design. You saw that in Chapter 1 when you used the developer view (obtained by pressing F12) in the browser to take look at the hidden program inside the `hello.html` web page. That HTML file contained a `script` element holding some JavaScript code. We used the console to run a JavaScript function. Now we are going to trigger a function by pressing a button.

Using a button

One way to create an active web page is by using a button. This HTML code creates a button that contains the text "Say Hello":

```
<button onclick="doSayHello();">Say Hello</button>
```

The button is displayed in the normal flow of the text in the page, as shown in **Figure 2-9**.

Figure 2-9   Say Hello button

The button has an onclick attribute. One of the great things about JavaScript is that most of the time, the names make sense. The onclick attribute specifies a function that is to be used when the button is clicked. In this case, the attribute specifies a JavaScript function called "doSayHello". A JavaScript function is a sequence of JavaScript statements that have been given a name. (We will take a detailed look at functions in Chapter 8.)

```
function doSayHello() {
   alert("Hello");
}
```

This function only performs a single action; it displays an alert that says "Hello" to the user when it is called. The line of JavaScript that displays the alert is called a *statement*. The end of a statement is marked by a semicolon character. A function can contain many statements, each of which is ended with a semicolon (;).

```
<!DOCTYPE html>
<html lang="en">
<head>
   <title>Ch02-06 Buttons</title>
</head>

<body>
   <h1>Buttons</h1>
   <p>
      <button onclick="doSayHello();">Say Hello</button>
   </p>

   <script>
      function doSayHello() {
         alert("Hello");
      }

   </script>
```

This is the complete HTML text of the web page. The <script> element is at the bottom of the body of the document. The page displays the Say Hello button, and when the button is pressed, the alert is displayed, as shown in **Figure 2-10**.

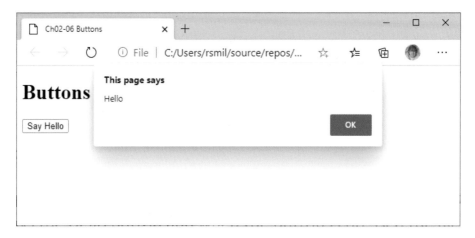

Figure 2-10 Say Hello alert

Reading input from a user

The `button` tag lets us create an element in a web page that responds to a user action. Next, we need a way of getting input from a user. The `input` tag lets us do just that:

```
<input type="text" id="alertText" value="Alert!">
```

It has three attributes:

- `type`   The `type` attribute tells the browser the type of input that is being read. In the code above, we are reading text, so the attribute type is set to `text`. If you set the type attribute to `password`, the contents of the input are replaced with other characters (usually * or .) as they are being typed in. This is how JavaScript programs read passwords in web pages.

- `id`   The `id` attribute gives an element a unique name. This name can be used in the JavaScript code to locate the element. If we had two input elements, we would use a different name for each. I've called the element `alertText` because this nicely reflects what the element is being used for.

- `value`   The `value` attribute specifies the value in this element tag. This is how we can prepopulate an input with text. When this input element is displayed, it will have the text "Alert!" in it. If we want the input to be blank when it is displayed, we can set the value to an empty string.

```
<p>
  <input type="text" id="alertInputText" value="Alert!">
  <button onclick="doShowAlert();">Show Alert</button>
</p>
<script>
  function doShowAlert() {
    var element = document.getElementById("alertInputText");
    alert(element.value);
  }
</script>
```

The web page contains the input element, a button element that will call a function to display the alert, and the function that uses the input text in an alert. The user can type their own text into the input and then press the **Show Alert** button to have the text displayed in an alert. **Figure 2-11** shows what the program looks like when it is used.

Figure 2-11

If you run the example, you will notice that when you press the **Show Alert** button, the text you have entered in the input area is displayed in the alert.

HTML and JavaScript

It's worth spending some time discovering how HTML and JavaScript work together, as this underpins almost all of the programs that we are going to write. The JavaScript program needs a way of interacting with the HTML document it is part of. This interaction is provided by *methods*, which are part of the *document object model*, or DOM, that the browser creates to represent the HTML document it is displaying for the user. The DOM is a *software object* that is held in the memory of the computer. The DOM contains methods alongside the HTML elements that make up the page. Our program uses the getElementByID method to get a reference to the element on the page. It then gets the text out of this element and displays that text in an alert.

If you're not sure about this, perhaps an analogy would help. Think of the HTML document as "Rob's Car Rental." When someone comes to pick up a car, they will say, "I've come to pick up car registration ABC 123." I will then hand them the keys and say "It's over in bay E6". They can then go find the car. I don't hand the car to the customer over the counter because I'm not strong enough for that. I just tell them where the car is, so they can go and find it.

In the case of the HTML document, each of the elements in the document is like a car in the parking lot for my rental business. An element can be given an ID just like a car has a registration plate. In our document, the ID is alertInputText. The method getElementById is the means by which a JavaScript program can ask the document where an element is:

```
var element = document.getElementById("alertInputText");
```

On the right-hand side of the statement above, you can see the use of getElementByID to get the location of the text element with the alertInputText ID. The left-hand side of the statement creates a *variable* to hold this location. The word var creates a JavaScript *variable*. A variable is a named location that stores some information that the program wants to remember.

At "Rob's Car Rental," I would offer to write down the location of a car for a customer who was afraid of forgetting where their car was. I'd give them a piece of paper with "Car Location" (the name of the "variable") and "Bay E6" (the value of the variable) written on it. In the JavaScript above, the variable we are creating is called element (because it refers to an element in the document) and the value is the location of the text input element. This operation is called an *assignment* because the program is assigning a value to a variable. An assignment operation is denoted using the equals (=) character. (We will discuss variables in detail in Chapter 4.)

Now that the program has a variable called element that contains a reference to the input, we can extract the text value from this element and store it in a variable called message:

```
var message = element.value;
```

The variable called message now contains the text that was typed into the input by the user. (Remember that we set this to "Alert!" in the HTML.) The program can now display this text in an alert:

```
alert(message);
```

It is very important that you understand what is going on here. Up until now, every-thing has seemed quite reasonable, and then suddenly, you've been hit with some-thing really complicated. I'm sorry about that. Just go through the code and try to map the statements back to what the program is trying to do. And remember that the equals character (=) means "set this variable to the value." It does not mean that the program is testing to see if one thing is equal to another.

If you are confused about how the various parts of the program fit together, consider that the program is doing exactly the same thing as if I had given a car rental cus-tomer the location of their car and then asked them to come back and tell me how much fuel there was in that car. That sequence would go as follows:

1. Get the location of the car.

2. Go to the car.

3. Get the value from the fuel-level display.

4. Bring that value back to me.

In the case of the JavaScript program that is displaying the message, the sequence is:

1. Use `getElementById` method to get a reference to the input element.

2. Follow the reference to the element.

3. Get the text value from the input element.

4. Display that text in an Alert.

CODE ANALYSIS

The doShowAlert function

```
function doShowAlert() {
  var element = document.getElementById("alertInputText");
  var message = element.value;
  alert(message);
}
```

We can build on our understanding of this important aspect of JavaScript by looking at this function and considering some questions.

Question: What would happen if you got the ID of the text element wrong?

Answer: The doShowAlert method uses an unspoken "contract" between the HTML and the JavaScript code. The doShowAlert function asks the getElementById to find an element with the alertInputText ID. If this contract is broken because the element has the wrong name, for example alertinputtext, the getElementById method will not be able to deliver a result. This is a bit like me telling a car rental customer to look for their car in a location that doesn't exist. In this case, the getElementById method will return a special value called "null" which means "I couldn't find anything." This would cause the rest of the doShowAlert function to fail. In the case of my car rental customer, they would come back and tell me that the location does not exist. In the case of the doShowAlert function, there would be no error reported to the user, but the alert would not be displayed. Later in this book, we'll look at how you can write code that will test for methods returning results that mean, "I couldn't find what you wanted."

In JavaScript, you tend to have to go hunting for the errors that you make. In some programming languages, you are told about errors when they occur. In JavaScript, things tend to fail silently or just do something that you were not expecting.

Question: What would happen if the user didn't type any text into the text area on the web page before pressing the button?

Answer: If you look at the HTML at the very start of this section, you will see that the value attribute of the text tag is set to "Alert!" If the user doesn't replace this with their message the word "Alert!" will be displayed.

Question: What would happen if I pressed the button several times?

Answer: The browser will block any activity on the web page until you clear the alert that is displayed. When you press the button again, the doShowAlert function would be called again. It would make two new variables called element and message and use them to display the appropriate message text.

Question: What does var do?

Answer: The word var is a command to JavaScript to create a *variable*. The name of the variable follows the word var. The variable holds a value that the program wants to make use of. A program can assign values to variables by using = to tell JavaScript to perform an assignment.

Display text output

In the previous section, we used a JavaScript program to read data from a web page by getting a reference to an element on the page and then reading information from that element. Displaying text on the screen is a similar process. A JavaScript program can use a reference to an object to change attributes of the element. We are going to write a program that changes the text in a paragraph into a string of text that we have entered. The complete HTML file looks like this:

```html
<!DOCTYPE html>
<html lang="en">
<head>
  <title>Ch02-08 Paragraph Update</title>
</head>

<body>
  <h1>Paragraph Update</h1>
  <p>
    <input type="text" id="inputText" value="">
    <button onclick="doUpdateParagraph();">Update the Paragraph</button>
    <p id="outputParagraph"></p>
  </p>

  <script>
    function doUpdateParagraph() {
      var inputElement = document.getElementById("inputText");
      var outputElement = document.getElementById("outputParagraph");
      var message = inputElement.value;
      outputElement.textContent = message;
    }
  </script>
</body>
</html>
```

Annotations:
- Input text element
- Button that calls doUpdateParagraph
- Paragraph for the output
- Function that updates the paragraph
- Gets a reference to the input
- Gets a reference to the output
- Reads the text from the input
- Writes the text into the output

This example is an extension of the previous one. Instead of displaying text using an alert, this example sets the `textContent` attribute of a paragraph to the text that the user enters into the dialog box. The behavior of this program is given in four lines.

```javascript
var inputElement = document.getElementById("inputText");
var outputElement = document.getElementById("outputParagraph");
var message = inputElement.value;
outputElement.textContent = message;
```

The first two lines set up variables that refer to the input and output elements. The third line gets the message to be displayed, and the fourth puts this message onto the web page, as shown in **Figure 2-12**.

Figure 2-12　Paragraph Update message

Work with object properties

You might be wondering what the `textContent` property does and how the program uses it, so it might be worth investigating this. We can use the JavaScript console in the Developer Tools to do this. Find the folder on your PC that contains the sample code for the book. (If you haven't downloaded the sample code, you can find the instructions in Chapter 1 in the "Getting the sample files" section.) Find the **Ch02 HTML/Ch02-08 Paragraph Update** folder. Double-click the **index.html** file in that folder. This should open your browser, and you should see a page that looks like the one in Figure 2-12 above.

Note that Edge will only open if it is the default browser on your computer. On a Windows PC, you can select which browser should open a page by right-clicking the page and then selecting **Open With** from the menu that appears. Once the page is open, do the following:

Press F12 to open the Developer Tools view. Select the **Console** tab. Enter the following JavaScript statement:

```
var outputElement = document.getElementById("outputParagraph");
```

This is the statement in our program that gets a reference to the outputParagraph in the document. We now have a variable called outputElement that refers to the output paragraph. We can prove this by using our new variable.

```
outputElement.textContent = "fred";
```

Take a look back at the web page. You should see that the word "fred" has appeared. By setting the value of the TextContent property of the paragraph, we can change the text in the paragraph. A JavaScript program can read properties as well as write them. Enter the following statement:

```
alert(outputElement.textContent);
```

This will make an alert box appear with "fred" in it (because that is the textContent of the element referred to by outputElement). Now let's see what happens if we make a mistake. Try this:

```
outputElement.tetContent="test";
```

This statement looks sensible, but I've mistyped "textContent" as "tetContent." The paragraph element does not have a tetContent property. However, this statement doesn't cause an error, but the word "test" is not displayed either. What happens is that JavaScript creates a new property for the outputElement variable. The new property is called "tetContent" and it is set to the value "test." You can prove this by entering the following:

```
alert(outputElement.tetContent);
```

This will display an alert showing the value in the tetContent property, which is the string "test." We will discover more about creating properties in objects in Chapter 9.

See if you can change the web page so that the name is displayed as a heading (<h1>) rather than as a paragraph. You can use Visual Studio Code to edit the HTML for the web page. Will you have to change the JavaScript or the HTML?

Egg timer

We now know enough to be able to create a properly useful program. We are going to create an egg timer. The user will press a button and then be told when five minutes (the perfect time for a boiled egg) have elapsed. We know how to connect a JavaScript function to an HTML button. The next thing we need to know is how to measure the passage of time. We can do this by using a JavaScript function called setTimeout. We have used functions already. The alert function accepts a string that it displays. The setTimeout function accepts two things: a function that will be called when the timer expires and the length of the timeout. The timeout length is given in thousandths of a second. The statement below will cause the doEndTimer function to run one second after setTimout was called.

```
setTimeout(doEndTimer,1000);
```

Our egg timer will use two functions. One function will run when the user presses a button to start the timer. This function will set a timer that will run the second function after five minutes. The second function will display an alert that indicates that the timer has completed.

```
function doStartTimer() {
   setTimeout(doEndTimer,5*60*1000);
}

function doEndTimer() {
   alert("Your egg is ready");
}
```

The doStartTimer function is connected to a button so that the user can start the timer. The doEndTimer will be called when the timer completes. I've added a calculation that works out the delay value. I want a five-minute delay. There are 60 seconds in a minute and a value of 1000 would give me a one-second delay. This makes it easier to change the delay. If we want to make a hard-boiled egg that takes seven minutes, I just have to change the 5 to a 7. Note that the * character is used in JavaScript to mean *multiply*. You will find out more about doing calculations in Chapter 4.

Investigate the egg timer

```
<!DOCTYPE html>
<html lang="en">
<head>
  <title>Ch02-09 Egg Timer</title>
</head>

<body>
  <h1>Egg Timer</h1>
  <p>
    <button onclick="doStartTimer();">Start the timer</button>
  </p>

  <script>
    function doStartTimer() {
      setTimeout(doEndTimer,5*60*1000);
    }

    function doEndTimer() {
      alert("Your egg is ready");
    }
  </script>
</body>
</html>
```

Let's take a look at how the egg timer works. Find the **Ch02 HTML/Ch02-09 Egg Timer** folder. Double-click the file **index.html** in that folder to open the page.

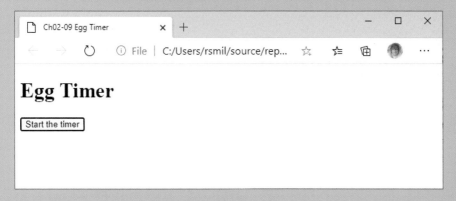

Click the **Start The Timer** button once. This version of the code only has a 10-second delay, so after 10 seconds, you would see the alert appear.

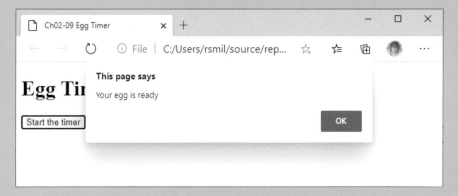

Click the **Start The Timer** button three times in succession. Wait and see what happens. Was this what you expected? It turns out that each time you press the button, a new timeout is created. Now press F12 to open the Developer Tools. Enter the following code and press Enter. What would you expect to see?

```
doEndTimer();
```

This is a call of the function that will run and display the end message. You should see the alert appear telling you that your egg is ready. Click **OK** in the alert to close it. Enter the following and press enter. What would you expect to happen?

```
setTimeout(doEndTimer,3*1000);
```

After three seconds the alert appears, because that is the length of the timeout. You should also have seen something else appear when the function runs. You will also see an integer displayed. If you repeat the `setTimeout` call, you will see another value displayed. It is usually one bigger than the previous one. This number is the "ID" of timer. This can be used to identify a timeout so that it can be canceled. We are not going to do that, so you can ignore this value.

See if you can change the web page so that it supports multiple cooking times. Add buttons for "Soft" (four minutes), "Normal" (five minutes), and "Bullet" (ten minutes). You will have to add two more buttons and two more JavaScript functions to the program.

If you want to see how I did it, open the **Ch02-09 Selectable Egg Timer** file. My solution even displays the status of the timer.

Adding sound to the egg timer

Our egg timer works fine, but it would be nice if it could do a little more than just display an alert when our egg is ready. A web page can contain an audio element that can be used to play sounds.

```
<audio id="alarmAudio">
  <source src="everythingSound.mp3" type="audio/mpeg">
  Your browser does not support the audio element.
</audio>
```

The audio element includes another element called src that specifies where the audio data is going to come from. In this case, the audio is stored in an MP3 file named everythingSound.mp3, which is stored on the server. The text inside the audio element is displayed if the browser does not support the audio element. I've given this element an ID so that the code in the doEndTimer function can find the audio element and ask it to play the MP3 file.

```
function doEndTimer() {
  alarmSoundElement = document.getElementById("alarmAudio");
  alarmSoundElement.play();
}
```

This code looks like the code in the **Ch02-08 Paragraph Update** example. In that case, the getElementById method was fetching a paragraph element to be updated. In the function above, getElementById is fetching an audio element to be played. An audio element provides a play method that starts it playing. The rest of the file is exactly the same as the original egg timer. If you try this program, you will hear quite an impressive sound when your egg is ready.

Controlling audio playback

The egg timer page does not display anything to represent the audio element. It is "hidden" inside the HTML. You can modify an `audio` element so that a player control is shown on the web page. To do this, you just have to add the word `controls` into the element tag:

```
<!DOCTYPE html>
<html lang="en">

<head>
  <title>Ch02-11 Sound playback</title>
</head>

<body>
    <audio controls>
        <source src="everythingSound.mp3" type="audio/mpeg">
      Your browser does not support the audio element.
    </audio>
    </body>
</html>
```

This is the complete source of an MP3 file playback page. If you visit the page you will see a simple playback control, as shown in **Figure 2-13**.

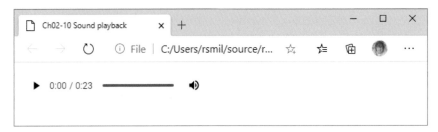

Figure 2-13   Sound playback

This is how the playback control looks when using the Edge browser. Other browsers will look slightly different, but the fundamental controls will be the same. You can start the playback by pressing the play control at the far left.

An image display program

The final example program in this chapter shows how JavaScript can change the content of an image displayed on the screen. You can use this technique to implement "slide shows" and also allow the user to select images for display. The image to be updated must be given an ID:

```
<img src="seaside1.JPG" id="pageImage"></p>
```

This `img` element displays the picture in the file `seaside.JPG`. A JavaScript program can change the displayed image by modifying the `src` attribute of the image and making it refer to a different image file:

```
var pic = document.getElementById("pageImage");
pic.src="fairground.JPG";
```

These two statements get a reference to the image and then set the `src` attribute of the `img` to refer to the image `fairground.jpg`. This will update the image displayed by the browser. Note that this is a repetition of a pattern that you've seen several times now. A program obtains a reference to a display element and then makes changes to it. You can find a complete image picker program in the **Ch02-12 Image Picker** example.

MAKE SOMETHING HAPPEN

Create your own pages

You now know enough to create your own pages that contain timers, images, and buttons. Here are some ideas for you to think about:

- **Make a "mood" page**   The page will display buttons labeled "Happy," "Sad," "Worried," and so on. When the user presses a button, the page will display an appropriate message and play a piece of appropriate music.

- **Make a "fitness" page**   Users will press a button to select an exercise length, and the page will display exercise instructions and start a timer for that exercise.

- **Make a slide show**   Users press a button, and the page will show a sequence of images. To do this, you can use a number of calls to `setTimeout` to trigger picture changes at different times in the future—perhaps one at two minutes, one at four minutes, and so on.

What you have learned

This chapter has given you a good understanding of what the World Wide Web is and how it works. Here are the major points you've covered in this chapter:

- The HTTP (Hypertext Transport Protocol) is used by *browsers* to request pages of data from web servers.

- Data arriving at the browser is *formatted* using HTML (Hypertext Markup Language) and a web page contains commands to the browser (for example *emphasize* this word) using tags (for example, `<em>`) to mark out *elements* in the text. Elements can contain text, images, audio, and preformatted text. Elements can also contain links to other web pages, which can be local to a page or on distant servers.

- HTML text can contain *symbol* definitions. Symbols include characters such as < (less than) and > (greater than), which are used to mark tags and can also be used to incorporate emojis into web pages.

- An HMTL document comprises a line that identifies the document as HTML, followed by header and body elements enclosed in an HTML element. The body of the document can contain a `<script>` element that holds JavaScript code.

- A web page can contain a button element that runs a JavaScript function when the button is activated.

- JavaScript code interacts with the HTML document via a document object containing all the elements of the page. The document provides methods that a program can call to interact with it. The document method `getElementById` can be used to obtain a reference to the page element with a particular ID.

- A JavaScript program can contain variables. These are named storage locations. A variable can be assigned a value, which it will store for later use. The assignment operation is denoted by the equals (=) character.

- A JavaScript function can locate elements in a document by their `id` attribute and then use element behaviors to change the attributes on the elements. This is how a JavaScript program could update the text in a paragraph or change the source file for an image.

- The `setTimeout` method can be used to call a JavaScript function at a given time in the future.

To reinforce your understanding of this chapter, you might want to consider the following "profound questions" about JavaScript, computers, programs, and programming.

What is the difference between the Internet and the World Wide Web?

The Internet is a mechanism for connecting large numbers of computers together. The World Wide Web is just one thing that we can use the Internet for. If the Internet were a railway, the World Wide Web would be one type of passenger train providing a particular service to customers.

What is the difference between HTML and HTTP?

HTTP is the Hypertext Transport Protocol. This is used to structure the conversation between a web browser and a web server. The browser uses HTTP to ask, "Get me a page." The server then gives a response, along with the page if it is found. The format of the question and the response is defined by HTTP. The design of the content of the page is expressed using Hypertext Markup Language. This tells the browser things like "put a picture here" or "make this part of the text a paragraph."

What is a URL?

A URL is the address of a resource that a browser wants to read. It starts with something that identifies what kind of thing is being requested. If it starts with HTTP, it means that the browser would like a web page. The middle part of the URL is the network address of the server that holds the web page to be read. The final part of the URL is the address on the server of the web page. This is a path to a file. If the path is omitted, the server will return the contents of a default file, which is sometimes (but not always) the file `index.html`

Where do I put things like image and audio files when I build a website?

The simplest place to put images and audio files is in the same folder as the website. So, the folder that contains `index.html` can also contain these images and sounds. However, a path to a resource can include folders, so it is possible to organize a website so all the images and sound files are held separately from the web pages. We will do this in the next chapter.

Why should I not use preformatted text for all my web pages?

The `<pre>..</pre>` element allows page designers to tell the browser that a block of text has already been formatted and that the browser is not to perform any additional layout. This can be useful for displaying such things as program listings that have a fixed format, but it does not allow the browser to make any allowance for the target device. One of the fundamentals of web page design is that the browser should be responsible for laying out the page. The page itself should contain hints such as "take a new paragraph here" and allow the browser to sort out the final appearance.

Why should I use `<em>` rather than `<i>`?

The `<i>` (italic) tag means "use italic text." The `<em>` tag means "make this text stand out." If the browser is running on a device that does not support italic text, it is much more useful for it to be asked to emphasize text (which it could do by changing color or inverting black and white), rather than select a character type that it is not able to display.

How are HTML tags and elements related?

A tag is the `<p>` marker that denotes that this text is an instruction to the browser rather than something to be displayed on a page. A complete sequence of tags (perhaps with a start and end tag) marks a complete element in a web page.

Does every HTML tag have to have a start and an end element?

No. Lots of tags do. For example, `<p>` marks the start of a paragraph and `</p>` marks the end. But some, for example `<br>` (create a new line), do not.

Can you put one element inside another?

Yes. A paragraph element may contain elements of emphasized text. And an audio element contains an element that identifies the source of the audio to be played.

What is the difference between an attribute and a property?

The HTML source of a web page contains elements with *attributes*. For example, `<img src="seaside1.JPG">` would create an image element with a `src` attribute set to the image in the `seaside1.JPG` file. Within JavaScript, the web page the program is part of is represented by a document object that contains a collection of objects. Each object represents one of the elements on the page. Each element object has a *property* that maps to a particular page attribute. A JavaScript program could change the `src` attribute of an image element to make it display a different picture. In short, attributes are the original values that are set in the HTML, and properties are the representations of these values that can be manipulated in a JavaScript program.

What is a reference?

In real life, a reference can be something that you follow to get somewhere. In a JavaScript program, a reference is used by a program to find a particular object. An object is a collection of data and behaviors that represent something our program is working with. JavaScript uses objects to represent elements on a web page. Each element is represented by an object. A reference is a lump of data that holds the location of a particular object.

What is the difference between a function and a method?

JavaScript contains functions, which are blocks of JavaScript code that have a name. We have written functions with names like `doEndTimer`. Methods are functions that are held inside objects. We have used the `getElementById` method, which is provided by the document object.

3
Cascading Style Sheets (CSS)

What you will learn

In the last two chapters, you've learned how to use HTML to design a web page and how to use JavaScript to add some behaviors to it. However, you've probably also noticed that the web pages that you've been creating don't look much like ones on the sites you usually visit. They are lacking in design and color. In this chapter, you'll discover how to manage the appearance of a web page to make it more appealing. Along the way, you'll pick up some important points abut JavaScript programming and make some nifty applications and games.

Putting on the style

We can start by considering what style is. Apparently, it is something that you either have or have not got. And I've been told many times that I don't have any. But in the case of web page design, I have a little bit, and I can tell you how to create and apply styles to the contents of web pages. The *style* of an element on a web page covers such things as the foreground and background color it has, the type of character design (font), the size of the text, and things like margins. You can think of a style as a collection of settings that you want to apply to something. We are going to start by styling some text. Once we've worked out how to apply style to a single element in a document, we will move on to consider how we can make it easier for us to change the style of all the elements in a document.

Splashing some color

We can start by adding a bit of color to a page. The definition of an HTML element on a web page can contain attributes that describe the element. We can add a *style* attribute to an element to set the foreground color for that element.

```
<p>This is an ordinary paragraph</p>
<p style="color:red">This is a red paragraph.</p>
```

Above, you can see how style is applied to a single paragraph. The first paragraph is ordinary. The second has been styled with red text. **Figure 3-1** shows how this appears on the page.

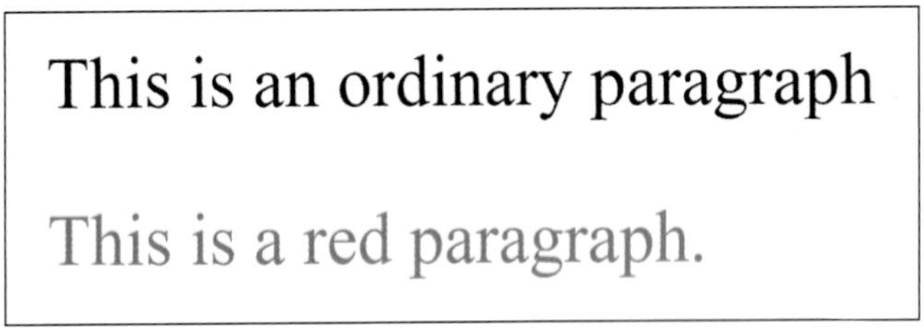

This is an ordinary paragraph

This is a red paragraph.

Figure 3-1   Styling text

The HTML standard contains a set of color definitions that you can refer to by name. Visual Studio Code will show you a tiny preview of the color when you are editing the text of your code, as shown in **Figure 3-2**.

```
<p>This is an ordinary paragraph</p>
<p style="color:■red">This is a red paragraph.</p>
```

Figure 3-2   Visual Studio color preview

Visual Studio Code will also produce a color menu when you start typing a color value into a style when you are editing your HTML source (see **Figure 3-3**).

Figure 3-3   Visual Studio color selector

There are very many style settings. The interactive help in Visual Studio will show you all the possible settings when you start typing a style command. Style settings can be combined in a single style description by separating them with the semicolon character. The style below would result in a tasteful display of red text on a yellow background.

```
<p style="color:red; background: yellow;">Red on Yellow.</p>
```

Color highlighting on mouse rollover

By now you should be used to a pattern of JavaScript program that works like this:

1. Attach a JavaScript function to an event.

2. When the function runs, it gets a reference to an element in the document.

3. The function then changes a property on the element to change the appearance of the document.

We've used this to make a program that responds to button clicks and another one that runs a function after a time interval has elapsed. Now we are going to use exactly same pattern to make a web page that highlights text when you roll the mouse over it. You definitely seen this used on web pages that you have visited. Take a look at the code below:

```html
<!DOCTYPE html>
<html lang="en">
<head>
<title>Ch03-02 Color Change on Mouse Over</title>
</head>
<body>
<p onmouseover="doMouseOver();" id="mouseOverPar">Roll your mouse over this paragraph.</p>
<script>
    function doMouseOver()
    {
        var par = document.getElementById("mouseOverPar");
        par.style="color: red";
    }
</script>
</body>
</html>
```

Can you work out which event we are using, and how the function doMouseOver changes the color of the text?

The event that we are using is called onmouseover and the program is using the style property of the paragraph to make it turn red. The browser will call the function doMouseOver when it detects that the mouse pointer is over the paragraph text. The function doMouseOver obtains a reference to the paragraph and then sets the style of that paragraph to include the color red.

Let's take a look at how the code works in practice. Find the **Ch03 HTML/ Ch03-02 Color Change on Mouse Over** folder. Double-click the **index.html file** in that folder to open the page. In the top-left corner, you will see a simple page with this message: "Roll your mouse over this paragraph." Roll your mouse over the text and note what happens. You should see the text turn red, which is exactly what you want, but you should notice something else, too. Is the behavior what you want? I think you would prefer it if the text turned back to black when the mouse was not over the paragraph.

We have found our first *bug*. A bug in a program is a behavior that you don't want. Finding and fixing bugs is a big chunk of software development. In this case, the bug came about because we didn't think through what rollover actually means. Perhaps we assumed that the browser would restore the original color of the text when the mouse left the paragraph, but that is not how the program works. How do you think we can fix this?

We can fix it by using another event. It turns out that an element on a web page can generate events when a mouse leaves it as well as when the mouse moves over it. The event that we need to use is called onmouseout, and we need to connect it to a function that sets the text color of the paragraph back to black. See if you can fix your copy of the program so that it works correctly. Edit the **index.html** file using Visual Studio Code, save it, and then test it with the browser.

If you want to see my fixed solution, take a look in the **Ch03 HTML/ Ch03-03 Color Change on Mouse Over Working** folder. This works, but later in the text, we will discover a much easier way to create a rollover effect.

PROGRAMMER'S POINT

Bugs are a fact of life for a programmer

You are going to have to get used to creating bugs. I've been programming for many years and I still write code with bugs in. And I expect to create many more bugs as I write more programs. The thing to remember is that creating a bug is fine, but creating a *fault* is not. You get a fault when a customer finds a bug in your program. Programmers spot bugs by testing. Programmers make faults by not testing enough, which leads to bugs making their way into the final product. Whenever you make something, you need to work out how to test it. In the case of our "paragraph highlight" program, the testing is obvious—just move the mouse over and see what happens. When we make some bigger programs, we'll discover that testing can be more complex.

Note that bugs are also the result of by poor specifications. Initially, I said that I wanted some text to change color when the mouse pointer is rolled over it. The first version of our program did this, so you could say it was free of bugs. It was only when we noticed that the text stayed highlighted when the mouse moved off the text that we decided that behavior was not what we wanted. This shows how important it is to think through exactly what you want a program to do before you start building it. It also shows the usefulness of "prototype" programs that can be used to determine whether the solution does exactly what the customer wants.

Work with fonts

Fonts are one of many things about computers where computer manufacturers have "agreed to differ."

They all agree that they need a font that looks like this.

(This is called a *serif* font because the lines in the character design have lines on the end.)

And they all agree that we need a font that looks like this.

(This is called a *sans-serif* font because it doesn't have extra lines and "sans" is French for "without.")

However, the manufacturers have not agreed on the names for them. For example, the "sans serif" font can be called "Arial" or "Helvetica."

Select a text font

This means that when we specify the font to use in a web page, we can't request a specific font because we don't know what type of computer is being used to view the page. Instead, we will specify a *font family*. This is specified in the style for an element. We can specify a list of fonts that we would like to use, and the browser will work through them in order looking for a font that it can use:

```
<p style="font-family:Arial, Helvetica, sans-serif">This is in sans-serif font</p>
```

The style above asks for **Arial**, followed by **Helvetica** and finally **sans-serif**. Most computers have a sans-serif font, so the last entry in the list acts as a "catch all." The first item on the list is a specific font, while the last item on the list will be a more abstract font type. If I were picking vegetables to have for dinner, the first item would be "chips" (a specific dish) and the last would be "potatoes" (a general catch-all for the particular vegetable I want). Font selection works in the same way. Note that when I select a font family, I get the designs for bold and italic versions of the characters in that font, too. See **Figure 3-4**.

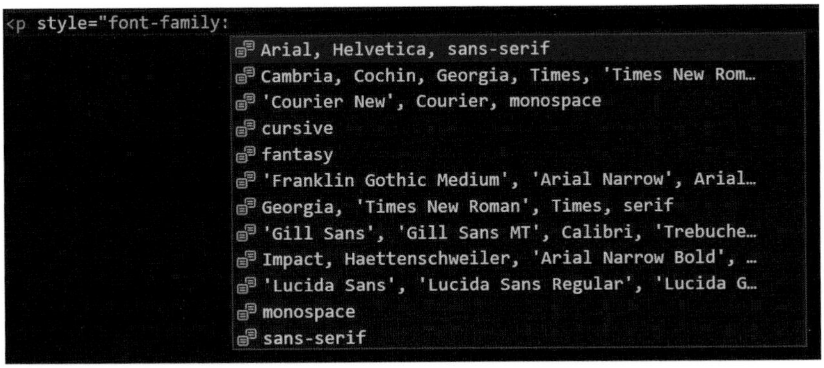

```
<p style="font-family:
                        Arial, Helvetica, sans-serif
                        Cambria, Cochin, Georgia, Times, 'Times New Rom…
                        'Courier New', Courier, monospace
                        cursive
                        fantasy
                        'Franklin Gothic Medium', 'Arial Narrow', Arial…
                        Georgia, 'Times New Roman', Times, serif
                        'Gill Sans', 'Gill Sans MT', Calibri, 'Trebuche…
                        Impact, Haettenschweiler, 'Arial Narrow Bold', …
                        'Lucida Sans', 'Lucida Sans Regular', 'Lucida G…
                        monospace
                        sans-serif
```

Figure 3-4   Visual Studio Code font selector

We have already seen how helpful Visual Studio Code is when selecting style colors. It also pops up suggestions for font families, which have been arranged in a sensible way. The suggested families give a good range of typefaces that you can use in your pages, as shown in **Figure 3-5** below. You can find the HTML code that generates this page in the example folder at **Ch03 HTML/ Ch03-04 Fonts in JavaScript**.

This is standard text.

Arial, Helvetica, sans-serif

Cambria, Cochin, Georgia, Times, Times New Roman, serif

cursive

fantasy

Franklin Gothic Medium, Arial Narrow, Arial, sans-serif

Georgia, Times New Roman, Times, serif

Gill Sans, Gill Sans MT, Calibri, Trebuchet MS, sans-serif

Impact, Haettenschweiler, Arial Narrow Bold, sans-serif

Lucida Sans, Lucida Sans Regular, Lucida Grande

monospace

Figure 3-5   Font examples

Fonts can be a minefield

I must admit that I find it difficult to spot the difference between the Cambria and Georgia fonts in **Figure 3.5** above. But some people can, and they may have strong opinions. Make sure that you agree with your customer about the fonts that you are going to use. I don't use many fonts in my pages. I usually use one serif font for headings and a sans-serif for normal text (or vice versa). Just because you *can* use lots of fonts in a page doesn't mean that you *should*.

You should make sure that if a font name contains spaces (for example, Times New Roman), you should enclose this name in single quotes in the font family setting. You should also note from **Figure 3.5** above that different fonts have quite different sizes, which can affect your page layout.

Select a font size

As I write this book, I'm not really worrying too much about the particular font size of the text. I know that the headings must be larger than "normal" text, but I don't concern myself too much with specific dimensions. When designing web pages, you should take a similar approach. In other words, if you want to display large text in a heading, select the H1 format for the heading, and don't change the size of the font in the heading.

If you want to specify the size of text in a web page, there are a number of units you can use. You can express the size in inches, centimeters, pixels, points, or as a percentage of the size of the display, but I would advise you to use the em unit. An em value of 1 means normal-sized text. If you want smaller text, use a value of em that is smaller than 1; for example, an em value of 0.5 would mean half the normal size. This makes all the font sizes *relative* rather than *absolute*. This is usually what you want. As the creator of a page, you want to make sure that the text will be readable on all devices. Setting an absolute size will make text that looks perfect on one device and wrong on every other. If you want text twice as big as the normal size for that font, you would set the em size to 2 and so on. You set the size of the text on the screen by setting a font-size in a style:

```
<p>This is normal text.</p>
<p style="font-size:1em">This is 1 em.</p>
<p style="font-size:2em">This is 2 em.</p>
<p style="font-size:0.5em">This is 0.5 em.</p>
```

Figure 3-6 shows the above HTML as it would appear on the page. (You can find the HTML code that shows these examples in **Ch03 HTML/Ch03-05 Font Sizes**.)

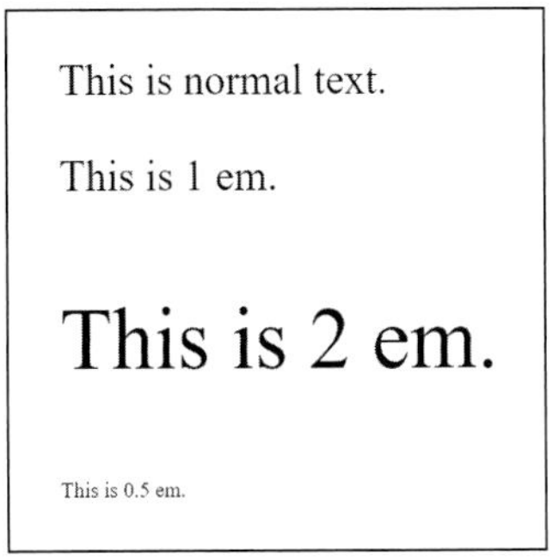

This is normal text.

This is 1 em.

This is 2 em.

This is 0.5 em.

Figure 3-6 Font sizes

Text alignment

You can also add an element to a style command to tell the browser how to lay out the text. By default (unless you specify otherwise), your text will be laid out with each line starting at the left-hand margin. You can add a `text-align` setting to a style, as shown below and in **Figure 3-7**.

```
<p style="text-
align: left;">This text is aligned at the left hand margin of the page and the words
    will wrap with a ragged edge.
    This is the normal format of text</p>
<p style="text-align: center;">This text is aligned in the center.
    Useful for headings and quotations.</p>
<p style="text-align: right;">This text is aligned at the right margin of the page.</p>
<p style="text-
align:justify;">This text is aligned at the left and right margins of the page.
    This makes the text look like the pages of a book or a column in a newspaper.</p>
```

This text is aligned at the left hand margin of the page and the words will wrap with a ragged edge. This is the normal format of text

This text is aligned in the center. Useful for headings and quotations.

This text is aligned at the right margin of the page.

This text is aligned at the left and right margins of the page. This makes the text look like the pages of a book or a column in a newspaper.

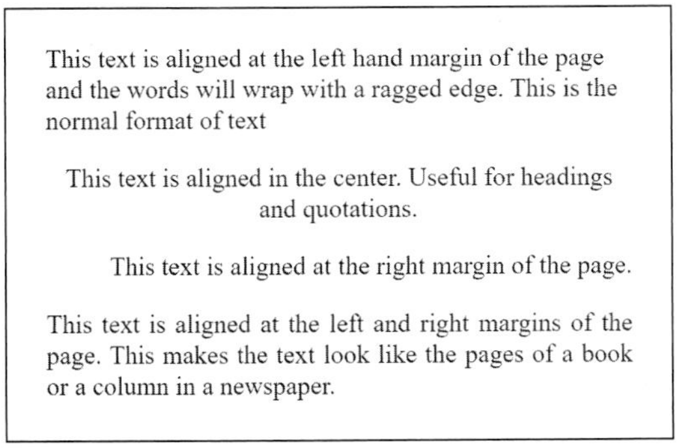

Figure 3-7 Text alignment

Make a ticking clock

We can use our ability to display large text on the screen to create a large ticking clock. However, to do this we need to know how a JavaScript program can obtain the current time (the value of hours, minutes, and seconds to be displayed by the clock). We also need to create a program that runs every second to update the clock display.

MAKE SOMETHING HAPPEN

Get the time for display

The programs that we have created so far have interacted with the Document object, which represents the HTML that makes up the web page. To get the time, we need to create another type of object, the Date object. Let's see how this works. Find the **Ch03 HTML/ Ch03-07 Clock Display** folder and double-click the **index.html** file in that folder to open the page. You should see a clock displaying 0:0:0. We are going to get the time and display it on the clock. Press F12 to open the Developer Tools view and move to the console window. Enter the following JavaScript statement:

```
var currentDate = new Date();
```

We've seen var before; it is how a program creates variables. The variable that is created is called currentDate and it is made to refer to a newly created Date object. The word new means "make a new object." We've not had to create any objects before because our programs have used objects that already exist when the program runs. The Date object is provided to allow JavaScript programs to work with dates and times.

When a new Date object is created, it is set with the current date and time. The variable currentDate is a reference that refers to the newly created Date object. We've used references before when we created a reference to a paragraph element in a web page that we wanted to update. Take a look at example **Ch02-08 Paragraph Update** if you need to refresh your understanding of this. We can ask an object questions by calling methods on the reference to it. Type the following:

```
alert(currentDate.getHours());
```

This statement uses the getHours method, which is part of a Date object. This method returns a number that contains the hours value of the date. The statement displays this in an alert. There are also methods to get the minutes and seconds values. Each method has a name that reflects what it does. See if you can use them to display these time values as well. Note that you must put the open and close brackets () after each method name so that JavaScript knows you want to call the method. We will find out more about making method calls in Chapter 7.

Now type in the following statements to set variables with the hours, minutes, and seconds values that we need for the clock:

```
var hours = currentDate.getHours();
var mins = currentDate.getMinutes();
var secs = currentDate.getSeconds();
```

We now have the hours, mins, and secs variables that we can use to build up a string to display as the time. The string will contain the time values separated by the : (colon) character. Type the following statement to create the time string:

```
var timeString = hours+":"+mins+":"+secs;
```

This statement creates a variable called timeString that contains the time that we want to display. The values in the hours, mins, and secs variables are converted into text. You can view this string using an alert:

```
alert(timeString);
```

If you check the time that appears in the alert, you will find that it is out of date because it will have taken you a few seconds to type all these statements. The value in currentDate is a *snapshot* of the date and time. This will not be a problem in our clock program because the time values will be displayed immediately after they have been read. We now know how to get the time value into a string that is ready for display. The HTML for the clock display program contains a paragraph that has the id timePar. Type the following statements:

```
var outputElement = document.getElementById("timePar");
outputElement.textContent=timeString;
```

We've used this pattern of statements before. The first one creates a variable that refers to the output element we want to use to display the time. The second statement sets the textContent property of that element to the contents of the timeString variable. This will cause the time to be displayed.

The HTML for this page contains a function that does everything we have just typed in. Type the following statement to call this function:

```
doClockTick()
```

You should see the date and time update to show the current date and time. Press F12 to close the **Developer Tools** in the browser.

Create a ticking clock

We now know how to create a string that contains the current time and then display that string in large text. Now we need a way to make the clock "tick." When we created the egg timer programs in Chapter 2, we used a function called setTimeout to call a JavaScript function after a specified timeout value. Another useful function in JavaScript is called setInterval, which calls a function at regular intervals. As with the setTimeout function, the interval is specified in milliseconds.

```
setInterval(doClockTick,1000);
```

The statement above would cause a method called doClockTick to be called every second. This is the function that will update our clock. The final piece of our application is a way of starting the interval timer. We could ask the user to press a button to start the clock (this is how the egg timer works), but it would be best if the clock starts ticking as soon as the page is opened. The onload event can be made to call a function when an element on a web page is loaded—in this case, a three-digit ticking clock, which is shown in **Figure 3-8**. You can find the HTML code below in the **Ch03 HTML/Ch03-08 Ticking Clock** example folder.

Figure 3-8 Ticking clock

```
<!DOCTYPE html>
<html lang="en">
<head>
    <title>Ch03-08 Ticking Clock</title>
</head>
```

```
<body onload=" ᴬdoStartClock();">                          Calls doStartClock when the page is loaded.
    <p id="timePar" style="font-size:10em;font-
family: 'Courier New', Courier, monospace;
    text-align: center;">00:00:00</p>              This is the paragraph that contains the clock display
    <script>
        function doStartClock()                              Function that starts the clock
        {
            setInterval(doClockTick,1000);               Call doClockTick every second
        }

    function doClockTick()                             Update the clock with the current time
    {
        var currentDate = new Date();
        var hours = currentDate.getHours();
        var mins = currentDate.getMinutes();
        var secs = currentDate.getSeconds();
        var timeString = hours+":"+mins+":"+secs;


        var outputElement = document.getElementById("timePar");
        outputElement.textContent=timeString;
    }
</script>
</body>
</html>
```

Ticking clock

You might have some questions about this code. And if you haven't, I have. It's important that you understand the answers because they underpin some important aspects of JavaScript programming.

Question: What is the difference between **var** and **new**?

> **Answer:** The commands `var` and `new` look very similar because they seem to be associated with the creation of something, but you might be confused about exactly what is going on. In the case of `var`, a program is creating a new variable:

```
var age=21;
```

This would create a variable called age, which is set to the number 21 (which is a bit optimistic in my case).

```
var outputElement = document.getElementById("timePar");
```

This would create a variable called outputElement, which is set to the result delivered by the getElementByID from the document object. (You can refresh your understanding of how this works by reading the section "HTML and JavaScript" in Chapter 2.) So, every time we want to create a variable (such as a named location into which we can store something), we use var. In the next chapter, we will consider variables in much more detail.

A program uses new when it wants to make a new object. The word new is followed by the name of the type of object that is to be created:

```
var currentDate = new Date();
```

This creates a new variable called currentDate (that's what var does) and then sets this variable to refer to a Date object created using new. So, var is used to create variables, and new is used to create objects.

Question: Do I have to put semicolons after each statement when I use the console?

Answer: You might have noticed that console commands still work if you leave off the semicolon at the end. When you type JavaScript statements into the console, you end each one by pressing the Enter key. This means that JavaScript knows when you have finished the statement because you have pressed Enter. However, if you wanted to enter multiple statements on one command line, you would have to separate them using the semicolon character. I like to always add a semicolon so that someone reading my code will know exactly when I intend to end my statements.

Question: Why is one function name enclosed in quotes, whereas the other is not?

Answer: The clock program uses two functions. One is called doStartClock and starts the clock running. The other function is called doClockTick and updates the clock every second. The function doStartClock is called when the page is loaded by using the onload attribute of the body element:

```
<body onload="doStartClock();">
```

The doClockTick function is called every second using the setInterval function:

```
setInterval(doClockTick, 1000);
```

You might be wondering why the name of doStartClock is enclosed in double quotes, whereas doClockTick is not. At least, I hope you are, because appreciating the distinction will help you a lot in understanding how JavaScript and HTML work together. In the case of the onload event in the HTML, the action to be performed is a string containing JavaScript statements that are obeyed when the element is loaded. The string that we are using calls the doStartClock method, but it could be any sequence of JavaScript statements:

```
<body onload="var x=99;alert(x);">
```

This is completely legal HTML. The JavaScript that is performed on loading creates a variable called x, sets the value to 99, and then displays an alert showing this value. However, the setInterval function is given a reference to a function to be called every second, not a string containing some JavaScript code. You might be wondering why these two things work in different ways. This is because the onload event is part of an HTML element, whereas the setInterval function is called from within the JavaScript program code.

Question: Why does the time take a second to appear when the clock starts?

Answer: If you load the example, page you will find that it takes a second for the time to appear. For a second after the page has loaded, the time is displayed as 0:0:0. If you think about it, this is exactly how the program works. The setInterval function calls the function doClockTick at one-second intervals, but this means that program must wait for this interval to elapse before the clock is displayed. Can you think of a way to solve this problem?

The solution is simple. The program must call doClockTick from the doStartClock function. Since the doStartClock method is called when the page is loaded, this will cause the display to be updated at the start. You can find my version of this in the **Ch03 HTML/Ch03-09 Clock Quick Start** folder.

Margins around text

Text on a printed page does not extend right to the edge of the paper. This book has *margins* around the paragraphs. Some paragraphs (for example, the "Code Analysis" sidebar above) have different margins from the rest of the text. This makes the paragraphs stand out. A style can express the size of margins around a paragraph. It can also describe a border for a paragraph. The paragraph above has an outer margin, a border, and then "padding" around the text inside the border.

```
<p style="margin: 20px;
    padding: 10px;
    border:1px;border-style: solid; border-color:blue;">
    This is some text in a blue box.</p>
```

The dimensions of the margins and the border are expressed in units we have not seen before called `px`, which is short for *pixel*.

I could have spent some time drawing a diagram to show how the margin, border, and padding values are used to control the layout of text on a page, but it turns out that the Edge browser will do this for me. In **Figure 3-9**, you can see the developer view of the HTML above, which you can find in the code folder **Ch03 HTML/ Ch03-10 Margins**. The diagram on the bottom right of Figure 3-9 shows how the margin, border, and padding elements all fit inside each other.

Figure 3-9   Margin display

I've specified the margin, border, and padding dimensions in the `px` unit, which is an *absolute* unit that equates to a single dot on the target display. We used these units when we specified the size of an image to be drawn on the screen. If you are concerned with precise layout, you can use these to lay out text and graphics exactly. The size of a px unit matches that used to set the size of images, so you can combine text and graphics to make precisely aligned pages. The HTML below, which you can find in the **Ch03 HTML/ Ch03-11 Fixed Width Paragraphs** code folder, puts an image and a descriptive paragraph inside a blue box, as shown in **Figure 3-10** below.

```
<p style="margin: 20px;
    border:1px;
    border-style: solid;
    border-color:blue;
    padding: 10px;
    width:400px;
    font-family: Arial, Helvetica, sans-serif;
    text-align: justify;
    ">
    <img src="seaside.JPG" alt="Waves crashing on a deserted beach" width="400">
    This picture was taken on New Year&quot;s Day 2020 at Hornsea sea front.
    Hornsea is a village on the north eastern coast of England.</p>
```

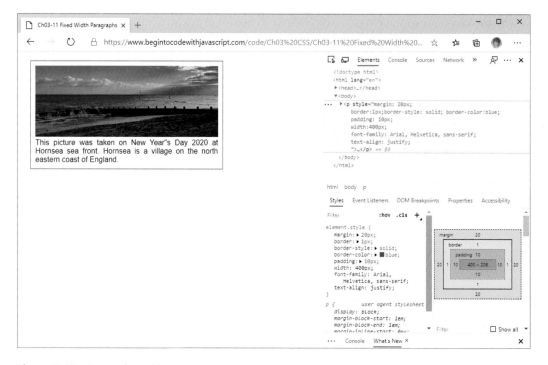

Figure 3-10   Text and graphics

There are lots more things you can do with styles. The best way to find out about them is to use the pop-up help in Visual Studio Code to get ideas for command options and then try them out.

Making a style sheet

An HTML document can use the `style` attribute to add style to any element in a document. However, it seems like hard work to have to add style elements to everything. Fortunately, HTML provides a way to simplify the application of a style to a document. We can add a *style sheet* to an HTML document to apply styles to elements in the document. The style sheet is added to the head of the document between the `<style>` and `</style>` tags, as shown below.

```
<!DOCTYPE html>
<html lang="en">

<head>
    <title>Ch03-12 Changing styles</title>
    <style>                                         ── Style element
        p {                                         ── Selector for the p style
            color: blue;
            font-family: Arial, Helvetica, sans-serif;
        }                                           ── End of settings for p
    </style>
</head>

<body>
    <p>
        This is a modified paragraph.</p>
</body>

</html>
```

We can use a style sheet to set style properties on elements. A style setting starts with a *selector*, which specifies the element that is being styled. We want to style the `<p>` element, so that is what we specified in the style sheet above. The changes the style sheet makes result in all `<p>` elements in the document being displayed in blue text using the Arial, Helvetica, or sans-serif fonts. A style sheet can provide style settings for many elements.

Creating a style sheet file

When a website is created the designers usually come up with a standard "house style" which is to be applied to all the pages. The house style settings could be included in the `<head>` section of each page as shown in the sample above, but this would make it hard to change the style of the site because each document would need to be edited. To make this easier the style settings can be stored in a separate file. A `<link>` element in the HTML header then specifies the style sheet file to be added.

```html
<head>
    <title>Ch03-13 Stylesheet File</title>
    <link rel="stylesheet" href="styles.css">
</head>
```

The HTML above shows how this works. The `link` element contains a `rel` attribute that tells the browser the type of resource that the link relates to. In this case, the link relates to a style sheet. The link to the file containing the style information is specified in the `href` attribute. In the case of the HTML page above, this is a local file called `styles.css`, which is held in the same folder as the HTML page. However, this file could be in a different folder, or it could even be on another server. The actual style sheet file contains the style instructions:

```css
p {
    color: blue;
    font-family:Arial, Helvetica, sans-serif;
}
```

PROGRAMMER'S POINT

It is a good idea to separate style from layout

A web page is made up of layout (what is on the page and where it is) and style (how the page looks). It is very sensible to separate these elements. I could have filled this entire book with a description of how to style web pages, but it would not be a very good read because I'm not very good at design. I'd much rather find a designer who is good with fonts and colors and ask them to sort those things out. Being able to put the styling information into a separate file means that I can design the layout and the behavior of the application entirely apart from the style.

Computer scientists talk about "separation of concerns" in a project, where different people work on different parts. At the start of the project, everyone agrees how the different components will work together, and then they can work on just their parts. In the case of HTML and style, I would tell the designer I was using <p>, <h1>, and <h2> for different levels of text, and then the designer could work on the look of these styles. Later, when we start writing larger JavaScript programs, we will discover a way of separating the program code from the HTML, which allows another level of separation.

Creating style classes

If we are making a simple web application, we might be able to express all our formatting requirements using the paragraph and heading styles. However, a more complex
application would need to contain other styles. For example, we might want to have a
different format for displaying an address. It might need to be red, in a monospaced
font, and aligned to the right-hand margin. We can add a new style class called
address to the style sheet for a document:

```
.address {
    color: red;
    font-family: 'Courier New', Courier, monospace;
    text-align:  right;
}
```

Notice that this looks like the way that we modified the styling of `<p>`, except that the
address class has a leading dot (.) to indicate that this is a newly created style class:
.address. We can then specify that this class provides the style of a paragraph:

```
<p class="address"> This is an address paragraph.</p>
```

The class attribute of an element specifies a CSS (Cascading Style Sheet) style class
that is to be used to style the element. This means that the text in the paragraph
above would be drawn in a red and monospaced font at the right-hand side of the
page. You can see this in action in the **Ch03 HTML/ Ch03-14 Address Style** folder.
You can create as many style classes as you need. If you were working with a designer,
you would both agree on the style names to be used for the various elements, and
then you could generate HTML files elements tagged with the classes that should be
used to format them.

Exploring style sheets

We can use the **Developer** menu in the browser to take a look at how the style sheets work. Find the **Ch03 HTML/Ch03-14 Address Style Class** folder and open the `index.html` file with your browser. This shows you the address paragraph formatted with a red monospaced font. Press **F12** to open the **Developer** menu. Then select the **Sources** tab in the dialog box at the top of the **Developer** menu.

You can now see the `index.html` and `style.css` files. If you click them, you can view their contents. When we start making more complex web pages, you'll find this view very useful. You can use it to view the sources of any web page you visit, but don't get discouraged by how complicated they seem.

Formatting parts of a document using `<div>` and `<span>`

We can add a `class` attribute to any element of text that we want to format, but sometimes it is useful to apply a style class to multiple items. In the case of the `address` style above, we would like to mark all the paragraphs in the address that we are displaying. We could mark each paragraph individually, but it would be nice if we could mark them all at once. The `<div>` and `<span>` elements make this possible. They are used to create regions to which classes can be assigned.

```
<!DOCTYPE html>
<html lang="en">

<head>
    <title>Ch03-14 Address Style</title>
    <link rel="stylesheet" href="styles.css">
</head>

<body>
    <div class="address">
        <p>Rob Miles</p>
        <p>18 Pussycat Mews</p>
        <p>London</p>
        <p>NE14 10S</p>
    </div>
</body>

</html>
```

The HTML above would format all the paragraphs of the address using the `address` class because they are enclosed in a division. The `div` element specifies a *division* in the document. Each `div` element marks the start and end of a paragraph of text. This means that we can't use a `div` element to set the style of some words in a paragraph. If we want to just format part of a paragraph using a particular style, we can use the `span` element.

```
<p>An HTML document can use the
<span class="codeInText">style</span>
attribute to add style to any element in a document.</p>
```

In the example above, I want the word style to stand out from the text because it is an HTML element name. I've created a class called codeInText and used it to apply a style to the word style in the sentence. I can't use div in this situation because this would break the sentence over several lines. The **Ch03 HTML/ Ch03-16 Code Style with span** example shows how it works. You can put span and div elements inside each other, but it doesn't make much sense to put a div inside a span because this would cause paragraph breaks in your line of text. You must, of course, make sure that any "nesting" is properly formatted. Take a look at the Programmer's Point "Don't abuse the browser" in Chapter 2 for more details on this issue.

Cascading styles

You might be wondering why they are called *cascading* style sheets. The name refers to the way styles "cascade" down from one element to all the elements it encloses. Consider the following HTML:

```
<!DOCTYPE html>
<html lang="en">
<head>
<title>Ch03-17 Cascading Styles</title>
</head>
<body style="color: blue;">
<p>This is an ordinary paragraph.</p>
<p style="color:red">This is a red paragraph.</p>
<p style="background: yellow;">This has a yellow background.</p>
</body>
</html>
```

The document contains three style elements. The first is applied to the body of the document. The next two are applied to elements inside the body of the text. The body element has been styled with the color blue. The body element encloses the two paragraph elements, so this setting *cascades* down onto these paragraphs, as shown in **Figure 3-11**.

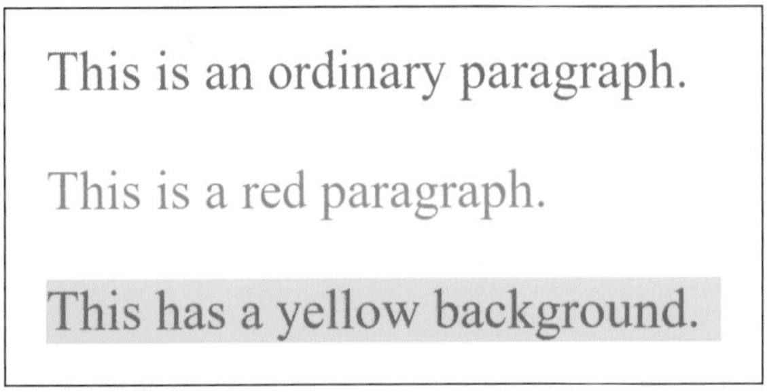

This is an ordinary paragraph.

This is a red paragraph.

This has a yellow background.

Figure 3-11   Cascading styles in action

The "ordinary" paragraph has blue text because of the style applied to the enclosing body element. The red paragraph is red because the color setting in the style for the paragraph *overrides* the cascading style. However, the text with a yellow background has blue text because the style on this paragraph does not modify the color in the enclosing one; instead, it modifies the color of the text background. The rule is that style settings are "inherited" from enclosing elements unless they are "overridden" in them.

PROGRAMMER'S POINT

Managing styles is all about design

As you go through this book, I want to you learn that a lot of solution development is about making your life easier. For example, you might have a problem if you showed your customer the solution you had built and they told you they want shocking-pink text on an orange background (it has been known). If you'd applied the text style to each HTML element, this would mean you would have to work through the entire document and make the requested changes. If you've used style sheets properly, you should be able to change just one file to make a change like this.

A huge amount of programming is about organization and planning. This chapter has introduced some excellent tools that you can use to create and manage the appearance of an HTML page.

Color highlighting using selectors

Earlier in this chapter, in "Make Something Happen: Color highlighting on mouse roll-over," we used the onmouseover event to trigger a JavaScript function to change the color of text in a paragraph. At the time, I said that there is a much easier way to make text appear as highlighted when the user rolls their mouse over it.

```
.rollover {
    color:black;
}

.rollover:hover {
    color:red;
}
```

The style sheet above creates a style called `rollover`. There are two definitions for the style. The first definition just sets the color as black. The second definition of `rollover` has an additional *selector*: `hover`. A selector indicates the circumstance in which this variant of the style should be used. The `hover` selector specifies that this style is to be used when the mouse is hovering over an element with the class set to `rollover`. This style sets the color to red. If you view this page in the **Ch03 CSS\Ch03-18 Rollover with CSS** folder, you will see how it works.

There is a lot more you can do with selectors. You can use them to set styles for unvisited links, or selected items, and you can even use them to set the first letter of a paragraph. You can find a full reference at the following Mozilla page. You will have to work hard to understand all of it (I did), but it is powerful stuff: *https://developer.mozilla.org/en-US/docs/Web/CSS/CSS_Selectors*.

What you have learned

This chapter has given you a good understanding of what style is and how to manage it. Here are the major points we covered in this chapter:

- The definition of an element in an HTML page can include a style attribute that describes how the element should be displayed, such as to make the text in a paragraph red.

- The definition of an element can also include event attributes that execute a piece of JavaScript code when a particular event occurs, such as the `onmouseover` event triggering code when the user moves the mouse pointer over the element.

- The style information for a text element can include the font to be used to draw the text. Fonts are specified as *families*, which include all the variants of the text to be displayed (such as italic and bold). It is conventional to provide a number of different `font-family` values when specifying font options because systems use different names for popular font designs.

- The size of elements in an HTML document can be specified in multiple ways. If the intention is to change the size of text relative to other text, the size should be expressed in em units, where an em value of 1 is "normal-sized" text.

- Text can be aligned across an HTML page using the text-align attribute.

- The setInterval function can be used to call a JavaScript function at regular intervals. We used this to create a ticking clock.

- The style of an element can include definitions for margin, padding, and border items. The margin is the outer margin around the element. The border can be drawn in a variety of styles and colors, and the border has a set thickness. The padding value sets how far the item is placed away from the border.

- When specifying the dimensions of borders and margins around HTML elements, the px unit can be used. A value expressed in px units represents a number of *pixels* and equates to the size of a pixel in an image. Using px units means that you can get absolute control over the layout of items at the expense of portability. (For example, the pages might look too large or too small on some devices.)

- A style sheet contains style settings that can be assigned to elements in an HTML document. Style settings can modify styles such as <p>, <h1>, and <h2>, or they can create completely new styles that can be assigned to elements using the class attribute.

- A style sheet can be held in a file that is separate from an HTML page. The page contains a link element in the page heading that identifies the style sheet file to be used. This allows complete separation between the content and the styling of a page.

- Styles are applied to elements in a way that cascades down from enclosing elements. For example, if the body of a document is styled with red text, that setting will cascade down into any elements in the document. However, a color style attribute in a paragraph inside the document will override this cascading setting.

- The div and span elements act as containers around other elements. Style attributes applied to the div and span elements cascade down into all the elements contained in them. When a div element is rendered, the browser will insert line breaks at the start and the end of the div. This does not happen with a span element, making the span element useful for applying styles to words in sentences.

To reinforce your understanding of this chapter, you might want to consider the following "profound questions" about styles and style sheets.

Can I add a style attribute to any element?

Yes. It might not be sensible to set the font of the script element in an HTML file, but it will not cause an error if you do.

What happens if I add an irrelevant style to an item?

Nothing. If you want to set a font for the `<script>` part of your HTML file, you can do that, and you will not get any errors, but it would not be a sensible thing to do.

What happens if I set conflicting style settings?

The most "recently" applied style will be the one that is enforced. In other words, if the text color of the body of the document is set to black, but the text color of the paragraph in the body is set to red, the text will be red. This is how "cascading" works.

Is a CSS file a program?

No. The JavaScript programs that we have written set out a sequence of actions to be performed. A CSS file contains a number of style settings items that are applied to HTML elements that are assigned to them.

Is redText a good name for a CSS style class?

I don't think so. If your customer decides that they really want to change to blue text for that style, you can't easily change the name of the class. The name of a class should reflect what you want a style to achieve. For example, you could have a class called `displayName`, which is used to display names, and you could have another class called `displayAddress` for addresses. If a style is being displayed as red, that's something that would be reflected in the settings for that style class, not in the name of the class itself.

Can I store CSS files on a different server from the HTML file that contains the web page?

Yes, you can. The link element that gets the CSS file contains a URL that can refer to a file on a distant machine.

When should I use div, and when should I use span?

Div is used if you want to control the style of some elements that make up a *division* in your page. By division, I mean something like an entire address, an order, or a report. The division will be separated from the rest of the page by line breaks. Span is used when you want to style a small portion of a paragraph. For example, you might use span to highlight the word code in this sentence. In this case, you don't want any line breaks in the text.

What is the difference between id and class?

An element on a web page can have a setting for an id value and a class value. The id value is unique for that element in the HTML document. JavaScript code that works with the document can locate an element by its id. The class value specifies the style to be applied to this element. A large number of elements in a document can have the same class value. This would make changing the style of these elements very easy because the designer would just have to change the definition of the class in the style sheet, and it would be applied to all the elements.

What is the difference between the em and px units?

This is confusing. Not least because em also means "emphasized" when applied to text. An em value of 1 refers to the size of a "normal" character in the current font. So, I can specify a size in em values so that I can make my text larger or smaller relative to the rest of the text. I don't want to use an absolute value for my text size because, as we have seen, different fonts have different "standard" text sizes, and I don't want everything to become too large or too small if the font changes. So em is very useful if you want to express that some things are bigger than others, but you don't want tie things to specific sizes.

A px value refers to a number of "pixels" on the screen. Modern high-resolution screens have pixels that are so small that this might not be an accurate mapping, but the idea is that px values give you the ability to place things more precisely, particularly in relation to images, which are also sized using pixel dimensions. So em is used if you want to lay elements out very precisely in relation to each other.

Is this all there is to CSS?

Absolutely not. We have barely scratched the surface in this chapter. You can perform animation, fade images in and out, and do all manner of other things too. The great thing is that the interactive help from tools like Visual Studio Code and the wonderful Developer Console in the browser allow you to experiment with styles to find out more. It is certainly worth doing this. As we have seen when we looked at the rollover style selector, we can replace JavaScript code with style sheet behavior. One of the rules of HTML development is that you should always check to see if a style sheet could be used to get the effect that you want before you write any JavaScript code. Just because you could write a program to get a particular effect doesn't mean that you should.

Part 2
Coding with JavaScript

In this part, we start writing JavaScript applications. We'll discover how to create complete programs that run inside the browser. We'll gain fundamental programming knowledge of data storage and processing in software. Then we'll move on to a discussion of how to structure solutions and break a large program into smaller components. Finally, we'll take a look at software objects and how they can be used to create custom data storage types that map program storage to real-world data.

4
Working with data

What you will learn

In this chapter, you'll build more JavaScript programs. You'll discover that a computer is fundamentally a data processor and that a program tells the computer what to do with the data. You'll see how programs store data using *variables*, and you'll learn how JavaScript manages diverse kinds of data that can be stored by a program. You'll also learn how JavaScript manages the *visibility* of variables within a program. By the end of this chapter, you'll be able to create useful programs.

Computers as data processors

Humans are a race of toolmakers. We invent things to make our lives easier, and we've been doing it for thousands of years. We started with mechanical devices, such as the plow, which made farming more efficient. In the last century, we've moved into electronic devices and, more recently, into computers.

As computers have become smaller and cheaper, they have found their way into things around us. Many devices (for example, the smartphone) are possible only because we can put a computer inside to make them work. However, we need to remember what the computer does; it automates operations that formerly required brain power. There's nothing particularly clever about a computer; it simply follows the instructions that it's been given.

A computer works on data in the same way that a sausage machine works on meat: Something is put in one end, some processing is performed, and something comes out the other end. A program tells a computer what to do in the same way that a coach gives instructions to a football or soccer team before a play. The coach might say something like, "If they attack on the left, I want Jerry and Chris to run back, but if they kick the ball down the field, I want Jerry to chase the ball." Then, when the game unfolds, the team will respond to events in a way that should let them outplay their opponents.

However, there is one important distinction between a computer program and the way a team might behave in a football game. A football player would know when he or she is given some senseless instructions. If the coach said, "If they attack on the left, I want Jerry to sing the first verse of the national anthem and then run as fast as he can toward the exit," the player would raise an objection.

Unfortunately, a program is unaware of the sensibility of the data it is processing, in the same way that a sausage machine is unaware of what meat is. Put a bicycle into a sausage machine, and the machine will try to make sausages out of it. Put meaningless data into a computer, and it will do meaningless things with it. As far as computers are concerned, data is just a pattern of signals coming in that must be manipulated in some way to produce another pattern of signals. A computer program is the sequence of instructions that tell a computer what to do with the input data and what form the output data should have.

Examples of typical data-processing applications include the following (as shown in **Figure 4-1**):

- **Smartphone**—A microcomputer in your phone takes signals from a radio and converts them into sound. At the same time, it takes signals from a microphone and makes them into patterns of bits that will be sent out from the radio.

- **Car**—A microcomputer in the engine takes information from sensors telling it the current engine speed, road speed, oxygen content of the air, accelerator setting, and so on. The microcomputer produces voltages that control the carburetor settings, the timing of the spark plugs, and other things to optimize engine performance.

- **Game console**—A computer takes instructions from the controllers and uses them to manage the artificial world that it is creating for the gamer.

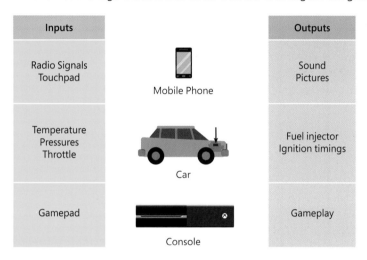

Figure 4-1   Computers in devices

Most reasonably complex devices created today contain data-processing components to optimize their performance, and some exist only because we can build-in such capabilities. The growth of the Internet of Things (IoT) is introducing computers into a huge range of areas. It's important to think of data processing as much more than working out the company payroll—calculating numbers and printing out results (the traditional uses of computers). As software engineers, we will inevitably spend a great deal of our time fitting data-processing components into other devices to drive them. These embedded systems mean many people will be using computers, even if they're not aware of it!

PROGRAMMER'S POINT
Software might be a matter of life and death

Remember that seemingly innocuous programs can have life-threatening capabilities. For example, a doctor may use a spreadsheet you have written to calculate doses of drugs for patients. In this case, a defect in the program could result in physical harm. (I don't think doctors do this—but you never know.) For a deeply scary description of how poor software design can cause injury and even death, search for **Therac-25** on the web.

Programs as data processors

Figure 4-2 shows what every computer does. Data goes into the computer, which does something with it, and then data comes out of the computer. What form the data takes and what the output means are entirely up to us, as is what the program does.

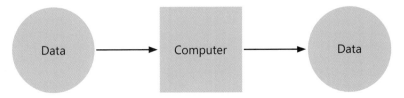

Figure 4-2   A computer as a data processor

Another way to think of a program is like a recipe, which is illustrated in **Figure 4-3**.

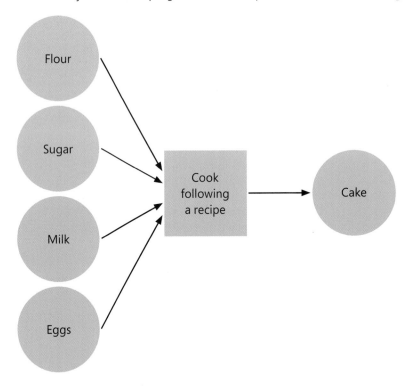

Figure 4-3   Recipes and programs

In this example, the cook plays the role of the computer, and the recipe is the program that controls what the cook does with the ingredients. A recipe can work with many different ingredients, and a program can work with many different inputs, too. For example, a program might take your age and the name of a movie you want to see and provide an output that determines whether you can go see that movie based on its audience rating.

JavaScript as a data processor

Figure 4-4 shows the workings of one of the early example programs, **Ch02-08 Paragraph Update**, from a data processing perspective. The input to the program is an input box on the HTML page, and the output from the program is the text in a paragraph in the HTML page. In this case, the JavaScript program code is in the function doUpdateParagraph, which runs when the user presses a button on the page. This function doesn't perform any processing on the data input; it simply transfers text from the input element to the output element.

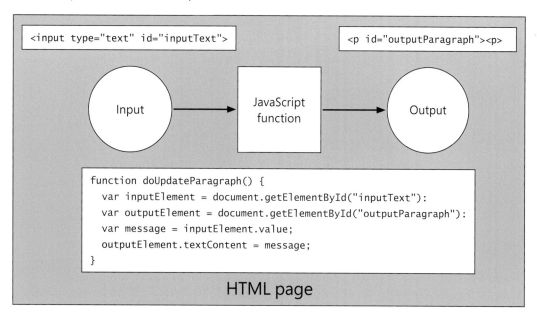

Figure 4-4 JavaScript as a data processor

This is a program structure that we will be using a lot in the next few chapters. We can change what a program does by changing the instructions in the functions that run inside the web page. Statements in a function will act on data and generate new values by evaluating *expressions*.

Process data with expressions

An expression can be as simple as a single value (for example `2` or `Rob Miles`), or it can contain *operators* and *operands*. **Figure 4-5** shows a simple expression with two operands and one operator. Things that do the actual work are called *operators*. In the case of 2+2, there are two operands (the two values of 2) and one operator (+). When you feed an expression into the JavaScript command prompt, it identifies the operators and operands and then works out the answer.

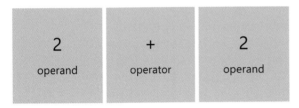

Figure 4-5   Expression

In Chapter 1 in "Our first brush with JavaScript," we entered some expressions and saw the results. Now let's enter some more.

CODE ANALYSIS

Evaluate expressions with JavaScript

The function shown previously in **Figure 4-4** doesn't process any data; instead, it simply transfers the text from the input to the output. Data processing in JavaScript is performed by the evaluation of *expressions*. An expression can be as simple as a single value (which is called a *literal* because it is taken exactly as it is). Alternatively, an expression could perform a complicated calculation. Let's do some expression evaluation to find out more.

Question: Can JavaScript work out 2+2?

> **Answer:** I hope so. Go to the example folder **Ch04 Working with data\Ch04-01 Empty Page**. Press F12 to open the **Developer View** of the web page and select the **Console** tab. Type the expression 2+2 and press Enter.

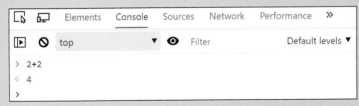

The JavaScript console always attempts to evaluate any expression you give it and then return the result. In this case, it has worked out that 2+2 equals 4. We can do some more experiments using the console to investigate expressions. From now on, rather than showing you screenshots of the browser, I'll just show the output that you'll see in the console. In other words, the previous expression would look like this.

```
>  2+2
<-  4
```

The typed text is shown in black, the output from JavaScript is shown in blue, and the command prompts are shown in brown.

Question: What do you think would happen if you tried to evaluate 2+3*4?

Answer: The * (asterisk) operator means multiply. JavaScript uses the asterisk in place of the × (multiplication symbol) used in math. In math, we always perform higher-priority operations like multiply and divide before addition, so I'd expect the expression above to display the value 14. The calculation 3*4 would be worked out first, giving an answer of 12, and this would be added to the value 2. If you try this in the console, you should see what you would expect:

```
>  2+3*4
<-  14
```

Question: What do you think would happen if you tried to evaluate (2+3)*4?

Answer: The parentheses enclose calculations that should be worked out first, so in the above expression, I'd expect to see the value 5 calculated (2+3) and then this value to be multiplied by 4, giving a result of 20.

```
>  (2+3)*4
<-  20
```

Question: What do you think would happen if you tried to evaluate (2+3*4?

Answer: This one is quite interesting. You should try it with the console. What happens is that JavaScript says to itself, "The expression I'm trying to work out is incomplete. I need a closing parenthesis." So, the console waits for more input from you. If you type the closing parenthesis and complete the expression, the value is calculated and the result is displayed. You can even add more sums on the second line if you want.

```
>  (2+3*4
     )
<-  14
```

Question: What do you think would happen if you tried to evaluate)2+3*4?

> **Answer:** If JavaScript sees a closing parenthesis before it sees an opening one, it instantly knows that something is wrong and displays an error.

```
>  )2+3*4
(x) Uncaught SyntaxError: unexpected token ')'
```

> Note that the command shell is trying to help you work out where the error is by identifying the incorrect character.

Scripting languages

We can use the console for having conversations like this because JavaScript is a "scripting" programming language (the clue is in the name). You can think of the console as a kind of "robot actor" who will perform whatever JavaScript statements you give it. In other words, you tell the console what you want your program to do using the JavaScript language. If the instructions don't make sense to the "robot actor," it tells us it can't understand them (usually with red text). The process of taking a program and then acting on the instructions in it is called *interpreting* the program. Actors earn a living interpreting the words of a play; computers solve problems for us by interpreting program instructions.

> **PROGRAMMER'S POINT**
>
> ## Not all programming languages run like JavaScript
>
> Not all programming languages are "scripting" languages, which are interpreted in the same way as JavaScript. Sometimes, program instructions are converted into the very low-level instructions that the hardware of your computer understands. This process is called *compilation*, and the program that performs this conversion is called a *compiler*. The compiled instructions can then be loaded into the computer to be executed. This technique produces programs that can run very fast because when the compiled low-level instructions are performed, the computer doesn't have to figure out what the instructions mean; they can just be obeyed.
>
> You might think this means that JavaScript is a "slow" computer language because each time a JavaScript program runs, the "robot actor" must work out the meaning of each command before performing it. However, this is not really a problem because modern computers run very, very fast, and JavaScript uses some clever trickery to compile your program as it runs.

Data and information

Now that we understand computers as machines that process data, and we understand that programs tell computers what to do with the data, let's delve a little bit deeper into the nature of data and information. People use the words *data* and *information* interchangeably, but it's important to make a distinction between the two, because the way that computers and humans consider data is completely different. Look at **Figure 4-6**, which shows the difference.

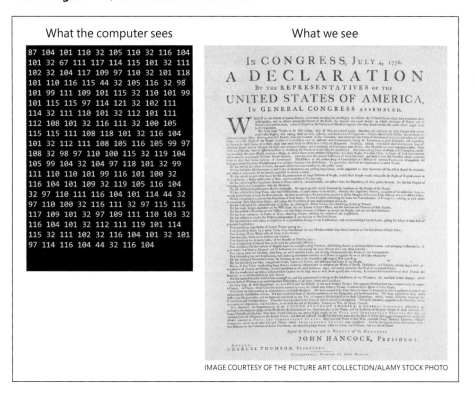

IMAGE COURTESY OF THE PICTURE ART COLLECTION/ALAMY STOCK PHOTO

Figure 4-6 Data and information

The two items in Figure 4-6 contain the same data, except that the image on the left more closely resembles how the document would be stored in a computer. The computer uses a numeric value to represent each letter and space in the text. If you work through the values, you can figure out each value, beginning with the value 87, which represents an uppercase W (in the "When" that begins the first regular paragraph in the document on the right).

Because of the way computers hold data, yet another layer lies beneath the mapping of numbers to letters. Each number is held by the computer as a unique pattern of on and off signals, or 1s and 0s. In the realm of computing, each 1 or 0 is known as a bit. (For a wonderful explanation of how computers operate at this level and of how these workings form the basis for all coding, see Charles Petzold's *Code: The Hidden Language of Computer Hardware and Software*.) The value 87, which we know means "uppercase W," is held as the following way:

```
1010111
```

This is the *binary* representation of the value. I don't have the space to go into precisely how this works (and Charles Petzold already did this!), but you can think of this bit pattern as meaning "87 is made up of a 1 plus a 2 plus a 4 plus a 16 plus a 64."

Each of the bits in the pattern tells the computer hardware whether a particular power of 2 is present. Don't worry too much if you don't fully understand this but do remember that as far as the computer is concerned, data is a collection of 1s and 0s that computers store and manipulate. That's *data*.

Information, on the other hand, is the interpretation of the data by people to mean something. Strictly speaking, computers process data and humans work on information.

For example, the computer could hold the following bit pattern somewhere in memory:

```
11111111 11111111 11111111 00000000
```

You could regard this as meaning, "You are $256 overdrawn at the bank" or "You are 256 feet below the surface of the ground" or "Eight of the thirty-two light switches are off." The transition from data to information is usually made when a human reads the output.

I am being so pedantic because it is vital to remember that a computer does not "know" what the data it is processing means. As far as the computer is concerned, data is just patterns of bits; it is the user who gives meaning to these patterns. Remember this when you get a bank statement that says you have $8,388,608 in your account when you really have only $83!

Data processing in JavaScript

We now know that JavaScript is a data processor. A script containing JavaScript statements is interpreted by the browser, which then produces some output. We also know that within the computer running a JavaScript program, data values are represented by patterns of bits (representing ons and offs). Now we need to discover how variables let our programs store and manipulate the data being processed.

Variables in programs

We have already used quite a few variables in our JavaScript programs. *Variables* are how programs remember things. You can think of a variable as a storage location you can refer to by name. What you store in the location and the name you give the location are up to you. You can create a variable in a JavaScript program by thinking of a name for the variable and then putting a value in the variable. Perhaps you know someone with a pressing need to add up some numbers. In this case, the first statement in your program might look like this:

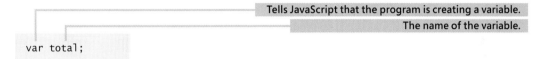

Tells JavaScript that the program is creating a variable.
The name of the variable.

```
var total;
```

If we want to add up a bunch of numbers, we will need something to store the total value. This statement creates a variable with the name `total`. The program will set the initial value of `total` to `0` and then add each number to it. To set the initial value of the total variable, we use an *assignment* statement:

```
total = 0;
```

The `=` in the statement tells JavaScript that the program is performing an assignment. The variable name on the left-hand side of the equals symbol specifies the destination of the assignment (meaning the place to put the result). The expression on the right-hand side provides the result to store in the variable. When JavaScript sees a variable name in an expression, it fetches the value out of the variable and uses that value. This means the following statement should make perfect sense to you:

```
total = total + 1;
```

The item on the right-hand side of the statement is an *expression*, which will generate a result. JavaScript gets the value of `total` and adds 1 to it. It then puts this result into the variable total. In other words, the effect of the statement above is to increase the value in `total` by 1.

Working with variables

Let's have a look at variables in JavaScript by using the Developer Tools. Start your browser and navigate to the page in the **Ch04 Working with data\Ch04-01 Empty Page** folder. Open up the **Developer View** by pressing F12. You can begin by creating a `total` variable.

```
> var total;
```

When you press Enter, JavaScript will create the variable. However, it gives a rather strange response:

```
> var total;
<- undefined
```

This response occurs because every time the console performs a statement, it then displays the value generated by that statement. Creating a new variable doesn't create a value, so the console displays the value as `undefined`. You can see this in action if you enter a statement that assigns a value to total. Enter the statement below and look at the result:

```
> total = 0;
<- 0
```

In JavaScript, the result of an assignment is the value that is assigned, so this statement will generate the value 0. Let's try performing the addition we saw in the text:

```
> total = total + 1;
<- 1
```

This statement works out the value of `total + 1` (which will be `0 + 1`) and then assigns this to the `total` variable. The effect of this is that `total` now contains the value 1. Perform the statement again.

```
> total = total + 1;
<- 2
```

Each time we perform the addition statement, the value in `total` gets larger by 1. This expression might appear confusing. If you've worked with mathematical equations, you'll remember that the equals character (=) means that one value is equal to another. From a mathematical point of view, the statement generated above is obviously wrong because the `total` cannot equal the `total` plus 1. However, it's important to remember that in JavaScript, the equals operator means "assign." So, the expression `total+1` is evaluated on the right side and then is assigned to the variable on the left side. In JavaScript, it is perfectly okay to create a variable and assign it a value immediately:

```
> var total=0;
```

If you do this, you will notice that the result displayed by the console is *undefined* because, as we saw at the start of this section, a statement that creates a variable does not return a value. If you haven't set a value into a variable, JavaScript marks that variable as holding the value `undefined`. Enter this statement to create a new variable called `test`.

```
> var emptyTest;
```

Now you can investigate the value that the newly created variable `emptyTest` holds. If you just enter the `emptyTest` variable, the console will hold the value stored in the variable `emptyTest`:

```
> emptyTest
<- undefined
```

Note that this does **not** mean that the variable `emptyTest` does not exist. Instead, it means that the variable `emptyTest` does not hold a value. The contents of `emptyTest` are undefined. We can pass the undefined value around as we would any other:

```
> emptyCopy=emptyTest;
<- undefined
```

Now I have a variable called `emptyCopy` that holds a copy of `emptyTest`. Both of these variables hold the undefined value. If I use an undefined value in a calculation, I won't get an error, but I will get a result that is not a number:

```
> emptySum=emptyTest + 1;
<- NaN
```

This kind of calculation will not cause a problem with your program, except that it will produce silly results. JavaScript makes a distinction between things that are not defined and things that do not exist. If you try to view the value in a variable that does not exist, something different happens. Enter the name notDefined and press Enter:

```
>notDefined
Uncaught ReferenceError: notDefined is not defined at <anonymous>:1:1
```

The variable notDefined does not exist, so JavaScript gives us an error.

JavaScript identifiers

Names of things in JavaScript are called *identifiers*. We used the identifier total for the first variable that we created. When you write a program, you must come up with identifiers for the variables in that program. JavaScript has rules about the way you can form identifiers:

An identifier must start with a letter, the dollar character ($), or the underscore character (_) and can contain letters, numerals (digits), or the underscore character.

The name total is a perfectly legal identifier, as is xyz. However, the identifier 2_be_or_not_2_be would be rejected with an error because it starts with a digit. Also, JavaScript views uppercase and lowercase letters differently; for example, FRED is regarded by JavaScript as different from fred.

PROGRAMMER'S POINT

Create meaningful identifiers

I find it terribly surprising that some programmers use identifiers such as X21 or silly or hello_mum. I don't. I work very hard to make my programs as easy to read as possible. So, I'll use ones such as length or, perhaps even better, windowLengthInInches. My window length identifier uses a format where the first letter of each word inside the identifier is a capital letter. This is called *camel case* because the capital letters in the name stick up like humps on the back of a camel. Another convention uses the underscore character to split up the words in an identifier: window_length_in_inches. I reckon either of these is okay, although camel case is more common in JavaScript. I don't care which one you use, but I do care that you use it consistently throughout your program.

I don't care which method you choose to make up your identifiers; I only care that you strive to create identifiers with meaning. If the identifier applies to a particular thing, then identify that thing. And if that thing has particular units of measurement, then then add those, too. For example, if I were storing the age of a customer, I'd create a variable called `customerAgeInYears`.

JavaScript allows identifiers of any length, and longer identifiers don't slow down a program. However, very long names can be a bit hard for humans to read, so you should try to keep them down to the lengths shown in the examples.

CODE ANALYSIS

Code errors and testing

By now, you should be getting used to the idea that if you give a JavaScript program the wrong instructions, the wrong thing will happen. However, consider the JavaScript below, which is supposed to add 1 to the value in the variable with the name `total`:

```
Total = total + 1
```

Question: There is an error in the statement above, which is supposed to add 1 to the variable `total`. What is the error?

> **Answer:** Earlier in this chapter, we used a statement that looks like this to add 1 to the value in a variable called `total`. It looks like we are doing the same thing here, but that's not the case. There is a crucial difference between this statement and the one we saw earlier. This statement assigns the result of the calculation to a newly created variable called `Total`. The error can happen because although we have used the word `var` to tell JavaScript that we are declaring a variable, this is not something that JavaScript insists on. If you assign something to a variable that JavaScript has not seen before, JavaScript will just create a new variable with the specified name.
>
> The statement would not generate any complaints from JavaScript when it runs, but it would also not update the value of `total` correctly. Instead it would create a new variable called `Total`. This is a *logic* error. The statement is completely legal as far as JavaScript is concerned, but it will do the wrong thing when it runs.
>
> I mentioned at the start of this book that JavaScript has some features that make me want to tear my hair out. This is one of them because it means that your punishment for a simple typing mistake is not an error or warning message. Instead you get a program that runs but doesn't work properly.

Question: How do we prevent logic errors?

Answer: The only way to attack logic errors is to test. We need to run a program with some known values (values for which we know the total) and then verify that the answers agree with the test total. If the answers make sense, we can start to build confidence in our code. However, even if a program passes all the tests, it could still be faulty because there might be a fault that is not picked up by those tests.

Tests don't prove that a program is good; tests simply prove that a program is not as bad as it would be if it had failed the tests.

Tests work best if they are added at the time the program is created. We'll talk about testing strategies every time we make a new program.

```
total = Total + 1
```

Question: The statement above also contains a misspelling of a variable named `total`. However, this time the name on the right-hand side of the equals is misspelled. What will happen when this program runs?

Answer: JavaScript will refuse to run this statement. It will tell you that you are using a variable with the name `Total`, which it hasn't seen yet. Sometimes, typing mistakes will be detected before your program runs, but other times, they might not.

You might be thinking that you've been set up to fail because I've suggested that you use long, meaningful names, and typing those long, meaningful names creates more opportunities for mistakes. For now, one way around this problem is to use the text copy feature of your editor to copy names from one part of the program to another.

Performing calculations

We know that JavaScript expressions are made up of operators and operands. The operators identify actions to be performed, and the operands are worked on by the operators. Now we can add a bit more detail to this explanation. Expressions can be as simple as a single value or as complex as a large calculation. Here are a few examples of numeric expressions:

```
2 + 3 * 4
-1 + 3
(2 + 3) * 4
```

These expressions are evaluated by JavaScript by working from left to right, just as you would read them yourself. Again, just as in traditional math, multiplication and division are performed first, followed by addition and subtraction. JavaScript achieves this order by giving each operator a priority. When JavaScript works out an expression, it finds all the operators with the highest priority and applies them first. It then looks for the operators next in priority, and so on, until the result is obtained. The order of evaluation means that the expression 2 + 3 * 4 will calculate to 14, not 20.

If you want to force the order in which an expression evaluates, you can put parentheses around the elements of the expression you want to evaluate first, as in the final example above. You can also put parentheses inside parentheses if you want—provided you make sure that you have as many opening parentheses as closing ones. Being a simple soul, I tend to make things clear by putting parentheses around everything.

It is probably not worth getting too worked up about expression evaluation. Generally speaking, things tend to be evaluated how you would expect. Here is a list of some other operators, with descriptions of what they do and their precedence (priority). The operators are listed with the highest priority first.

OPERATOR	HOW IT'S USED
–	Unary minus. This is the minus that JavaScript finds in negative numbers.
*	Multiplication. Note the use of the * rather than the more mathematically correct but confusing **X**.
/	Division. Because of the difficulty of drawing one number above another during editing, we use this character instead.
+	Addition.
–	Subtraction. Note that we use the same character as for unary minus.

This is not a complete list of the operators available, but it will do for now. Because these operators work on numbers, they are often called *numeric operators*. However, one of them, the + operator, can be applied between strings, as you've already seen.

Work out the results

Question: See if you can work out the values of a, b, and c when the following statements have been evaluated:

```
var a = 1;
var b = 2;
var c = a + b;

c = c * (a + b);
b = a + b + c;
```

Answer: a=1, b=12, c=9. The best way to work this out is to behave like a computer would and work through each statement in turn. When I do this, I write down the variable values on a piece of paper and then update each as I go along. Doing this means that you can predict what a program will do without having to run it.

Whole numbers and real numbers

We know that JavaScript is aware of two fundamental kinds of data—text data and numeric data. Now we need to delve a little deeper into how numeric data works. There are two kinds of numeric data—whole numbers and real numbers. Whole numbers have no fractional part. Up until now, every program that we have written has made use of whole numbers. A computer stores the value of a whole number exactly as entered. Real numbers, on the other hand, have a fractional element that can't always be held accurately in a computer.

As a programmer, you need to choose which kind of number you want to use to store each value.

Whole numbers versus real numbers

You can learn about the difference between whole numbers and real numbers by looking at a few situations in which they might be used.

Question: I'm building a device that can count the number of hairs on your head. Should I store this value as a whole number or as a real number?

   Answer: This should be a whole number because there is no such thing as half a hair.

Question: I want to use my hair-counting machine on 100 people and determine the average number of hairs on all their heads. Should I store this value as a whole number or as a real number?

   Answer: When we work out the result, we'll find that the average includes a fractional part, which means that we should use a real number to store it.

Question: I want to keep track of the price of a product in my program. Should I use whole numbers or real numbers?

   Answer: This is very tricky. You might think that the price should be stored as a real number—for example, $1.50 (one and a half dollars). However, you could also store the price as the whole number, 150 cents. The type of number you use in a situation like this depends on how that number is used. If you're just keeping track of the total amount of money you take in while selling your product, you can use a whole number to hold the price and the total. However, if you are also lending money to people to buy your product and you want to calculate the interest to charge them, you would need a fractional component to hold the number more precisely.

PROGRAMMER'S POINT

The way you store a variable depends on what you want to do with it

It seems obvious that you would use a whole number to count the number of hairs on your head. However, one could argue that we could also use a whole number to represent the average number of hairs on 100 people's heads. This is because the calculated average would be in the thousands. Fractions of a hair would not add much useful information, so we could drop any fractional parts and round to the nearest whole number. When you consider how you are going to represent data in a program, you must take into account how it will be used.

Real numbers and floating-point numbers

Real number types have a fractional part, which is the part of the number after the decimal point. Real numbers are not always stored exactly as they are entered into JavaScript programs. Numbers are mapped to computer memory in a way that stores a value that is as close as possible to the original. The stored data is often called a *floating-point* representation. You can increase the accuracy of the storage process by using larger amounts of computer memory, but you are never able to hold all real values precisely.

This is not a problem, however. Values such as pi can never be held exactly because they "go on forever." (I've got a book that contains the value of pi to 1 million decimal places, but I still can't say that this is the exact value of pi. All I can say is that the value in the book is many more times more accurate than anyone will ever need.)

When considering how numbers are stored, we need to think about *range* and *precision*. Precision sets out how precisely a number is stored. A particular floating-point variable could store the value 123456789.0 or 0.123456789, but it can't store 123456789.123456789 because it does not have enough precision to hold 18 digits. The range of floating-point storage determines how far you can "slide" the decimal point around to store very large or very small numbers. For example, we could store the value 123,456,700, or we can store 0.0001234567. For a floating-point number in JavaScript, we have 15 to 16 digits of precision, and we can slide the decimal point 308 places to the right (to store huge numbers) or 324 places to the left (to store tiny numbers).

The mapping of real numbers to a floating-point representation does bring some challenges when using computers. It turns out that the value 0.1 (a tenth) may not be held accurately by a computer. The value stored to represent 0.1 will be very close to that value, but not the same. This has implications for the way we write programs.

CODE ANALYSIS

Floating-point variables and errors

We can find out more about how floating-point values work by doing some experiments using the JavaScript **Developer View** in the browser. If we just type numeric expressions, we can view the results that JavaScript calculates.

Question: What happens if we try to store a value that can't be held accurately as a floating-point value?

Answer: We know that the value `0.1` can't be held accurately in a computer, so let's enter that value into the **Developer View** and see what comes back. Go to the console in browser and enter the following:

```
>  0.1
<- 0.1
```

At this point, you might think that I've been lying to you because I said that the value `0.1` can't be held accurately, and now this example shows JavaScript returning the value `0.1`. However, I'm not lying to you—JavaScript is. The JavaScript print routine "rounds" values when it prints them. In other words, it says that if the number to be printed is `0.10000000000000000551115` or thereabouts (which it is), then it will just print `0.1`.

Question: Does this "rounding" really happen?

Answer: At the moment, you've just got my word for it that values are rounded when printed and that errors are being hidden from us as a result. However, if we perform a simple calculation, we can introduce an error that is large enough to escape being rounded. Enter the following calculation into the JavaScript Shell and note what comes back.

```
>  0.1+0.2
<- 0.30000000000000004
```

The result of adding `0.1` to `0.2` should be `0.3`, but because the values are held as binary floating-point values, the result of the calculation contains an error large enough to escape being rounded.

However, this lack of accuracy is not a problem in programming because we don't usually have incoming data that is particularly precise anyway. For example, if I refine my hair counting device to measure hair length, it would be difficult for me to measure hair length with more than a tenth of an inch (2.4 millimeters) of accuracy. For hair data analysis, we need only around three or four digits of accuracy.

It is also worth noting at this point that these issues have nothing to do with JavaScript. Most, if not all, modern computers store and manipulate floating-point values using a standard established by the Institute of Electronic and Electrical Engineers (IEEE) in 1985. All programs that run on a computer will manipulate values in the same way, so floating-point numbers in JavaScript are no different from those in any other language.

The only difference between JavaScript floating-point values and those in other languages is that a floating-point variable in JavaScript occupies 8 bytes of memory, which is twice the size of the float type in the languages C, C++, Java, and C# (but not Python). A JavaScript floating-point variable equates with a *double precision* value in those languages.

Creating random dice

We can explore the difference between integer and floating-point values in JavaScript by creating a "random dice" web page. This will display a value between 1 and 6 when the user presses a button. JavaScript has a built-in library of Math functions including one called random, which generates a real number that ranges from 0 to 1 (but does **not** include the value 1). Let's investigate how this works.

 MAKE SOMETHING HAPPEN

Random numbers

Let's have a look at random numbers in JavaScript. Start your browser and navigate to the page in the **Ch04 Working with data\Ch04-02 Computer Dice** folder. Press the button and note that you get a different dice roll each time.

Digital Dice

Roll the Dice

Rolled: 4

Open the **Developer View** by pressing F12. You can begin by displaying a random number by calling the random function from the Math library:

```
> Math.random()
```

When you press Enter, JavaScript will calculate a "pseudorandom" number and display the result. The number is called "pseudorandom" because it is calculated as one of a sequence of values generated from a particular "seed" value. The seed value is chosen by JavaScript using the current time, so a program will get a different sequence each time it runs.

```
> Math.random()
<- 0.01479622790601498
```

I would be very, very surprised if you got the same number as the one printed above (you would have to run your program at exactly the same time I did). You will see a number between 0 and 1. Call random a few more times and note that you get a different number each time. If you tried it enough times, it is possible you could see a value 0 but you would **never** see a value of 1. That is important to us.

The random function returns a value between 0 and 1. We can expand the range of the random number by multiplying it by the range that we want; in this case, that range is 6. Try entering this:

```
> Math.random()*6
```

This will generate a result that ranges from 0 up to but not including 6 (because random() can never return 1). Try it.

```
> Math.random()*6
<- 1.342641962710725
```

The next thing we need to do is get rid of that fractional part. JavaScript provides another Math function, called floor, which chops the fractional off a number. No matter how large the fractional part, it is always discarded. Try this:

```
> Math.floor(1.9999)
```

The value 1.9999 is very close to 2, but the floor function throws away the entire fractional part. We can apply the floor function to our random value. Try this:

```
> Math.floor(Math.random()*6)
```

This is an important thing to learn. I can feed an expression into a function call. The above statement gets a value from the `random` function, multiplies it by 6, and then feeds the result into the `floor` function. If you repeat this statement lots of times, you should see the values 0, 1, 2, 3, 4, and 5 appearing at random. We want a value between 1 and 6, so we just add 1 to this:

```
> Math.floor(Math.random()*6)+1
```

This is the "brains" of our program. Click the **Elements** tab in the **Developer View** and then expand the `<script>` element to view the `doRollDice` function.

```
⌖  ⬚   Elements   Console   Sources   Network   Performance   Memory   Application

<!DOCTYPE html>
<html lang="en">
▶ <head>…</head>
▼ <body>
    <h1>Digital Dice</h1>
  ▶ <p>…</p>
    <p id="outputParagraph" class="numberDisplay">Rolled: 2</p>
    <p></p>
  ▼ <script>
…        function doRollDice() {
             var outputElement = document.getElementById("outputParagraph");

             var spots = Math.floor(Math.random()*6)+1;
             var message = "Rolled: " + spots;
             outputElement.textContent = message;
         }
```

In the middle of the function there is a statement that sets the value of the `spots` variable to a random number between 1 and 6. How would you change the program to produce a number between 1 and 20?

```
> Math.floor(Math.random()*20)+1
```

This turns out to be very easy; the program must multiply the random value by 20 rather than 6.

Working with text

We now know how to use variables that hold numbers. A program can also create a variable that holds a string of text.

```
var customerName = "Fred";
```

This statement looks exactly like the statement we used to create the `total` variable except that the value being assigned is a string of text. The string being assigned is enclosed in double quote characters that define the limits of the text. The double quote characters are called *delimiters* because they define the limits of the text. The delimiters are not part of the string being stored, so the `customerName` variable just contains the word `Fred`.

The `customerName` variable is different from the `total` variable in that it holds text rather than a number. We can use this variable anywhere we would use a string.

```
var message = "the name is " + customerName;
```

In the expression being assigned, the text in the `customerName` variable is added onto the end of the `"the name is "` string. As `customerName` currently holds the string `"Fred"` (we set this in the previous statement), the above assignment would create another string variable called `message`, which contains `"the name is Fred"`. We have seen that the + operator before when we used it to add numbers together. In this context it is performing *concatenation*, which means adding two strings together.

JavaScript string delimiters

The " character can act as a delimiter that marks the start and the end of a string in the program. But what if we want to enter a string that contains a " character? In that case, we can use a single quote (') to mark the start and end of the string:

```
var message = 'Read "Begin to code with JavaScript". It is an amazing book';
```

If you want to enter a string that contains both single and double quotes, you can use backticks (`)—also known as an acute—to delimit the string:

```
var message = `Read "Begin to code with JavaScript". It's an amazing book`;
```

If you have a need to enter a string that contains both kinds of quotes and backticks, then it must be an amazing string. You can enter that by using *escape sequences*.

Escape sequences in strings

You can include quote characters in a string by using an *escape sequence*. Normally, each character in a string represents that character. In other words, an A in a string means 'A'. However, when JavaScript sees the escape character —the backslash (\) character—it looks at the text following the escape character to decide what character is being described. This is called an escape sequence. There are many different escape sequences you can use in a JavaScript string. The most useful escape sequences are shown in the following table.

ESCAPE SEQUENCE	WHAT IT MEANS	WHAT IT DOES
\\	Backslash character (\)	Enters a backslash into the string
\'	Single quote (')	Enters a single quote into the string
\`	Backtick (`)	Enters a single backtick into the string
\"	Double quote (")	Enters a double quote into the string
\n	Unicode Line Feed/New Line	End this line and take a new one
\t	Unicode Tab	Move to the right to the next tab stop
\r	Unicode Carriage return	Return the printing position to the start of the line

If you're wondering what Unicode means, it is a mapping of numbers to character designs. We saw it in Chapter 2 in the "Display symbols" section.

Working with strings and numbers

You can create expressions involving strings, but the only operator that can be used between two strings is the + operator that we saw earlier. You can also create expressions involving strings and numbers, but you need to be a bit careful when you do this.

CODE ANALYSIS

Combining strings and numbers

We can find out more about how strings and numbers can be combined in a JavaScript program by using the **Developer View** to answer some questions.

Question: What happens if I add a number to a string?

Answer: We know that JavaScript regards numbers and strings as different types of data. Let's see what happens when we add them together:

```
> "hello" + 99
<- "hello99"
```

This statement adds the numeric value 99 to the string "Hello". JavaScript automatically converts the number into a string giving the result that you see above. However, this can lead to strange behavior if you add lots of numbers to a string...

Question: What happens if I add lots of numbers to a string?

Answer: The way that JavaScript performs the conversion of numbers to strings can result in some interesting consequences:

```
> 1 + 2 + "hello" + 3 + 4
<- "3hello34"
```

JavaScript works along the expression. It adds the 1 and the 2 to produce the value 3. Then it sees a string and thinks, "Oh. I need to make this number into a string." It converts the value 3 into a string and adds it to "hello". Then it converts everything else it finds into strings, too, and adds them together. If you want to force the calculations to be performed before the values are converted into strings, you can use brackets.

```
> (1+2) + "hello" + (3+4)
<- "3hello7"
```

Note that this is not the kind of programming I approve of, because it is a bit confusing. If I really wanted to create an output like what's shown above, I would break it down into a number of separate statements.

```
var calc1 = 1 + 2;
var calc2 = 3 + 4;
var result = calc1 + "hello" + calc2;
```

This makes it very clear to the reader of my program that I wanted the values to be calculated before I displayed them.

Converting strings into numbers

We have seen that JavaScript regards numeric and text variables as different types of data. We have also seen that JavaScript will automatically convert from a number into a string when it thinks this is appropriate (although it may sometimes get this wrong). Sometimes our programs will need to convert from a string into a number. For example, we might want to create an adding machine web page. The user enters two values and presses a button, which causes the sum of the numbers to be displayed. **Figure 4-7** shows how the page can be used to solve the age-old question "What is 2+2?"

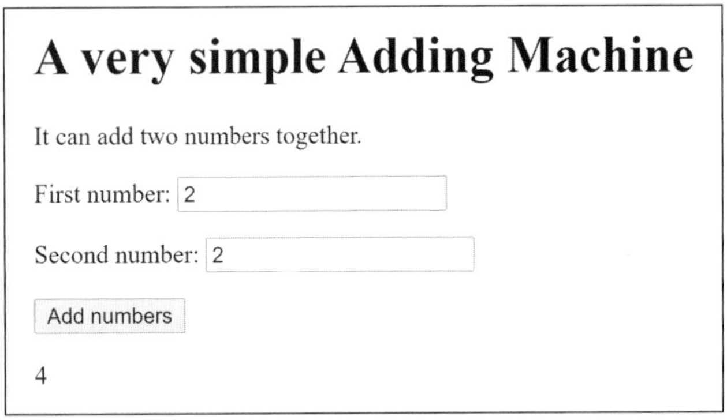

A very simple Adding Machine

It can add two numbers together.

First number: 2

Second number: 2

Add numbers

4

Figure 4-7   Adding machine

The page contains two input fields for the values to be entered, a button to request a calculation, and a paragraph element that displays the result. We know how to create almost every part of this application except for one thing. The user will enter the numbers to be added as text strings. We need a way of converting these strings into numbers that can be added together.

 MAKE SOMETHING HAPPEN

Converting strings into numbers

JavaScript makes a distinction between numbers and values. Let's investigate how this works. Open the web page in the example folder **Ch04 Working with data\Ch04-03 Adding Machine**. This displays an adding machine. Enter two numbers and press the **Add Numbers** button. Note that the right answer appears. Now press F12 to open the **Developer View**. Click the **Console** tab to view the console prompt. Type the following sum and press Enter:

```
>  2+2
```

The console shows the result of the expression you would expect:

```
<- 4
```

Now enter a different sum:

```
> "2"+"2"
```

This is adding the string "2" to the string "2".

```
<- 22
```

We can see this distinction in action when we create variables. Create the two variables by entering the following:

```
> var stringTwo = "2"
> var numberTwo = 2
```

JavaScript provides a function called typeof, which will tell you the type of a variable you supply to it. Use it to investigate the type of the variables name and age.

```
> typeof(stringTwo)
<- "string"
> typeof(numberTwo)
<- "number"
```

JavaScript provides a function called Number, which will attempt to convert whatever you give it into a number. Let's use this to convert the string version of 2 into a number version:

```
> var convertedTwo = Number(stringTwo)
```

This statement creates a new numeric variable convertedTwo, which contains the number held in stringTwo. The type of convertedTwo is a number:

```
> typeof(convertedTwo)
<- "number"
```

Leave the **Developer Tools** window open for later.

Make an adding machine

Now that we know we can use the `Number` function to convert from a string type into a numeric type, we can create our adding machine. The HTML for the elements on the page is as follows:

```
<h1>A very simple Adding Machine</h1>
<p>It can add two numbers together.</p>
<p>
  First number: <input type="text" id="no1Text" value="0">
</p>
<p>
  Second number: <input type="text" id="no2Text" value="0">
</p>
<p>
  <input type="button" value="Add numbers" onclick="doAddition();"></button>
</p>

<p id="resultParagraph">
  Result displayed here.
</p>
```

First number input

Second number input

Button to trigger the calculation

Paragraph to display the answer

You can map each of the elements in the HTML onto items on **Figure 4-7**. There are two text input areas for the user to type in the values that are to be added. These areas have IDs that are `no1text` and `no2text`. There is also an output paragraph that will be used to display the output. The output paragraph has the `resultParagraph` ID. When the user clicks the button, the function `doAddition` will be called to calculate the result and display it. This function takes the text out of the inputs, converts it into numbers, and then does the calculation.

The `input` element reads a string of text from the user. This works if we just want to read names. However, it is not so useful if we want to read in numbers.

```
var no1Element = document.getElementById("no1Text");
var no1Text = no1Element.value;
var no1Number = Number(no1Text);
```

Get a reference to the element holding the user input

Get the text from the user input element

Convert the text into a number

This is the code that gets the user input for the first value and converts it into a number that can be used in calculations. The `Number` function performs the conversion; the first two statements get a reference to the input element holding the number text and then get the text from that element. The program uses a similar sequence of statements to get the value entered in the second input element.

```
var result = no1Number + no2Number;
```

This is the statement that calculates the addition and stores it in a variable called result. This is the part of the program where the data processing is performed. The rest of the HTML and JavaScript are there to provide a means of input and output. The last thing the function needs to do is display the result for the user. We have written several functions that do this; the result is displayed by modifying the text in a paragraph on the web page.

```
var resultElement = document.getElementById("resultParagraph");
resultElement.innerText = result;
```

The first statement gets a reference to the resultParagraph element. The second statement sets the innerText to the value of the result that was calculated. Note that the result variable holds a number, but JavaScript will automatically convert this to text for display. You have seen this automatic conversion of numbers to text before.

WHAT COULD GO WRONG

Entering invalid numbers

When you create a program, you have to think of ways that it could go wrong. For example, after being asked to type 2 into a text entry in our adding machine, it is perfectly possible for a user to type this instead:

First number: two

We are using the function Number to convert text into a numeric value. It would be very impressive if the Number function could convert "two" into the value 2, but unfortunately it can't. Instead, it decides that "two" is not a number, and so it returns NaN, which means "not a number." Any JavaScript calculations involving something that is not a number generate a result of NaN, so an attempt to use text like this would result in the display below:

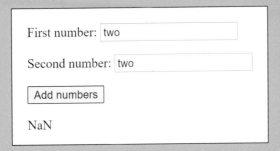

First number: two

Second number: two

Add numbers

NaN

The good news is that at least the program didn't output a number like –8399608 when the user upset it like this, but it is still less than perfect. In the next chapter, we will discover how a program can decide when a number is valid and display a suitable alert message. However, the best way to remove an error like this is to do something that ensures it can never happen. We can tell the browser that a given input element is a number rather than text.

```
First number: <input type="number" id="no1Text" value="0">
```

The HTML above shows how we do this. The `type` of the input is now `number`. If we do this, the input element will only accept numbers when the user types things into it. If you used this input area on your smartphone, you'd be given a numeric keypad to enter the value, rather than a full keyboard. On a Windows PC, the Microsoft Edge browser even shows up and down buttons that you can use to change the numeric value of the element.

It can add two numbers together.

First number: 2

Second number: 2

Note that even though we have specified that the type of the input field is `number`, we still get a text string from the input field when we use it in our programs. However, we can be sure that the text that we get from the element only contains digits. You can try this version of the page in the **Ch04 Working with data\Ch04-04 Number Adding Machine** example folder.

PROGRAMMER'S POINT

Error handling is a big part of programming

Professional programmers spend at least as much time thinking about how things can go wrong as they do writing program code. They also spend a lot of time deciding how they can prove that their program works by testing it. This is one reason why what look like simple programs can take a long time to create.

Making applications

We now know enough programming to be able to make some useful applications, so let's make some.

Calculating a pizza order

Rigorous scientific research conducted by me at many hackathons I've attended has arrived at a figure of exactly 1.5 people per pizza. In other words, if I get 30 students, I'll need 20 pizzas, and so on. I decided to make a web page that works out how many pizzas I need to order for a given number of students. The user types in the number of students and presses the **Calculate Pizzas** button to display the result. The code for my first version is shown below, and the result is shown in **Figure 4-8**.

```html
<!DOCTYPE html>
<html>

<head>
    <title>Ch04-05 Pizzcalc Vesion 1</title>
    <link rel="stylesheet" href="styles.css">          Using a style sheet to add some style
</head>

<body>
    <h1>&#x1f355; Pizza Calculater</h1>
    <p>Calculates the number of pizzas you&rsquo;ll need.</p>
    <p>                                                 Input element for the
                                                        number of students
    Number of students: <input type="number" id="noOfStudentsText" value="0">
    </p>
    <p>
    <input type="button" value="Calculate pizzas" onclick="doPizzaCalc();"></button>
    </p>
                                                        Button to press to display result

    <p id="resultParagraph">                            Paragraph to display the result
    Result displayed here.
    </p>

    <script>
    function doPizzaCalc() {                            Function that calculates the result

        var noOfStudentsElement = document.getElementById("noOfStudentsText");
        var noOfStudentsText = noOfStudentsElement.value;
```

```
        var noOfStudents = Number(noOfStudentsText);          Get the number of students

        var noOfPizzas = noOfStudents / 1.5;                  Perform the calculation
                                                      Get the paragraph that displays the result
        var resultElement = document.getElementById("resultParagraph");
        resultElement.innerText = "You need " + noOfPizzas + " pizzas.";

      }                                                        Display the result
    </script>
  </body>

</html>
```

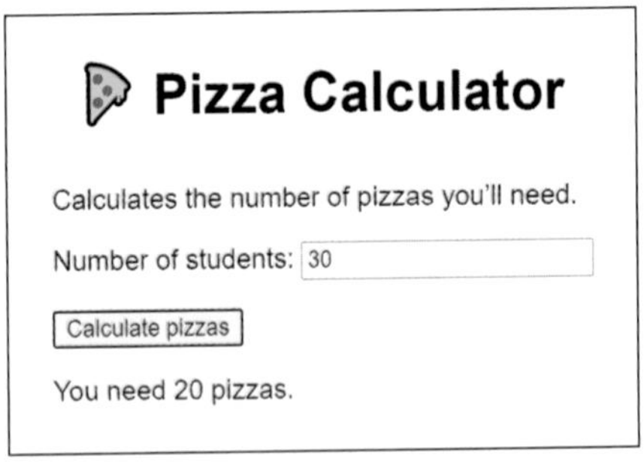

Figure 4-8   Pizza calculator

This is my first version. I'm using the Pizza emoji symbol (🍕) to get a nice pizza slice for the heading. The page works fine with the data above. If I say there are 30 students, the program will tell me I need 20 pizzas. However, there are problems with some numbers of pizzas, as you can see in **Figure 4-9**.

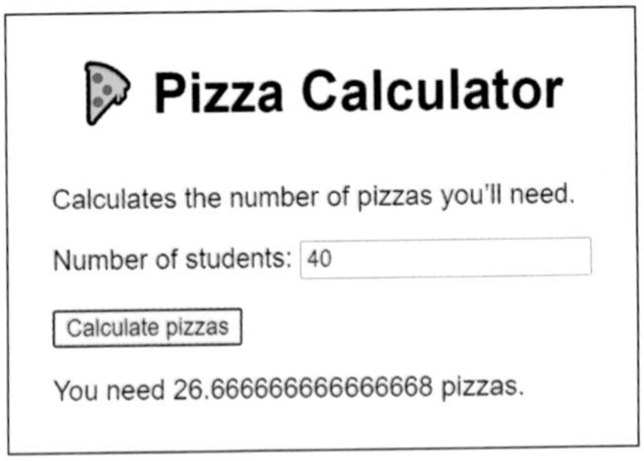

Figure 4-9   Pizza fractions

I can't ask the pizza place for a fraction of a pizza, so I need a way of converting the number of pizzas to an integer. At this point, I also must decide what the conversion will do. If I just use the `floor` function we used in the dice program, this will result in an order for 26 pizzas because the `floor` function truncates the floating-point value. This effectively means that I'll have pizza for only 39 people rather than 40, leaving one hungry student. There are several ways to address this problem. I might think the best way to attack the problem is to add one extra pizza to the order to take care of any "spares."

```
var noOfPizzas = Math.floor(noOfStudents / 1.5) + 1;
```

MAKE SOMETHING HAPPEN

Fix the pizza program

Load the example program in the folder **Ch04 Working with data\Ch04-05 Pizzacalc Version 1** and modify it using the above statement so that when you tell it there are 40 students, the program suggests that you buy 27 pizzas. Then change the program to make it less generous. Make the program always round down to the nearest integer number of pizzas to order. You can find my generous version in **Ch04 Working with data\Ch04-05 Pizzacalc Version 2**.

The program uses a style sheet to modify the style of the `<h1>` and `<p>`. You could modify these styles to make it look even better.

PROGRAMMER'S POINT

Never assume that you know what a program is supposed to do

If you wrote the pizza calculator for a customer, you should *not* decide for yourself what the program should do if it must order a fraction of a pizza. Your customer might want to "round down" the number of pizzas to keep their costs down. If this is the case, they will complain when your program adds an extra pizza. Alternatively, they might want to establish a reputation as a generous person, in which case the program should be made to "round up" the value.

As a programmer, never assume that you know what the program should do. You must always ask the customer. Otherwise, you might find yourself paying for over-ordered pizzas.

Converting between Fahrenheit and centigrade

An interesting thing about the adding machine program and the pizza calculator is that they have similar structures. The adding machine takes an additional input (the second number to be added), but the way that it works is just the same as the pizza calculator. We can use this same pattern to make a third program that converts temperature readings between Fahrenheit and centigrade. Have a go at creating a conversion web page. The following sections offer some hints.

Conversion formula

To convert a temperature from Fahrenheit to centigrade, you subtract 32 from the Fahrenheit value and then divide the result by 1.8. The statement below shows how this would work. It assumes that you have created a variable called `fahrenheit` that contains the temperature in Fahrenheit.

```
var centigrade = (fahrenheit-32)/1.8;
```

Truncating the displayed temperature value

We saw in the pizza calculator example that JavaScript likes to display lots of decimal places when it shows you a number. It would be distracting if the program displayed 60 degrees Fahrenheit as 15.55555555 degrees Centigrade. The `toFixed` method can be used on a numeric variable to create a string with a particular fixed number of decimal places. The statement below would create a variable called `resultString` that contains a number string that only contains one decimal place. In other words, a temperature of 15.5555555 would be converted to a string containing 15.6.

```
var resultString = centigrade.toFixed(1);
```

Displaying a thermometer emoji

You might want to add a thermometer emoji to your web page. This requires you to add two symbols to your HTML source. The HTML below will display a heading with a thermometer emoji.

```
<h1>&#x1f321;&#xfe0f; Fahrenheit to Centigrade</h1>
```

You can find my version of the solution in this folder: **Ch04 Working with data\ Ch04-07 Fahrenheit to Centigrade**. You can now write any kind of conversion program you like, converting feet to meters, grams to ounces, or liters to gallons.

Adding comments

As soon as you start to make useful programs, I think you should start adding comments to make it clearer what your program is doing. You don't write comments for the computer; you write comments for someone reading your program:

```
/* Based on each pizza feeding 1.5 students. We divide the number
   of students by 1.5 to get the number of pizzas. Then we drop
   the fractional part and add 1 to round up the number
   Note that this means we might buy slightly too much
   pizza for some numbers of students.
*/
var noOfPizzas = Math.floor(noOfStudents / 1.5) + 1;
```

The comment in the program above makes it very clear exactly how we are calculating the number of pizzas and the reasoning behind the statement. If the comment weren't there, you'd have to know that 1.5 was there because we have decided that is how many students each pizza will feed. You can write a comment that spreads over several lines by enclosing your comment text in the characters /* and */. When the browser sees the character sequence /* in a JavaScript program, it ignores the following text, up to the point where it sees a */ that ends the comment text. You can put comments anywhere in your program. The browser will completely ignore them. You can also create single-line comments:

```
var centigrade = (fahrenheit-32)/1.8; // using standard conversion formula
```

The comment above is a single-line comment. It starts at the character sequence // and finishes at the end of that line. We can add these kinds of comments on the end of a statement or on a line by themselves. If you use Visual Studio Code to write your programs, you'll find that comments are displayed in green to make them stand out.

It is important that programs be written in a way that makes it easy for humans to understand what is going on. We have seen that when choosing identifiers for variables we need to make sure that the name describes what the variable is being used for. We can also make programs clearer by adding comments.

Some people say that writing a program is a bit like writing a story. I'm not completely convinced that this is true. I have found that some computer manuals are works of fiction, but programs are something else. I think that while it is not a story as such, a good program text does have some of the characteristics of good literature:

1. It should be easy to read. At no point should the hapless reader be forced to back-track or brush up on knowledge that the writer assumes is there. All the names in the text should impart meaning and be distinct from each other.

2. It should have good punctuation and grammar. The various components should be organized in a clear and consistent way.

3. It should look good on the page. A good program is well laid out. The different parts should be indented, and the statements spread over the page in a well-formed manner.

4. It should be clear who wrote it and when it was last changed. If you write something good, you should put your name on it. If you change what you wrote, you should add information about the changes that you made and why.

A big part of a well-written program is the comments that the programmer puts there. A program without comments is a bit like an airplane that has an autopilot but no windows. There is a chance that it might take you to the right place, but it will be hard to tell where it is going from the inside.

Be generous with your comments. They help to make your program much easier to understand. You will be surprised to find that you quickly forget how you got your program to work. You can also use comments to keep people informed of the particular version of the program, when it was last modified and why, and the name of the programmer who wrote it—even if it was you. From now on, the example code that you see will have what I consider an appropriate level of comments.

PROGRAMMER'S POINT

Don't add too much detail in your comments

Writing comments is a very sensible thing to do, but don't go mad. Remember that the person who is reading your program can be expected to know JavaScript and doesn't need things explained to them in too much detail:

```
goatCount = goatCount + 1; // add one to goatCount
```

This is plain insulting to the reader, I reckon. If you chose sensible names, you should find that quite a lot of your program will express what it does directly from the code itself.

HTML comments

Note that these comments only work in the `<script>` part of the program. You can add comments to the HTML, as we saw in Chapter 2, but you use a different character sequence to mark the start and end of the comments:

```
<!-- Rob's Pizza Calculator Page Version 1.0 -->
```

The start of the comment is marked by the sequence `<!--` and the end of the comment by the sequence `-->`. As with JavaScript comments, the text between the two sequences is ignored by the browser.

Global and local variables

At the start of this section, we wanted to make a totalizer program that can be used to add up a bunch of numbers. We can now create this. Let's assume that we are creating a solution for a customer who really does want to totalize some numbers. You have sat down with her and agreed on the following design for the application.

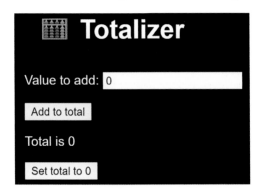

Figure 4-10   Totalizer

Your customer would like a stylish black background containing the Abacus emoji. We can create this by using a style sheet that sets the color scheme for the application and finding the symbol number for the abacus (🧮).

She wants to be able to type in a value and press the **Add to total** button to add the value to the total. She also wants a button she can use to set the total back to zero when she has finished adding one set of values. You agree on the design shown in **Figure 4-10** above.

Getting a good specification is vital

The sample page shown in **Figure 4-10** is a good start for the specification of the Totalizer application. It is very important that you get a solid specification for any work that you perform, even (or perhaps especially) if you are working for someone you know. The nice thing about the screenshot of the application is that it sets out exactly what the solution should look like. However, there are some questions I'd want answered, too.

I would like to know if there is any upper limit to the amount to be added to the total. I'd also like to know if the Totalizer should accept negative numbers to be subtracted from the total or whether the total should always be increased. The answers to these questions tell me whether the Totalizer should detect and reject invalid input values. The customer might be assuming that negative values should not be added (or might never have thought about this issue). Either way, as the builder of the solution, you need to know how it should work. Otherwise, you might end up having conversations with your customer that include phrases such as, "It isn't supposed to do that...".

Global variables

The Totalizer program is interesting because it is the first program we have written that needs to "remember" something between function calls. Until now, every program that we have created takes data from the input elements, does something to it, and then displays the result. Any variables that we have created to store data in a function during data processing are discarded as soon as the process has finished. For example, consider the temperature conversion program, which takes a temperature entered in Fahrenheit and converts it to centigrade.

```
function doTempConvert() {
                                          Get a reference to the input element

    var fahrenheitElement = document.getElementById("fahrenheitText");
    var fahrenheitText = fahrenheitElement.value;    Get the text from the input element
    var fahrenheit = Number(fahrenheitText);         Convert the text into a numeric value


    var centigrade = (fahrenheit-32)/1.8;            Convert the value into Centigrade
                                                     Get a reference to the output element
    var resultElement = document.getElementById("resultParagraph");
    var resultString = centigrade.toFixed(1) + " degrees Centigrade";
    resultElement.innerText = resultString;          Build the result string
}
                                                     Put the result string on the output element
```

All the variables in this function will be destroyed once the function has finished. They are described as *local* because they are local to the function. This is how the JavaScript manages variables created using var. Most of the time, this is exactly what you want. We don't want the program to use any values left over from a previous use of the function. However, the Totalizer program needs to retain the total value for use in successive calls of the function that adds values to it. In other words; we want to write some code like this:

```javascript
var total=0; // Global variable to hold the total

/* This function reads the value from the valueText element
   and adds it to the global total value */
function doAddToTotal() {

  var valueElement = document.getElementById("valueText");
  var valueText = valueElement.value;
  var value = Number(valueText);

  total = total + value; // update the global total value

  // Display the updated total
  var resultElement = document.getElementById("resultParagraph");
  var resultString = "Total is " + total;
  resultElement.innerText = resultString;
}
```

The variable total is special. It exists outside any JavaScript functions. We call it a *global* variable because it can be used by any function in my application. I've added a comment above the declaration of the total variable. This is because I like my global variables to stand out in the code.

> **PROGRAMMER'S POINT**
>
> ## Global variables are a necessary evil
>
> If you talk to some programmers, they might tell you that your programs should never use global variables. This is because a global variable represents a possible failure point that is out of your control. I can be sure that all the variables in my functions contain correct values. This is because each time a function runs, it makes clean new copies of every variable, but a global variable exists in outside my functions. I can't regard it as "clean" because I don't know what other functions might have been doing with it. Mistakes by other programmers could make my functions do the wrong thing, and that is bad. If another

function changes, the contents of total my function could display a result that is incorrect. However, in the case of the Totalizer program, a global variable is the simplest way I can make it work.

Programmers talk about functions having *side effects*. These are things that the function does that change the state of the system in which they are running. In the case of the Totalizer, the doAddToTotal function has a side effect that increases the value of total by the amount entered by the user. This is a side effect that is present by design. It is important to avoid unintended side effects.

CODE ANALYSIS

Global variables and side effects

It is important that you understand the difference between local and global variables, so here are some questions you might have considered.

Question: How can I tell if a variable is global?

> **Answer:** A global variable is declared outside of any function. The total variable below is not part of any function, therefore it is global. The variable is also set to 0 when it is created.

```
var total=0;
```

> In Chapter 3, in the "Create a ticking clock" section, we discovered a JavaScript function called onload, which runs when a web page is loaded. A program could initialize (but of course not declare) global variables in that function.

Question: Is the value of a global variable retained if I reload the web page?

> **Answer:** No. When the page is reloaded, the JavaScript environment is reset and new global variables are created.

Question: Is a single global variable shared between multiple tabs of the same page being viewed in a single browser? In other words, if I opened several views of the Totalizer program, would the value of total be shared between them?

> **Answer:** No. Each web page runs a separate JavaScript environment.

Question: Do any other functions in the Totalizer have side effects?

Answer: Yes. The function that is called to clear the total back to 0 will set the value of `total` back to 0.

```
/* This function clears the total value and updates the display
*/
function doZeroTotal(){
  total=0; // set the global total to 0

  // update the display
  var resultElement = document.getElementById("resultParagraph");
  resultElement.innerText = "Total is 0";
}
```

This function sets the value of `total` to 0 and then updates the display to reflect this.

Question: How could I create a Totalizer that stored the total value when the page was not being used?

Answer: The browser provides a feature called "local storage," which can be used to store values when a web page is not active. In Chapter 9, we will use this to create an address book. A totalizer program could use local storage to hold a total value that would persist when the totalizer page was not being used.

You can find my version of the Totalizer program in the **Ch04 Working with data\ Ch04-08 Totalizer** folder. This includes the style sheet that sets up the requested color scheme.

 MAKE SOMETHING HAPPEN

Make some party games

There is no better way to show off your programming skills than by using them to make some silly party games. At least, that's what I think. We can create a good-looking party game using our skills with CSS and JavaScript. The basis of many games is randomness. We know how to use JavaScript to create random numbers, so let's see if we can make some games using this.

"Nerves of Steel"

We can use our ability to make random numbers, coupled with the `setTimeout` function we used to make egg timers in Chapter 2, to create a "Nerves of Steel" party game. The game works like this:

1. One player presses the **Start Game** button.

2. The program displays **Players stand**.

3. The program then pauses for a random time between 5 and 20 seconds. While the program is paused, players can sit down. The players need to keep track of the last person to sit down.

4. When the time interval expires, the program displays "`Last to sit down wins.`" Players still sanding are eliminated, and the winner is the last person to sit down.

This is a variant of the egg timer program from Chapter 2. Rather than set a timeout for a fixed duration (5 minutes), the program selects a random time for the duration. You can make the game properly skillful if the game displays the selected time at the start of the game. You can also improve it using sound effects to mark the start and end of the timeout session.

High and Low

Another way of using random numbers is to create a "High and Low" game. The game works like this:

1. One player presses the **Next Round** button.

2. The program displays a number between 1 and 10, inclusively.

3. The program then sleeps for 20 seconds. While the program is asleep, the players are invited to decide whether the next number will be higher or lower than the number just printed. Players who choose "high" stand on the right. Players who choose "low" stand on the left.

4. The program then displays a second number between 1 and 10, and anyone who was wrong is eliminated from the game. The program is then re-run with the players that are left until you have a winner.

This game can get very tactical, with players taking a chance on an unlikely number just so that they will be one of the people to go forward to the next round.

Adding sound

You can add sound to the game. You can have a ticking clock sound effect while the players are waiting and a "ding" sound when the timer expires. To do this the program will have to start and stop the audio playback. It will also have to "reset" the ticking sound so that it plays from the beginning of the sound sample. A sound in HTML provides play and pause methods that can be used to control playback. It also provides a currentType property that a program can use to read or set. This is the tickAudio element in my version of the program:

```html
<audio id="tickAudio">
    <source src="tick-track.mp3" type="audio/mpeg">
</audio>
```

I can start the playback as follows. The first statement sets the playback position at 0 so that the playback begins at the start of sound. The second statement plays the sample.

```javascript
tickSoundElement.currentTime=0;
tickSoundElement.play();
```

When I want the ticking sound to stop (when the timer has expired), I use the following:

```javascript
tickSoundElement.pause();
```

Note that there is no command to stop the playback of a sound. You can find my versions of the games in the folders **Ch04 Working with data\Ch04-09 Nerves of Steel** and **Ch04 Working with data\Ch04-10 High and Low**. You can use these as the basis of any other games you might like to create.

What you have learned

This chapter has given you a good understanding of how JavaScript programs store and manipulate data. Here are the major points you have covered in the chapter:

- A computer is fundamentally a data processor. A program receives data, does something with it, and outputs more data. What the computer does with the data is determined by the program itself.

- The JavaScript programs that we have created take data in from input elements and display data by updating the text displayed by a paragraph element.

- Data processing in a computer is performed by the evaluation of expressions. An expression contains operands (values to be worked with) and operators (which specify what is to be done with the operands). In the expression 2+3 the operands are the literal values 2 and 3. The operator is +.

- A program is unaware of the nature of the data that it is processing. Meaning is added when humans interpret the data as information.

- A variable is a named storage location that holds a value that a program is working with. Variables can be created using `var`.

- Variables can be used as operands in expressions. The assignment operator is used to set a value in a variable.

- Variables can be created before they are used, in which case, they contain a value denoted as "undefined." When assigned to a value, a variable will acquire a type appropriate to the value. The two types we have used so far are number (a numeric value) and string (a string of text)

- Operators in an expression are evaluated according to their priority. This priority can be overridden by using brackets.

- Numbers in a program can be real numbers (with a fractional part) or whole numbers (integers). JavaScript provides `Math` functions for creating whole numbers from floating point numbers. The `floor` function removes the fractional part, whereas the `round` function rounds up to the nearest whole number.

- Text in program source code can be delimited by the double quote ("), single quote ('), or backtick (`) characters. Escape characters (\)are used in strings for the entry of delimiter characters and some nonprinting characters.

- If an expression involves string and numeric values, the numeric values are automatically converted into strings.

- The JavaScript function `Number` is used to convert a string into a numeric value. If this conversion is not possible, the `Number` function returns the value NaN (not a number). All numeric calculations involving the value NaN will generate a result of NaN.

- Comments can be added to a program by delimiting them with /* and */ character sequences. A single-line comment is started by the character sequence // and extends to the end of the line containing the comment.

- A variable is made global by declaring it outside any JavaScript function. Global variables are useful because they allow values to be shared between functions, but they should be used with care as they represent a way in which a fault in one function could set a global variable to a value, which could cause other functions to fail. Changes made by a function to the contents of a global variable are known as "side effects."

To reinforce your understanding of this chapter, you might want to consider the following "profound questions" about variables.

Do all computer programs have to have an input from the user?

Many programs have an input from the user that they use to produce an output. However, not all programs have an input. The "Nerves of Steel" and "High and Low" games get their input from random numbers before displaying them.

What is the difference between "undefined" and "not a number"?

A JavaScript variable normally holds a value. However, it can also hold the special values undefined and NaN (not a number). A variable is "undefined" if it has been created but it has not been assigned a value yet. The value NaN (not a number) is used to represent a situation when a calculation did not create a numeric result. The Number function is used to convert a string of text into a number and will return a result of NaN if conversion was impossible because the supplied string does not contain digit characters.

Do long variable names slow my program down?

No, but they do speed up the process of understanding what the program does.

What is the difference between an operator and an operand?

An operator is a doing thing (in the English language the verbs are a bit like the operators). An operand is the thing that is operated on. In the sentence "The cat sat on the mat," I would say that the operands are "cat" and "mat," and the operator is "sat."

What is the difference between a real number and a whole number?

A real number has a fractional part. The value of Pi is a real number as it has a fractional component (3.1416). A whole number has no fractional part. Whole number values are used in programs for things like counting (how many sheep in a field). Real numbers are used for calculated values (the average weight of the sheep in a field).

What is the length of the longest string that a program can hold?

A string can be very, very long. You could store an entire book in a single string if you wish.

Can I create a global variable inside a JavaScript function?

No. The important thing about a global variable is that it exists outside all functions. The variables created inside a function body are discarded when the function stops running. However, we sometimes need variables whose value is persisted between function calls. These are declared as global and can be accessed by all functions.

How can I create a string that contains the double quote characters that delimit it?

My programs usually use double quotes to mark the start and end of strings in the program text. If I want to include a double quote in the string there are two ways I can do this. The first is to use an escape sequence (\") in the string. The other way would be to use either single quote (') or back tick (`) to delimit the string with the double quote characters in it.

5
Making decisions in programs

What you will learn

I've described a computer as a sausage machine that accepts an input, does something with it, and then produces an output. This is a great way to start thinking about computers, but a computer does a lot more than that. Unlike a real-life sausage machine, which simply tries to create sausage from anything you put in it, a computer can respond to different inputs in different ways. In this chapter, you'll learn how to make your programs respond to different inputs. You'll also learn about the responsibility that comes with making the computer work in this way because you must be sure that the decisions your programs make are sensible.

Boolean thinking

In Chapter 4, you learned that programs use variables to represent different types of data. I like to think that you will forever associate the number of hairs on your head with whole numbers (integers) and the average length of your hair with real numbers (floating-point values). Now it's time to meet another way of looking at data values: Boolean. Data that is Boolean can only have one of two values: true and false. You could use a Boolean value to represent whether a given person has any hair.

Boolean values in JavaScript

A program can create variables that can hold Boolean values. As with other JavaScript data types, JavaScript will deduce the type of a variable from the context in which it is used.

```
var itIsTimeToGetUp = true;
```

The above statement creates a variable called itIsTimeToGetUp and sets its value to true. In my world, it seems that it is always time to get up. In the highly unlikely event of me ever being allowed to stay in bed, we can change the assignment to set the value to false:

```
var itIsTimeToGetUp = false;
```

The words true and false are keywords. These are words that are "built in" to JavaScript. There are 63 different keywords. You've already seen a few of them. For example, function is a keyword. When JavaScript sees the keywords true or false, it thinks in terms of Boolean values.

JavaScript regards values that are numbers or text as being either "truthy" or "falsy." Values are regarded as "truthy" unless they are zero, an empty string, Not a Number (NAN), or undefined—in which case, they are "falsy."

CODE ANALYSIS

Boolean values

Boolean values are a new type of data that a program can manipulate. But of course, we have questions about them.

Question: What do you think would happen if you displayed the contents of a Boolean value?

```
alert(itIsTimeToGetUp);
```

Answer: When you display any value, JavaScript will try to convert that value into something sensible for us to look at. In the case of Boolean values, it will display true or false.

Question: Is there a JavaScript function called Boolean that will convert things into Boolean values, just like there is a Number function that will convert things into a number?

Answer: Indeed, there is. The Boolean function applies the rules of "truthy" and "falsy" to the value supplied to it.

```
> Boolean(1);
<- true
> Boolean(0);
<- false
```

Applying Boolean to 0 gives the result false. Any other numeric value would be regarded as true.

Question: Are negative numbers regarded as false?

Answer: No. It is best to regard "truthy" as meaning "the presence of a value" rather than something that is positive or negative. Applying Boolean to a negative number will produce a result of true.

```
> Boolean(-1);
<- true
```

Question: Is the string `false` regarded as `true`?

Answer: Yes. If you understand this, you can call yourself a "truthy ninja." Any string other than an empty string is regarded as `true`.

```
> Boolean("false");
<- true
> Boolean("");
<- false
```

Question: Is the value `infinity` regarded as `true` or `false`?

Answer: In our first encounter with JavaScript in Chapter 1, we tried dividing 1 by zero to see what happened. We discovered that this type of invalid calculation produces a value of `infinity` as a result. The best way to discover whether `infinity` is `true` or `false` is to ask JavaScript:

```
> Boolean(1/0);
<- true
```

The calculation `1/0` generates a result of `infinity`, which is regarded by the `Boolean` function as `true`.

Question: We know that if we ask JavaScript to perform a silly calculation, such as dividing a number by a string, the result is a special value called Not a number (NaN). Is NaN regarded as `true` or `false`?

Answer: JavaScript regards NaN as `false`. Dividing the number 1 by the string Rob produces NaN as a result. If we feed this into the `Boolean` function, it decides this value is `false`.

```
> Boolean(1/"Rob");
<- false
```

Question: What happens if a program combines Boolean values with other values?

Answer: In Chapter 4, in the section "Working with strings and numbers," we discovered that when we combine numbers with strings, the numeric value is automatically "promoted" to a string. Something similar happens when logical values are combined with values of other types. A value that is `true` equates to the number 1 and the `true` string. A value of `false` equates to 0 and `false`.

```
> 1 + true;
<- 2
> "hello" + true;
<- "hellotrue"
```

Note that, as with numbers, this conversion does not work the other way. Just as we had to use the Number function to convert a string into a number, we have to use the Boolean function to convert values of other types into values that obey the "truthy" and "falsy" rules.

In Chapter 3, we created a ticking clock that displayed the time. The program in Chapter 3 used the Date object that JavaScript provides to get the current date and time:

```
var currentDate = new Date();
var hours = currentDate.getHours();
var mins = currentDate.getMinutes();
var secs = currentDate.getSeconds();
```

The statements above get the hours, mins, and secs values for the current time. We could use these values to write some JavaScript that would decide whether I should get up. Note that the hours value is supplied as a 24-hour clock value, meaning it goes from 0 to 23 over the day.

Boolean expressions

We've said that JavaScript expressions are made up of operators (which identify the operation) and operands (which identify the items being processed). **Figure 5-1** shows our first expression, which worked out the calculation 2+2.

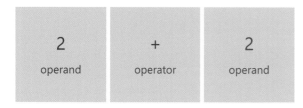

Figure 5-1   An arithmetic operator

An expression can contain a comparison operator, as shown in **Figure 5-2**.

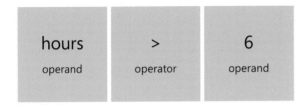

Figure 5-2   A comparison operator

An expression containing a comparison operator evaluates to a result that is either `true` or `false`. The `>` operator in this expression means "greater than." If you read the expression aloud, you say "hour greater than six." In other words, this expression is `true` if the hour value is greater than 6. I need to get up after 7, so this is what I need for my alarm clock. Expressions that return either `true` or `false` are called logical expressions.

Comparison operators

These are the comparison operators that you can use in JavaScript programs.

OPERATOR	NAME	EFFECT
>	Greater than	**True** if the value on the left is greater than the value on the right
<	Less than	**True** if the value on the left is less than the value on the right
>=	Greater than or equals	**True** if the value on the left is greater than or equal to the value on the right
<=	Less than or equals	**True** if the value on the left is less than or equal to the value on the right
==	Equality	**True** if the value on the left and the value on the right can be promoted to values that are equal
===	Identity	**True** if the values on the left and the value on the right are the same type and hold the same value
!=	Not equals	**True** if the value on the left and the value on the right cannot be promoted to values that are equal
!==	Not identical	**True** if the values on the left and the value on the right are not the same type or do not hold the same value

A program can use comparison operators in an expression to set a Boolean value.

```
itIsTimeToGetUp = hours > 6;
```

This statement will set the variable itIsTimeToGetUp to the value true if the value in hours is greater than 6 and false if the value in hours is not greater than 6. Remember that an operator that is a single equals character performs an assignment, not a test. If this seems hard to understand, try reading the statement and listen to how it sounds. The statement "itIsTimeToGetUp equals hour greater than six" is a good explanation of the action of this statement.

CODE ANALYSIS

Examining comparison operators

Question: How does the equality operator work?

> **Answer:** The equality operator evaluates to true if the two operands hold the same value.

```
> 1==1;
<- true
```

The equality operator (==) can be used to compare strings and Boolean values, too.

```
> "Rob"=="Rob";
<- true
> true == true;
<- true
```

We've seen that JavaScript "promotes" values when they are used in expression. This happens with the equality operator, too. The logical value true is promoted to the value 1 when it is used in an expression with the equality operator.

```
> 1 == true;
<- true
```

JavaScript returned true because the value true was promoted to 1 before the comparison was performed. Note that comparing true for equality with any other value would return false, because true is always promoted to 1.

```
> 2 == true;
<- false
```

Question: What is the difference between equality and identity?

Answer: We've just seen how the `==` (equality) operator above promotes values before comparing them. This means that the operator can compare values of different types.

```
> true == 1;
<- true
```

In the example above, the statement compares a logical value with a number. This generates a `true` result because the true value is "promoted" to the integer value `1` before being compared.

The identity comparison `===` does not perform any promotion before comparing two values. If we use the identity comparison to compare the logical value of `true` with `1`, a result of `false` is produced.

```
> true === 1;
<- false
```

JavaScript returned `false` because once side of the identity operator holds a logical value (`true`), and the other holds a number (`1`). If, like me, you are the kind of programmer who thinks that programs should never compare numbers and logical values for equality and get a result of `true` (because comparing numbers and logical values directly is not a meaningful thing to do), then you can use the `===` comparison operator to make sure of this.

Question: How do I remember which relational operator is which?

Answer: When I was learning to program, I associated the `<` in the `<=` operator with the letter L, which reminded me that `<=` means "less than or equal to."

Question: Can we apply relational operators between other types of expressions?

Answer: Yes, we can. If a relational operator is applied between two string operands, it uses an alphabetic comparison to determine the order.

```
> "Alice" < "Brian";
<- true
```

JavaScript returned `true` because the name Alice appears alphabetically before Brian.

Equality and floating-point values

In Chapter 4, we saw that a floating-point number is sometimes only an approximation of the real number value our program is using. In other words, some numbers are not stored precisely.

This approximation of real number values can lead to serious problems when we write programs that test to see whether two variables hold the same floating-point values. Consider the following statements, which I've typed into the Developer View in the Edge browser:

```
> var x = 0.3;
> var y = 0.1 + 0.2;
```

These statements create two variables, x and y, which should both hold the value 0.3. The variable x has the value 0.3 directly assigned, whereas the second variable, y, gets the value 0.3 as the result of a calculation that works out the result of 0.1 + 0.2. What do you think we will see if we test the two variables for equality?

```
> x == y;
<- false
```

This expression uses the equality operator (==), which will produce a result of true if its two operands hold the same value. However, JavaScript decides that x and y are different because the variable x holds the value 0.3, and the variable y holds the value 0.30000000000000004. This illustrates a problem with program code that compares floating-point values to determine whether they are equal. The tiny floating-point errors mean values we think are the same do not always evaluate that way.

If a program needs to compare two floating-point values for equality, the best approach is to decide they are equal if they differ by only a very small amount. If you don't do this, you might find that your programs don't behave as you might expect.

The date and time values returned from the JavaScript Date object are supplied as integers so you can test these for equality without problems.

Logical operators

At the moment, my test to determine whether it is time to get up is only controlled by the hour value of the time.

```
itIsTimeToGetUp = hours > 6;
```

The above statement sets the value of `itIsTimeToGetUp` to `true` if the hour is greater than 6 (meaning from 7 and onward) but we might want to get up at 7:30. To be able to do this, we need a way of testing for a time when the hour is greater than 6 and the minute is greater than 29. JavaScript provides three logical operators we can use to work with logical values. Perhaps they can help solve this problem.

OPERATOR	EFFECT
!	Evaluates to True if the operand it is working on is False Evaluates to False if the operand it is working on is True
&&	Evaluates to True if the left-hand value and the right-hand value are both True
||	Evaluates to True if the left-hand value and the right-hand value are both True

The `&&` (and) operator is applied between two Boolean values and returns `true` if both values are `true`. There is also an `||` (or) operator, which is applied between two Boolean values and returns `true` if one of the values is `true`. The third operator is the operator `!` (not), which can be used to invert a Boolean value.

CODE ANALYSIS

Logical operators

We can investigate the behavior of logical operators by using the Developer View in the Edge browser. We can just type in expressions and see how they evaluate. Please don't be confused by the way that the < and > characters are used in the devleoper console samples below.

Question: What does the following expression evaluate to?

```
<- !true;
```

Answer: The effect of `!` is to invert a Boolean value, turning the `true` into a `false`.

```
> !true;
<- false
```

Question: What does this expression evaluate to?

```
> true && true;
```

Answer: The operands on each side of the `&&` are `true`, so the result evaluates to `true`.

```
> true && true;
<- true
```

Question: What does this expression evaluate to?

```
> true && false;
```

Answer: Because both sides (operands) of the `&&` (and) operator need to be `true` for the result to be `true`, you shouldn't be surprised to see a result of `false` here.

```
> true && false;
<- false
```

Question: What does this expression evaluate to?

```
> true || false;
```

Answer: Because only one side of an `||` (or) operator needs to be `true` for the result to be `true`, the expression evaluates to `true`.

```
> true || false;
<- true
```

Question: So far, the examples have used only Boolean values. What happens when we start to combine Boolean and numeric values?

```
> true && 1;
```

Answer: It turns out that JavaScript is quite happy to use and combine logical and numeric values. The above combination would not return `true`, however. Instead, it will return 1.

```
> true && 1;
<- 1
```

This looks a bit confusing, but it gives us an insight into how JavaScript evaluates our logical expression. JavaScript will start at the beginning of a logical expression and then work along the expression until it finds the first value it can use to determine the result of the expression. It will then return that value.

In the above expression, when JavaScript sees the left-hand operand is `true`, it says to itself "Aha. The value of the && (and) expression is now determined by the right-hand value. If the right-hand value is `true`, the result is `true`. If the right-hand value is `false`, the result is `false`." So the expression simply returns the right-hand operand. We can test this behavior by reversing the order of the operands:

```
> 1 && true;
<- true
```

We know that any value other than 0 is `true`, so JavaScript will return the right-hand operand, which in this case is True. We can see this behavior with the || (or) operation, too. JavaScript only looks at the operands of a logical operator until it can determine whether the result is `true` or `false`.

```
> 1 || false;
<- 1
> 0 || True;
<- True
```

You might wish to experiment with other values to confirm that you understand what is happening.

We want to make some JavaScript that takes in hour and minute values and decides whether to sound the alarm. We could try to make an alarm that triggers after 7:30 by writing the following statement:

```
var itIsTimeToGetUp= hours>6 && minutes>29;
```

The && (and) operator is applied between the result of two Boolean expressions and returns true if both of the expressions evaluate to true. The above statement would set the variable itIsTimeToGetUp to true if the value in hours is greater than 6 and the value in minutes is greater than 29, which you might think is what we want. However, this statement is incorrect. We can discover the bug by designing some tests:

HOURS	MINUTES	REQUIRED RESULT	OBSERVED RESULT
6	00	False	False
7	29	False	False
7	30	True	True
8	0	True	False

The table shows four times, along with the required result (what *should* happen), and the observed result (what *does* happen). One of the times has been observed to work incorrectly. When the time is 8:00, the value of itIsTimeToGetUp is set to false, which is wrong.

The condition we are using evaluates to true if the hours value is greater than 6 and the minutes value is greater than 29. This means that the condition evaluates to false for any minute value that is less than 29, meaning it is false at 8:00. To fix the problem, we need to develop a slightly more complex test:

```
var itIsTimeToGetUp= (hours>7) || (hours==7 && minutes>29);
```

I've added parentheses to show how the two tests are combined by the || (or) operator. If the value of hours is greater than 7, we don't care what the value of minutes is. If the hours value is equal to 7, we need to test to see whether the minutes value is greater than 29. If you try the values in the table with the above statement, you will find that it works correctly. This illustrates an important point when designing code intended to perform logic like this. You need to design tests that you can use to ensure that the program will do what you want.

The **if** construction

Suppose I want to make a program that will display a message telling me whether it's time to get out of bed. We can use the Boolean value we just created to control the execution of programs by using JavaScript's if construction. **Figure 5-3** shows how an if construction fits together.

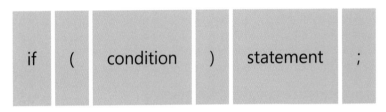

Figure 5-3   If construction

The condition controls the execution of the statement. In other words, if the condition is "truthy," the statement is performed; otherwise, it is not performed.

```
if (itIsTimeToGetUp) alert("It is time to get up!");
```

The statement above would display an alert if it were time to get up. You can see this in use in the example **\Ch05 Making Decisions in Programs\Ch05-01 Alarm Alert**, which displays the alert if you visit the page after 07:30 in the morning.

```
<!DOCTYPE html>
<html lang="en">

<head>
    <title>Ch05-01 Alarm Alert</title>
</head>

<body onload="doCheckAlarm()">
    <script>
        function doCheckAlarm() {
            var currentDate = new Date();
            var hours = currentDate.getHours();
            var mins = currentDate.getMinutes();
            var itIsTimeToGetUp = (hours>7) || (hours==7 && minutes>29);
```
The if construction that controls the alert
```
            if (itIsTimeToGetUp) alert("It is time to get up!");
```

```
        }
    </script>
</body>

</html>
```

This is the full text of the alarm alert page. Note that the statement that implements the "intelligence" of the program is only one tiny part of the code.

The behavior of the `if` construction is controlled by the condition. The condition does not have to be a variable; it can also be a logical expression:

```
if ((hours>7) || (hours==7 && minutes>29)) alert("It is time to get up!");
```

This statement removes the need for the `itIsTimeToGetUp` variable. However, I quite like using the variable because it helps the user understand what the program is doing.

Adding an else part

Many programs want to perform one action if a condition is `true` and another action if the condition is `false`. The `if` construction can have an `else` element added, which identifies a statement to be performed if the condition is `false`. See **Figure 5-4**.

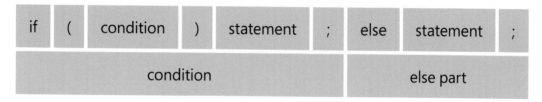

Figure 5-4   If construction with `else`

The `else` part is added onto the end of a conditional statement. If comprises the keyword `else` followed by the statement to be performed if the condition is `false`. We could use it to make our alert program display a message when we can stay in bed.

```
if(itIsTimeToGetUp)
    alert("It is time to get up!");
else
    alert("You can stay in bed");
```

This program displays a different message depending on the time of day that the user runs the program. Note that although I've spread the statement over several lines, the content matches the structure in Figure 5-4.

If constructions

Question: Must an if construction have an else part?

> **Answer:** No. They are very useful sometimes, but it depends on the problem that the program is trying to solve.

Question: What happens if a condition is never true?

> **Answer:** If a condition is never true, the statement controlled by the condition never gets to run.

Question: Why is the statement underneath the if condition in my example indented by a few spaces?

> **Answer:** This statement doesn't need to be indented. JavaScript would be able to understand what we want the program to do even if we put everything on one line. The indentation is there to make the program easier to understand. It shows that the statement underneath the if construction is being controlled by the condition above it. Indenting like this is such common practice that you will find the behavior "baked in" to the Visual Studio Code editor. In other words, if you start typing an if construction and press the Enter key at the end of the condition part, Visual Studio Code will automatically indent the next line.

Creating blocks of statements

The if condition controls the execution of a single statement. However, sometimes you might want to perform multiple statements if a condition is true. For example, we might what to play an alarm sound as well as displaying an alert message when it is time to get up. To do this, a program needs to control multiple statements from a single condition. You write code for a task like this by creating a block of statements.

A block of statements is a sequence of JavaScript statements enclosed in a pair of curly braces—the { and } characters. You have already seen blocks of statements in the programs we've examined and written. In those programs, the statements in all the functions are enclosed in a block. You can create a block anywhere in a program, and it is equivalent to a single statement.

```
if (itIsTimeToGetUp) {
    alarmAudio.play();
    outputElement.textContent = "It is time to get up!";
}else {
    outputElement.textContent = "You can stay in bed";
}
```

The code above displays a message and plays an alarm sound. You can find the working program in the example **Ch05 Making Decisions in Programs\Ch05-03 Alarm Alert with sound block**. This uses the "everything sound" as an alarm, which some might feel a bit harsh, but it certainly wakes me up. Note that in the above code, I've used curly braces to enclose the statements for both the `if` and `else` parts of the condition, even though there is no need to do this for the else part as it only contains one statement. I do this to make it clear what is going on. It also means that it is easier to add extra statements controlled by the `else` part because I can just put them inside the block.

Use decisions to make an application

Now that you know how to make decisions in your programs, you can start to make more useful software. Let's say your next-door neighbor is the owner of a theme park and has a job for you. Some rides at the theme park are restricted to people by age, and he wants to install some computers around his theme park so that people can find out which rides they may go on. He needs some software for the computers, and he's offering a season pass to the park if you can come up with the goods, which is a very tempting proposition. He provides you with the following information about the rides at his park:

RIDE NAME	MININUM AGE REQUIREMENT
Scenic River Cruise	None
Carnival Carousel	At least 3 years old
Jungle Adventure Water Splash	At least 6 years old
Downhill Mountain Run	At least 12 years old
The Regurgitator (a super scary roller coaster)	Must be at least 12 years old and less than 90

You discuss with him the design of the program user interface. The user interface is what people see when they use the program and the steps that they go through when they are using it. In this application, users will specify the ride they want to go on and enter their age. They then click a button and are told whether they can go on that ride (see **Figure 5-5**).

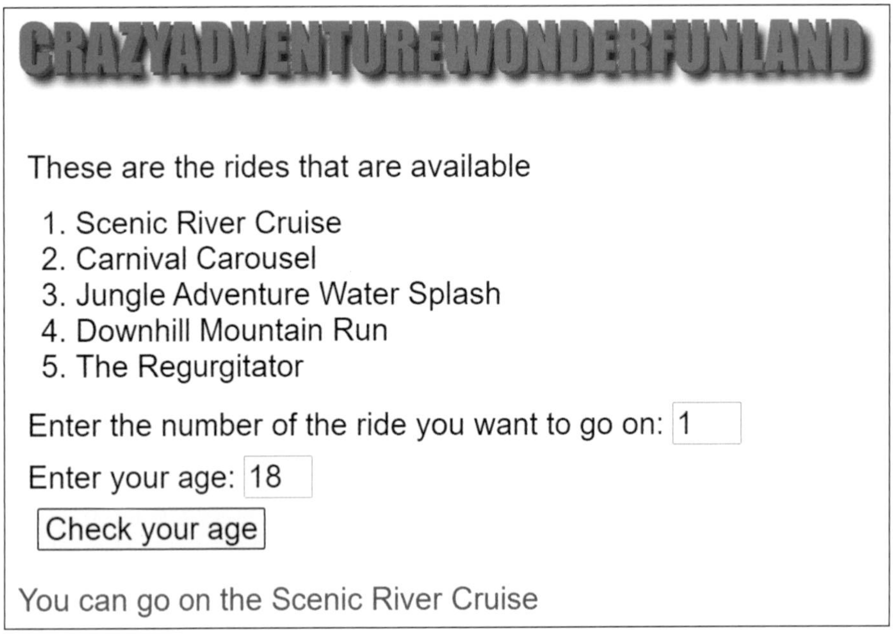

CRAZYADVENTUREWONDERFUNLAND

These are the rides that are available

1. Scenic River Cruise
2. Carnival Carousel
3. Jungle Adventure Water Splash
4. Downhill Mountain Run
5. The Regurgitator

Enter the number of the ride you want to go on: 1

Enter your age: 18

Check your age

You can go on the Scenic River Cruise

Figure 5-5   Theme park rides

PROGRAMMER'S POINT

Design the user Interface with the customer

You might think that an interface like this would be simple to design and that the customer will have no strong opinions on how the user interface looks and functions. I've found this to be wrong. I've had the awful experience of proudly showing my finished solution to a customer only to be told that it was not what they wanted and that it is "hard to use." I now understand that this was my fault. Rather than showing only my finished design, I should have created the design with the customer. That would have saved me a lot of work.

Build the user interface

The first thing we need to do is create the HTML web page and the style sheet for the application. In Chapter 3, we decided that it was a good idea to separate the style sheet file, which holds the style of the page elements, from the page layout. It is also a good idea to separate the JavaScript program code from the HTML layout. We do this by putting the JavaScript into a file with the language extension ".js." We can then add an element in the head of the HTML file that specifies this file name:

```
<script src="themepark.js" ></script>
```

The HTML above is added to the `<head>` part of an HTML document and includes the contents of the JavaScript file `themepark.js` in an HTML page. You can see it in use in the HTML below.

```
<!DOCTYPE html>
<html lang="en">

<head>
    <title>Ch05-04 Theme Park Ride Selector</title>
    <link rel="stylesheet" href="styles.css"> ———————— Include the CSS file
    <script src = "themepark.js" ></script> ———— Include the JavaScript file
</head>

<body>
    <p class="menuHeading">CRAZYADVENTUREWONDERFUNLAND</p>
    <p class="menuText">These are the rides that are available</p>
    <ol class="menuRideList"> ———————————————— Start of numbered list of rides
        <li>Scenic River Cruise</li>
        <li>Carnival Carousel</li>
        <li>Jungle Adventure Water Splash</li>
        <li>Downhill Mountain Run</li>
        <li>The Regurgitator</li>
    </ol>
    <p class="menuText">Enter the number of the ride you want to go on:
      <input class="menuInput" type="number" id="rideNoText"
      value="1" min="1" max="5"> </p>
    <p class="menuText">Enter your age:
      <input class="menuInput" type="number" id="ageText"
      value="18" min="0" max="100"> </p>
```

```
    <button class="menuButton" onclick="doCheckAge()">Check your age</button>

    <p class="menuAnswer" id="menuAnswerPar"></p>
</body>

</html>
```

This is the HTML file for the Theme Park Ride Selector application. It uses some features of HTML that we've not seen before. We can create an ordered list of items by using the `<ol>` tag to enclose some `<li>` list elements. The browser will automatically number the elements for us. Each element on the page is assigned a class that has a specific style. The settings for each of the styles are in a separate CSS style sheet file called `styles.css`. A part of this file is given below:

```
.menuHeading {
    font-size: 4em;
    font-family: Impact, Haettenschweiler, 'Arial Narrow Bold', sans-serif;
    color: red;
    text-shadow: 3px 3px 0 blue, 10px 10px 10px darkblue; ————  This style adds shadows
}                                                                          to the text
                                                      ┌─ These settings will be applied to all the classes.
.menuText,.menuRideList, .menuButton, .menuInput, .menuYes, .menuNo
{
    font-family:Arial, Helvetica, sans-serif;
    font-size: 2em;
    color:black;
}

.menuYes
{
    margin: 30px;
    color:green;
}
... remainder of classes are defined here ...
```

The `menuHeading` class is in the HTML used to format the heading. It uses the Impact font and adds two shadows to the text. The first shadow is blue and close to the text, which provides a 3D effect for each character. The second shadow is more diffuse and darker blue so that it makes the characters appear to stand out from the page. You can see the effect in Figure 5-5. Each shadow is defined by a color value preceded by three values. The first two values give the x and y offsets of the shadow from the text. The third value determines how "diffuse" the shadow is. The first shadow is not diffused at all, whereas the second has a diffusion size of 10px, leading to the text shown earlier in Figure 5-5.

The style sheet also applies some shared settings to all the menu input classes. This means that the font is set once for all those classes, making it easy to change the font if required. It is a good idea to group classes in this way if they all have a set of common characteristics. Remember that classes accumulate setting values, which are then used on the HTML elements that are assigned to that class. So, for example, the menuYes class will bring together the following settings—some from those shared by other menu settings, and some specific to that class:

```
font-family:Arial, Helvetica, sans-serif;
font-size: 2em;


color: green;
```

Add the code

Now that we have the user interface complete, we need to add the JavaScript that implements the behavior that the application needs. When the user presses the button to check their age, the doCheckAge function runs. This function gets values for the number of the selected ride and the age of the person wishing to use it. The function then tests these values to see whether the combination is valid. The first part of this function works in the same way as the adding machine that we created earlier. It fetches text from the input elements in the HTML and uses the Number function to convert the text into a number.

```
var rideNoElement = document.getElementById("rideNoText");
var rideNoText = rideNoElement.value;
var rideNo = Number(rideNoText);              Get the ride number that was entered

var ageElement = document.getElementById("ageText");
var ageText = ageElement.value;
var ageNo = Number(ageText);                  Get the age of the person
```

When these statements have completed, the variables `rideNo` and `ageNo` contain the number of the ride and the age of the guest. The next thing the function does is get a reference to the paragraph that will be used to display the result. If you look at the HTML for the user interface, you'll see that this paragraph has the ID `menuAnswerPar`:

```
var resultElement = document.getElementById("menuAnswerPar");
```

Now that the program has the input data and somewhere to put the output, it can make decisions about the use of the rides. If the user has selected ride number 1, there are no age restrictions for the Scenic River Cruise, so this code is a single test for a ride number of 1. If the user has selected this ride, we set the style class for the result element to the `menuYes` class. This has the effect of changing the style of that element so that the text is now green. Then the inner text for the paragraph is set to `You can go on the Scenic River Cruise` so that this is displayed for the user.

```
if(rideNo==1) {
    // This is the Scenic River Cruise
    // There are no age limits for this ride
    resultElement.className="menuYes";
    resultElement.innerText = "You can go on the Scenic River Cruise";
}
```

If the user has not selected ride number 1, the program must test to see whether ride number 2 has been picked.

```
if(rideNo==2) {
    // This is the Carnival Carousel
    // riders must be 3 or over
    if(ageNo<3) {
        resultElement.className="menuNo";
        resultElement.innerText = "You are too young for the Carnival Carousel";
    }
    else {
        resultElement.className="menuYes";
        resultElement.innerText = "You can go on the Carnival Carousel";
    }
}
```

The code above shows how this works. The program works by nesting one conditional statement inside another. Note how I've used the layout of the program to make it clear which statements are controlled by which condition.

Now that you have code that works for the Carnival Carousel, you can use it as the basis for the code that handles some of the other rides. To make the program work correctly for the Jungle Adventure Water Splash, you need to check for a different ride number and confirm or reject the user based on a different age value. Remember that for this ride, a visitor must be at least six years old.

```
if(rideNo==3) {
    // This is the Jungle Adventure Water Splash
    if(ageNo<6) {
        resultElement.className="menuNo";
        resultElement.innerText =
            "You are too young for Jungle Adventure Water Splash";
    }
    else {
        resultElement.className="menuYes";
        resultElement.innerText = "You can go on Jungle Adventure Water Splash";
    }
}
```

You can implement the Downhill Mountain Run very easily by using the same pattern as for the previous two rides. But the final ride, the Regurgitator, is the most difficult. The ride is so extreme that the owner of the theme park is concerned for the health of older people who ride it and has added a maximum age restriction as well as a minimum age. The program must test for users who are older than 90 as well as those who are younger than 12. We must design a sequence of conditions to deal with this situation.

The code that deals with the Regurgitator is the most complex piece of the program that we've had to write so far. To make sense of how it needs to work, you need to know more about the way that if constructions are used in programs. Consider the following code:

```
if(rideNo==5) {
    // This is the Regurgitator
```

The condition is true when the user has selected ride number 3, and all the statements we add to the block of code controlled by this condition will run only if the selected ride is the Regurgitator. In other words, there is no need for any statement in that block to ask the question "Is the selected ride the Regurgitator?" because the statements are run only if this is the case. The decisions leading up to a statement in a program determine the context in which that statement will run. I like to add comments to clarify the context:

```
if(rideNo==5) {
    // This is the Regurgitator
    if(ageNo<12) {
        resultElement.className="menuNo";
        resultElement.innerText = "You are too young for the Regurgitator";
    }
    else {
        // get here if the age is 12 or above
        if(ageNo>90) {
            resultElement.className="menuNo";
            resultElement.innerText = "You are too old for the Regurgitator";
        }
        else {
            resultElement.className="menuYes";
            resultElement.innerText = "You can go on the Regurgitator";
        }
    }
}
```

These comments make the program slightly longer, but they also make it a lot clearer. This code is the complete construction that deals with the Regurgitator. The best way to work out what it does is to work through each statement in turn with a value for the user's age. You can find all the sample code in the folder **Ch05 Making Decisions in Programs\Ch05-04 Theme Park**.

Using the switch construction

The program code for the ride selector is a sequence of if constructions controlled by the value of rideNo. This pattern appears frequently in programs, so JavaScript contains an additional construction to make it slightly easier. This is something we've not seen before. Up until now, everything we have learned is about making something possible.

However, the `switch` construction is all about making something easier. Programs can use a switch to select different behaviors based on the value in a single control variable. Take a look at this code, which implements the Theme Park Ride Selector.

```
switch(rideNo)
{
    case 1:
    // This is the Scenic River Cruise
    // There are no age limits for this ride
    resultElement.className = "menuYes";
    resultElement.innerText = "You can go on the Scenic River Cruise";
    break;

    case 2:
    // This is the Carnival Carousel
    // .. statements for Carnival Carousel go here
    break;

    case 3:
    // This is the Jungle Adventure Water Splash
    // .. statements for Jungle Adventure Water Splash go here
    break;

    case 4:
    // This is the Downhill Mountain Run
    // .. statements for Downhill Mountain Run go here
    break;

    case 5:
    // This is the Regurgitator
    // .. statements for the Regurgitator go here
}
```

The code above shows how the `switch` would be used. The value in `rideNo` is used as the control value for the `switch`, and the program will select the `case` that matches the control value. You can put as many statements as you like in a particular case, but you must make sure that the last statement in the case is the `break` keyword, which ends the execution of the code for that case. You can find my switch-powered solution for the Theme Park ride selector in the **Ch05 Making Decisions in Programs\Ch05-05 Switch Theme Park Ride Selector** folder.

You can use the `switch` statement with strings and integer values, which can be a convenient way of selecting an option. A `switch` construction can have a `default` selector, which is obeyed if none of the cases match the control value. You can also use multiple case elements to select a particular behavior. The switch below is controlled by a variable called `commandName`. The commands `Delete`, `Del`, and `Erase` all result in the erase behavior being selected:

```
var commandName ;

switch(commandName)
{
    case "Delete":
    case "Del":
    case "Erase":
        // Erase behavior goes here
        break;

    case "Print":
    case "Pr":
    case "Output":
        // Print behavior goes here
        break;

    default:
        // Invalid command behavior goes here
        break;
}
```

Missing breaks in switches can cause mayhem

```
switch(rideNo)
{
    case 1:
    // This is the Scenic River Cruise
    // There are no age limits for this ride
    resultElement.className = "menuYes";
    resultElement.innerText = "You can go on the Scenic River Cruise";

    case 2:
    // This is the Carnival Carousel
    if (ageNo < 3) {
        resultElement.className = "menuNo";
        resultElement.innerText = "You are too young for the Carnival Carousel";
    }
    else {
        resultElement.className = "menuYes";
        resultElement.innerText = "You can go on the Carnival Carousel";
    }
    break;
}
```

The code above is part of my switch-controlled version of the Theme Park ride selector. It has a dangerous bug in it. The bug will not cause JavaScript to crash, but it will cause the program to do the wrong thing. The bug is caused by a missing break keyword between case 1 and case 2. When the user selects ride number 1, the program will perform the statements for case 1 and then go straight through and perform the statements for case 2. This means that if the user selects the Scenic River Cruise (option 1), the program will behave as if the Carnival Carousel (option 2) was selected. Bugs like this that cause a program to "mostly work" are particularly dangerous, and you should make sure to test for every input to make sure that you have no missing breaks in your switches.

Improve the ride selector

You can use the application in **Ch05 Making Decisions in Programs\Ch05-04 Theme Park** as the starting point for a really good ride selector program—but it is not perfect. It would benefit from some testing of the input values to prevent the user from entering invalid ride numbers or age values. You could even design custom graphics for each ride and then display them when the ride is selected. You could even add suitable sound effects for each ride, too.

Fortune Teller

The `Math.random` function can be used in `if` constructions to make programs that perform in a way that appears random.

```
var resultString = "You will meet a ";

if(Math.random()>0.5)
   resultString = resultString+"tall ";
else
   resultString = resultString+"short ";

if(Math.random()>0.5)
   resultString = resultString+"blonde ";
else
   resultString = resultString+"dark ";

resultString = resultString + "stranger.";
```

The `if` constructions test the value produced by a call to the `Math.random` function. This produces a value in the range 0 to 1. If the value is less than 0.5, the program selects one option; otherwise, another option is picked. This is repeated to produce a random seeming program. You can build on this sequence of such conditions to make a fun fortune teller program. You could also create some graphical images to go along with the program predictions.

What you have learned

This chapter has introduced you to the use of Boolean values in programs and showed you how to make code that can take decisions. Here are the major points we have covered:

- Boolean data has one of only two possible values—true or false. JavaScript contains the keywords `true` and `false` that can be used to represent these values in programs.

- JavaScript can regard variables of other types in terms of their "truthy" or "falsy" nature. Any numeric value other than 0 is regarded as `true`. Any string other than an empty string is regarded as `true`. The value that represents Not a Number (NaN) is regarded as `false`, but the value that represents Inifinity is regarded as `true`.

- The JavaScript function `Boolean` can be used to convert a variable of any type into the Boolean value `true` or `false`, according to the ways of "truthy" and "falsy."

- Programs can generate Boolean values by using comparison operators such as `<` (less than) between values of other types. Care should be exercised when comparing floating point values (numbers with a fractional part) for equality because they might not be held accurately.

- JavaScript provides two ways to test if things are the same. The equality comparison operator (`==`) will promote values before comparing them. Comparing the values `true` and `1` for equality would give a `true` result because the logical value true would be promoted to `1` before the comparison. The identity comparison operator (`===`) will always return `false` when comparing values of different types, so comparing `true` and `1` for identity would return `false`.

- JavaScript also provides Boolean operators such as `&&` (and) that can be used between Boolean values.

- The `if` construction is used in programs to select statements based on Boolean expression used as a condition. The `if` construction can have an `else` part, which specifies a statement to be performed if the condition is `false`. Conditional statements can be nested.

- JavaScript statements can be enclosed in curly braces ({ and })to create blocks that can be controlled by a single condition in an `if` construction.

- It is possible to store the JavaScript component of an application in a separate code file that is included in an HTML page.

- The switch construction is an easier way to create code that selects a behavior based on the content of a single control variable.

Here are some questions that you might like to ponder about making decisions in programs:

Can a program test two boolean values to see if they are equal?

Yes, it can. The equality operator (==) will work between two values that are either `true` or `false`.

Why does JavaScript provide equality and identity logical operators?

The identity operator (===) can be said to be "stricter" than the equality operator (==) because attempts to compare values of different types (for example compare a number with a Boolean value) will always return `false`. This is why some programmers (including me) use identity (===) in preference to equality (==).

Can JavaScript regard any value in terms of "truthy" and "falsy"?

Yes. Essentially, if there is something there (a value other than zero or a non-empty string) then this will be regarded as `true`. Otherwise, it will be `false`.

Must every `if` construction have an `else` part?

No. If an `else` is present, it will "bind" to the nearest `if` construction in the program. If you write a program in which only some conditions have an `else` part, you need to make sure that an `else` binds to the correct `if`.

Is there a limit to how many `if` conditions you can nest inside each other?

No. JavaScript will be quite happy to let you put 100 `if` statements in a row (although you would have a problem editing them). If you find yourself doing this, you might want to step back from the problem a bit and see if there is a better way of attacking the problem.

How long can a block be?

A block of code can be very long indeed. You could control 1,000 lines of JavaScript with a single if condition. However, very long blocks can make code hard to understand. If you want to control a large amount of code with a condition, you should put the code into a function. We will learn about functions in Chapter 8.

Does the use of Boolean values mean that a program will always do the same thing given the same data inputs?

It is very important that, given the same inputs, the computer does the same thing each time. If the computer starts to behave inconsistently, this makes it much less useful. When we want random behavior from a computer (for example, when writing a fortune teller program), we have to obtain values that are explicitly random and make decisions based on those. Nobody wants a "moody" computer that changes its mind (although, of course, it might be fun to try to program one using random numbers).

Will the computer always do the right thing when we write programs that make decisions?

It would be great if we could guarantee that the computer will always do the right thing. However, the computer is only ever as good as the program it is running. If something happens that the program was not expecting, it might respond incorrectly. For example, if a program was working out cooking time for a bowl of soup, and the user entered 10 servings rather than 1, the program would set the cooking time to be far too long (and probably burn down the kitchen in the process).

In that situation, you can blame the user (because they input the wrong data), but there should probably also be a test in the program that checks to see if the value entered is sensible. If the cooker can't hold more than 3 servings, it would seem sensible to perform a test that limits the input to 3.

This part of a program is called "input validation," and it is a very important that programs do this. When you write a program, you need to "second guess" what the user might do and create decisions that make your program behave sensibly in each situation.

6

Repeating actions in programs

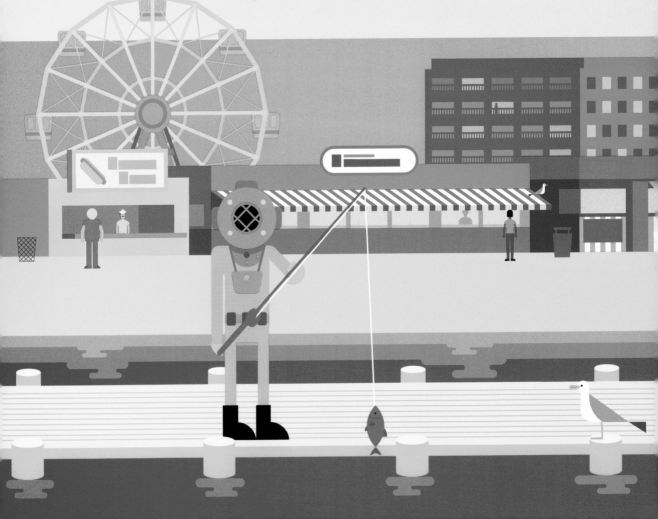

What you will learn

In the last chapter, you learned how a program can make decisions and change its behavior according to the data that it is given. In this chapter, you are going to discover how to make a program repeat a sequence of actions using the JavaScript *loop* constructions. Along the way, we're going to explore some new features of HTML and JavaScript. We are also going to discover some ways that programs can go wrong and how good design can reduce the chances of a program failing.

App development

Our starting point is the Theme Park Ride Selector program developed in Chapter 5. This program uses conditional (if) constructions to display whether a rider can go on their selected ride.

Figure 6-1 shows the solution in use. The rider entered their age as 18 and selected ride number 1, the Scenic River Cruise, which they can go on. The program works, but the owner of the theme park wants changes. She wants to remove the need for the ride selection and have the program display the ride names in red or green to indicate which ones can be ridden for a given age. She has created a new design and wants you to rewrite the application to match.

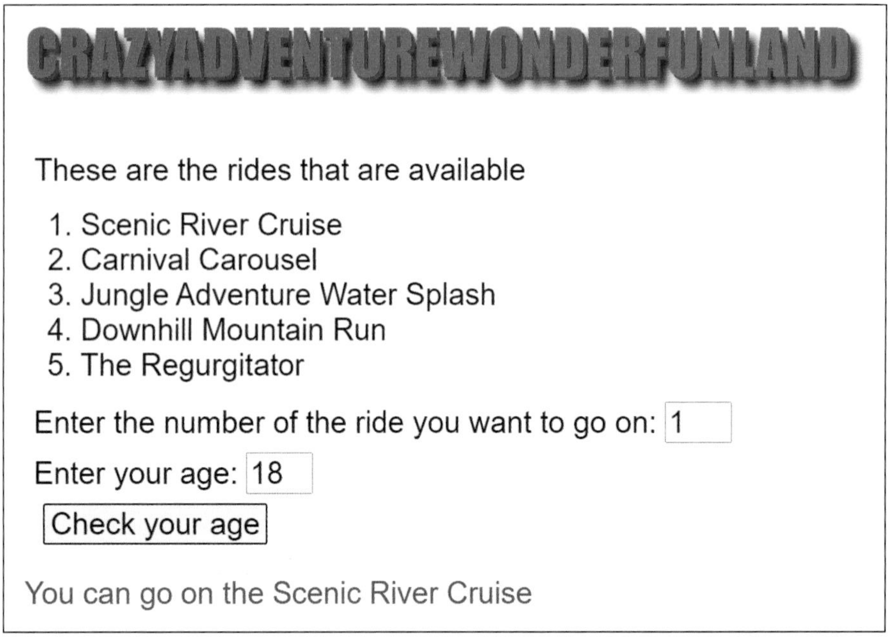

Figure 6-1   Theme Park Ride Selector

Figure 6-2 shows how the updated application will work. The rides that are available to an 8-year-old are shown in green. The first thing we need to do is remove the ride numbers from the ride display. The previous application used a numbered list because the rider had entered their chosen ride number. However, the new application doesn't need ride numbers.

```
<ul class="menuRideList" id="rideList">
    <li id="scenicRiver">Scenic River Cruise</li>
    <li id="carnivalCarousel">Carnival Carousel</li>
    <li id="jungleAdventure">Jungle Adventure Water Splash</li>
    <li id="downhillMountain">Downhill Mountain Run</li>
    <li id="regurgitator">The Regurgitator</li>
</ul>
```

CRAZYADVENTUREWONDERFUNLAND

These are the rides that are available

- Scenic River Cruise
- Carnival Carousel
- Jungle Adventure Water Splash
- Downhill Mountain Run
- The Regurgitator

Enter your age: 8

Check your rides

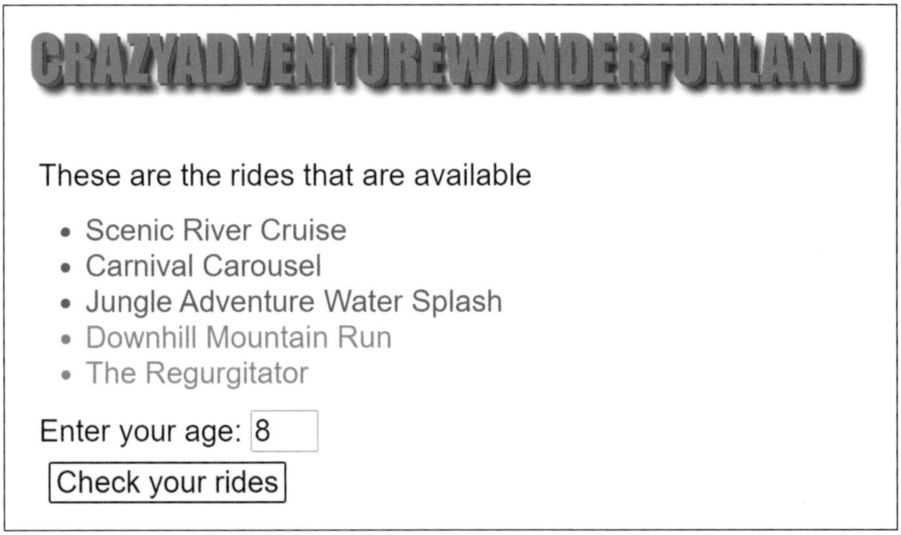

Figure 6-2   Proposed New Design

This is the HTML that we will use to display the names of the rides in the updated application. It uses an unordered list element— <ul>—that holds a collection of list elements (<li>) for rides. These are not displayed with numbers. Now we need to modify the program in the JavaScript code that controls the behavior of the application. The program will get the age of the rider and then use it to indicate whether the rider can go on each ride.

```
                                                    Get a reference to the ride name display
    var jungleAdventureElement= document.getElementById("jungleAdventure");
    if (ageNo < 6) {                                                    Test the age value
        jungleAdventureElement.className = "menuNo";          Turn red if the ride can't be used
    } else {                                              Performed if the ride can be used
        jungleAdventureElement.className = "menuYes";        Turn green if the ride can be used
    }
```

This code shows how the program displays the results for the Jungle Adventure ride. It follows a pattern that we have seen many times before:

1. Get a reference to the document element that will display the result for the rider to see.

2. Update a property of this document element to show the result.

The code above sets a variable called jungleAdventureElement to refer to the element holding the text being displayed for the Jungle Adventure ride. (This is the list item with the ID jungleAdventure.) It then uses a conditional statement controlled by the value in ageNo to update the className property of jungleAdventureElement to an appropriate style. The ageNo variable contains the age of the rider.

When the program runs, the className property of jungleAdventureElement is set to menuNo if the value in ageNo is less than 6. If the value in ageNo is greater than or equal to 6, the else part of the conditional statement is performed, and the className property of the element is set to menuYes. The className property of an element gives the style sheet class to be used to format this element. These two classes are defined in the styles.css file for this application, and they look like this:

```
.menuYes {
    color: green;
}

.menuNo{
    color: red;
}
```

This combination of JavaScript and style sheet will cause the text for the Jungle Adventure to change to red if the age of the ride user is less than 6 and to green for any other age. We must implement this construction for all the other rides in the theme park. A friend of ours is looking for some free access to the Theme Park, so we decide to subcontract the work to him. He is an experienced programmer (or at least he has read a couple more books than we have). He does the work, gets his Theme

Park tickets, and hands over the finished program. The new program seems to work well, and the owner of the theme park is pleased with it at first. However, after a while, he starts to get complaints from riders about incorrect displays for the Downhill Mountain Run ride. We need to find out what has gone wrong.

PROGRAMMER'S POINT

Always respond constructively to fault reports

I've had my share of bugs over the years. I learned quickly that customers appreciate a positive response to their fault reports. It is important to remember that when you are fixing a fault, your loyalty is to solving the problem, not finding out who caused it. I never made a fuss when a bug turned out not to be my fault, and I always accepted responsibility when it was. By being constructive in my approach to fault reports, I could turn a negative into a positive, so that my customers would end up praising my fault-fixing skills rather moaning about my buggy code.

CODE ANALYSIS

Fixing faults

Programs contain bugs because they are created by fallible humans. We get a *bug* when, for whatever reason, a program does something that it should not. A bug becomes a *fault* when it affects the user in some way. It seems that there is a bug in the ride program that is causing the faulty display. Let's open the program in the **Ch06 Repeating actions\Ch06-01 Broken Ride Selector** folder and take a look.

Question: What age values don't work?

> **Answer:** We've been told that the Downhill Mountain Run ride display is not working properly. Only riders who are 12 years or over can use this ride. Let's start with an age that is less than 12:

These are the rides that are available

- Scenic River Cruise
- Carnival Carousel
- Jungle Adventure Water Splash
- Downhill Mountain Run
- The Regurgitator

Enter your age: 8

Check your rides

This test shows that the program is working correctly for 8-year-old riders. They should not be allowed on the Downhill Mountain Run or the Regurgitator. Let's try 12—an age that should work.

These are the rides that are available

- Scenic River Cruise
- Carnival Carousel
- Jungle Adventure Water Splash
- Downhill Mountain Run
- The Regurgitator

Enter your age: 12

Check your rides

Aha! The bug is exposed. The Downhill Mountain Run is displayed in red, which is incorrect. A rider who is 12 years old should be allowed to go on this ride.

Question: What could cause the error?

Answer: Now we can see the bug we can investigate the cause. Use Visual Studio Code to open the **themepark.js** program file in the example folder and investigate the code. The part that you need to find is the part that handles the Downhill Mountain Run ride. There is a bug here. Can you see it?

```
var downhillMountainElement= document.getElementById("downhillMountain");
if (ageNo < 12) {
    downhillMountainElement.className = "menuNo";
} else {
    jungleAdventureElement.className = "menuYes";
}
```

The program is supposed to set the Downhill Mountain element to red if the age is less than 12; otherwise, it should set the element to green. The logic is the same as that used for the Jungle Adventure ride, but this code is broken. Have you spotted the error yet?

```
var downhillMountainElement= document.getElementById("downhillMountain");
if (ageNo < 12) {
    downhillMountainElement.className = "menuNo";
} else {
    jungleAdventureElement.className = "menuYes";
}
```

The error is in the `else` part. I've highlighted it above. Rather than setting the `className` on the `downhillMountainElement`, it instead works on the `jungleAdventureElement`. The program is deciding correctly that the rider can go on the Downhill Mountain Run ride, but then it is displaying the result on the wrong element.

Question: How do we fix the bug?

Answer: This bug is easy to fix. We just need to change it so that the correct element is updated when the rider can go on the ride.

```
var downhillMountainElement= document.getElementById("downhillMountain");
if (ageNo < 12) {
    downhillMountainElement.className = "menuNo";
} else {
    downhillMountainElement.className = "menuYes";
}
```

Question: How would you make a mistake like this?

Answer: It seems very strange to type a completely wrong name. But this kind of bug is quite likely. Consider how the code would be written. Our programming friend created the code for the Jungle Adventure ride and then copied it for the Downhill Mountain Run ride. He should have changed all the identifiers, but he missed one out and caused the bug.

Question: How do we prevent mistakes like this?

Answer: The primary cause of the fault was a lack of proper testing. If the program had been properly tested, the fault would have shown up. However, the practice of using block copy when writing the code made the bug possible. We should try to write our solutions in a way that reduces the number of ways they could go wrong. This includes not using block copy to repeat sections.

The importance of well-designed code

A bridge made of random pieces of wood nailed together that shudders and creaks as you cross it is probably not built to a particularly good design. You can consider software in design terms, too. The theme park ride application we have created is like a badly made bridge. It works, but the internal structure is not good. As we have seen above, using multiple copies of the same if construction makes mistakes likely when writing the code. There is also another possible source of error. The names of the rides are held in the HTML file, but the age limits for the riders are held in the JavaScript file. If we want to add more rides or adjust the age limits for the rides, we must edit both and make sure that their contents line up. Any mistakes will show up as more bugs.

Design is important

You might think that worrying about the internal design of a program is a waste of time. If the program works, why do we need to care about how it fits together? However, it is important that you always strive to make your code well designed. If you are still not convinced, consider the implications of a bug in the Theme Park Ride Selector that allowed a three-year-old to go on the Regurgitator ride. The child might be injured, and the Theme Park owner would be in a lot of trouble. An investigation might conclude that we were at fault for not using best practice when creating the code.

When we make a solution, we should try to make it easy to understand how it works. Bugs can appear when one programmer modifies the work of another and doesn't fully understand how the original code worked. The easier that program is to understand and the smaller the number of required changes, the lower the likelihood of bugs being introduced. We will look at design techniques throughout the rest of this book.

Adding data attributes to HTML elements

We can start to improve the structure of our application by putting all the data that controls it in the same place. This will remove one possible cause of errors. We are going to do this by putting the age limits inside the elements that display the ride information in a web page. This is a powerful feature of HTML and JavaScript that we will use a lot in later programs. The feature we are going to use is called a *data attribute*.

We have seen that an HTML element can contain attributes that modify it in some way. For example, to display red text, I add a `style` attribute to a paragraph to select red.

```
<p style="color:red">This is a red paragraph.</p>
```

An attribute is something that modifies an element. Each HTML element uses a particular set of attributes: A p element has a `style` attribute that sets the text style (as we saw above), and an `image` element has a `src` attribute that specifies the source file containing an image (as we saw when we displayed images). An element can also contain data attributes.

```
<ul class="menuRideList" id="rideList">
    <li data-MinAge="0" data-MaxAge="120" id="scenicRiver">Scenic River Cruise</li>
    <li data-MinAge="3" data-MaxAge="120" id="carnivalCarousel">Carnival Carousel</li>
```

```
    <li data-MinAge="6" data-MaxAge="120"
        id="jungleAdventure">Jungle Adventure Water Splash</li>
    <li data-MinAge="12" data-MaxAge="120"
        id="downhillMountain">Downhill Mountain Run</li>
    <li data-MinAge="12" data-MaxAge="90" id="regurgitator">The Regurgitator</li>
</ul>
```

The HTML above is like the earlier list of theme park rides, but each of the list items now has a `data-MinAge` and a `data-MaxAge` attribute. These give the age limits for each of the rides. This information about rides and ages is now all held in one place. The JavaScript program can use the `getAttribute` method provided by an element to read the contents of a data attribute.

```
// Get the carnival element
var carnivalCarouselElement = document.getElementById("carnivalCarousel");

// Get the min age from the carnival element data attribute ── Read the min age attribute
var carnivalMinAgeText = carnivalCarouselElement.getAttribute("data-MinAge");
var carnivalMinAgeNo = Number(carnivalMinAgeText)

// Get the max age from the carnival element data attribute
var carinvalMaxAgeText = carnivalCarouselElement.getAttribute("data-MaxAge");
var carinvalMaxAgeNo = Number(carinvalMaxAgeText);          Read the max age attribute
```

The code above shows how this would work for the Carnival Carousel ride. Note that the value of an attribute is a string of text, so the `Number` function is used to convert the text into a numeric value. Once the program has the maximum and minimum ages, it can then update the display to indicate whether the rider can go on the ride.

```
if(ageNo<carnivalMinAgeNo){
    carnivalCarouselElement.className="menuNo";
} else {
    if(ageNo>carinvalMaxAgeNo){
        carnivalCarouselElement.className="menuNo";
    } else {
        carnivalCarouselElement.className="menuYes";
    }
}
```

Data attributes

You may have some questions about data attributes. Let's see if we can answer them by looking at some code. Start with the sample application in the **Ch06 Repeating actions\Ch06-03 Data Ride Selector** example folder. Open this in your browser. Enter an age of **2** and click **Check Your Rides**. You will see the display below.

These are the rides that are available
- Scenic River Cruise
- Carnival Carousel

Enter your age: 2

Check your rides

Question: Why are the two ride names shown in different colors?

> **Answer:** The Scenic River Cruise text is green because the minimum age attribute for Scenic River Cruise list item is 0, and an age of 2 is greater than 0. The Carnival Carousel text is red because an age of 2 is less than the minimum age for that ride, which is 3.

Question: What is the upper limit for the age of the Carnival Carousel ride?

> **Answer:** We can answer this question by looking at the data attributes on the Carnival Carousel list element in the HTML document. Press F12 to open the Developer View. Now type in the following JavaScript statement:

```
> var carnivalCarouselElement = document.getElementById("carnivalCarousel");
```

This statement creates a variable called `carnivalCruiseElement` that refers to the Carnival Carousel list element in the web page. Press Enter to run it.

```
> var carnivalCarouselElement = document.getElementById("carnivalCarousel");
<- undefined
```

When you press Enter, the variable is created, and the statement that created the variable returns a value of `undefined`. Now we can use the `getAttribute` method to get data out of this element. Enter the following statement:

```
> carnivalCarouselElement.getAttribute("data-MaxAge");
<- "120"
```

This returns the value 120, which is the contents of the data-MaxAge attribute in the Carnival Carousel element. This means that the maximum age for that ride is set to 120 years. You can use the same method to read the minimum age value.

```
> carnivalCarouselElement.getAttribute("data-MinAge");
<- "3"
```

Question: What happens if we ask getAttribute to find a data attribute that doesn't exist?

Answer: Let's try it. Enter the statement below, which looks for a data attribute called data-SillyAge:

```
> carnivalCarouselElement.getAttribute("data-SillyAge");
<- null
```

This call of getAttribute returns null, which is how JavaScript indicates that a reference value doesn't refer to anything. In other words, the getAttribute method couldn't find anything, and so it returned a value that indicates that nothing was found. We could use an if construction to test for a value of null, so our program could do something sensible if a data attribute is not found.

Question: Can I set the value of a data attribute in an element?

Answer: Yes, you can. There is a method called setAttribute that is provided with the name of a data attribute and the value to be set in the attribute. It sets the data attribute to that value. Enter the following statement to set the maximum age for the ride to 99.

```
> carnivalCarouselElement.setAttribute("data-maxAge", "99");
<- undefined
```

We can test this by reading back the value of the maximum age:

```
> carnivalCarouselElement.getAttribute("data-MaxAge");
<- "99"
```

Question: Can a program create new data attributes on an element?

Answer: Yes. This can be used to "bind" data to elements. The setAttribute method will create a new attribute if the one being set does not exist. Try the following statements, which create a test data attribute called `data-test` on the Carnival Carousal element:

```
> carnivalCarouselElement.setAttribute("data-test", "test string");
<- null
> carnivalCarouselElement.getAttribute("data-test");
<- "test string"
```

Question: Does the name of a data attribute have to start with the characters "data-"?

Answer: JavaScript does not enforce this rule, but it is a very sensible convention so that someone reading the code does not mistake a data attribute for a "normal" attribute of that element.

Question: Can my program add data attributes to any HTML element?

Answer: Yes, it can. This is a good way to store data values inside your web page.

Using an unordered list as a container

The code in the **Ch06 Repeating actions\Ch06-03 Data Ride Selector** example folder only handles two rides. The reason for this is that I just didn't feel like copying the Carnival Carousel code for the other rides. It seemed like too much hard work, and I was concerned I might make a mistake. It turns out that there is a much easier way of handling all the other rides that uses a loop to work through the list of rides.

```
<ul class="menuRideList" id="rideList">
    <li data-MinAge="0" data-MaxAge="120">Scenic River Cruise</li>
    <li data-MinAge="3" data-MaxAge="120">Carnival Carousel</li>
    <li data-MinAge="6" data-MaxAge="120">Jungle Adventure Water Splash</li>
    <li data-MinAge="12" data-MaxAge="120">Downhill Mountain Run</li>
    <li data-MinAge="12" data-MaxAge="70">The Regurgitator</li>
</ul>
```

The HTML above shows the list of rides in the Theme Park as they are displayed. Each of the rides is described by a list item (`<li>`) element and all the lists are enclosed inside an unnumbered list (`<ul>`) element. The `<ul>` element is a *container* element that holds other elements. In this case, the list contains five list items. These list items are called the *children* of their container elements. HTML elements provide methods that can be used to access the children of an element. Let's investigate.

Investigate list elements

Start by opening the application in the **Ch06 Repeating actions\Ch06-04 Theme Park Ride For Loop** folder in the example code. This is a fully working ride selector that uses a `for` loop. We'll discover how the `for` loop works later in this section. For now, we are going to take a look at the list container. Open the Developer View by pressing the function key F12. Now we can start typing commands into the JavaScript command prompt. The first thing we are going to do is get a reference to the list that holds the ride names:

```
> var rideListElement= document.getElementById("rideList");
<- undefined
```

When you press Enter, the JavaScript console returns the result as `undefined` because, as we know, the process of creating a variable does not return a value. However, the variable `rideListElement` now refers to the list of rides. To prove this, just type the name `rideListElement`, and the Developer View will show you the HTML in the element it refers to:

```
> rideListElement
<    ▶<ul class="menuRideList" id="rideList">…</ul>
```

When you press Enter this time, the JavaScript console displays the element. Click the little right-pointing arrow to expand the display.

```
> rideListElement
<    ▼<ul class="menuRideList" id="rideList">
        <li data-minage="0" data-maxage="120" class="menuYes">Scenic River Cruise</li>
        <li data-minage="3" data-maxage="120" class="menuYes">Carnival Carousel</li>
        <li data-minage="6" data-maxage="120" class="menuYes">Jungle Adventure Water Splash</li>
        <li data-minage="12" data-maxage="120" class="menuYes">Downhill Mountain Run</li>
        <li data-minage="12" data-maxage="70" class="menuYes">The Regurgitator</li>
     </ul>
```

The list has five children, which are the list items. These children are held in a property of the list, which is called `children`. We can use an *index* to specify which of the children we want to look at. The index is expressed as a number enclosed in square brackets (`[]`): Let's have a look at the element at the start of the list. Type in the statement below.

```
> rideListElement.children[0]
```

Note that this is the element with an index of 0. When counting items in a container, JavaScript starts counting at zero, not one. When you press Enter, the list item for the Scenic River Cruise is displayed.

```
<- <li data-MinAge="0" data-MaxAge="120">Scenic River Cruise</li>
```

You can use this technique to obtain any of the items in the list. The statement below will view the list item for the Regurgitator. I tried it with a different number:

```
> rideListElement.children[4]
<- <li data-MinAge="12" data-MaxAge="70">The Regurgitator</li>
```

Remember that because JavaScript counts elements from 0, the final element in a list containing four elements will have an index of 4. You might be wondering what will happen if you try to access an element that isn't there. Try this:

```
> rideListElement.children[5]
```

There is not a fifth element in the list (although the film *The Fifth Element* is a classic). The result of trying to find a non-existent element is the undefined value:

```
<- undefined
```

We can find out how many children there are by using the length property of children. Try this statement to see how it works:

```
> rideListElement.children.length
```

There are five children, and so the length property will be 5:

```
<- 5
```

Leave your browser open for now, as we will be using it to investigate loops a little later.

The JavaScript for loop

Now that we know how to get hold of the list items in the ride list, the next thing we need to be able to do is use the items in our application. What we need is language construction that will loop round a block of code and count each time around the loop. It turns out that JavaScript has just the thing. It is called the for loop. **Figure 6-3** shows the elements of a JavaScript for loop.

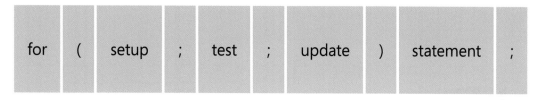

Figure 6-3 For loop

1. **setup** The setup (sometimes called initialization) element is performed once when the for loop is started.

2. **test** The test element is performed before every pass through the code in the loop. If the test has a JavaScript "truthy" value of true, the loop will continue. If the test has a "truthy" value of false, the loop will end, and the program will continue at the statement after the for loop.

3. **update** The update element is performed after each execution of the loop.

4. **statement** The statement is a JavaScript statement that is to be repeated by the for loop. This can be a block of statements enclosed in curly braces if you want the loop to perform more than one statement.

A for loop is usually used with a *control variable*. This variable counts the number of times the loop has been performed. The setup element puts a starting value in the control variable. The test element tests the value of the control variable and will stop the loop when the control variable reaches a particular value. The update element increases the value of the control variable.

Figure 6-4 shows a complete for loop. This causes the loop statement to be performed 10 times. Let's take a proper look at it.

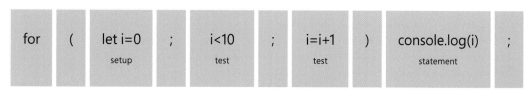

Figure 6-4 For loop counter

The for loop

We can use the Developer View in the browser to investigate what a for loop does. Open the application in the **Ch06 Repeating actions\Ch06-04 Theme Park Ride For Loop** folder (if you haven't already) and then open the Developer View by pressing F12.

Question: What does the for loop we have created actually do?

Answer: We can start by typing in the JavaScript that you have just seen in Figure 6-4:

```
> for(let i=0;i<10;i=i+1)console.log(i);
```

You know (because I've told you) that this should repeat the statement console.log(i) 10 times—whatever that does. Press Enter to see what happens.

```
> for(let i=0;i<10;i=i+1)console.log(i);
0
1
2
3
4
5
6
7
8
9
<- undefined
```

The console.log statement is a useful tool for debugging a program. It logs values on the Developer View console. In this case, it is logging the value of i each time it is called. The value of i starts at 0. Each time around the loop, the value in i is increased by 1. The loop also tests the value in i using the condition i<10. When i reaches the value 10, this condition is no longer true (the value 10 is not less than 10) and so the loop stops.

Question: Why does the for loop display undefined at the end.

Answer: The for loop does not display this message. This message is displayed because the console always displays the value of a statement. A for loop construction does not generate a result in the same way that creating a variable using var does not generate a result. In both cases, the value undefined is displayed by the console.

Question: Can I use a `for` loop to control lots of statements?

Yes. A `for` loop can control a block of statements enclosed in curly braces (`{}`) in the same way as an `if` construction.

Question: What does the word `let` mean in front of the declaration of `i`?

Answer: Up until now, we have created our variables using the JavaScript keyword `var`. However, we can also create a variable by using the keyword `let`. Variables created using `var` can be used anywhere in the program after they have been declared. Variables created using `let` are only useable in the block where they were declared. The value in `i` is only used inside the statement controlled by the `for` loop, so it should only exist inside that `for` loop. To prove that this has happened, enter the following statement to try and look at the value in `i`:

```
> i;
```

This variable no longer exists because it was deleted when the `for` loop was completed.

```
<-Uncaught ReferenceError: i is not defined at <anonymous>:1:1
```

Question: Why is it a good idea for variables to disappear like this?

Answer: This is another piece of good design. I tend to use a variable called `i` for counting. Other programmers working on this code might decide to use a variable called `i` for something else. I don't want these two variables to clash, so I make sure that my version of the variable only exists when I use it.

Question: What happens if JavaScript is given a loop that will never run?

```
> for(let i=0;i>10;i=i+1)console.log(i);
```

Answer: This loop is silly. The loop sets `i` to `0` and then continues while the value of `i` is greater than `10`. Because the value of `i` is not greater than `10`, the loop will never be performed. If you run this code, you will discover that it does not produce any output.

```
> undefined
```

Question: What happens if I put in a loop that will never end? (Please don't actually run this statement before reading the answer.)

```
> for(let i=0;i<10;i=i-1)console.log(i);
```

Answer: This loop is also silly. Each time around the loop, the value of i is reduced by 1 rather than increased by 1. This means that the value of i will never reach 10, so the loop will run forever. If you run this statement (and I don't advise it), you will notice that the console will be filled with ever-decreasing numbers, the fan on your computer will come on, and your browser will become strangely unresponsive as it tries to run this loop as quickly as possible. The only way to stop this that always works is to close the browser tab holding the program. Sometimes when you visit a web page, you find that your browser gets "stuck." Now you know one way that it can happen.

Now that we know about for loops, we can write the code for the Theme Park Ride Selector.

```javascript
function doCheckAge() {

    // get the age that was input
    var ageElement = document.getElementById("ageText");
    var ageText = ageElement.value;
    var ageNo = Number(ageText);

    // get the list of rides
    var rideListElement= document.getElementById("rideList");

    // get the number of child list items
    var noOfRides = rideListElement.children.length;

    // make a loop to count round the rides
    for(i=0; i < noOfRides; i=i+1){                    This is the for loop that updates the list
        // get the ride element out of the list
        let rideElement = rideListElement.children[i];

        // get the minimum age
        let minAgeText = rideElement.getAttribute("data-MinAge");
        let minAgeNo = Number(minAgeText)

        // get the maximum age
        let maxAgeText = rideElement.getAttribute("data-MaxAge");
        let maxAgeNo = Number(maxAgeText);

        // test the age and update the component
        if(ageNo<minAgeNo){
```

```
                rideElement.className="menuNo";
        } else {
            if(ageNo>maxAgeNo){
                rideElement.className="menuNo";
            } else {
                rideElement.className="menuYes";
            }
        }
    }
}
```

I love this code. I really like how it works. You should spend some time looking through it to make sure that you understand how it fits together. To appreciate how well designed it is, consider what changes you would have to make to the program if the theme park added another ride. The wonderful answer is that you would not have to change this code at all. You would just have to add another item to the list in the HTML file. You also don't have to change the program code if the age rating on one of the rides is changed. You just change the data in the HTML file and the program keeps going. The example solution in the folder **\Ch06 Repeating actions\Ch06-05 Lots of Theme Park Rides** has lots of additional rides, but the JavaScript program code is the same.

PROGRAMMER'S POINT

Great programmers are "constructively lazy"

You can spot a great programmer by the way that they use their skills to avoid hard work. I call this "constructive laziness." If I find myself having to write lots of code or worrying about synchronizing different parts of a solution, I will try to find a way of using a loop and bringing things together into one place.

Work through collections using for-of

We've seen how we can use a for loop to count through a range of values. We might find a use for this a bit later in the chapter, but we can also use a new form of the for loop to directly work through the items in a container. The for - of loop was not added to make something possible; we already know how to solve the problem. It was added to make something easier.

```javascript
for (let rideElement of rideListElement.children) {
    // get the minimum age
    let minAgeText = rideElement.getAttribute("data-MinAge");
    let minAgeNo = Number(minAgeText)

    // get the maximum age
    let maxAgeText = rideElement.getAttribute("data-MaxAge");
    let maxAgeNo = Number(maxAgeText);

    // test the age and update the component
    if (ageNo < minAgeNo) {
        rideElement.className = "menuNo";
    } else {
        if (ageNo > maxAgeNo) {
            rideElement.className = "menuNo";
        } else {
            rideElement.className = "menuYes";
        }
    }
}
```

The loop above shows how it would be used. The loop will be performed for each of the children of the ride list. Each time round the loop the value of `rideElement` is set to the next child. There is no need to create a control variable and the code is much simpler. You can see a `for-of` loop in action in the example in **Ch06 Repeating actions\Ch06-06 For of loop**.

Building web pages from code

The Theme Park Ride Selector makes good use of the way that a JavaScript program can interact with the elements in a web page. Now let's take this technique even further and find out how a JavaScript program can create new elements on the page when it runs. Then we can make web pages that construct themselves when they are loaded. For example, perhaps we might be asked to create a program to help people learn their multiplication tables. Users enter a number and get a display of the multiplication table for that number.

Figure 6-5 shows how the program is used. The user enters the number of the multiplication table that they want, and the program displays it. This program looks a lot like the Theme Park Ride Selector that we have already created.

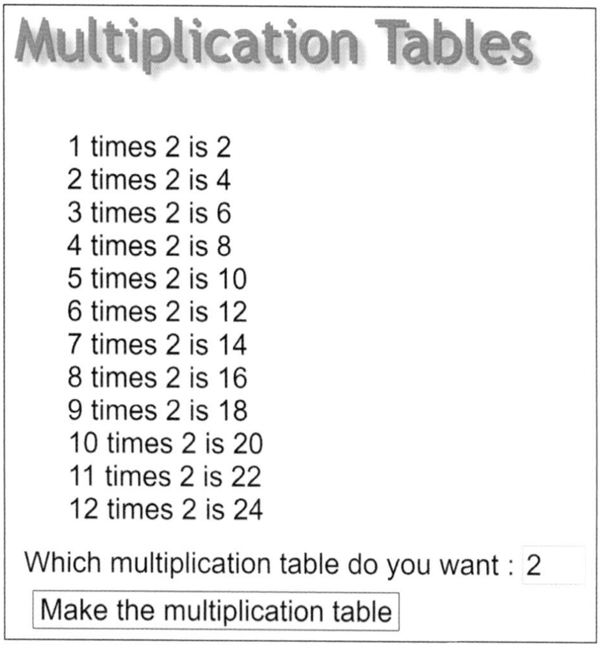

Multiplication Tables

1 times 2 is 2
2 times 2 is 4
3 times 2 is 6
4 times 2 is 8
5 times 2 is 10
6 times 2 is 12
7 times 2 is 14
8 times 2 is 16
9 times 2 is 18
10 times 2 is 20
11 times 2 is 22
12 times 2 is 24

Which multiplication table do you want : 2

Make the multiplication table

Figure 6-5 Multiplication tables

We could use a 12-element list to hold the results and then update the text in the list items with the multiplication table that the user has requested in the same way that we update the color of each ride entry. However, that would mean we would have to type in a 12-element list, and that sounds like a bit too much work to me. So let's start with an empty HTML document and then write some JavaScript to fill in the multiplication table results by creating list items.

```
<!DOCTYPE html>
<html lang="en">

<head>
    <title>Ch06-07 Multiplication Tables HTML generator</title>
    <link rel="stylesheet" href="styles.css">
    <script src="multiplicationtables.js"></script>
</head>
```

```
<body>
    <p class="menuHeading">Multiplication Tables</p>
    <!- Multiplication table list will be built by code-->
    <ul class="menuMultiplicationTableList" id="multiplicationTableList">
    </ul>                              Empty list to hold the multiplication table results
    <p class="menuText">Which multiplication table do you want :
        <input class="menuInput" type="number" id="timesTableText" value="2"
        min="2" max="12"> </p>              Input for the required multiplication table

    <button class="menuButton" onclick="doMultiplicationTables()">Make the
    multiplication table</button>      Button that is pressed to produce the multiplication table
</body>

</html>
```

This is the HTML page for the multiplication table application. Note that in the middle there is an empty list with the ID multiplicationTableList. This is going to hold the multiplication table that the program will generate. The user will press the Make the multiplication table button, which will call the JavaScript function doMultiplicationTable to create the table. Let's have a look at that.

```
function doMultiplicationTables() {

    // get the multiplication table number from the web page
    var tableTextElement = document.getElementById("tableNumberText");
    var tableNumberText  = tableTextElement.value;
    var tableNumber = Number(tableNumberText );

    // get the multiplication table list from the web page
    var multiplicationTableListElement =
        document.getElementById("multiplicationTableList");

    // count through the  table producing results
    for (let i=1; i<=12;i=i+1) {
        // calculate the result
        let resultNunber = tableNumber * i;

        // create a result strung
        let resultString = i + " times " + tableNumber + " is " + resultNunber;

        // make  new list item
        let listItem = document.createElement("li");
```

```
        // set the text of the new list item to the result string
        listItem.innerText=resultString;
        // add it to the multiplication table list
        multiplicationTableListElement.appendChild(listItem);
    }
}
```

The most interesting part of this function is the last three statements, which create a new element and add it to the list. Let's take a look at how they work.

CODE ANALYSIS

Building HTML from JavaScript

Take as your starting point the example application in the **Ch06 Repeating actions\Ch06-07 Times Tables HTML generator** folder. Open this application and then press F12 to open the Developer View.

Question: Does the program work?

Answer: You can test the program by entering a multiplication table value into the web page and pressing the **Make the multiplication table** button. You will see a display like the one shown previously in Figure 6-5.

Question: How do we create new web page elements?

Answer: The method createElement is provided by the document object. The method will make a new HTML element. Let's make another list item to add to the multiplication table list. We give createElement a string that specifies the type of element we want. In this case, we want a list item, so we use the string "li." Type in the following and press Enter:

```
> var newElement=document.createElement("li");
```

Now that we have our new element, we can set the innerText that it contains. Type in the following and press Enter:

```
> newElement.innerText="Hello world";
```

We now have an HTML element that is a list item containing the text **Hello world**.

Question: How do we add a web page element to an element on the page?

Answer: We can add a new child to any HTML element using the appendChild method to add a new child to the element. First, we need to find the element we want to add to. Type the following statement and press Enter:

```
> var multiplicationTableListElement = document.
getElementById("multiplicationTableList");
```

We now have a variable called multiplicationTableListElement that refers to the list holding the multiplication table. Let's add our new element to this. Type in the following statement and press Enter.

```
> multiplicationTableListElement.appendChild(newElement);
```

If you look back at the web page you will discover a new line has appeared underneath the last line of the times table. This line was added by us just now:

12 times 2 is 24
Hello world

Which multiplication table do you want : 2

Make the multiplication table

This new element is not part of the HTML file; it is part of the document object that is being maintained by the browser.

Question: Can we just keep adding lines to the list?

Answer: Yes, you can. In fact, there is a bug in our solution, which means that it just keeps adding multiplication tables to the list. If you press the **Make the multiplication table** button again, you will discover that another table will be added to the page:

11 times 2 is 22
12 times 2 is 24
Hello world
1 times 2 is 2
2 times 2 is 4

Question: Can a program delete items from an element?

Answer: Yes, it can. We can delete the element at the start of the list by entering the following:

```
> multiplicationTableListElement .removeChild(timesTableListElement.children[0])
```

The removeChild method is given a reference to an element that is then removed from the list. In the statement above, the reference that is supplied is a reference to the element at the start of the list. If you look at the web page display, you will find that the first result has been removed.

Deleting elements from a document

In the preceding Code Analysis, we discovered a bug in the multiplication table application. When you select a new multiplication table, the results are added to the end of the existing one. Fortunately, we also discovered a method we can use to remove children from an element. We can use this method to "clean up" the list prior to adding new elements. To do this, we can use another loop construction called a while loop. A while loop repeats a statement as long as a condition is true.

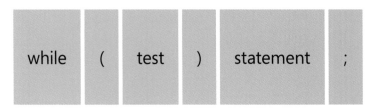

Figure 6-6   While loop

Figure 6-6 above shows the structure of a while loop. The while loop will perform the test and then, if the test is "truthy," it will perform the statement. It will then loop back and repeat this process until the test is "falsey." We can use this to create some JavaScript that will delete child elements until there are none left:

```
while(multiplicationTableListElement.children.length > 0)
    multiplicationTableListElement.
    removeChild(multiplicationTableListElement.children[0]);
```

If this looks a little hard to understand, try converting it into English: "While the number of children is greater than 0, delete a child." There is a working example of the Times Table program in the **Ch06 Repeating actions\Ch06-08 Multiplication Tables HTML generator cleanup** folder in the sample programs.

 MAKE SOMETHING HAPPEN

More multiplication table fun

Here are some ideas that you might like to investigate.

20s multiplication table

Some people like to show off by knowing their 20s multiplication table. Can you make a change to the program above to make a version that displays the 20s multiplication table? You should be able to do this by changing just one number in the program. If you can't work out how to do this, you can find my version in the **Ch06 Repeating actions\Ch06-09 Twenty times table** folder.

Multiplication Table Tester

> **Multiplication Table Tester**
>
> 1 times 2 is 2
> 2 times 2 is 4
> 3 times 2 is 5
> 4 times 2 is 8
> 5 times 2 is 11
> 6 times 2 is 12
> 7 times 2 is 14
> 8 times 2 is 16
> 9 times 2 is 18
> 10 times 2 is 19
> 11 times 2 is 22
> 12 times 2 is 24
>
> Which multiplication table do you want : 2
>
> Make the multiplication table   Check the multiplication table

The Multiplication Table Tester produces a multiplication table with some wrong numbers and then challenges the user to find them all. Then the user can press the **Check The Multiplication Table** button to check which ones are correct. The JavaScript random number generator can be used to decide if a given value is to be displayed incorrectly. The program could work by using a data attribute in each list item that holds the value being displayed by that item. The marking process would be rather like the Theme Park Ride program. It would change the color of the list item depending on whether the displayed value is correct. You can find my version in the **Ch06 Repeating actions\Ch06-10 Multiplication Table Tester** folder.

What you have learned

This chapter has shown you how to use loops in JavaScript programs. You've also picked up some useful programming design tips and discovered how JavaScript code can change the structure of the document being displayed by the browser.

1. You only really learn how a program should work by making something and trying to use it. If you make a solution for someone, you must be prepared to change the way it works when they think of a better way of using it.

2. Bugs are a natural consequence of software development. When a fault is reported, your loyalty should be to the process of fixing it, not assigning blame or responsibility.

3. Some software writing processes, such as repeating behaviors by copying blocks of code, make bugs more likely.

4. HTML elements can be given data attributes. This allows a program to bind data values directly to items in the document and for data to be embedded in the web page text.

5. HTML elements can act as containers for other elements. Elements contained in an element are the child elements of the parent. Individual child elements can be accessed using an index value. The index values start at 0.

6. A JavaScript `for` loop construction is used to repeatedly perform a statement. The `for` loop has `setup`, `test`, and `update` behaviors. The `setup` behavior is performed at the start of the loop. The `test` is performed after each loop and also before the first loop. If the `test` evaluates to `false`, the loop stops. The `update` behavior is performed after each loop.

7. A JavaScript `for` loop construction can be used to manage a control variable counter that can count between two values, allowing a program to work through the children of a container element.

8. JavaScript provides a `for-of` construction to work through the elements in a container.

9. There are JavaScript functions that can be used to create new page elements (`document.createElement`) and add them as children to existing elements (`appendChild`). These elements are then rendered by the browser. This makes it possible for JavaScript code to create the contents of a web page programmatically.

10. There is a JavaScript function (`removeChild`) that can be used to remove child elements from a container element.

11. The `while` loop construction allows a program to repeat a block of statements while a controlling logical expression evaluates to `true`.

Here are some questions that you might like to ponder about the content of this chapter:

Does every program contain bugs?

It is almost impossible to prove that a given program does not contain any bugs. Testing only ever proves that bugs exist, not that they don't. The good news is that not all bugs affect the behavior of the program when in normal use.

Why are lists indexed starting at zero?

This is just the way that JavaScript works. Some languages index their collections starting at 1, but JavaScript starts at 0. You can think of the index as the "distance" down the storage that you need to go to get to the item.

Can any HTML element be a container for other elements?

Yes. The HTML element in a document contains the HEAD and BODY elements. It is also possible for the child of an element to have children of its own, allowing for a hierarchy to be created.

Does adding an attribute to an HTML element change the contents of the web page file?

No. You can think of the HTML file as defining the starting point of the document object that is displayed by the browser. Changes to this object will affect the appearance of the page but they will not change the contents of the HTML file.

What is the difference between `let` **and** `var`**?**

Both keywords are used to create variables. Variables created with `var` exist from that point in the program. Variables created with `let` are destroyed when program execution leaves the block where they were declared. Declaring variables using `let` is a good idea, as it reduces the chances of variables being reused by mistake.

Could I create an entire web page using JavaScript code?

Yes. Lots of web pages you visit work this way. Rather than having HTML text stored on the server, a site contains a small HTML file and a JavaScript program that loads data from the web and then uses it to build the website. We will be doing more of this in future chapters.

7
Creating functions

What you will learn

Functions are an essential part of program design. You can use functions to break up a large solution into individual components and to create libraries of behaviors that can be used by your programs. We have used some built-in functions (for example, `alert`) and created event handler functions (for example, `doCheckAge`). In this chapter, you'll learn how to create and use functions of your own. You'll see how to give functions data to work on and how a program can receive results that a function returns. Along the way, you will pick up some tips about error handling.

What makes a function?

A function is a chunk of JavaScript that has been given an identifier. A function should be *defined* before it is used. When JavaScript encounters a function definition, it takes the statements that provide the behavior of the function and stores them, so they are ready for use by the program. A program can *call* the function and the statements in the function will be performed. We've created and called functions already, but now is the time to take a detailed look at how they work. Let's start with a look at a simple function that just says "hello."

```html
<!DOCTYPE html>
<html lang="en">

<head>
<title>Ch07-01 Greeter Function</title>
</head>

<body>
    <h1>Greeter</h1>
    <p>
    <p id="outputParagraph"></p>
    </p>

    <script>
      function greeter() {
        var outputElement = document.getElementById("outputParagraph");
        outputElement.textContent = "Hello";
      }
    </script>
</body>
</html>
```

style sheet function

Find the display element

Set the display text to "Hello"

This web page contains a function called greeter. The function finds an element on the screen with the ID outputParagraph and displays Hello in that element. Once the function has been defined, a program can call it. A call of a function runs the statements given when the function was defined. The greeter function doesn't do much, but you can create functions that contain many statements. Remember that your program must define the function before it can be called.

Investigating functions

Start by opening the application in the **Ch07 Functions\Ch07-01 Greeter Function** example code folder. This application contains an HTML page with the output paragraph and a script section containing the greeter function. Open the Developer View by pressing F12.

Question: How do I call a function in my program?

> **Answer:** Up until now, our programs have used functions that have been provided for us by JavaScript (for example, the alert function). But the greeter function is one that we have written. However, we can call it in the same way, simply by entering the name of the function, followed by a pair of braces.

```
> greeter();
```

When you press Enter, the greeter function is called. This function does not return a result (we will look at this later) and so the console displays undefined.

```
<- undefined
```

However, you will notice that the word "Hello" has now appeared in the browser display. This was displayed by the greeter function when it ran.

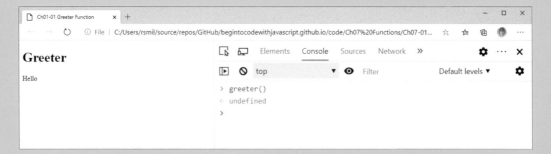

Question: Can we define functions in the console?

> **Answer:** Yes, we can define our own functions in the console. Type the statement below, which creates a function called alerter.

```
> function alerter() { alert("hello"); };
```

Press Enter when you've typed the above statement, **exactly** as it is shown. Make sure to use the right kinds of brackets for each part.

```
<- undefined
```

The application now contains a new function called `alerter`. The process of defining a function does not return a value, so the console shows the result as `undefined`.

The JavaScript that you have just typed contains a statement that calls the `alert` function, but this has not run because this statement is in the body of the `alerter` function. Now enter a statement that calls the newly created function:

```
> alerter();
```

When you press Enter, the statement will call `alerter`, which will display an alert:

```
<- undefined
```

Question: Can one function call another function?

    Answer: Yes, it can. Consider the following functions:

```
function m2(){
    console.log("the");
}

function m3(){
    console.log("sat on");
    m2();
}
```

```
function m1(){
    m2();
    console.log("cat");
    m3();
    console.log("mat");
}
```

If m1 is called what will be logged in the console? The best way to figure this out is to work through the functions one statement at a time, just like the computer does when it runs the program. Remember that when a function is complete, the program's execution continues at the statement following the function call. These functions are in the JavaScript for the Greeter page. You can find out what happens by calling function m1:

```
> m1();
```

When you press enter the m1 function is called. This then calls m2 and so on. The output is what you would expect:

```
the
cat
sat on
the
mat
```

Question: What happens if a function calls itself? For example, what if the m1 function called m1?

Answer: Making a function call itself is a bit like arranging two mirrors so that they face each other. In the mirrors, you see reflections going off into infinity. Does JavaScript go off into infinity when a function call itself? Let's create a function and find out. Enter the following function definition:

```
> function mirror() { mirror(); };
```

The mirror function just contains one statement that calls the mirror function. What happens when we create the function. Press Enter to find out.

```
<- undefined
```

Answer (*cont.*)

Nothing happens. Creating a function is not the same as running it. However, we now have a function called `mirror` that calls itself. Let's call `mirror` and see what happens:

```
> mirror();
```

When you press Enter, JavaScript will find the `mirror` function and start obeying the statements in it. The first statement in `mirror` is a call of the `mirror` function, which JavaScript will start to execute. The program is stuck in a loop, but it does not get stuck forever. After a while, the console stops with an error:

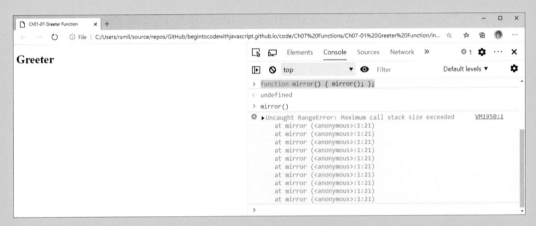

Each time a function is called, JavaScript stores the return address (the place it must go back to) in a special piece of memory called the "stack." The idea is that when a running program reaches the end of a function, it grabs the most recently stored return address from the top of the stack and returns to where that address points. This means that as functions are being called and returned, the stack grows and shrinks.

However, when a function calls itself, JavaScript repeatedly adds return addresses to the stack. Each time the function calls itself, another return address is added to the stack, at the top. The stack is finite in size, and when this size is exceeded, JavaScript stops the program.

Programmers have a name for a function that works by calling itself: *recursion*. Recursion is occasionally useful in programs, particularly when the program is searching for values in large data structures. However, I've been programming for many years and have used recursion only a handful of times. I advise you to regard recursion as strong magic that you don't need to use now (or hardly ever). Loops are usually your best bet for repeating blocks of code.

Figure 7-1 shows the form of a JavaScript function definition. We can work through each of these items in turn. The keyword `function` tells JavaScript that a function is being defined. JavaScript will allocate space for the function and get ready to start storing function statements. The word `function` is followed by the identifier of the function. We must create an identifier for each function we define. Because a function is associated with an action, it's a very good idea to make the name reflect this. I give functions names in the form `verbNoun`. The verb specifies the action the function will perform, and the noun specifies the item it will work on. An example would be `doMultiplicationTables`.

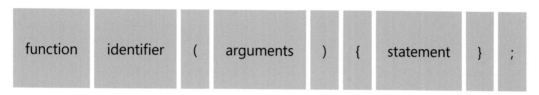

| function | identifier | (| arguments |) | { | statement | } | ; |

Figure 7-1 Function definition

After the function identifier, we have the arguments that are fed into the function. The arguments are separated by commas and enclosed within parentheses. Arguments provide a function with something to work on. So far, the functions we've created haven't had any arguments, so there has been nothing between the two parentheses. Finally, the definition contains a block of JavaScript statements that form the body of the function. These are the statements that will be obeyed when the function is called.

Give information to functions

The `greeter` function shows how functions can be used, but it isn't really that useful because it does the same thing each time it's called. To make a function truly useful, we need to give the function some data to work on. You've already seen many functions that are used in this way. The `alert` function accepts a string to display in the alert box. The `Number` function accepts an input to be turned into a numeric value. We could make a version of the `greeter` function that accepts a message to be displayed:

```
function greeter(message) {
  var outputElement = document.getElementById("outputParagraph");
  outputElement.textContent = message;
}
```

Investigating arguments

The new version of greeter is in the example application **Ch07 Functions\Ch07-02 Greeter Arguments**. Open this application and then open the Developer View by pressing F12.

Question: How do I give a function call an argument?

> **Answer:** We can give a function an argument by putting something between the braces in the call of the function:

```
> greeter("Hello from Rob");
```

> When you press Enter, the greeter function is called and the string Hello from Rob is passed as an argument to the function call.

```
<- undefined
```

> The greeter function does not return a value, so the console displays undefined. However, you will notice that the phrase Hello from Rob has now appeared on the browser display. This was displayed by the greeter function when it ran.

Question: What happens if I omit the argument from the function call?

> **Answer:** This is bad programming practice. We've told JavaScript that the greeter function accepts an argument, and then we failed to supply an argument when we called it. Let's try it. Enter a call of greeter with no arguments.

```
> greeter();
```

You might think that this would cause an error. The `greeter` function is expecting to receive something that is missing from the call. If you've used other programming languages, for example C++ or C#, you will be used to getting errors if you make this mistake. However, it turns out that JavaScript is much more relaxed about this. There is no error, but there's no greeting either:

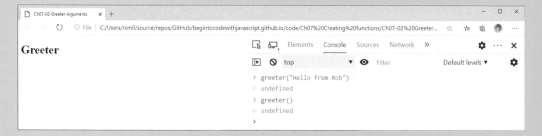

This is what has happened:

1. The JavaScript system notices that there is an argument missing from the call.

2. It supplies the function with the value `undefined` for the missing argument.

3. The function sets the `textContent` property of the output paragraph to `undefined`. This is not displayed by the browser, so the text on the screen disappears.

If we are concerned about calls with missing arguments, we can make a version of the `greeter` function that checks to see if it has been given an argument:

```
function errorGreeter(message) {
  if(message == undefined) {
    alert("No argument to greeter");
  }
  else
  {
    let outputElement = document.getElementById("outputParagraph");
    outputElement.textContent = message;
  }
}
```

The function above is called `errorGreeter`. It checks the message it has been supplied with and if the message is undefined it displays a warning alert. Otherwise, it displays the message. This function is in the scripts of the example program. Try calling `errorGreeter` in the browser console with a missing argument:

```
> errorGreeter();
```

When you press Enter, you will see an alert because the function was not supplied with an argument.

If you call errorGreeter with an argument, you will see that it displays the message as it should.

Question: What happens if I call a function with too many arguments?

Answer: We could try this:

```
> greeter("Hello world", 1,2,3, "something else");
```

If you call greeter as above, JavaScript will not produce any errors, but the greeter function will ignore the extra arguments.

Arguments and parameters

From the title of this section, you might expect that we will have a difference of opinion, but in JavaScript, the word *argument* has a particular meaning. In JavaScript, "argument" means "that thing you give to the call of a function."

```
greeter("Hello world");
```

In the above statement, the argument is the string Hello world. So when you hear the word "argument," you should think of the code that is making a call of the function. In JavaScript, the word *parameter* means "the name within the function that represents the argument." The parameters in a function are specified in the function definition.

```
function greeter(message)
```

This is the definition of a `greeter` function that has a single parameter. The parameter has the identifier `message`. When the function is called, the value of the `message` parameter is set to whatever has been given as an argument to the function call. Statements within the function can use the parameter in the same way as they could use a variable with that name.

 MAKE SOMETHING HAPPEN

Parameters as values

When a function is called, the value of the argument is passed into the function parameter. What exactly does this mean? The following program contains a function (with the interesting name `whatWouldIDo`) that accepts a single parameter. The function doesn't do much; it just sets the value of the parameter to `99`.

```
function whatWouldIDo(inputValue) {
    inputValue = 99;
}
```

This function is part of the application in the **Ch07 Creating functions\Ch07-03 Parameters as values** folder in the example code. Open this application and then open the Developer View by pressing F12. First, we are going to create a variable and put a value into it:

```
> var test=0;
```

When you press Enter, the console will create a variable called `test` that contains the value `100`. We can use the `test` variable as an argument to the `whatWouldIDo` function:

```
> whatWouldIDo(test);
```

When the function has been called, the question we must consider is "What value does `test` now contain?" Does it contain `0` (the value set when it was created), or does it contain `99` (the value set in the function `whatWouldIDo`)? We can answer the question by asking the console to display the value of `test`:

```
> test
<- 0
```

When a function is called, the value in the argument is *copied* into the parameter. So any changes to the parameter will not affect the argument at all.

Multiple parameters in a function

A function can have multiple parameters. We might want a `greeter` function that can display text in different colors. We could add a second parameter that contains a color name:

```
function colorGreeter(message, colorName) {
  var outputElement = document.getElementById("outputParagraph");
  var elementColorStyle = "color:"+colorName;
  outputElement.textContent = message;
  outputElement.style=elementColorStyle;
}
```

This function creates a style element using a supplied color name. The style is then applied to the output element along with the greeting text. We then provide arguments giving the string to be displayed and the color of the text:

```
colorGreeter("Hello in Red", "red");
```

 WHAT COULD GO WRONG

Muddled arguments

The `colorGreeter` function has two arguments that are mapped onto the two parameters that are used inside the function. The first argument has the greeting text, and the second argument has the name of the color to be used for the text. It is important that these arguments are supplied in the correct order.

```
colorGreeter("red", "Hello in Red");
```

This call of `colorGreeter` has supplied the color name before the greeting text. In other words, they are the wrong way round. This would result in the `colorGreeter` trying to display the message "red" in the color "Hello in Red." This would not cause an error, but it would result in the program not doing what you want. So when we make calls to functions, we need to make sure that the arguments that are supplied are given in the same order as the parameters. You can find the `colorGreeter` function in the **Ch07 Creating functions\Ch07-04 Color Greeter** folder.

Using references as function arguments

In a JavaScript program there are essentially two kinds of variable. There are variables that contain a value and variables that contain a reference to an object.

```
var age=12;
```

This statement creates a variable called age, which contains a number with the value 12.

```
var outputElement = document.getElementById("outputParagraph");
```

This statement creates a variable called outputElement, which contains a reference to an HTML element in the page document. This is how our JavaScript programs have located the page elements to be used to display information for the user. We can pass references into function calls as arguments:

```
<!DOCTYPE html>
<html lang="en">

<head>
  <title>Ch07-05 Reference arguments</title>
</head>

<body>
  <h1>Reference Arguments</h1>
  <p>
  <p id="outputParagraph">This is output text</p>          Paragraph element for output
  </p>

  <script>
    function makeGreen(element) {                           makeGreen function
      element.style = "color:green";        Set the color of the element parameter to green
    }

  </script>
</body>

</html>
```

The HTML page above contains a function called `makeGreen`. The function `makeGreen` has a parameter called `element`. The function sets the style of the `element` parameter to the color `green`. A program can use this function to make any given HTML element green.

```
makeGreen(outputElement);
```

Reference arguments

The function `makeGreen` is declared in the example application **Ch07 Creating functions\Ch07-05 Reference arguments** folder in the example code. Open this application and then open the Developer View by pressing F12. First we are going to get a reference to the display paragraph.

```
> var outputElement = document.getElementById("outputParagraph");
```

When you press Enter, a variable called `outputElement` is created that contains a reference to a paragraph on the screen. Now use this variable as an argument to a call of `makeGreen`:

```
> makeGreen(outputElement);
```

This will cause the text of the paragraph on the web page to turn green because the `makeGreen` function has set the `style` property of the element to which it has received a reference:

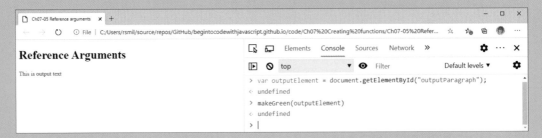

What happens if we give `makeGreen` the wrong kind of argument? Try this:

```
> makeGreen(21);
```

The result of this statement is that nothing happens. No error is produced even though it is not meaningful to try to set the style of a numeric value to 21. Any mistakes that you make with function arguments will not produce errors; instead, the program will just keep running.

Arrays of arguments

There is another way that we can pass arguments into a JavaScript function—an *array* of items. We will discuss arrays in detail in the next chapter. An array is a form of *collection*. We have already seen one form of collection. The unordered list that we used to display ride information in the Theme Park in Chapter 6 held elements in the form of an array of items. We used the `for-of` loop construction to work through the array. If you're not sure about how this works, take a moment to return to Chapter 6 and read "Work through collections using `for-of`." Within a function, the keyword `arguments` means the array of arguments that were given when the function was called.

```
function calculateSum(){
  let total = 0;                                            Set the total to 0
  for (value of arguments){                        Work through the arguments
    total = total + value;          Add each value in the arguments to total
  }                                       Get a reference to the output element
  var outputElement = document.getElementById("outputParagraph");
  outputElement.textContent=total;                   Display the output element
}
```

The function `calculateSum` shows how this works. It uses a `for-of` loop to calculate the total of all the arguments given to the function call. This total value is then displayed on the page. The function can be called with any number of numeric arguments:

```
calculateSum(1,2,3,4,5,6,7,8,9,10);
```

This would display the value 55. Of course, if you do something silly, you might not get what you expect.

```
calculateSum(1,2,3,"Fred","Jim","Banana");
```

This call of the function would not cause an error. It would display the result 6FredJimBanana. This is because of the way that JavaScript combines strings and numbers. You can find out more in Chapter 4 in the section "Working with strings and numbers." You can find this sample code in **Ch07 Creating functions\Ch07-06 Argument arrays**.

Returning values from function calls

A function can return a value. You have seen this in many of the programs we've written. Here's an example:

```
var ageNo = Number(ageText);
```

This statement uses the `Number` function. The function accepts an argument (text expressing a number) and returns a value (the text as a numeric value). We can write our own functions that return a value.

Dice spots method

In Chapter 4, we created an application that displays random dice. Each time we wanted a random dice value, we had to perform some calculations. It would be useful to have these calculations in a function that we could use to get a random number of spots.

```
function getDiceSpots() {
    var spots = Math.floor(Math.random() * 6) + 1;        Calculate the random result
    return spots;                                          Return it to the caller
}
```

This is the function `getDiceSpots`, which calculates a random number of spots. (Check out the section "Creating random dice" in Chapter 4 for details of how this works.) The last statement in the function uses the JavaScript `return` keyword to return the calculated number to the caller. This function can be used whenever an application needs a dice value.

```
function doRollDice() {                                 Get a reference to the output paragraph
    var outputElement = document.getElementById("outputParagraph");
    var spots = getDiceSpots();                          Get the number of spots to display
    var message = "Rolled: " + spots;                    Build the message to display
    outputElement.textContent = message;                 Display the message
}
```

The function `doRollDice` is called to display a dice value. It calls `getDiceSpots` to get the value and then display it. You can see this in action in the example application **Ch07 Creating functions\Ch07-07 Returning values**, which works in exactly the same way as the dice example in **Ch04 Working with data\Ch04-02 Computer Dice**, but it uses the doRollDice function.

Creating customizable dice

Sometimes, a program needs a random number in a different range from the 1 to 6 provided by a die. We could use our newfound skills to make a function that accepts minimum and maximum values and then returns a random integer in that range.

```
function getCustomDiceSpots(min, max) {
    var range = max - min + 1;                              Calculate the range of values
    var spots = Math.floor(Math.random() * (range)) + min;     Calculate the random value
    return spots;                                                     Return result
}
```

The function getCustomDiceSpots is given two parameters that specify the minimum and maximum values of the required random number. It works out the range of numbers that are required (the difference between the maximum and minimum values), calculates a random number in this range, and then adds that number to the minimum value to produce the number of spots. This number is then returned. One of the nice things about functions is that you don't have to understand how they work to use them.

```
var health = getCustomDiceSpots(70,90);
```

The above statement creates a variable called health, which contains a random number in the range 70 to 90. It could be used in a video game to set the initial health value of a monster that fights the player. Sometimes, the monster would be slightly harder to kill, which would make the game more interesting to play.

The customizable dice app

I've used the getCustomDiceSpots function to make a dice application where the user can select the minimum and maximum values for random numbers that they want to use to play a particular game.

Figure 7-2 shows how the application is used. The user fills in the text boxes for the **Min** and **Max** values for the random number that they want and presses the **Roll The Dice** button to display a random number in that range.

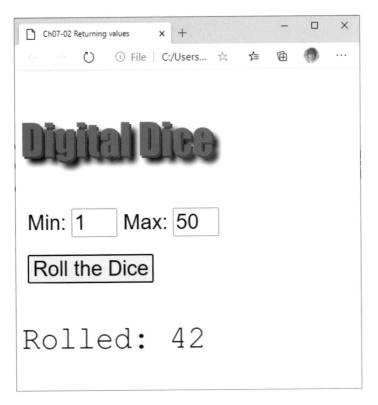

Figure 7-2   Customizable dice

The settings in Figure 7-2 will produce a value in the range 1 to 50 that could be used to play a bingo game. Let's take a look at the code.

```
<!DOCTYPE html>
<html lang="en">

<head>
  <title>Ch07-07 Returning values</title>
  <link rel="stylesheet" href="styles.css">          The style sheet for the application
  <script src="customdice.js"></script>              The JavaScript source file for the application
</head>

<body>
  <p class="menuHeading">Digital Dice</p>
```

```
<p class="menuText">
  Min:
  <input class="menuInput" type="number" id="minNoText" value="1" min="1" max="100">
  Max:
  <input class="menuInput" type="number" id="maxNoText" value="6" min="2" max="100">
  <p>
    <button class="menuText" onclick="doRollDice('minNoText','maxNoText',
    'outputParagraph');">
    Roll the Dice</button>
  </p>
</p>

<p id="outputParagraph" class="numberDisplay">Press the roll button</p>
</p>
</body>

</html>
```

Min input

Max input

Button that rolls the dice

Output paragraph

We have seen this kind of page before. There is some text to tell the user about the application. There are two input fields, which are used to get the minimum and maximum values for the random number to be produced. There is a **Roll the Dice** button to trigger the generation of the value and an output paragraph that displays the result. This page is very similar to the one used by the Theme Park Ride Selector application in Chapter 6. The function doRollDice is called when the user clicks the button to roll the dice.

```
onclick="doRollDice('minNoText','maxNoText', 'outputParagraph');"
```

This is the onclick attribute for the **Roll the Dice** button. This attribute contains a string of JavaScript code that will be obeyed when the button is clicked. If you're not clear on how this works, take a look in the section "Using a button" in Chapter 2 for a refresh. The JavaScript that runs when the button is clicked makes a call of the function doRollDice.

```
doRollDice('minNoText','maxNoText', 'outputParagraph');
```

The doRollDice function has three arguments, which are the ID strings for the minNoText, maxNoText, and outputParagraph elements in the web page. The function gets the minimum and maximum values from elements identified by the first two arguments to the function call. It then calculates the random result and then displays the result using the output element identified in the third element. We can take a look at this function to see how it works:

```
function doRollDice(minElementName, maxElemementName, outputElementName) {

    var min = getNumberFromElement(minElementName);          Get the minimum value
    var max = getNumberFromElement(maxElemementName);         Get the maximum value


    var spots = getCustomDiceSpots(min, max);                 Get the number of spots


    var message = "Rolled: " + spots;                         Build the output message
                                                              Get the output element

    var outputElement = document.getElementById(outputElementName);
    outputElement.textContent = message;                      Display the number
}
```

The function looks very small. It gets in the minimum and maximum values, calls getCustomDiceSpots to get the random value, and then displays the result. The function is small because it uses another function called getNumberFromElement to get the maximum and minimum values:

```
function getNumberFromElement(name)
{
    var element = document.getElementById(name);       Get the input element
    var text = element.value;                          Get the text from the input element
    var result = Number(text);                         Convert the text into a result
    return result;                                     Return the result
}
```

This function is given the identifier of an input element on the web page as a parameter. It fetches a number from the specified input element. We can use this function in any program that needs to read numbers from the user. It gets a reference to the element with the identifier that has been supplied as a parameter, gets the text from this element, converts the text into a number, and then returns the number to the caller. The function is called twice in the dice application—once to read the maximum value and once to read the minimum value. If I had an application that needed 10 inputs to be read from the screen, I could call this function 10 times in the application.

Designing with functions

Functions are a very useful part of the programmer's toolkit and form an important part of the development process. Once you've worked out what a customer wants the application to do, you can start thinking about how you'll break down the program into functions. Once you've specified the behavior of each function in the application, you can write the function headers (in other words, pick the function name, the parameters, and any return value), and then you could even get someone else to write that function for you.

Functions save you from writing too much code. Often, you find that as you write a program, you write code that repeats a particular action. If you do this, you should consider taking that action and turning it into a function. There are two reasons why this is a good idea:

First, it saves you writing the same code twice; and secondly, if a fault is found in the code, you only need to fix it in one place.

Functions also make a program easy to test. You can regard each function as a "data processor." Data goes into the function via the arguments, and output is produced via the return value. We can write what is called a "test harness" to call a function with test data and then check to ensure the output is sensible. In other words, we can make a program that tests itself. We will look at this later in the book.

Add error handling to an application

The Digital Dice program works well as long as we use it correctly. However, it is not without its problems. It is quite easy to enter invalid values for the minimum and maximum values. You can experiment with the application in the examples folder **Ch07 Creating functions\Ch07-08 Custom dice** to discover what happens when it fails.

Figure 7-3 shows how the application can be used incorrectly. A minimum value of 50 and a maximum value of 2 is not correct. To make matters worse, the application has displayed a result that might be incorrect. We have no way of knowing if it has worked correctly because we are not sure how the `getCustomDiceSpots` function behaves if it is given incorrect maximum and minimum values. It turns out that there are also other ways to cause the program problems. A user could press **Roll The Dice** when the **Min** and **Max** input areas are both empty. We need to fix all these things. Fortunately, we have the JavaScript skills that we need to sort this out.

Figure 7-3 Dice errors

Finding all the errors in advance

One thing that separates a good programmer from a great programmer is the way that they handle errors. A great programmer will start a project by thinking of all the things that could go wrong when the user starts to use their program. It's unlikely that they will think of every possible error (users can be very inventive when it comes to breaking things), but they will write down all the errors they can think of and then set out to deal with each error. Then, as the project continues, a great programmer will keep looking for possible errors and keep making sure that the errors that they know about are being handled correctly. In the case of the Digital Dice application, I can think of three things that might go wrong:

1. The user might not enter anything into the Max or Min inputs.

2. The user might enter a number outside the correct range for one of the Max or Min inputs.

3. The user might enter a Min value that is greater than or equal to the Max value.

Now that we have identified the errors, the next thing we need to decide is what the program should do when they are detected. If you are writing a program for a customer, you **must** discuss with them what is supposed to happen. Do they want the program to assume default values (perhaps a Min of 1 and a Max of 6), or do they want error messages to be displayed? Do they want the error to be a message on the screen or a pop-up alert? These are all important questions that the programmer alone can't answer. The worst thing that can happen is that you make an assumption concerning what the customer wants. In my experience, making assumptions is a neat way of doubling your workload. You show the customer what you've made, they tell you it is not what they want, and you have to do it again. In the case of our customer, we have been told that the program should display a message and turn any invalid input areas on the screen red so that the user knows what to fix. So let's see how we can use our JavaScript skills to solve this problem.

Let's start with the error display. These are two style classes that I'm going to use to on the input elements on the web page. The menuInput style is the "normal" style. The program will set the menuInputError style to an input element that contains an invalid entry. Note that this has the background color set to red.

```css
.menuInput {
    background-color: white;
    font-size: 1em;
    width: 2em;
}

.menuInputError {
    background-color: red;
    font-size: 1em;
    width: 2em;
}
```

Our application uses a function called getNumberFromElement to get a number from an input element. Let's have a look at an improved function to deal with input errors:

```javascript
function getNumberFromElement(elementID){
    var element = document.getElementById(elementID);    ──── Get the input element
    var text = element.value;                            ──── Get the text from the input element

    var result = Number(text);                           ──── Convert the text into a number

    if(isNaN(result)){                                   ──── Make sure that we have a number
        // fail with bad number input
        element.className="menuInputError";             ──── Indicate an error
        return NaN;
    }
}
```

```
// get the max and min values from the input field
var max = Number(element.getAttribute("max"));
var min = Number(element.getAttribute("min"));

if(result>max || result<min){                              Make sure that the number is in range
    // fail because outside range
    element.className="menuInputError";
    return NaN;
}

// if we get here the number is valid
// set to normal background
element.className="menuInput";

return result;
}
```

The getNumberFromElement function

This function bears closer inspection. Here are answers to some questions about it:

Question: What does NaN mean? And what is the isNan function doing?

    Answer: We first saw NaN in Chapter 4 when we wrote our first JavaScript to read numbers from the user. It is how JavaScript represents a value that is "not a number." In this case, the function is using the Number function to convert the text entered by the user into a number. If the Number function fails, either because the text is not numeric or the text is empty, the Number function returns the value NaN because it could not create a number result. The isNaN function takes an argument and returns true if the argument is not a number. The getNumberFromElement function uses isNaN to test the result value produced by the call to Number. If the result is not a number, the function sets the style of the element to indicate that the input was in error and then returns the value NaN to the caller to indicate that a number could not be read.

Question: What are the min and max attributes? Where do they come from?

    Answer: We can add min and max attributes to an HTML input element to help the browser validate numbers entered by the user. However, the browser does not enforce minimum and maximum values completely; our program must also play a part in making sure that numbers are entered in the correct range.

```
<input class="menuInput" type="number" id="minNoText" value="1" min="1" max="99">
```

The HTML above is the input element for the minimum value. The `min` and `max` attributes are set to 1 and 99 respectively. The `getNumberFromElement` function can get the values of these attributes and then use them to perform input validation:

```
var max = Number(element.getAttribute("max"));
var min = Number(element.getAttribute("min"));
```

The function can then use these values to validate the number entered by the user.

```
if(result>max || result<min){
    // fail because outside range
    element.className="menuInputError";
    return NaN;
}
```

This is a really good way of handing minimum and maximum values because the values are obtained from the elements on the HTML page and are not held in the JavaScript code.

Question: Why does the function sometimes return the value NaN?

Answer: We've discovered that it is possible for the `getNumberFromElement` function to be unable to deliver a result. This happens when the user doesn't type in a numeric value or when the value they enter is out of range. The function needs a way of informing the caller that it does not have a valid result, and returning NaN is how you do this in JavaScript. This makes using a function that returns a value that is a kind of "buyer beware" proposition, as the code that called the function must test to make sure that the delivered result was valid. We will see this in action when we look at the error handing version of `doRollDice`.

These changes to the `getNumberFromElement` function have addressed the first two errors that we identified. The user must now enter a valid number or the `getNumberFromElement` function returns the value NaN (not a number). Now the `doRollDice` function needs to be updated. This version checks that the minimum and maximum values are both numbers. It also checks that the minimum value is less than the maximum value. If either of these conditions is not met, the function displays an alert.

```
function doRollDice (minElementName, maxElemementName, outputElementName) {
                                                                          Get the output element
    var outputElement = document.getElementById(outputElementName);

    var minRand = getNumberFromElement(minElementName);                   Get the minimum value
    var maxRand = getNumberFromElement(maxElemementName);                 Get the maximum value

    if (isNaN(minRand) || isNaN(maxRand)) {                               Check for non-numbers
        outputElement.textContent="Invalid range values";                Display error message
        return;
    }

    if (minRand >= maxRand) {                                             Check maximum and minimum
        outputElement.textContent="Minimum above maximum";                Display error message
        return;
    }

    var spots = getCustomDiceSpots(minRand, maxRand);                     Get the spots value
    var message = "Rolled: " + spots;                                     Build the reply
    outputElement.textContent = message;                                  Display the reply
}
```

Figure 7-4 shows the error handling in action. Note that I've also made another change to the application, so that it now shows the user the minimum and maximum values that are allowed for each input. This is a great way to reduce the chances of any errors in the first place.

Figure 7-4   Error handling

Local variables in JavaScript functions

Imagine several cooks working together in a kitchen. Each cook is working on a different recipe. The kitchen contains a limited number of pots and pans for the cooks to share. The cooks would need to coordinate so that two of them didn't try to use the same pot. Otherwise, we might get sugar added to our soup and custard instead of gravy on our roast beef.

The designers of JavaScript faced a similar problem when creating functions. They didn't want functions to fight over variables in the same way that two cooks might fight over a particular frying pan. You might think that it would be unlikely that two functions would try to use variables with the same name, but this is actually very likely.

Many programmers (including me) have an affection for the variable name i, which they use for counting. If two functions use a variable called i and one function calls the other function, this could lead to programs that don't work properly because the second function might change i to a value that the first function didn't expect.

JavaScript solves this problem by providing a way for each function to have its own local variable space. This is the programming equivalent of giving each cook their own personal set of pots and pans. Any function can declare a local variable called i that is specific to that function call. We declare a variable as local by using the keyword `var`.

```
function fvar2() {
   var i=99;
}

function fvar1(){
   var i=0;

   fvar2();

   console.log("The value of i is:" + i);
}
```

When a function returns, all local variables are destroyed. The code above shows two functions that contain local variables. Both fvar1 and fvar2 use a variable called i. If we call f1var, JavaScript follows this sequence:

1. The function fvar1 is called.

2. The first statement of fvar1 creates a variable called i and sets it to 0.

3. The second statement of fvar1 makes a call to fvar2.

4. The first and only statement of fvar2 creates a variable called i and sets it to 99.

5. The function fvar2 finishes and control returns to the third statement of fvar1.

6. The third statement of fvar1 prints out the value of i.

The question we must consider is this: "What value is displayed in the console?" Is it the value 0 (which is set inside fvar1), or is it 99 (which is set inside fvar2)? If you've read the first part of this section, you know the value that will be printed is 0. The variables both have the same name (they are both called i), but they each "live" in different functions.

JavaScript uses the word *scope* when talking about variable lifetimes. The scope of a variable is that part of a program in which a variable can be used. Each version of i has a scope that is limited to the function body in which it is declared This form of isolation is called encapsulation. Encapsulation means that the operation of one function is isolated from the operation of other functions. Different programmers can work on different functions with no danger of problems being caused by variable names clashing with each other. Now take look at this pair of functions:

```
function f2() {
  i=99;
}

function f1(){
  i=0;

  f2();

  console.log("The value of i is:" + i);
}
```

Can you spot the difference? These two functions don't use the keyword var to declare their variables. Is this important? **Yes.** It turns out that variables declared without the var keyword are made global to the whole application, so f1 and f2 are now sharing a single global variable called i. If we call the function f1, it will print the value 99 because the call of f2 will change the value of the global variable i. This means that you should always use var to declare variables in your functions unless you specifically want to share them. In Chapter 4, in the section "Global and local variables," we discovered a situation where a program needs to have a variable that has *global scope*. Now we are starting to understand how this works.

Local variables using let

In Chapter 6, in the section "The JavaScript for loop," we discovered that we could declare local variables using the keyword let. Variables declared using let are discarded when a program leaves the block of statements where they were declared, whereas variables declared using var are discarded when the program leaves the function in which they are declared.

```
function letDemo(){
  var i=0;                                          This version of i exists for the whole function
  {
    let i=1;                                        This version of i only exists in this block
    var j=2;                                        j exists for the whole function
    console.log("The value of let i is:"+i);
  }

  console.log("The value of var i is:"+i);
  console.log("The value of var j is:"+j);
}
```

The function `letDemo` shows how this all works. It contains two versions of `i`. The first version is declared as `var` and exists for the entire function. The second version is declared inside a block and is discarded when the program leaves that block. Note that within the block it is not possible to use the outer version of `i` because any references to `i` will use the local version. In this case, we say that the outer variables is *scoped out*. The function also contains a variable called `j`, which is declared inside the inner block. However, because `j` is declared as `var`, it can be used anywhere inside the function. These functions are declared in the example program in the **Ch07 Creating functions\Ch07-10 Variable scope** folder.

If you find this confusing, then I apologize. The best way to understand it is to consider the problem that they are trying to solve (stopping lots of cooks fighting over the same pots and pans) and then work from there. The most important point is to always use `var` or `let` when you create a variable. Otherwise, you may find yourself a victim of very strange bugs in your programs.

MAKE SOMETHING HAPPEN

Double dice

Quite a few games use two dice rather than one. Make a version of the dice program that displays the results from two dice. You could even make this super-customizable so that the user can select the range of values to be produced by each die. If you are bit stuck with this, remember that there is nothing wrong with the `onClick` behavior of a button calling two methods. And that two dice are just one dice (or die) times two. Take a look at my example solution in the examples at **Ch07 Creating functions\Ch07-11 Two Dice** to discover the sneaky way I made the program work.

What you have learned

In this chapter, you learned how to take a block of code and turn it into a function that can be used from other parts of the program.

1. You've seen that a function contains a header that describes the function, and a block of code that is the body of the function. The function header supplies the name of the function and any parameters that are accepted by the function. When a function is called, the programmer supplies an argument that matches each parameter.

2. Parameters are items that the function can work on. They are passed by value, in that a copy is made of the argument given in the function call. If the function body contains statements that change the value of the parameter, this change is local to the function body. When an object (for example, a paragraph that has been obtained using the `getElementById` method) is used as an argument to a function call, the function receives a reference to the object. This allows code in the function body to interact with attributes in the objects, as we saw with the `makeGreen` function above.

3. A function can regard parameters as an array and can work through the arguments supplied to the function by using the `arguments` keyword.

4. A function returns a single value. This is achieved by using the `return` statement, which can be followed by a value to be returned. If no value is returned or the function does not perform a return statement, the function will return a special JavaScript value called `undefined`, which is used to denote a missing value.

5. The scope of a variable in a program is that part of the program in which the variable can be used. Variables created inside the body of a function using the keyword `var` have a scope that is local to the function and cannot be used by statements outside that function.

6. When creating software, it is important to consider potential errors at the start of the project rather than finding out about them later.

Here are some questions that you might like to ponder about the use of functions in programs:

Does using functions in programs slow down the program?

Not normally. There is a certain amount of work required to create the call of a function and then return from it, but this is not normally an issue. The benefits of functions far outweigh the performance issues.

Can I use functions to spread work around a group of programmers?

Indeed, you can. This is a very good reason to use functions. There are several ways that you can use functions to spread work around. One popular way is to write place-holder functions and build the application from them. A function will have the correct parameters and return value, but the body will do very little. As the program develops, programmers fill in and test each function in turn.

What is the maximum number of arguments that you can give to a function call?

We have seen that you can add lots of arguments to a call of a function. JavaScript does not place a limit on how many arguments you can pass in, but if you find yourself passing more than seven or eight, I'd advise you to think about how you are delivering the information to your function. If you want to pass a number of related items into a function, you might want to create an object (which we will explore in the next chapter) and pass in a reference to the object, rather than passing in lots of different values.

What is the difference between var **and** let **when creating variables inside a function body?**

Great question. Both keywords can be used to create a variable that exists within the block of code that is a function body. The difference between the two is that a variable created using var will exist within the function body from that point onward. A variable created using let will disappear at the end of the block in which it is created.

I'm still not clear on the difference between var **and** let **in JavaScript. Why do we have them?**

Remember that the problem that we are solving is that we don't want a program to fail because programmers put values with different meanings into the same variable. If one part of a program used a variable called total to hold the total sales and another part used a variable called total to hold the total price, the program would fail. You would have the same problems if you used a single pan to make both custard and gravy while cooking a meal.

A variable created with the let keyword only exists within the block where it is declared, which means that it cannot be affected by statements running outside that block. This would be like you grabbing a clean pan, making the custard, and then washing the pan and putting it away before it was used for anything else. The var keyword allows you to create a variable that exists from the point of declaration and can be used to share a value around parts of a program or function.

Generally, you should create variables by using the `let` keyword and only use `var` if you really want the value in the variable to be used in other places in the function body. Note that a variable in a function that was created with the keyword `var` will disappear when the program exits the function.

How do I come up with names for my functions?

The best functions have names given in a verb-noun form. `getNumberFromElement` is a good name for a function. The first part indicates what it does, and the second part indicates where the value comes from. I find that thinking of function names (and variable names, for that matter) can be quite hard at times.

What do I do if I want to return more than one value from a function?

JavaScript functions can only return a single value. However, in the next chapter we will discover how to create data structures that can contain multiple values that can be returned by functions.

8

Storing data

What you will learn

You might find this surprising, but you've already learned most of what you need to know to tell a computer what to do. You can write a program that gets data from the user, stores it, makes decisions based on data values, and repeats behaviors using loop constructions. You also know how to use functions to break a solution down into components. These are the fundamentals of programming, and all programs are built on these core capabilities.

However, there is one more thing you need to know before you can write most any kind of program. You need to be able to write programs that can manage large amounts of data. In this chapter, you'll learn just that, along with some extremely powerful JavaScript techniques for working with the HTML Document Object Model (DOM) that underpins the display of a page.

Collections of data

Your fame as a programmer is beginning to spread far and wide. Now the owner of an ice-cream parlor comes to you and asks that you write a program to help her track sales results. She currently has six stands around the city selling ice cream treats. What she wants is quite simple—she wants a program where she can enter the sales value from each stand and then get the total sales from all of them, as well as the best and worst sales. She wants to use this analysis to help her plan the location of her stands and reward the best sellers. If you get this right, you might be getting some free ice cream, so you agree to help.

As usual, the starting point for your program is a design that shows how the application should look. **Figure 8-1** shows what the customer has drawn up. She wants to enter the sales values and then press a **Calculate** button to display the analysis. Because you have read Chapter 7 and you know about error handling, you ask her about the upper and lower limits on the data values and what the program should do if any of the values are out of range. Your customer hasn't thought of this, but you discuss the application and agree on some additions to the design as shown in **Figure 8-2**.

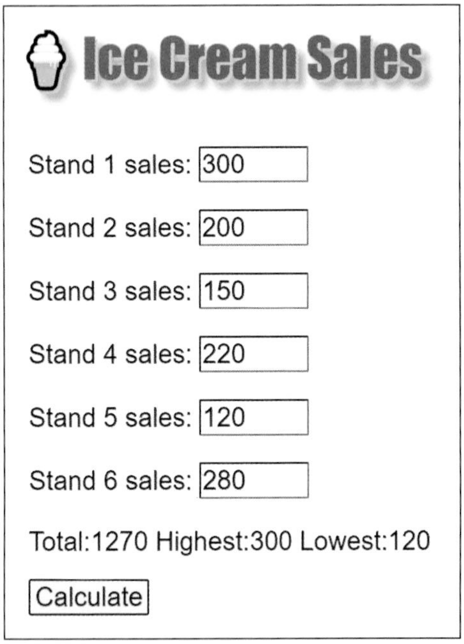

Figure 8-1   Ice cream calculator

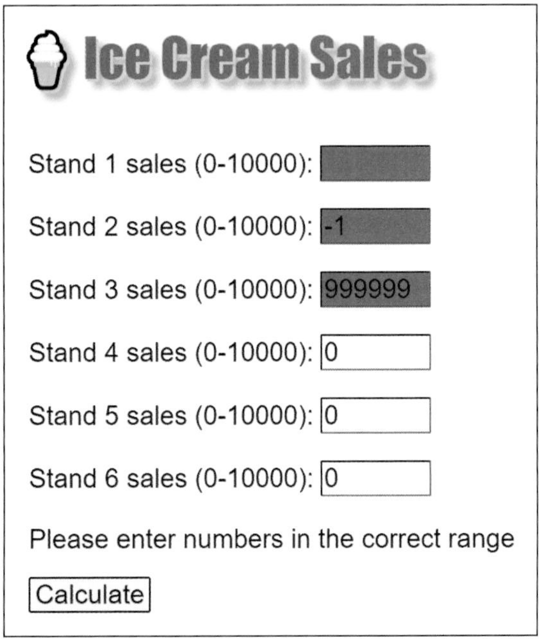

Figure 8-2   Ice cream calculator errors

Ice cream sales

Now that you have a specification, all you must do now is write the actual program itself. The program will need variables to hold the sales values entered by the user, and it can use logical expressions to compare sales values and choose the largest (so that it can find the biggest and smallest sales). You also know from earlier chapters how to display results to the user by setting the innerText of a paragraph in the page. We could start with the HTML for the application:

```html
<!DOCTYPE html>
<html lang="en">

<head>
  <title>Ice Cream Sales</title>
  <link rel="stylesheet" href="styles.css">
  <script src="icecreamsales.js"></script>
</head>

<body>
  <p class="menuHeading"> &#127846; Ice Cream Sales</p>

  <p>
    <label class="menuLabel" for="s1SalesText">Stand 1 sales (0-10000):</label>
    <input class="menuInput" type="number" id="s1SalesText" value="0" min="0"
    max="10000">
  </p>

  <p>
    <label class="menuLabel" for="s2SalesText">Stand 2 sales (0-10000):</label>
    <input class="menuInput" type="number" id="s3SalesText" value="0" min="0"
    max="10000">
  </p>

  <p class="menuText" id="outputParagraph">
  </p>

  <p>
    <button class="menuText" onclick="doCalc()">Calculate</button>
  </p>

</body>

</html>
```

This HTML contains an input field for each of the six sales that are to be entered by the user. (The listing above only shows the first two to save space.) Each input field has an `id` attribute so that the program can find it and load the value stored in it. The input field uses a new feature of HTML that we have not seem before, the `label`, as shown in **Figure 8-3**.

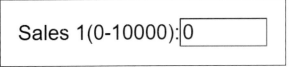

Figure 8-3   Single data entry element

Labeling HTML input elements

Each of the elements on the application has a label next to it. In Figure 8-3, the label shows that the input is for the sales of ice cream stand number 1. In earlier programs, we have just displayed text next to the input element to label it, but it turns out that there is a better way to label inputs on an HTML page. We can use the `label` element to explicitly link a label with an input.

```
<p>
    <label class="menuLabel" for="s1SalesText">Stand 1 sales (0-10000):</label>
    <input class="menuInput" type="number" id="s1SalesText" value="0" min="0"
    max="10000">
</p>
```

The `label` and the `input` are held inside a paragraph. The `label` contains the label text for the `input`. It also contains a `for` attribute that matches the `id` of the target of the label. Both the `label` and the `input` are assigned style sheet classes to manage their appearance on the page.

Calculate total ice cream sales

The HTML contains a button that the user presses to perform the calculation. When this is pressed, the JavaScript function doCalc is called. This function must get the values from the input elements on the HTML page and then calculate the results that the user wants to see.

```
Function doCalc() {
    var sales1, sales2, sales3, sales4, sales5, sales6;
    sales1 = getNumberFromElement("s1SalesText");
    sales2 = getNumberFromElement("s2SalesText");
    sales3 = getNumberFromElement("s3SalesText");
    sales4 = getNumberFromElement("s4SalesText");
    sales5 = getNumberFromElement("s5SalesText");
    sales6 = getNumberFromElement("s6SalesText");        Get the sales values from the inputs

    var total = sales1 + sales2 + sales3 + sales4 + sales5 + sales6;
```

This is the first part of the function doCalc. The function runs when the user presses the Calculate button. It calls another function with the name getNumberFromElement that we created in the "The customizable dice app" section in Chapter 7. This function is supplied with a string containing the id of the element in the HTML, and it returns the value that the element contains. Once each sales value has been obtained, the program then works out the total sales value by adding all the sales together.

Find the highest ice cream sales

Finding the total sales was easy, so now we need to add the code to find the highest and the lowest sales. Fortunately, we know about the use of relational operators to compare values and logical expressions to combine the comparisons. You can refresh you understanding of these in Chapter 5 in the "Boolean expressions" section. With that knowledge, we can write a JavaScript statement that can determine whether the sales from ice cream stand 1 are the largest:

```
var highestSales;

if(sales1>sales2 && sales1>sales3 && sales1>sales4 &&
    sales1>sales5 && sales1>sales6) {
    highestSales = sales1;                          Test to see if sales1 is the highest sales
}
```

The code above uses an if construction to decide whether the sales from stand 1 are the largest. The sales from stand 1 are largest if sales1 is greater than the sales values from the other five stands. The logical expression checks to see whether the sales from stand 1 are greater than the sales from stand 2, stand 3, stand 4, and stand 5. The expression sets the variable highestSales to the value in sales1 if sales1 is the largest value.

One problem with this design is that our program needs a test like this for all six sales values, so we need to write five more tests. Then we need another six tests to determine the lowest sales value, and if the ice cream parlor owner sets up more ice cream stands, this would make our program even more complex.

We have hit this problem because we have started from the wrong place. Sometimes, it is a good idea to use an existing program as the basis of a new one, but we have discovered that a design created to work with two values (the maximum and minimum values for a random number) does not scale up very well. We must do a lot of work to extend this structure to read in and manipulate six values.

I've watched a lot of people learn to program, and I've seen quite a few work much harder than they needed to because they took something that they know how to do and tried to extend it to do a different task. This is a bit like trying to dig the foundations of a house with a spoon just because you know how use a spoon but don't fancy learning how to drive the mechanical digger. We have already decided that the best programmers are "creatively lazy." This might be a good point to try for some creative laziness. If you find yourself having to repeat chunks of code, you might want to stop and think about a better way of doing this. If you really want to do this the hard way, I've put my partially completed version of the program in the **Ch08 Storing data\ Ch08-01 Unworkable Ice Cream Sales** folder.

Creating an array

JavaScript also provides an *array* component that can be used to create indexed storage of a collection of data values. Each item in an array is called an *element*. A program addresses a particular element in the array by using an *indexer*, which is a number that identifies the element in the array. Some programmers refer to an indexer as a *subscript*. Let's investigate how arrays work.

 MAKE SOMETHING HAPPEN

Investigating arrays

Start by opening the application in the **Ch08 Storing data\Ch08-02 Array Ice Cream Sales** folder in the example code. This application works, so you can enter some data and check the results. We are just going to investigate arrays from the developer console. Open the Developer View by pressing the function key F12. Now we can start typing commands into the JavaScript command prompt. The first thing we are going to do is create an empty array. Type in the statement below:

```
> var sales = [];
```

When you press Enter, the JavaScript console creates an empty array with the identifier sales. This action does not return a result, so the console displays the message undefined:

```
> var sales = [];
<- undefined
```

We can ask the JavaScript console to show the contents of any variable by entering the name of that variable. This works with an array, too. Type in the identifier sales and press Enter.

```
> sales
<- []
```

The console shows us that the sales array is empty by displaying two brackets with nothing between them. Now lets store a sales value in the array. This statement will add an element at the start of the array:

```
> sales[0] = 100;
```

When you press the Enter key, JavaScript must store the value 100 in the array element with the index 0.

```
> sales[0] = 100;
<- 100
```

This element does not exist, so JavaScript adds it to the array automatically. Because an assignment statement returns the value that is assigned, the console displays the value 100, which is what was assigned to the array element. We can view the contents of the array again to see what has changed. Type in the identifier sales and press Enter.

```
> sales
<- [100]
```

The console shows us that the sales array now contains a single value. We can use an array element as we would use any other variable. What do you think the following statement would do? Type it in and find out.

```
> sales[0] = sales[0] + 1;
<- 101
```

This statement adds 1 to the element at the start of the array. Let's add a second element to the array. We create the new element just by storing something in it.

```
> sales[1] = 150;
<- 150
```

This element does not exist, so JavaScript adds it to the array automatically. Because an assignment statement returns the value assigned, the console displays the value 150. Let's see what has changed in the array. Type in the identifier sales and press Enter.

```
> sales
<- [101, 150]
```

JavaScript shows us the element at the start of the array (which has 101 in it) and the next element (which has 150 in it). JavaScript will add new elements to the array each time whenever it needs to. You can think of the array as "stretching" to hold whatever items it needs to.

The JavaScript in the **Ch08 Storing data\Ch08-02 Array Ice Cream Sales** example program uses arrays to store the sales values. Below, you can see the statements in the program that get the data into the array for analysis.

```
var sales = [];                                            Create the sales array

sales[0] = getNumberFromElement("s0SalesText");            Store sales values in each
sales[1] = getNumberFromElement("s1SalesText");            element of the array
sales[2] = getNumberFromElement("s2SalesText");
sales[3] = getNumberFromElement("s3SalesText");
sales[4] = getNumberFromElement("s4SalesText");
sales[5] = getNumberFromElement("s5SalesText");
```

The statements above create an array called sales and then set elements in the array with the sales values from the elements on the HTML page. Note that because the array elements are indexed from 0, I've changed the IDs for the input elements to match. In other words, the element at the start of the array has an index value of 0 and is assigned a value from an element with an ID that matches.

```
sales[0] = getNumberFromElement("s0SalesText");
```

Counting from zero is just something you will have to get used to

If you are used to counting from 1, you will find that the way that arrays count from zero is a bit irritating. However, you will just have to get used to it, as it is how JavaScript (and lots of other programming languages) work. Just remember that an array containing six elements (like the sales array above) will index these in the range 0 to 5. Note that this means that sometimes you will have count in one way for the program (array elements 0 to 5) and another for the user (ice cream stands 1 to 6).

Processing data in an array

Storing the sales in an array makes it easy for a program to work through the elements in it. We can access individual elements by using index values, or we can use the `for-of` loop to work through the elements.

```
total = 0;                              Set the total to zero

for(let saleValue of sales) {           Work through the sales array
    total = total + saleValue;          Add each sales value to the total
}
```

The statements above work through the `sales` array and calculate the total number of sales. The great thing about this code is that it would work for any size of array.

Finding the highest and lowest sales values

Another request the customer made was for the program to find the highest and lowest sales in the set of results. Before you write the code to do this, it's worth thinking about the algorithm to use. In this case, the program can implement an approach very similar to one that a human would use. If you gave me some numbers and asked me to find the highest value, I would compare each number with the highest value I had seen so far and update the current highest value each time I found a larger one. In programming terms, this algorithm would look a bit like the following. (This is not JavaScript as such; a description like this is sometimes called *pseudocode*. It looks something like a program, but it is there to express an algorithm, not to run inside a computer.)

```
if(new value > highest I've seen)
   highest I've seen = new value
```

At the start, we set the "highest I've seen" value to the value of the element at the start of the array because this is the highest we've seen at the start of the process. I can put this behavior into a function that will calculate the highest value in any array that is passed into it.

```
function getHighest(inputArray){

    var max = inputArray[0];                    ———— Set the maximum to the start element

    for(let value of inputArray) {              ———— Work through the input array
        if(value>max){                          ———— Test for a new maximum
            max = value;                        ———— Set the maximum to the new value
        }
    }
    return max;                                 ———— Return the maximum value
}
```

A program can use the getHighest function to get the highest value from any array of values. We can create helper functions called getHighest, getLowest, and getTotal to use in our application.

```
function doCalc() {

    var sales = [];

    sales[0] = getNumberFromElement("s0SalesText");
    sales[1] = getNumberFromElement("s1SalesText");
    sales[2] = getNumberFromElement("s2SalesText");
    sales[3] = getNumberFromElement("s3SalesText");
    sales[4] = getNumberFromElement("s4SalesText");
    sales[5] = getNumberFromElement("s5SalesText");

    var totalSales = getTotal(sales);
    var highestSales = getHighest(sales);
    var lowestSales = getLowest(sales);

    var result = "Total:" + totalSales + " Highest:" + highestSales +
                " Lowest:" + lowestSales ;

    var outputElement = document.getElementById('outputParagraph');

    outputElement.textContent = result;
}
```

The completed version of `doCalc` is shown above. It creates a `sales` array, uses the analysis functions to create the results, and then displays them. You can find this version of the program in the **Ch08 Storing data\Ch08-02 Array Ice Cream Sales** examples folder.

WHAT COULD GO WRONG

Detecting invalid sales values

The ice cream sales application configures the input elements in the HTML document to have an input type of number.

```
<input class="menuInput" type="number" id="s0SalesText" value="0" min="0" max="10000">
```

However, using this input type would not stop the user from directly entering invalid values:

Stand 1 sales (0-10000): -100

In this case, the user has accidentally pressed the minus key when typing in the number and entered a negative value. The good news is that the `getNumberFromElement` function that the program is using to read the sales value will return a result of NaN (not a number) when it reads a value outside the min and max settings for an element. (You can learn more about how this works in Chapter 7 in the section "Add error handling to an application.")

The bad news is that our program will not handle this correctly. We can fix the problem by using the way that JavaScript works with numbers. Remember that any mathematical calculation involving the value "not a number" will return a result of "not a number." So if the total of all the sales values is not a number this means that at least one of the sales values is not a number. This is something our program can test for.

```
var totalSales= getTotal(sales);

var result;

if (isNaN(totalSales)) {
    result = "Please enter numbers in the correct range"
}
else {
```

```
    var highestSales = getHighest(sales);
    var lowestSales = getLowest(sales);

    result = "Total:" + totalSales + "Highest:" + highestSales +
             "Lowest:" + lowestSales;
}
```

The code above shows how this works. If the `totalSales` value is not a number, the `result` variable is set to an error message. Otherwise, `result` is set to the calculated values. You can find this version of the program in the example folder **Ch08 Storing data\Ch08-03 Error handling Ice Cream Sales**.

Build a user interface

The program that we have created meets the specification set by the customer. Which makes the next phone call from our customer rather unwelcome. She says she has some good news. Her company has just got another two ice cream stands. This means that we will have to add two extra elements to the HTML for the application and then make sure that the data analysis program loads these new values in correctly.

A way to make our lives easier, in terms of both creating the HTML data entry page and processing the data, is to make more use of the Document Object Model (DOM) that underpins the application. In Chapter 6, in the "Building web pages from code" section, we made some use of this when we created the Multiplication Table Generator application, which generates HTML output elements using a `for` loop and adds the elements to the document for display to the user. If you are not sure how this works, take a look at the Code Analysis section "Building HTML from JavaScript" in Chapter 6.

```
<!DOCTYPE html>
<html lang="en">

<head>
  <title>Ice Cream Sales</title>                          Title for the page
  <link rel="stylesheet" href="styles.css">               Style sheet for the application
  <script src="icecreamsales.js"></script>
</head>
                                                           Function called to build the page
<body onload="doBuildSalesInputItems('salesItems',0, 10000, 6);">
  <p class="menuHeading"> &#127846; Ice Cream Sales</p>    Heading for the page
```

```
<div id="salesItems">                                    Container for the sales items
</div>

<p class="menuText" id="outputParagraph">                Output paragraph

</p>

<p>
  <button class="menuText" onclick="doCalc('salesItems','outputParagraph')">
  Calculate</button>
</p>

</body>
</html>
```

This is the HTML page for a version of the ice cream sales program that automatically generates the input paragraphs. The paragraphs will be generated by the doBuildSalesInputItems method, which is connected to the onload event. We first saw the onload event in Chapter 3 in the "Create a ticking clock" section when we used onload to start the clock ticking when the clock page was loaded.

For the ice cream sales application, the onload event will trigger the creation of the input items when the page is loaded. The input items will be added as children of the div element with the salesItems ID. A div element is an HTML element that is used to group things. We first saw div in Chapter 3 in the "Formatting parts of a document using div and span" section.

```
doBuildSalesInputItems ('salesItems',0, 10000, 6);
```

The doBuildSalesInputItems function is called with four arguments:

1. **The ID string of the element that will contain the input items to be created.** The input items will be added to the children of that element.

2. **The minimum value that can be input to this element.** This value is used to create the input element. In the case of our application, the smallest number of sales is 0.

3. **The maximum value that can be input to this element.** In the case of our application, the customer has said that sales of more than 10,000 are impossible.

4. **The number of input paragraphs that are to be created.** The statement above will create six input elements.

Now that we've seen how the `doBuildSalesInputItems` function is called, let's look at the function code itself.

```
function doBuildSalesInputItems(containerElementID, min, max, noOfItems)
{                                                          Find the container element
    var containerElement =  document.getElementById(containerElementID);
                                                     Loop round for each item to be added
    for(let itemCount=1; itemCount<=noOfItems; itemCount=itemCount+1){
        let labelText="Sales "+itemCount;                    Build the label for the item
        let itemPar=makeInputPar(labelText, min, max);    Get the paragraph to be added
        containerElement.appendChild(itemPar);          Add the paragraph to the container
    }
}
```

The function uses a `for` loop to generate each input paragraph in turn by calling the function `makeInputPar`. The end point of the loop is determined by the `noOfItems` parameter. The values of the `min` and `max` parameters are passed into the function `makeInputPar`. Let's have a look at how this works.

Create an input paragraph

The program must build the HTML elements into which the user will enter the data. I've created this as a function so that we can use it anywhere we want to read a value from a user. Figure 8-3 shows the display that the input paragraph should produce. This reads in the sales for ice cream stand number 1.

The HTML that describes this input paragraph is shown below:

```
<p>
    <label class="menuLabel" for="s1SalesText">Stand 1 sales (0-10000):</label>
    <input class="menuInput" type="number" id="s1SalesText" value="0" min="0" max="10000">
</p>
```

The input paragraph is composed of a label element that contains the Stand 1 sales (0-10000) label and an input element to receive the data. The label and the input elements are assigned style classes to make it easy to manage their appearance. The input element has `min` and `max` attributes that are used by the browser to limit the values that the user can enter.

In our first version of this application, the input paragraphs were defined in the HTML file for the application. There were six such paragraphs, one for each of the ice cream stands. However, we can simplify the application by using JavaScript to make the input paragraphs.

```
function makeInputPar(labelText, min, max) {                    Create the enclosing paragraph
    let inputPar = document.createElement("p");                       Create the input label
                                                                        Add the max and
                                                                         min to the label
    let labelElement = document.createElement("label");
    labelElement.innerText = labelText + " (" + min + "-" + max + "):";
    labelElement.className = "menuLabel";                     Set the style class for the label
    labelElement.setAttribute("for", labelText);                   Connect the input label
    inputPar.appendChild(labelElement);                         Add the label to paragraph
    let inputElement = document.createElement("input");          Create the input element
    inputElement.setAttribute("max", max);                       Set the maximum value
    inputElement.setAttribute("min", min);                       Set the minimum value
    inputElement.setAttribute("value", 0);                       Set the initial value to 0
    inputElement.setAttribute("type", "number");               Set the input type to number
    inputElement.className = "menuInput";                     Set the style class for the input
    inputElement.setAttribute("id", labelText);               Set the ID to connect to the label
    inputPar.appendChild(inputElement);              Add the input to the enclosing paragraph

    return inputPar;
}
```

The function `makeInputPar` uses the `createElement` function provided by the `document` object to create a paragraph element (`inputPar`) and give the paragraph two child elements. The children are a label element (`labelElement`) and an input element (`inputElement`). The `makeInputPar` function is supplied with three parameters:

1. The label to be used for the input

2. The maximum input value

3. The minimum input value

A program could make the input element for the first ice cream stand by making the following call:

```
var stand1input = makeInputPar("Sales 1", 0, 10000);
```

However, we are not going to do this because we are using a loop to create the inputs and add them to a container.

CODE ANALYSIS

Input generation

We can see this input generation in action by using the JavaScript console. We might also have some questions about it. Start by opening the application in the **Ch08 Storing data\ Ch08-04 Input Generation** folder in the example code. This application contains an HTML page which has been generated by the `doBuildSalesInputItems` function. Open the Developer View by pressing F12.

Question: Can we look at the HTML that was generated by the `doBuildSalesInputItems` function?

> **Answer:** Yes we can. If we click the **Elements** tab in the Developer View it will display a view of the document object. We can then open up the view to see the HTML for each element.

Question: Can we add another input element to the document from the console?

> **Answer:** Yes, we can. Click the **Console** tab to open the console. First, we need a reference to the container element that holds the input paragraphs. Type in the following and press Enter:

```
> var containerElement = document.getElementById('salesItems');
```

Next, we need to create a new input item. The function `makeInputPar` will do this for us. We will look at how this function works in the next section. Call the function to make a new input item called "New Sales" with a min of 1 and a max of 99:

```
> var newPar=makeInputPar("New Sales", 1, 99);
```

Now that we have our new paragraph, the next thing we do is add it to the children of the container element:

```
> containerElement.appendChild(newPar);
```

This adds our newly created paragraph to the page. You should see it appear. It will have the label "New Sales" and an input range of 1 to 99.

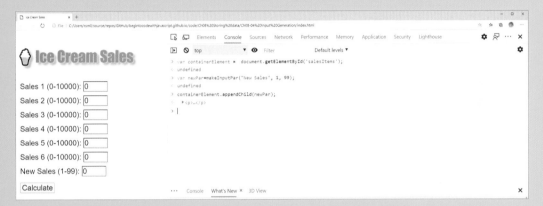

Above, you can see the new element (with the caption "New Sales") that has been added at the bottom of the list.

Question: How would I increase the number of ice cream stands?

Answer: Using a loop to generate the page makes it very easy to change the number of ice cream stands. If you take a look at the HTML code you will find the call of the function doBuildSalesInputItems. The final argument of this call is the number of stands to be created, which is presently six. If we want to handle 12 stands, we just have to change the HTML to reflect this. We don't need to make any changes to the JavaScript program.

```
doBuildSalesInputItems('salesItems',0, 10000, 6);
```

Now we need to move on to how we can make a JavaScript program that can process the data that has been entered. To do that, we need to write some code to create a sales array from the contents of the input elements in the document.

Read back the values

In the previous version of the ice cream program, we had a separate statement that created an array element for each sales value. Below is the statement that got the sales for the initial two ice cream stands.

```
sales[0] = getNumberFromElement("s0SalesText");
sales[1] = getNumberFromElement("s1SalesText");
```

If the customer added more stands, we would then have to modify the program and add more statements. For 12 ice cream stands, we would need 12 of these statements. There is a better way to do this. We can use a loop to read the values from the HMTL elements. The loop will work through all the input paragraphs on the page. The input paragraphs are children of the sales item element.

Figure 8-4 shows how these elements are structured. On the left, we have the `div` element with the ID `salesElements` that contains all the elements. The `div` element contains six paragraphs, one for each ice cream stand. The first paragraph gets the input for ice cream stand 1. It contains a `label` and an `input` item. To get the user input, the program must work through the sales items and extract the data from the input element.

```
▼<div id="salesItems">
  ▼<p>
     <label class="menuLabel" for="Sales 1">Sales 1 (0-10000):</label>
     <input max="10000" min="0" value="0" class="menuInput" id="Sales 1">
  </p>
  ▶<p>...</p>
  ▶<p>...</p>
  ▶<p>...</p>
  ▶<p>...</p>
  ▶<p>...</p>
</div>
```

Figure 8-4   Input paragraphs

The program can use a `for-of` loop to work through the children and extract the value of each item. The code above shows how this works.

```
var sales = [];                                              Create an empty array
var salesPos = 0;                                   Start at the beginning of the array

var salesElement = document.getElementById('salesItems');    Get a reference to the element
                                                             containing the sales items

for (let item of salesElement.children) {           Work through the children of this element

    let salesValue = getNumberFromElement(item.children[1]);    Get the number from the
                                                                input element

    sales[salesPos] = salesValue;                   Store the number in the array

    salesPos = salesPos + 1;                         Move on to the next element in the array
}
```

Reading numbers

Question: What is this code doing?

Answer: Good question. When the user presses the **Calculate** button, they have just typed in the sales values and want to see the total, highest, and lowest values displayed. The first thing the program needs to do is get the values out the input elements on the page and into the sales array. The input elements are children of the paragraphs that are themselves children of the `salesItems` element. Think of the `salesItem` element as a grandfather element. The grandfather has six children. These are the paragraphs that were generated when the page was built. Each of the six children has two more children, which are the label and the input elements.

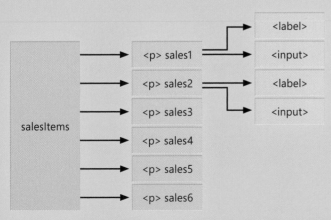

The `for-of` loop will work through each of the child elements of the `salesItems` container. Each time around the loop, the variable `item` refers the next paragraph element in the `salesItems`. Each paragraph element contains two children: the label for the input and the input itself. The input element that we need is the second child of the sales paragraph, which will have index number 1 (because indexes always start at 0).

```
let salesValue = getNumberFromElement(item.children[1]);
```

This version of the `getNumberFromElement` function is supplied with a reference to the element it is reading, so it fetches the value input and returns the result as a number.

Question: What happens if the input element contains an invalid value?

> **Answer:** The input element contains max and min attributes that are used by `getNumberFromElement` to validate the number that the user types in. If the number the user has entered is outside this range, or the user has not entered a number, the `getNumberFromElement` function returns a result of Not a Number (NaN).

Question: Would I have to change this code if we added more ice cream stands?

> **Answer:** No. That's the great thing about this loop. It will work through any number of input paragraphs.

 MAKE SOMETHING HAPPEN

Use the debugger to see code run

You might be finding the code above a little hard to follow. You might be thinking that it would be wonderful to be able to watch it execute and see what each statement does. It turns out that you can do just that by using the *debugger* which is built into the Developer View in the browser. In this case we are not debugging the program because there's something wrong with it; we just want to see how it works. Start by opening the application in the **Ch08 Storing data\Ch08-04 Input Generation** folder in the example code. This application contains an HTML page which has been generated by the `doBuildSalesInputItems` function. Enter some sales figures for the ice cream stands and then open the Developer View by pressing F12. Select the **Sources** tab in the Developer View.

The **Sources** tab will show you all the files that make up the application. Note that the browser display that you see might not match the one above. I've changed the arrangement of the windows in the browser and zoomed in on the Developer View to make it clearer for the book. However, you can drag the window borders around to get a similar view.

We want to take a look at the JavaScript code which is in the file `icecreamsales.js`. Click this file name (it is highlighted in darker gray in the figure above).

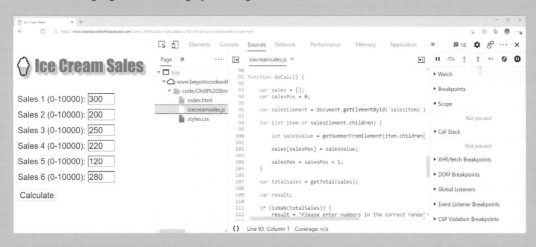

The Sources view now shows us the JavaScript code in a window. Use the scroll bars to move down the code to find the `doCalc` function. This function is called from the HTML when the Calculate button is pressed. We are going to put a *breakpoint* at the first statement of this function. When the program reaches the breakpoint, it will "takes a break." It will pause and we will be able to investigate what the function is doing and even run through the statements one at a time. We set a breakpoint by clicking just to the left of the line number in the listing.

```
91  function doCalc() {
92
93      var sales = [];
94      var salesPos = 0;
95
```

The display will show a red dot at that position as shown above. Click to add a breakpoint. If you click in the wrong place, you can remove a breakpoint by clicking the red dot. Once you have set the breakpoint, click the **Calculate** button in the application to run the function. The browser will call the `doCalc` function and then pause when it hits the breakpoint.

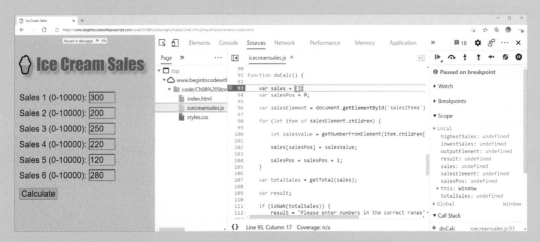

The program is paused at the statement where we set the breakpoint. You can see it high-lighted in blue. We can use the transport controls to make the program run one statement at a time.

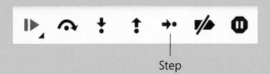

Step

The transport controls look a bit like Egyptian hieroglyphics. They are in the top right-hand area of the screen in my browser, but they might be somewhere else on yours. We will find out more about each control as we go. For now, we want to use the **Step** control, which is indicated above. Click this, and the program will execute the indicated statement and then move on to the next one.

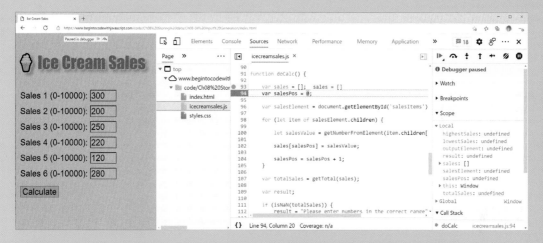

Note that the content of the `sales` array is shown for you. If you press the Step button again you are shown the contents of the `salePos` variable. You can keep pressing the button (or use the function key F9) to step through the program. You can watch the program get a reference to the sales element and then enter the `for` loop, which will work through the elements. When the program calls the `getElement` function you will find that the view moves into that function and you step through the statements in that.

```
62  function getNumberFromElement(element) {   element = input#Sales 1.menuInp
63
64      var text = element.value;   text = "300", element = input#Sales 1.menu
65
66      var result = Number(text);   result = 300, text = "300"
67
68      if (isNaN(result)) {
69          // fail with bad number input
70          element.className = "menuInputError";
71          return NaN;
72      }
```

The `getNumberFromElement` function reads the text from an input element and converts it into a number. Here, you can see that the text is 300 as a string, and the result is 300 as a value. If you look back at the application you will find that the first sale value is 300.

You can use another transport button to step out of the `getNumberFromElement` function and return to where it was called.

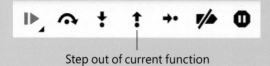

Step out of current function

When you have seen enough you can press the transport control that resumes normal program execution. If you leave the breakpoint set, you will find that if you press the **Calculate** button in the application, it will stop at the breakpoint the next time around.

Continue running

You can spend as much time as you like working through code. You can also use this technique to put breakpoints in any of the other sample programs and watch what they do, too.

Now that you know how the program works, you can make the change that adds two new ice cream stands to the system. The good news is that you only have to change the value 6 to the value 8 somewhere in the application. You can find my version in the examples in the **Ch08 Storing data\Ch08-05 Eight Stand Version** folder.

Your customer has had another idea. Rather than the application asking for the sales of Stand 1, she would like the application to show named locations, as shown in **Figure 8-5**.

Ice Cream Sales

Riverside Walk (0-10000): [0]

City Plaza (0-10000): [0]

Central Park (0-10000): [0]

Zoo Entrance (0-10000): [0]

Main Library (0-10000): [0]

North Station (0-10000): [0]

New Theatre (0-10000): [0]

Movie House (0-10000): [0]

[Calculate]

Figure 8-5 Named stands

Arrays as lookup tables

This looks like it might be quite hard to achieve, but it turns out that we can use arrays to help. In this case, we are going to use an array to hold a list of place names. When we first created an array, we used the following statement:

```
var newArray=[];
```

The characters [and] mark the start and end of the array that is being created. This statement creates an empty array, because there is nothing between the [and the]. We set the values into an array when we create it by putting values here:

```
var newArray=[1,2];
```

This statement creates an array called newArray that contains two numbers. The element at the start of the array contains the value 1, and the next element contains the value 2. This statement is exactly equivalent to these three:

```
var newArray=[];
newArray[0]=1;
newArray[1]=2;
```

We can also create arrays of strings. Consider the following statement:

```
var standNames = ['Riverside Walk','City Plaza','Central Park','Zoo Entrance',
    'Main Library','North Station','New Theatre','Movie House'];
```

This statement creates a variable called standNames that contains the names of all the stands. The item on the right of the assignment is the actual array. We can also use arrays like this in function calls:

```
doBuildSalesInputItems('salesItems',0, 10000,
    ['Riverside Walk', 'City Plaza', 'Central Park', 'Zoo Entrance',
    'Main Library','North Station','New Theatre','Movie House']);
```

This statement calls the function `doBuildSalesItems`. The final parameter to this call is an array that contains the names of all the ice cream stand locations. This version of the function can then use these names to build the HTML page:

```
function doBuildSalesInputItems(containerElementID, min, max, placeNames) {
    var containerElement = document.getElementById(containerElementID);
                                                    Get the container that will hold the items
    for (placeName of placeNames) {                 Work through the place names
        let itemPar = makeInputPar(placeName, min, max);  Create an input par
        containerElement.appendChild(itemPar);      Add the input par to the children in
                                                    the container
    }
}
```

Rather than creating the name "Sales x," where x is the number of the stand, this version of the function just works through the place names and feeds each name in turn into the `makeInputPar` function. The function `doBuildSalesInputItems` is called from the HTML when the page is loaded by the browser. The function call is triggered by the `onload` event:

```
<body onload="var standNames = doBuildSalesInputItems('salesItems',0, 10000,
    ['Riverside Walk', 'City Plaza', 'Central Park','Zoo Entrance',
     'Main Library','North Station','New Theatre','Movie House']);">
```

The text above comes from the HTML file for the application. The `body` element can contain an attribute called `onload`, which contains a string of JavaScript to be obeyed when the page is loaded by the browser. For this application, the string of JavaScript calls the `doBuildInputSalesItems` to create the input paragraphs for the sales values. You can find this function used in the example program in the **Ch08 Storing data\ Ch08-06 Named Stands** folder.

Creating named ice cream stands

This is all rather clever stuff. But you might have some questions:

Question: What is passed into a function when an array is used as an argument to a function?

> **Answer:** The parameter in the function is a reference to the array. This means that if the function changes the contents of the array (by assigning something to a value in the array or by adding a new element on the end of the array), this will change the array because there is only ever one copy of the array itself. Consider this function:

```
function changeArrayElement(inputArray)
{
    inputArray[0]=99;
}
```

> The function `changeArrayElemenent` has a single parameter, which is an array. It changes the value in the start of the array to 99.

```
var testArray = [0];
```

> This statement creates an array called `testArray`, which contains a single element that is set to the value 0.

```
changeArrayElement(testArray);
```

> This statement calls the `changeArray` method and gives it `testArray` as an argument. The question that we need to consider is: "What is the value in element 0 of `testArray` after the call of `changeArrayElement`?" The answer is that it contains 99 because the parameter to the function is a reference to the array. When the function runs, the reference is used to find the array and change the element in it. If you think about it, passing arrays by reference makes very good sense. Otherwise, a program would have to make a copy of an array to pass into a function call.

Question: How would I add another ice cream stand location to the application?

> **Answer:** This application design means that to add another stand to the application, we just have to add the name of the new stand to the array value that is passed into the call of `doBuildInputSalesItems`. The JavaScript code does not have to be changed at all.

Question: Can an array hold numbers and strings in different elements?

Answer: Yes, it can. You can regard each element of an array as a totally separate variable that can hold any value. It can be confusing if you use arrays in this way, so in the next chapter, we will discover how to design variables that collections of items of different types.

Question: What is the maximum size of an array?

Answer: An array can be very, very large. There is a limit, which will be determined by the amount of memory inside the computer running JavaScript. Modern computers have huge amounts of memory, so it is really unlikely that your program will ever have a problem with array size being too large.

Creating fixed width layouts

If you run the program in the **Ch08 Storing data\Ch08-06 Named Stands** folder, you will notice that it works perfectly well, but the layout of the input elements is not very consistent, as you can see in **Figure 8-6**.

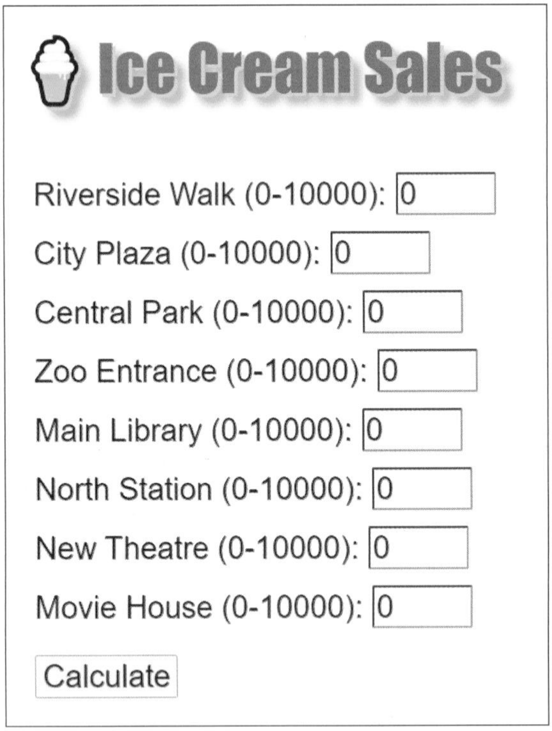

Figure 8-6   Poor layout

The input elements are not lined up vertically because the names of the different locations are of different lengths. This is not a programming problem, so we don't need to make changes to the JavaScript, but it would be useful to be able to modify the style of the labels for each item so that they are the same size.

```css
.menuLabel {
    display:inline-block;
    width:12em;
    margin: 10px;
}
```

> **Display this element as a block inline with the text**
>
> **Set the width of the block to 12 characters**

The CSS text above is the definition of the `menuLabel` style class, which is used to style the menu label (hence the name). I've added two new attributes to the style definition. The first tells the browser that this element is a block that should be displayed inline with enclosing elements. The second item sets the width of the element to 12 characters. If we make these changes to the style sheet, the input display matches what the customer requested in Figure 8-6. You can find this version of the application in the **Ch08 Storing data\Ch08-07 Named Stands fixed width** example folder.

MAKE SOMETHING HAPPEN

Highlight the best and worst sales locations

Your customer (who, by now, has given you a lot of ice cream) has one final request. She would like the program to highlight the best and worst sales locations in the display. She would like the highest sales to be highlighted yellow and the lowest to be highlighted in blue.

Hint: to do this the program must make a second pass through the sales elements after it has determined the highest and lowest values. Any sales elements with a sales value that matches the highest can be assigned a yellow style class. Any sales elements with a sales value that matches the lowest can be assigned a blue style class. This is the best way to do it because it is possible to have several sales values that are the highest or the lowest. You can find my version in the examples in the folder **Ch08 Storing data\Ch08-08 Highlight High and Low**.

Interactive Multiplication Tables Tester

Multiplication Table Tester

1 times 13 is: `13`

2 times 13 is: `26`

3 times 13 is: `39`

4 times 13 is: `52`

5 times 13 is: `65`

6 times 13 is: `68`

Which multiplication table do you want : `13`

How many lines do you want : `6`

`Make the multiplication table`   Check the multiplication table

We can use our new skills to improve the multiplication table tester application that we created in Chapter 6. The version above generates a multiplication table for any value and then checks what the user enters. You can find the working application in the **Ch08 Storing data\ Ch08-08 Multiplication Table Tester** example folder.

It has been suggested that the program could be improved if it displayed the scores at the end:

You got 2 correct out of 6

To make this work, you have to add a new paragraph to the HTML to display the result and then work through the program to find out where the table is scored. Have a go yourself and then take a look at my version in the **Ch08 Storing data\Ch08-09 Multiplication Table Tester with scores** example folder.

What you have learned

In this chapter, you discovered how a program can use arrays to store large amounts of data. You've also built on your knowledge of how a JavaScript program can generate document elements and display them.

1. A variable can be declared as an array and acts as a container for multiple values. Each value in an array is stored in an element, and a particular element can be identified by an index value. An index is sometimes called a *subscript*.

2. Elements in an array with a particular index value are created when a value is assigned to that element. There is no need to specify the size of an array when it is created.

3. An array value exposes a length property that gives the number of elements in the array.

4. Element index values start at 0 and extend up to the value of (length-1). This range of index values is called the *bounds* of the array. There is no element with an index value of the length of the array.

5. If a program uses an index value outside the bounds of the array, a value of `undefined` is returned.

6. A program can use the `for-of` loop construction to work through the elements in an array. A program can also work through elements of an array by creating a variable that counts through the index values in the array.

7. An array with a number of elements can be created using a single statement.

8. Inputs in an HTML document can be assigned `label` elements that display a prompt for that input.

9. The Developer Console in the browser can be used to step through JavaScript programs and view the contents of variables held in them.

Here are some questions that you might like to ponder about the use of functions in programs:

How do I find out the size of an array?

An array variable provides a property called `length`, which contains the number of elements in the array.

Does every element in an array have to be the same kind of data?

No. An array can contain numbers, strings, and references to other objects.

Do I have to put a value into every element?

No. For example, you could create an element with index 0 and another element with index 5. All the elements in the middle (meaning those with index values 1, 2, 3, and 4) would be set to `undefined`.

Can I store a table of data as an array?

A JavaScript array has only one dimension—the length of the array. You can think of it as a row. Some programming languages allow you to create "two-dimensional arrays." You can think of these as a grid with width and height. JavaScript does not allow you to create two-dimensional arrays. However, you could create a table data structure by creating an array that has an array as each element.

What happens to my program if I used an index value outside the range of the array?

If the program is storing data in this location, the array will be extended to hold the value at the new index. If the program is reading data from this location, the array access will return the value undefined.

Can I use indexes on other data items?

Yes. You can use an index to obtain the individual characters in a string.

What happens if I don't initialize the elements in a new array?

Any elements that you don't initialize are set to the `undefined` value.

What happens if I add two arrays together using the + operator?

It would be nice if adding two arrays together created a long array with one set of elements appended to the other. Unfortunately, this does not happen. Instead Java JavaScript creates the string version of each array and then appends one string to the other. However, JavaScript array objects provide a `concat` method that can be used to concatenate (add) an array onto the end of another.

Can I use an image as a label for an input item?

Yes, you can. The content of a label can be an image or some text and an image.

What is the difference between the children of an HTML element and a JavaScript array?

They are implemented in slightly different ways, but you can use an index to access values in each, and they both expose a length property. You can also use the `for-of` loop construction to work through the elements in either.

Can I use an array to allow a function to return more than one value?

What a good question. Yes, a program can return an array, which can contain multiple values. However, the function and the caller would have to agree on what was in each of the array elements. In the next chapter, we will discover a much neater way of creating objects that contain named data items.

Can I use the JavaScript debugger to debug the JavaScript in any web page?

Yes. If you press F12 when viewing your favorite web page, you can then open up the JavaScript files and take a look at them.

9
Objects

What you will learn

Programs can work with many different types of data, including integers, floating-point numbers, and strings of text. They can also create arrays of a particular data type. However, the data that programs need to work with is often more complex than single values. In this chapter, you'll learn how to use objects to store related data items. You will discover how software can create custom objects, and you will have your first go at solving a real computing problem.

Make a tiny contacts app

Suppose one of your friends is a lawyer who wants someone to create a personal contacts app. The client wants a tiny, "lightweight" application to provide a quick way of storing contact details—names, addresses, and telephone numbers—for her important clients. You sit down with her and decide how the application will work:

Figure 9-1 shows how the application will look. It has three text boxes for data entry and two buttons. When the Save Contact button is pressed, the data entered into the text boxes is stored. To find a contact, the user enters the name and then presses the Find Contact button. The program then searches the contact store for a contact with that name. If the contact is found, the program displays the address and phone number information. If the contact is not found, the program displays an alert, as shown in **Figure 9-2**.

Figure 9-1   Tiny Contacts prototype

Figure 9-2   Contact not found

Prototype HTML

The best way to show the lawyer what her program will look like is to create a prototype that behaves in the same way as the finished product. We can do this by creating an HTML page and then adding just enough JavaScript to allow us to demonstrate how the program will be used.

```html
<!DOCTYPE html>
<html lang="en">

<head>
  <title>Tiny Contacts</title>
  <link rel="stylesheet" href="styles.css">
  <script src="tinycontacts.js"></script>
</head>

<body>
  <p class="menuHeading"> &#128199; Tiny Contacts</p>

  <p>
    <label class="inputLabel" for="name">Name:</label>
    <input class="inputText" id="name">
  </p>

  <p>
    <label class="inputLabel" for="address">Address:</label>
    <textarea class="inputTextarea" rows="5" cols="40" id="address"></textarea>
  </p>

  <p>
    <label class="inputLabel" for="phone">Phone:</label>
    <input class="inputText" id="phone">
  </p>

  <p>
    <button class="menuButton" onclick="doFind()">Find Contact</button>
    <button class="menuButton" onclick="doSave()">Save Contact</button>
  </p>

</body>

</html>
```

The style sheet for the application

The JavaScript program for the application

Call doFind to find a contact

Call doSave to save a contact

This is the HTML for the prototype application. It defines the three input areas and the two buttons. There is one new element on this page—the `textarea` element.

The `textarea` element

If you look at Figure 9-1, you will see that the address of a contact can be entered as multiple lines of text. We can't use an `input` element to read multi-line text because an input element only supports a single line. A `textarea` is configured by two attributes called `rows` and `cols`, which define the size of the data entry area on the screen. The Tiny Contacts application uses an area that has 5 rows and 40 columns.

```
<textarea class="inputTextarea" rows="5" cols="40" id="address"></textarea>
```

The `textarea` will display a scroll bar if the user enters more than five lines of text, and a `textarea` will automatically wrap text if the user types off the end of the line. A JavaScript program can use the `value` property of a `textarea` to interact with the content of the text area.

Prototype style sheet

The HTML file contains the elements that make up the application display. The CSS (Cascading Style Sheet) file controls how the display will look. Your customer would like a clean black and white display, so you propose this style sheet:

```
.menuHeading {
    font-size: 4em;
    font-family: Impact, Haettenschweiler, 'Arial Narrow Bold', sans-serif;
    color: black;
    text-shadow: 3px 3px blue, 10px 10px 10px grey;   Style class for the application heading
}


.inputLabel,.inputText, .inputTextarea, .menuButton
{                                         These settings are applied to all the text style classes
    font-family:Arial, Helvetica, sans-serif;
    font-size: 2em;
    color:black;
}


.inputLabel
{                                         These settings are only applied to the label style classes
```

```
display:inline-block;──────────────────────── Make the label into an inline block
vertical-align: top;────────────────────────── Put the text at the top of the block
width:6em;──────────────────────────────────────── Fix the width of the label
}
```

The CSS file defines a style for the heading. It then contains settings shared by all the other text styles in the document, followed by settings, which are only applied to the labels. This makes it easy to change the font, size, or color of all of the text. It also makes it possible for a designer to change the style of any element on the page without changing the HTML file at all.

Prototype JavaScript

The third component of the tiny contacts application is the JavaScript that provides the behaviors. The prototype application doesn't do much. It just displays contact information if the user searches for "Rob Miles" and displays `Contact not found` if the user searches for any other name. The Save Contact button just displays an alert when it is pressed.

```
function displayElementValue(id, text){──── Display the text in the element with the specified ID
    var element = document.getElementById(id);
    element.value = text;
}


function getElementValue(id){──────────── Get the data value from the element with the specified ID
    var element = document.getElementById(id);
    return element.value;
}


function doSave() {────────────────────────────── Save the contact details
    alert("Saves a contact in the store");
}

function doFind() {──────────────────────────────────── Find a contact
    var name = getElementValue("name");──────────────── Get the name value
    if(name=="Rob Miles")──────────────────────────── Is the name "Rob Miles"
    {
        displayElementValue ("addressText", "18 Pussycat Mews\nLondon\nNE1 410S");
        displayElementValue ("phoneText", "+44(1234) 56789");
    }
```

```
    else {                                        Clear the details if the name is not "Rob Miles"
        displayContactNotFound ();
    }
}
```

You can find the prototype application in the **Ch09 Objects\Ch09-01 Tiny Contacts Prototype** sample folder. You can use it to enter and search for contact information. The application will only display output if you search for a contact named "Rob Miles," and it doesn't store any entered data. However, it's very useful for demonstrating how the application will work. Your client agrees that the application can work like this and says you can start building it.

Helper functions

If you look closely at the prototype JavaScript code, you'll notice a pair of tiny functions. I've written these to help move data between the HTML page and the application:

```
function displayElementValue(id, text){
    var element = document.getElementById(id);        Get the element being changed
    element.value = text;                             Set the value in the element
}

function getElementValue(id){
    var element = document.getElementById(id);        Get the element being read
    return element.value;                             Return the value in the element
}
```

The function `displayElementValue` accepts two arguments: the `id` of the element and the text to be displayed. It is used to display values on the HTML page. The call of the function below would display the phone number text on the page. Note that although the phone number is described as a number, the data itself is a string of text.

```
displayElementValue("phoneText", "+44(1234) 56789")
```

The function `getElementValue` accepts a single argument: the `id` of the input element to be read. The call of the function below would get the name that had been entered into the HTML page and store it in a variable called `name`.

```
var name = getElementValue("name");
```

You might wonder why I wrote such small functions. They don't make the program much smaller. If I were to write the application without these functions, it would only add a few statements. However, I think they do make the program much clearer because the functions express exactly what is being done without the distraction of how they work. For example, consider the function that is called when contact information is not found. At the time the function is called, we can tell from the name of the function exactly what the program is doing.

```
function displayContactNotFound()
{
    alert("Not found");
}
```

Another advantage of using a function like this is that it makes it easy to change what the program does when a contact is not found. If the customer says that she would like a sound to be produced when the item is not found, we can just add this to the `displayContactNotFound` function without having to work through the entire program to find the code that deals with finding contacts.

Storing contact details

Now that the customer has agreed how the program should work and we have built the HTML page and style sheet files, we can start to create the code. However, before we can write the code to save a contact, we need to decide how the contact information will be stored. There will be lots of contacts. When we wrote the ice cream sales application, we used an array to hold the sales information. One way to store the contact details would be to use three arrays: one for the name, one for the address, and third for the phone number:

```
var contactNames = [];
var contactAddresses = [];
var contactPhones = [];
```

The data for a contact would be held in array elements with a particular index value. In other words, contactNames[0] would hold the name of the contact at the start of the storage, contactAddresses[0] would hold the address, and contactPhones[0] would hold the phone number. **Figure 9-3** shows how this works.

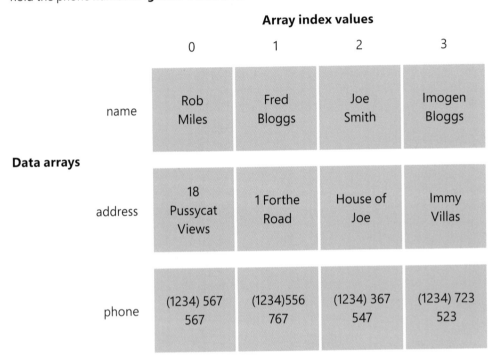

Figure 9-3 Array storage

The elements at index 0 in each array hold the details for Rob Miles. We can use the elements at a given index to build up a set of contact information for a specific person. For example, Imogen Bloggs lives at Immy Villas and has a phone number of (1234) 723523. We can write a function that stores a contact at a particular index position in all the arrays:

```
function storeContact(pos){
    contactNames[pos] = getElementValue("name");       Store the name
    contactAddresses[pos] = getElementValue("address");   Store the address
    contactPhones[pos] = getElementValue("phone");     Store the phone number
}
```

The function `storeContact` accepts an argument that gives the position in the array. This is where the contact will be stored. In other words, if the value of the argument is 0 the contact will be stored at the start of the storage.

Each statement in the function fetches data from an element on the HTML page and stores it at the given index in the array that holds the data for that type of data. Remember that a JavaScript program automatically creates an array element at the specified index when the program stores a value in that element. The first contact will be stored at the element with index 0 (remember that arrays are indexed from 0). The next will be stored at index 1 and so on. The statement below saves contact information on the HTML page into the elements at the start of the array.

```
storeContact(0);
```

Finding contacts

Now that we know how to store contact information, the next thing we can work on is finding it. The customer wants to be able to search for contacts by name. We need something that works through the stored contacts and finds the position of the one we want to display. In other words, if asked to find the entry for "Joe Smith" in the contact store shown in Figure 9-3, it would return the value 2.

```
function findContactPos(name) {
    for(let pos=0; pos<contactNames.length; pos= pos+1){       Count through the array elements
        if(contactNames[pos]==name) {          See if the stored name matches the parameter
            return pos;                         If the name matches return the index value
        }
    }
    return NaN;                        Return Not a Number (NaN) if the name was not found
}
```

The `findContactPos` returns the position in the array of the contact with the name supplied as a parameter. It uses a `for` loop to work through the `contactNames` array, comparing each element in the array with the name it is searching for.

The `findContacts` function

The `findContacts` function is a very important part of the application. You might have some questions about it.

Question: What does the `for` loop do?

> **Answer:** The function must look at each element in the `contactNames` array to see if it matches the name the function is searching for. If I asked you to search through a row of pigeonholes to find the one with my name on it, you'd start at the first pigeonhole, check its name, and then move on to the next one if there was no match. The `for` loop controls the contents of a variable called `pos` (an abbreviation for "position"). The value of `pos` starts at 0, and the loop ends when the value in `pos` reaches the length of the array.

Question: What would happen if the `contactNames` array is empty when the `findContacts` function is called?

> **Answer:** The loop only runs as long as the value of `pos` is less than the length of the array. An empty array has a length of 0. The initial value of `pos` is set to 0 when the loop is set up. This means that the loop is never performed if the array is empty because 0 is not less than 0.

Question: What happens when a match is found for the name being searched?

> **Answer:** When the program finds a matching name, the value of the index variable is returned to the caller. This is the position in the array of the name.

```
var pos = findContactPos("Fred Bloggs");
```

> For example, using the data store in Figure 9-3, the above statement would create a variable called `pos`, which would be set to 1 by the call of `findContactPos`.

Question: What does the `findContactPos` function do if the name is not found in the `contactNames` array?

> **Answer:** If the name is not found in the array, the `for` loop will complete without finding a match. The program would then move on to the statement after the `for` loop, which returns the value Not a Number (NaN) to indicate that the name was not found. It is perfectly sensible for a function to contain more than one return statement. Note that it is up to the program calling `findContactPos` to check to see if the name was found.

This type of search behavior is common in systems that you use every day. Whenever you use a credit card to pay for something, the bank's computer will use the credit card number to search for your bank account information so that the transaction can be authorized and added to your statement.

Displaying contacts

The final function that we need is one that displays the contact on the HTML page. This function is given a position in the contacts store and displays the elements in each array at that position. It uses the displayElementValue function that we saw earlier to display each item:

```
function displayContact(pos){
    displayElementValue("name", contactNames[pos]);
    displayElementValue("address", contactAddresses[pos]);
    displayElementValue("phone", contactPhones[pos]);
}
```

Saving a contact

The final pieces of code that we need are the functions that respond to the button presses in the application. When the user clicks the Save Contact button, the function doSave is called by the browser. This function must work in two different ways:

1. It must create a new contact store for a new contact.

2. It must update the contact information for an existing contact.

The doSave function gets the contact name from the web page and then uses the findContactPos function to see if the contact store already contains someone with that name. The findContactPos returns a value, which is stored in a variable called pos. If the value of pos that is returned is not a number (NaN), the function sets the value of pos to the length of the array, so that the contact information will be stored at the end of the array. Otherwise, the newly saved data will overwrite the existing data. I've added some comments to this code to make it clear what each section is doing.

```
function doSave() {

    // get the name of the contact being saved
    var name = getElementValue("name");
```

```
    // find the position of the name to save
    var pos = findContactPos(name);

    if(isNaN(pos)){
        // if we didn't find an existing contact name
        // we store the contact on the end of the array
        pos = contactNames.length;
    }

    storeContact(pos);
}
```

CODE ANALYSIS

The doSave function

The doSave function implements the editing behavior of the application. You might have some questions about it.

Question: Why does the findContactPos function sometimes return NaN?

Answer: We know that the JavaScript language provides a variable value called "not a number" or NaN. This is used by JavaScript itself. If we ask the JavaScript Number function to convert the string Fred into a numeric value, it will return NaN. In the Tiny Contacts application, I'm using the value NaN in the findContactPos function to indicate that a position could not be found. If I asked you to search through a row of pigeonholes to find the one with my name on it, and you couldn't find it, you'd say: "Sorry, Rob. I can't find it." The value NaN is how findContactPos indicates that it couldn't find what it had been asked to look for. I could have used a different flag value if I wanted, such as –1 (which would not be meaningful as an index into an array). This form of notification relies on the user of a function checking the reply of the function. Later in this book, we will look at ways that a program can explicitly stop running by raising an exception when things go wrong.

Question: What does the function use the length of the contactNames array for?

Answer: If the findContactPos function indicates that it can't find a contact with that name (which it does by returning NaN), this means that the store does not contain a contact with this name. The contact information must be stored in a new location. When the program is first run, the length of the array is 0, so the first contact will be stored at element 0, which is the start of the array; the next contact will be stored at element 1 (because the length of the array is now 1); and so on.

Question: What happens if the user changes the name of a contact and then saves it?

Answer: This is a very good question. It points to a potential bug in the application. We can answer the question by working through the code with an example. If the user opens a contact called "Rob," changes the name to "Rob Miles," and then presses the Save Contact button, what will the doSave function do? The function will fail to find a contact with the name "Rob Miles," and then it will create a new contact with that name. This could be dangerous because there would now be two contact entries for the same contact. If the user searches for the old name by mistake, they might see data that is out of date.

This kind of issue crops up frequently when software is being created. As you write the program code, you discover questions that you didn't consider when you discussed the design of the application. The only way to resolve this issue is to ask the customer what she wants to happen. She says that she will never need to change the name of a contact, so she is okay with the program being left as it is.

Finding a contact

The doFind function runs when the user clicks the Find Contact button. It can use the findContactPos function to search for a contact with a name that matches the one entered. If a contact is found, the contact contents are displayed. If a contact is not found, the function must display a message:

```
function doFind() {

    var name = getElementValue("name");

    var pos = findContactPos(name);

    if(isNaN(pos)){
        displayContactNotFound();
    }
    else{
        displayContact(pos);
    }
}
```

You can find the complete application in the **Ch09 Objects\Ch09-02 Array Tiny Contacts** folder. If you try it, you will discover that it works fine. You can enter contact details, save them, and search for them.

Use an object to store contact details

As you've seen, we can create a perfectly workable Tiny Contacts application by using a list for each piece of information we want to store for our contact. However, working with data stored in this way is not as easy as we might like. If we ever add a new data item for a contact (perhaps we want to add their email address), we would need to add a new list and then make sure that items in it were managed correctly.

We want a way of holding all the information about a contact in one place. We need some kind of "container" that can hold the name, address, phone number, and any other items we want to store. One possible solution might be to use an array to store information about each customer, but this wouldn't make it very easy to access specific detail items. Instead, we'll use a JavaScript object.

You'll hear a lot about objects over the next few chapters, as they are one of the fundamental building blocks that underpin the language. You might have heard the term "object-oriented programming." Now you are going to find out what an object is and how to use it in a JavaScript program.

 MAKE SOMETHING HAPPEN

Create an object

We can start our description of objects by making some using the JavaScript console in the browser. Open the example application in the **Ch09 Objects\Ch09-03 Object Tiny Contacts** examples folder and press F12 to open the Developer View. Select the **Console** tab in the view.

In JavaScript, we can create an empty object by using a pair of open and close braces ({}). Type in the statement below and press Enter. Do not use a pair of brackets ([and])—they are for creating arrays.

```
> var contact = {};
```

The process of creating an object does not return a value, so when you press Enter, you will see a familiar undefined message:

```
> var contact = {};
<- undefined
```

As usual with the JavaScript console, you can view the contents of a variable simply by typing the name of the variable. Type in `contact` and press Enter:

```
> contact
```

JavaScript shows you that the `contact` object does not contain any properties.

```
> contact
<- {}
```

Let's add a name property to the `contact` object. Type in the statement below, which sets the `name` property of the `contact` object to the string Rob Miles. Press Enter.

```
> contact.name = "Rob Miles";
```

This is an assignment operation (that's what the = means); an assignment expression always returns the value being assigned, so JavaScript replies with the string "Rob Miles".

```
> contact.name = "Rob Miles";
<- "Rob Miles"
```

Let's take a look at what has changed in the object. Type in `contact` and press Enter to view the contents of the `contact` object:

```
> contact
```

The `contact` object contains one property which is the name of the contact.

```
> contact
<- {name: "Rob Miles"}
```

We can add a second property to the contact by setting an `address` property in exactly the same way as we added the name. Type in the statement below and press Enter.

```
> contact.address = "18 Pussycat Mews";
```

The address is added to the contact, and the console shows us the value assigned as before.

```
> contact.address = "18 Pussycat Mews";
<- "18 Pussycat Mews"
```

Type in the statement below to view the contact, and press Enter to see what has been added to the contact.

```
> contact
```

The contact object now contains a name and address. We could keep adding properties to match the requirements of our application.

```
> contact
<- {name: "Rob Miles", address = "18 Pussycat Mews}
```

Objects are managed by *reference*. In other words, the contact variable we have created refers to a location in computer memory where the contact object is stored. We can create a new variable and set it to refer to the same location as the contact variable. Type the statement below, which creates a variable called refDemo, which refers to the same object as contact. Press Enter when you've typed in the statement.

```
> var refDemo = contact;
```

Creating a new variable always returns a result of undefined, which the console will now show us.

```
> var refDemo = contact;
<- undefined
```

Now let's take a look at the object that refDemo refers to. Type in refDemo and press Enter to get the console to display the object that refDemo refers to.

```
> refDemo
```

Because refDemo refers to the same object as contact you will see the same properties displayed.

```
> refDemo
<- {name: "Rob Miles", address = "18 Pussycat Mews}
```

The refDemo variable refers to the same object as contact. We can prove this. Enter the following statement and press Enter:

```
> refDemo.name = "Rob Bloggs"
```

This statement changes the name property of the object referred to by refDemo. As with other assignments, it displays the value being assigned.

```
> refDemo.name = "Rob Bloggs";
<- "Rob Bloggs"
```

Now, view the contents of the contact variable by typing its name and pressing Enter:

```
> contact
```

Both contact and refDemo refer to the same object, so changes made via refDemo will also change the object that contact refers to.

```
> contact
<- {name: "Rob Bloggs", address = "18 Pussycat Mews}
```

The name property is now Rob Bloggs. This change was not made via the contact reference; instead, it was made via the refDemo reference.

Use an object in the Tiny Contacts program

We can use an object to simplify the Tiny Contacts program. The program now only needs a single array to hold all the contact information.

```
var contactStore = [];
```

Each of the objects in the `contactStore` array will have a set of properties that are the stored data for that contact. To make this work, we will have to modify some of the functions in our program. Rather than storing the different parts of contact data in individual arrays, the `storeContact` function now adds the elements as properties, which are added to a contact object:

```
function storeContact(pos){
    var contact = {};                                   Create an empty object
    contact.name = getElementValue("name");             Add the name
    contact.address = getElementValue("address");       Add the address
    contact.phone = getElementValue("phone");           Add the phone number
    contactStore[pos]=contact;                          Store the contact in the array
}
```

The `displayContact` function now displays the properties in a contact object rather than elements from the three arrays that store contact data.

```
function displayContact(pos){
    var contact = contactStore[pos];
    displayElementValue("name", contact.name);
    displayElementValue("address", contact.address);
    displayElementValue("phone", contact.phone);
}
```

The example program in the **Ch09 Objects\Ch09-03 Object Tiny Contacts** folder contains a version of the Tiny Contacts program that uses an object rather than separate arrays. If you take a careful look at the JavaScript code, you will discover that some of the functions are completely unchanged.

Store data in JavaScript local storage

The Tiny Contacts program works perfectly well except for one thing. There is no way of persisting the contacts data. Each time the user opens the page, it starts with an empty set of contacts. For the Tiny Contacts program to be properly useful it needs a way of storing data. Some computer languages can save and load data in the file storage on the system they are running on. A JavaScript program running inside a browser is not usually allowed to interact with files stored on the host computer. JavaScript programs are often part of pages downloaded from anywhere on the Internet, and it would be very dangerous to give these programs access to files on your computer.

However, JavaScript does provide local storage. This is managed by the browser, and our JavaScript applications can use it to store reasonable amounts of data.

You can think of local storage as a data object that is persisted by the browser on the host computer. This means that every machine has its own copy of local storage. Fortunately, our customer only has one computer, a laptop that is used for everything, so this is not a problem. Later in this book, we'll discover how we can use network storage to store data.

Each browser program has its own implementation of local storage, which means that items stored when using the Edge browser would not be accessible when using the Chrome browser. The browser maintains an object called `LocalStorage`, which has methods that are used to save items in local storage and get them back.

 MAKE SOMETHING HAPPEN

Investigate local storage

The example program in the **Ch09 Objects\Ch09-04 Local Storage Tiny Contacts** folder uses local storage to store contact information. Let's find out how it works. Open the application in your browser.

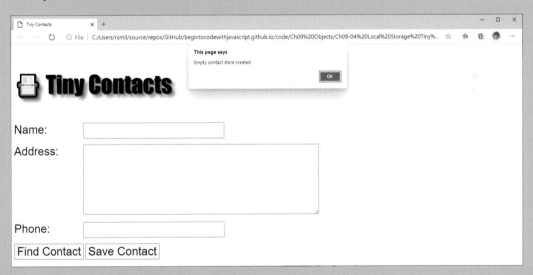

The first time the contacts page is opened, there will be no contacts store. The page displays an alert to indicate this. Click **OK** in the alert to clear it and press the F12 key to open the Developer View. Now move to the **Console** tab so that you can enter some JavaScript. Programs use local storage by placing strings of text in named locations. The method to store an item in local storage is called `setItem`. Type the statement below and press Enter.

```
> localStorage.setItem("test", "This is some test data we are storing");
```

When you press Enter, the method `setItem` will run and store the string `This is some test data we are storing` at the location `test`. The `setItem` method returns the value `undefined`.

```
> localStorage.setItem("test", "This is some test data we are storing");
<- undefined
```

We can use the method `getItem` to view the contents of an item stored in local storage. Type in the statement below.

```
> localStorage.getItem("test");
```

When you press Enter, the `getItem` method will run and return the contents of that location.

```
> localStorage.getItem("test");
<- "This is some test data we are storing"
```

The content of location test will still be there if we return to this web page after having shut down the browser. It will even be present after we have rebooted our computer. We can see how the data storage for our Tiny Contacts application works. Type some contact details into the application and press the **Save Contact** button. The contact information is held in a location called `TinyContactsStore`. Type in the following statement to read the contents of this location.

```
> localStorage.getItem("TinyContactsStore");
```

When you press Enter, you will see the contents of the contacts store now contains the data that was entered.

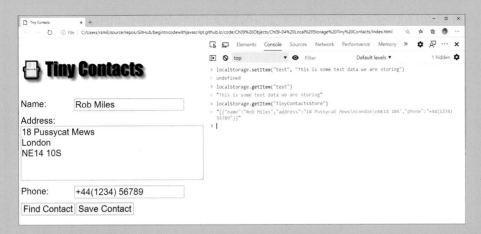

If you store some more contacts, you will find that they are added to the stored item. If you restart your PC and then load the same application, you will find that the contact information has been retained.

The functions `setItem` and `getItem` can be used to store and retrieve data in local storage. If you want to remove the contents of a local storage, the `removeItem` function can be used to remove an item. The statement below would remove the `TinyContactsStore` item from the browser storage.

```
localStorage.removeItem("TinyContactsStore");
```

Use JSON to encode object data

Now it is time to discover how JavaScript programs can store data as formatted text. This is one of the most powerful features of the language, and it underpins many JavaScript applications that store and transfer data around the Internet. It also makes it possible for JavaScript applications to exchange data with applications written using other programming languages. The technology is called JSON—JavaScript Object Notation. In the previous "Make Something Happen," we saw that the contacts store for our application is retained as a string of text. This text is encoded using JSON.

```
[{"name":"Rob Miles","address":"18 Pussycat Mews\nLondon\nNE14
10S","phone":"+44(1234) 56789"}]
```

The JSON string above represents a contact store that contains a single contact. If you look at it carefully, you can see some strings that are the names of properties (for example, phone) and some strings that are values (for example, +44(1234) 56789). The string above actually creates an array (which is why the outer characters are square brackets—[and]). The array contains a single object (which is the element enclosed in braces—{ and }) inside the array.

 MAKE SOMETHING HAPPEN

Working with JSON

You should still have your browser open at the example program in the **Ch09 Objects\ Ch09-04 Local Storage Tiny Contacts** folder. If you haven't, open the application, press F12 to open Developer View, and select the Console tab. We can start by making an object and adding some properties to it. Type the following statement and press Enter:

```
> var contact = {name: "Rob", address: "Rob's House", phone: "1234"};
```

This is a quick way of creating JavaScript objects that we have not seen before. Rather than creating an empty object, we have populated a new object with three properties. Each property is given as the name of the property, followed by a colon (:) and the value for that property. Successive properties are separated by the comma (,) character. We now have a variable called contact, which contains my details. If we just type the name of the variable, the console will show us the contents:

```
> contact
<- {name: "Rob", address: "Rob's House", phone: "1234"}
```

The console is showing us the JavaScript representation of the contact object. We can convert the object into a JSON string by using the stringify method provided by the JSON object. Type the following statement and press Enter:

```
> var jsonContact = JSON.stringify(contact);
<- undefined
```

The stringify method acts on a JavaScript object and returns a string of JSON text that describes it. The variable jsonContact now contains a JSON formatted string that represents the contents of contact. Type in jsonContact and press Enter to view it:

```
> jsonContact
<- "{"name":"Rob","address":"Robs House","phone":"1234"}"
```

The JSON string version of an object looks very like the JavaScript representation, with the difference that the names of properties are also enclosed in double quotes ("). Another method, called parse, can be used to convert this string back into an object:

```
> var decodedContact = JSON.parse(jsonContact)
<- undefined
```

We now have a new variable called decodedContact, which contains the contact information that was stored in the string jsonContact. We can view this by just entering the name of the variable:

```
> decodedContact
<- "{"name":"Rob","address":"Robs House","phone":"1234"}"
```

So, in this Make Something Happen, we have "round tripped" a contact object. We have converted it into a string of text by using the wonderfully named stringify method, and we have converted the string back into an object by using the parse method.

We can combine local storage and JSON to make two methods that will save and load the contacts in the Tiny Contacts application.

```
var contactStore = [];                              Array that holds the contacts

var storeName;                                      Constant variable that holds the name in local storage

function saveContactStore(){                         Saves the contacts

    var storeJson = JSON.stringify(contactStore);    Convert the contacts to a string

    localStorage.setItem(storeName, storeJson);      Store the string in local storage
}

function loadContactStore(){                          Loads the contacts

    var dataString = localStorage.getItem(storeName); Get the string from local storage
```

```
        if(dataString==null){
            contactStore = [];
            return false;
        }

        contactStore = JSON.parse(dataString);

        return true;
}
```

The `loadContactStore` function is called when the page is first loaded. The `saveContactStore` function is called each time a contact is saved. The name of the local storage item to be used to store the contact data is held in a variable called `storeName`. The value in this variable is set when the application is started.

```
function doStartTinyContacts(storeNameToUse){
    storeName = storeNameToUse;

    if(!loadContactStore()){
        alert("Empty contact store created");
    }
}
```

The function `doStartTinyContacts` is called to start the contacts store and load the contact values. If the load fails, the function displays an alert to indicate that the program has made an empty contact store. The HTML page for the application calls the `doStartTinyContacts` function when the page is loaded.

```
<body onload='doStartTinyContacts("TinyContactsStore");'>
```

The string `"TinyContactsStore"` is given as an argument to the call of `doStartTinyContacts` from within the web page. This makes it easy for us to change the location of the stored data. You can find this code in the example application in the **Ch09 Objects\Ch09-04 Local Storage Tiny Contacts** samples folder.

Using JSON

JSON makes it much easier to move data between JavaScript applications and also to store data in the form of strings. But you might have some questions about it:

Question: Where is the JSON standard defined?

> **Answer:** One of the great things about JSON is that it is human readable. You can see how property names and values go together. If you want to see the standard that defines what a JSON document can contain, you can find it at *https://www.json.org/.*

Question: What types of data can a JSON document store?

> **Answer:** A JSON document can hold strings of text (which are enclosed in quote characters), numeric values, and the logical values `true` and `false`.

Question: How long can a JSON string be?

> **Answer:** Strings in JavaScript can extend to many thousands of characters, so you can use JSON to store large objects if required.

Question: What happens if I store a reference in the JSON string?

> **Answer:** The reference is followed and the contents of the object are inserted into the JSON. We've seen this in action already. The `contactStore` in the Tiny Contacts application is an array of references to objects. When it is converted into objects, each reference is followed, and the object contents are inserted into the string.

Question: What happens if a program tries to store an invalid value like Not a Number (NaN) in a JSON string?

> **Answer:** We've seen that JavaScript variables can hold values such as Not an Number (NaN) or infinity. These values are stored in a JSON string as the special value `null`, which is used in JSON to indicate that a value is missing.

Question: What happens if the program tries to parse a string that does not contain valid JSON text?

> **Answer:** The `JSON.parse` method expects to be given a string of JSON to work on. If the `parse` method can't decode the string, it does something we haven't seen before. It throws an *exception* and ends the execution of the program. Exceptions are a way of forcing a program to respond to an error. We will discuss them in the next chapter.

Use property accessors

This section has perhaps the most confusing heading in the whole book. JavaScript programs can use property accessors to work with the properties in an object. Before we talk about property accessors, let's refresh our understanding of what a property is.

```
var contact = {};
contact.phone  = "+44(1234) 56789";
```

A JavaScript program can create an empty object and then add properties to it. The two statements above create a contact object and adds a phone property to the object. The new property is the string "+44(1234) 56789". We have seen that programs can add properties to an object. The object acts as a container for the property values that have been added to it. We can identify these properties in the program by name as you can see above, where we create a property called phone. This method is called dot notation because the name of the property is given after a dot (.) in the program text.

A property accessor looks a lot like an array indexer. It is called bracket notation because the property identifier is enclosed in square brackets. It works a bit like an array, except that the item used as an index can be any value. This makes a JavaScript object behave like a dictionary. One of my favorite jokes is to tell someone that the word "gullible" is not in the dictionary and then watch as they look up the word and proudly read it out to me. A dictionary lets you look up definitions starting from a given word. If you look up the word "gullible," you will get a result along the lines of "easily persuaded to believe something." In JavaScript, if you look up a property accessor, you get the value of the property with the specified name:

```
var contact = {};                              ──── Create an empty object
contact["phone"]  = "+44(1234) 56789";  ──── Add a phone property to the
                                                 object using a property accessor
```

The statements above show this works. The first statement creates an empty object called contact. The second statement adds a property "phone" to the empty object by using a property accessor. Note that the property accessor is the string "phone." This is a very powerful feature of JSON, but it can also be a confusing one, particularly when you try to compare JavaScript objects with JavaScript arrays. Let's see if we can't make things clearer.

Investigating property accessors

Open the application in the example folder **Ch09 Objects\Ch09-05 Universal Tiny Contacts**. It is a contact manager that works in the same way as previous ones. Press F12 to open Developer View and select the **Console** tab. First, we want to investigate property accessors. Let's start by making an empty contact. Type the following statement and press Enter:

```
> var contact = {};
```

Creating a new variable does not return a value, so the console displays the familiar message undefined.

```
> var contact = {};
<- undefined
```

We now have an object called contact, which has no properties. We can view the contents of contact by entering its name and pressing Enter :

```
> contact
```

JavaScript will tell us that the contact object is empty by printing a pair of curly brackets with nothing between them.

```
> contact
<- {}
```

Now, let's add a name property to the contact object. Enter the following and press Enter:

```
> contact.name = "Rob";
```

This statement returns the value being assigned, so the console prints the value "Rob".

```
> contact.name = "Rob";
<- "Rob"
```

The contact object now contains a property called name, which contains the value "Rob". Now let's add another property, but this time, we will refer to the property using a *property accessor*. Type in the statement below and press Enter.

```
> contact.["address"] = "House of Rob"
```

This statement adds a property called address, which is set to the value "House of Rob". It also displays the value being assigned, as usual.

```
> contact.["address"] = "House of Rob"
<- "House of Rob"
```

If we look at the contents of the contact object, we will see both of these properties. Type in the statement below and press Enter to take another look at the contents of the contact object:

```
> contact
```

The contact object now contains name and address properties.

```
> contact
<- {name: "Rob", address: "House of Rob"}
```

At this point, you might start to think that a property accessor makes every object look like an array. Let's see what happens if we try to use an object in the same way we would an array. The following statement tries to store the string "Hello world" at element 0 of an array. Let's try to do that with the contact object. Type in the statement below and press Enter.

```
> contact[0] = "Hello world";
```

JavaScript does not produce an error message, so the statement must have done something. The value "Hello world" has now been added as a property of the contact object.

```
> contact[0] = "Hello world";
<- "Hello world"
```

Let's take a look at the contents of the `contact` object. Type in the object name and press Enter:

```
> contact
```

This is very confusing. The `contact` object now has a property called 0, which contains the string `"Hello world"`.

```
> contact
<- 0: "Hello world", name: "Rob", address: "House of Rob"}
```

The next thing to do is to try and use 0 as a property identifier in our program. The statement below is trying to access a property called 0. Type it in and press Enter to see what it does:

```
> contact.0
```

JavaScript will not let you use a number as an object property identifier, so this will generate an error:

```
> contact.0
VM142:1 Uncaught SyntaxError: Unexpected number
```

Property identifiers in a program must obey the same rules that are applied to all JavaScript identifiers. However, we can still access this property by using 0 as a property accessor. Type this statement and press Enter to prove this:

```
> contact[0]
```

You have correctly identified a property and so JavaScript shows you the value it holds:

```
> contact[0]
<- "Hello world"
```

Please remember that I am in no way recommending that you should use anything other than strings of text as property accessors. As with lots of things in life, just because you can do something does not mean that you should try to do it.

We have discovered that we can use strings of text as property accessors rather than putting property names in the program code. This is interesting, but at the moment, we are not sure why it is so useful. It turns out that property accessors give us a lot of power. Our programs can be made to create their own object designs. Consider these two statements:

```
var propertyName = "phone";
contact[propertyName]  = "+44(1234) 56789";
```

The first statement creates a variable called propertyName that contains the word "phone" as a string of text. The second statement uses the contents of propertyName as property accessor. The effect of these statements would be to change the phone property of the contact variable. If I want to create an object with a particular set of properties, I can now do this from within the program, rather than having to create the code by hand. Why is this useful? Because it is how we can create a schema that describes the design of an object and then use that schema to create the objects themselves.

Use a data schema

Your Tiny Contacts program is becoming quite popular. A friend has seen you working on it and would like you to create a program to keep track of his video game high scores. Another friend wants a program to store her recipes. In fact, there are lots of people who seem to be looking for simple data stores. You could create all these different programs by editing the Tiny Contacts application, modifying the HTML elements, and then changing the JavaScript code to match. However, this is looks like it might be hard work.

A much better way forward would be to build something that describes the data storage needed by each application. Programmers call this a schema. The schema for the Tiny Contacts application would include name, address, and telephone items for each contact. The schema for a video game high score application would include video game name, high score, date, and time items for each high score. The schema would be designed at the start of the project. Then when the program runs, it can create the data storage objects by using property accessors that are described in the schema.

Design the system before you build it

If you were making an airplane, you would make sure you had a design before you started putting the wings on. The same is true with a software project. It is vital that you consider what data is to be stored and how it fits together before you start to write any code.

A large software system will contain many different components. At the start of the design process, a programmer will focus on identifying the components and how they are related. For example, a banking application would contain customers, accounts, addresses, statements, and transactions. The first part of the design process would be deciding the relationships between these components in the system. For the bank, we might decide that a customer can have multiple accounts but only one home address. At this point, we are working at a high level of abstraction. You can think of abstraction as a way of "stepping back" from the problem you are trying to solve and trying to think about the "bigger picture" surrounding the code that you are writing.

As soon as we had a high-level design, we would work with the customer to make sure that the design can be made to do what they want. Then we would move on to creating schemas for each of the components, making sure to check with the customer that each component holds the data that is required.

We are trying to avoid a situation right at the end of the project when the customer asks something like, "Where do you hold the date of each transaction?" If we had created the software as soon as we thought we knew what was needed, this might be the first time we've heard of this requirement, and it would need a lot of work to add it to the finished system.

JavaScript property accessors let us create data objects that describe the data items that are to be stored. These can then be used by the application to create objects that will hold the data. We've already done this kind of thing in the multiplication table and ice cream sales applications, where an application creates the HTML page that will be used to enter data. Now we are extending this process to allow an application to create bespoke objects to hold data. If you look in the HTML page of the **Ch09 Objects\Ch09-05 Universal Tiny Contacts** application, you will find a call of a function—doBuildPage.

Build HTML from a schema

The doBuildPage function takes two arguments. The first argument is the name of the display element on the HTML page that is to contain all the HTML that will be generated to provide the user interface. We've used this technique before in the ice cream sales application, where the program generates the input fields for all the ice cream stands.

```
doBuildPage( "contactItems",
[ { id:"name", prompt:"Name", type:"input"},
{ id:"address", prompt:"Address", type:"textarea", rows:"3", cols:"40"},
{ id:"phone", prompt:"Phone", type:"input"} ] );
```

Container object on the web page for the HTML

Description of the name entry

Description of the phone entry

Description of the address entry

The second argument is an array of objects, each of which describes one of the items to be stored. The schema above is for the Tiny Contacts application, and it defines three data items—the name, address, and phone number items. All the descriptions contain at least three property values:

1. The `id` to be used to identify the property in the object that will store a contact.

2. The `prompt` gives the text that is to be displayed in the HTML when this property is being edited.

3. The `type` gives the type of the item. There are two types of property. An `input` type uses the input HTML element to read a single line of text. The `textarea` type uses a text area. For a `textarea`, the description also contains `row` and `col` values to specify the size of the text area to be used.

The `doBuildPage` function works through each of the items in the schema and creates an HTML element for each item. This is then added to the `container` element to build the display. This function is called when the page is loaded.

```
function doBuildPage(containerElementID, schema){

    // store the schema for use later by the application
    dataSchema = schema;

    // get a reference to the element containing the edit items
    var containerElement = document.getElementById(containerElementID);

    // work through each of the items in the schema
    for (item of dataSchema) {
        // make an element for that item
        let itemElement = makeElement(item);
        // add the element to the container
        containerElement.appendChild(itemElement);
    }
}
```

The `doBuildPage` function uses a function called `makeElement` to make each HTML element for display on the page. This function uses the description from the schema to decide which what kind of element to make.

```
function makeElement(description) {
    // Create the enclosing paragraph
    var inputPar = document.createElement("p");

    // Create the label for the element
    var labelElement = document.createElement("label");
    labelElement.innerText = description.prompt + ":";
    labelElement.className = "inputLabel";
    labelElement.setAttribute("for", description.id);
    inputPar.appendChild(labelElement);

    // decide what kind of element to make
    switch (description.type) {
        case "input":
            inputElement = document.createElement("input");
            inputElement.className="inputText";
            break;

        case "textarea":
            inputElement = document.createElement("textarea");
            inputElement.className = "inputTextarea";
            inputElement.setAttribute("rows", description.rows);
            inputElement.setAttribute("cols", description.cols);
            break;
        // add new kinds of element here
    }

    // set the id for the element
    inputElement.setAttribute("id", description.id);
    // give the element an initial value
    inputElement.setAttribute("value", "");
    // add the element to the paragraph
    inputPar.appendChild(inputElement);
    // return the whole paragraph
    return inputPar;
}
```

The code in `makeElement` is very similar to the code in the function `makeInputPar` that we created in the "Create an input paragraph" section in Chapter 8. It creates an HTML paragraph that contains a label and an input element. The function is supplied with an object that describes the kind of input that is required. The object contains the three properties of `id`, `type`, and `prompt` that we saw earlier. These are used to build the HTML display.

Build a data object from a schema

When the user presses the **Save Contact** button, the `storeData` function is used to read data from the HTML elements on the page and create properties in a new data object that is then stored.

```
function storeData(pos){
    // Create an empty data item
    var newData = {};

    // Work through the data schema
    for(property of dataSchema){
        // Get the data out of the HTML element
        let itemData = getElementValue(property.id);
        // Create a property to store that data
        newData[property.id] = itemData;
    }
    // put the new data in the storage array
    dataStore[pos]=newData;

    // save the data store
    saveDataStore();
}
```

The schema array holds the application together. It describes each of the data items to be displayed by the editor and it is used to build the HTML page and also to create each data object for storage. We can extend the schema design by adding new types of data input, perhaps a number input type.

Create your own data storage

In this Make Something Happen, I want you to investigate some working programs and try to produce your own schema for a data store. The example application in the **Ch09 Objects\ Ch09-05 Universal Tiny Contacts** folder holds a tiny contacts data manager that uses the schema above. The example application in the **Ch09 Objects\Ch09-06 Recipe Store** folder holds a recipe storage program. Both programs use the same JavaScript and style sheet files. The only file that is changed for each application is the HTML file that contains the schema for the application. Take a look at both these applications and use what you find out to create a third application that can store video game scores. The items to be stored are:

- The name of the video game

- The high score reached

- The time in minutes that the game lasted

- A details panel that can accept 5 lines of text that are 40 columns wide

You should be able to achieve this by only changing the contents of the HTML file. If you get stuck, you can take a look at my version, which you can find in **Ch09 Objects\Ch09-07 Game Scores**.

Improving the user interface

We now have a working data store, but it is not very easy to use. When searching for an item, the user must enter an exact match for the item name for it to be found. If they mistype a letter of the name, perhaps by typing "rob" rather than "Rob," the name will not be matched. These problems are caused by the simple nature of the function that finds items in the data store:

```
function findDataPos(name) {
    for(let pos=0;pos<dataStore.length;pos=pos+1){
        let storedName=dataStore[pos].name;
        if(storedName==name) {              Very simple test for a name match
            return pos;
        }
    }
    return NaN;
}
```

We can make the find process much easier by making the test ignore whether the text was typed in UPPERCASE or lowercase. This can be achieved by converting the search string and all the items it is searching for to lowercase before performing the test:

```
function findDataPos(name) {
    name=name.toLowerCase();
    for(let pos=0;pos<dataStore.length;pos=pos+1){
        let storedName=dataStore[pos].name;
        storeName = storedName.toLowerCase();
        if(storedName==name) {
            return pos;
        }
    }
    return NaN;
}
```

The version of Tiny Contacts in the **Ch09 Objects\Ch09-08 Tiny Contacts Improved Search** example folder uses this version of the function.

Add "Super Search" to Tiny Contacts

You show the improved search to your lawyer customer and she is very pleased. However, after a while, she comes to see you, saying that she has had an awesome idea to make the application even better. She doesn't like having to type in the entire name to search for a contact. Instead, she wants to type in just the first part of the name and then use the **Find Contact** button to step through all the contacts that start with that part. For example, she might type just the letter "R," and then repeated presses of the **Find Contact** button would find the entries for "Rob", "Ronald," and "Rita." She calls this her "Super Search" feature, and she would really like you to add it to the Tiny Contacts program.

PROGRAMMER'S POINT

User ideas are often the best kinds of ideas

Making a great application is only the first step in making a successful one. You also have to work hard to engage with your users and make them into your sales force. We have seen that one way to do this is to always respond constructively to error reports. Another good technique is to engage with users and encourage them to suggest improvements. This is a win-win proposition. They get a solution tailored to their needs, and you get another feature that you can use to sell your solution.

Solve a problem

Making Super Search work is an interesting problem. I suppose you could call it our first "proper" programming problem. By that, I mean that it is not obvious how we can solve it. With all the other applications we have created, we have been automating a behavior that we know how to do. We knew how to calculate multiplication tables and add up ice cream sales before we went anywhere near a computer. But for this problem, we don't know how to do what is being requested. So the best possible answer we can give our lawyer friend is that we will think about it and get back to her later.

The first step toward solving a problem is to determine whether the problem can be solved. Trying to do the impossible never ends well. In this case, I can tell you that I've used systems that work in a similar way to that suggested by the lawyer, so it is possible. So with that useful knowledge, let's work out how we can solve the problem. The first step to solving the problem is to write down the sequence of actions that need to be performed to use the action in the application:

1. Type part of the name into the name input. (for example, "R").

2. Press the **Find Contact** button. The first contact (meaning the one nearest the start of the `contactStore` array) with a name that starts with R will be displayed.

3. If the user presses **Find Contact** again, the next contact with a name that starts with R will be displayed.

4. If the user enters a new name, the Find behavior resets, and the **Find Contact** button now searches for the new name.

After thinking about it, I found three things that the application needs to be able to do to make these behaviors work:

1. The application needs to be able to test whether one string starts with the search string. This is so it can match the contact with the name "Rob" to the search string "R."

2. The application needs to store the search string and the search position it has reached in the `connectStore` array. This needs to happen because when the user presses **Find Contact**, the application knows what to search for and where to start the search from.

3. The application needs to know when the user types in a new name. This needs to happen because when the name changes, the application can reload the search string and restart the search at the start of the data array.

Find out if one string starts with another

The JavaScript string object provides a method called `startsWith` that returns `true` if the string starts with another string.

```javascript
var name="Rob";
if(name.startsWith("R")){
    alert("Rob starts with R!")
}
```

The JavaScript code above shows how this works. So now we know that we can search the contacts for names that start with a string, and then we can move on to the next problem. The program needs to store the current search string and the position it has reached in the array of contacts.

Retain the find string and find position

These two variables hold the string we are finding, as well as the current find position. They are global variables that are declared outside any function so that they are visible to all the functions in the application.

```javascript
var findString = "";
var findPos = 0;
```

We start by setting the find string (`findString`) to an empty string (`""`) and the find position (`findPos`) to `0`. This means that if the user presses the **Find Contact** button as soon as the application has been started, the search will match all the contacts (all names start with an empty string) and search from the start of the contact store. (Remember, arrays are indexed from 0.)

When the user presses the Find Contact button, the `doFind` function is called to search. We can make this function start searching with the find string at the current find position:

```javascript
function doFind() {

    var pos = findStartsWithDataPos(findString,findPos);         Search for a contact

    if(isNaN(pos)){                                              Have we found a match?
        displayDataNotFound();              Display a message if no contacts match the search
    }
```

312   Chapter 9   Objects

```
    else{
        displayData(pos);                                    Display the contact that was found
        findPos = pos+1;                                     Store the find position that we have reached
    }
}
```

This `doFind` function uses a function called `findStartsWithDataPos`, which is given the current `findString` (perhaps the string "R") and the current value of `findPos` (perhaps the position 0). If `findStartsWithDataPos` doesn't find a match, it returns Not a Number (`NaN`), and the `displayDataNotFound` function is called to tell the user about this.

The `findStartsWithDataPos` function is provided with a name to search for and a start position. It searches for a contact that has a name that starts with the search string. It starts the search at the supplied start position.

```
                                                             Start the search at the search position
function findStartsWithDataPos(name, startPos) {
    name=name.toLowerCase();                                 Convert the name to lowercase
    for(let pos=startPos;pos<dataStore.length;pos=pos+1){
        let storedName=dataStore[pos].name;                  Get the name out of the search contact
        var lowerCaseStoredName = storedName.toLowerCase();
        if(lowerCaseStoredName.startsWith(name)) {           Check for a match
            return pos;                                      Return the search result
        }
    }
    return NaN;                                              If the search fails return this
}
                                                             Convert the name to lowercase
```

Our application can use these two functions to search through the datastore array for contacts that start with a particular string. Each time `doFind` is called, it will use `findStartsWithDataPos` to find the next contact to display. The final piece of the solution is code that restarts the search each time the user changes the contents of the `name` input field.

Detect changes to the name input

This is perhaps the easiest part of the solution. We have seen that HTML elements can be made to call JavaScript functions when something happens in the document. We've used the `onload` attribute to specify a JavaScript function to be called when an HTML document is loaded into the browser. HTML provides an `oninput` function that will call a JavaScript function when the user inputs text into an input field. We can use this to specify a method to run when the user changes the name of a contact when using the application:

```
<input class="inputText" oninput="resetFind();" id="name" value="">
```

This is a very powerful feature. If you've ever used a web page that automatically updates or checks your text as you type it in, you now know how it works. The resetFind function sets up a new search:

```
function resetFind(){
    nameString=getElementValue("name");      Get the name from the HTML input element
    findString=nameString.trim();            Remove leading and trailing spaces
    findPos=0;                                Set the find position to the start of the array
}
```

The resetFind function gets the name element from the HTML document and then uses a JavaScript string feature that we've not seen before. The trim function returns a version of the string that has had all its leading and trailing spaces removed. It would convert " R " to " R." This is very useful. The user will become confused if a search for "Rob" doesn't find "Rob," and this prevents that problem from happening. The value of findString is then set to this trimmed value, and findPos is set to 0 to make the next search start at the beginning of the stored contacts.

CODE ANALYSIS

Investigating Super Search

The Super Search version of Tiny Contacts is in the **Ch09 Objects\Ch09-09 Tiny Contacts Super Search** examples folder. Let's open it and take a look inside. Open the application in your browser and press F12 to open the Developer View of the application.

Question: Does it work?

Answer: Good question. Try it. Enter some data, save it, enter the first letter of one of the names into the name field, and press **Find Contact**. The application will display the first match and continue to display matches up to the end of the data.

Question: What happens if I enter an empty name to search for?

Answer: Try it. The behavior of the startsWith function means that all strings start with an empty string. So the findStartsWithDataPos function will match every contact. The user of the Tiny Contacts program will really like this, as it provides them with a way of stepping through all the saved contacts.

Question: How does the application add the `oninput` behavior to the `name` input field?

> **Answer:** Changes to the `name` input field must be detected and used to update the search string. If you use the **Elements** tab in the Developer View to take a look at the web page HTML, you will see that the `oninput` attribute has been added to the `name` input field. However, it has not been added to the address underneath. How does this work?

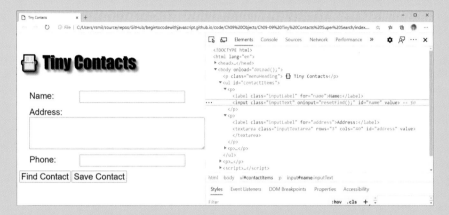

I've made a tiny change to the function that generates the HTML for each data item that needs to be stored. The `makeElement` function regards the element, which has the `id` `name` as special. When it generates that element, it adds the attribute to it. Open the **Sources** tab in the Developer View and take a look in the `tinyData.js` file.

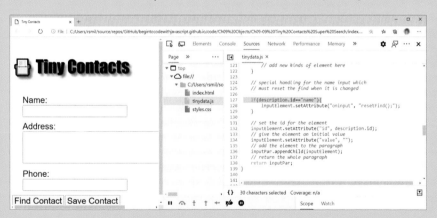

The statement that I have highlighted tests the `id` of the element being created and adds the `oninput` attribute if it is the `name` element.

Question: How hard would it be to add this feature to the Recipe and Video Game Score applications?

> **Answer:** The wonderful thing about the way that our solution works is that such a change would require no programming effort at all. We simply have to update the versions of `tinydata.js` with the Super Search version.

Improving data storage

At this point, your lawyer friend has lots of ideas about how the application could be made better. She even suggests some kind of partnership where she takes a stake in the business and gets a share of any income that you get from selling the application. This sounds reasonable to you because it is always useful to have a good lawyer on your side when you are writing software. Here are a few of the ideas that she would like you to add.

- She would like to add an "email" input so that the program can keep track of the email address of each contact.

- She would like a button that clears the HTML form to make it easy to enter new contacts.

- She would like the search to "wrap around," so that when she searches through to the end of the list, she then returns to searching at the start.

See if you can make these features work. If you need ideas, you can take a look at my solution, which you can find in the **Ch09 Objects\Ch09-10 Super Tiny Contacts** examples folder.

As a further exercise, you might like to make a datastore application that can hold data that you would like to store.

What you have learned

In this chapter, you learned how JavaScript objects allow programs to store related items as properties of a single object and how to make programs that work with objects.

1. An object can contain any number of named property values. Each property value can be regarded as a variable holding a particular kind of value. An object can contain numbers, text, and references to other objects.

2. A program can create an empty object using a pair of braces with nothing between them—{}.

3. A populated object (one with properties) is created if the braces enclose a comma-separated list of property values. Each property value is expressed as the name of the property followed by a colon and the property value. For example,

you could create the following implausible object: {name:"Rob Miles",age:21}. This object contains two properties called name and age.

4. Objects are managed by reference. A variable can contain a reference to an object. A single object can have multiple reference variables referring to it. An object can contain a property that is a reference to another object. This allows a program to build data structures such as lists.

5. An object reference can be given as an argument to a function call and then passed into the function as a parameter of that function. This allows the function to interact with the properties in the object and to add additional properties to the object.

6. A program can store a large amount of structured data by using an array of object references.

7. The browser maintains a *local storage* area for each different website the user visits. Values placed in local storage are maintained when the browser is not running, and the host machine is switched off. The values that are stored are strings of text. Each string is accessed by using a string that gives the item a name.

8. JavaScript Object Notation is a standard for encoding JavaScript variables into strings of text. The JSON object provides a stringify method to convert a variable into a JSON string and a parse method to convert JSON strings into variables.

9. There are two ways that a program can access a property. Dot notation uses a dot to separate the object variable name and the property name (contact.name). Bracket notation uses a property accessor (usually a string) enclosed in square brackets (contact["name"]).

10. A data schema is an object that contains a design for other objects. Schemas can be used in association with bracket notation property accessors (see above) to allow a program to dynamically create custom software objects.

11. JavaScript provides functions to convert text in a string to uppercase and lowercase (toLowerCase and toUpperCase) and also to remove leading and trailing spaces (trim).

12. JavaScript provides a startsWith function that can be used to detect whether one string stars with another.

13. A JavaScript function can be made to run when the user of an application changes the text inside an input element in the document. This is achieved using the onchanged attribute of the input or textarea element.

Here are some questions that you might like to ponder regarding the things you have learned in this chapter:

What is the difference between a `textarea` **element and an** `input` **element in HTML?**

Both elements have a `value` attribute that can be used by a JavaScript to read and write their contents. A `textarea` can be made to span an area of the HTML document to allow multiple lines of text to be entered. The `textarea` element can be given `rows` and `cols` attributes that specify the size of the area on the page.

How does a `textarea` **represent multiple lines of text?**

When the `value` attribute of a `textarea` is read by a JavaScript program the browser separates each line using the line feed character. We first saw line feed in Chapter 4 in the "Escape sequences in strings" section. The line feed character can be used in a string to mark the end of a line of text in the string. The `textarea` also uses line feed characters to arrange the display of any text loaded into it. The `textarea` will also break text and display scroll bars as appropriate to make the text fit on the screen.

Can I add a property to any JavaScript variable?

No. JavaScript will not complain if your program tries to do this, but properties added to variables containing Boolean values, strings, or numbers are not stored with the variable. If you want to add properties to an object, you need to tell JavaScript that your program is creating an object by using the {} notation.

Can I use an object as an argument to a function call?

Yes. We have done this many times in our programs already. The argument is passed as a reference to the object.

What happens if an object in memory has no variable referring to it?

Good question. As a program runs, variables that refer to an object could be reassigned to refer to different objects. In addition, variables defined using `let` and `var` may be discarded as program execution moves in and out of blocks of code. This can lead to objects in memory that no longer have any variables that refer to them. The browser that is running the JavaScript program also runs a special process called the "garbage collector," which searches for objects that have no references and reclaims the memory used by them. This is an automatic process as far as our programs are concerned, although we should be careful not to write code that create and discard large numbers of objects, so that our applications are not slowed down by the garbage collector having to come in and clean up all the time.

Does a browser only keep one local storage area on a given machine?

A browser keeps one local storage area per web connection origin. Two websites on the same host will be on the same origin, so the sites *https://robmiles.com/blog* and *https://robmiles.com/javascript* would share the same local storage. JavaScript programs running from pages stored on a particular PC will all share the same local storage on that PC.

How do property accessors really work?

A property accessor uses an accessor value to get the name of a property on an object. For example `contact["name"]` would access the `name` property of an object referred to by the variable `contact`. A program can also use other value types to access a property of an object. For example, `contact[99]` would also access a property (using a number as an accessor) as would `contact[true]` (using a Boolean value as an accessor). JavaScript manages this by converting the property to a string and then using this to search the properties of the object. However, you should not use anything other than a string as a property accessor. Just because something is possible does not mean that you should do it.

Can I use a reference as a property accessor?

This would be legal JavaScript, but it would be a very dangerous thing to do because when JavaScript converts the reference to a string (see above), it gets the same string for all object references.

What happens if a program uses an accessor value that does not exist?

If JavaScript can't find a property with a particular accessor name, it returns the value `undefined`.

What is the difference between `[]` and `{}`?

A pair of square brackets creates an empty array object. A pair of braces (curly brackets) creates an empty object. Arrays can use indexers to access array elements. and JavaScript will automatically create array elements as a program populates the array. Objects use property accessors to access properties.

Can I use a variable to identify the property to be accessed?

Yes, you can. If the program creates a string variable that contains the name of the property, a program can use the string contents as a property accessor.

Can I use a single object to store all the tiny contacts by using the name of a contact as a property accessor?

Good question. We could write something like `contacts["Rob Miles"] = robMilesContact`. This would make a "Rob Miles" property of the `contacts` object that contains a reference to `robMilesContact`. This would remove the need to have an array of contacts, but it would also make for strange behavior because the name of the contact would be used to locate it in the contact store. If the `name` property of the contact were changed, we would have to make sure that the `name` property was also changed. Otherwise, the user would find it difficult to locate the contact. I try to make sure that I store a single piece of data in one place only, rather than having two pieces of linked data elements that have to be kept synchronized. A better idea would be to assign each contact a unique number that we can use to index them in the contact store.

Part 3
Useful
JavaScript

In the final part, we take our JavaScript knowledge to the next level, starting by picking up some new design skills and using them to build a complete "business worthy" application. Then we move on to investigate the popular node.js platform and use it to create a JavaScript web server. Next, we will write some applications that can consume network services. And we'll round off the book by having some serious fun with a look at game creation in JavaScript. We start by drawing simple graphics and then move on to create a complete game with computer-controlled artificial intelligence (AI) opponents.

10
Advanced JavaScript

What you will learn

In this chapter, we are going to take our JavaScript knowledge to the next level. We are going to discover how applications manage errors with exceptions and how to design data storage with classes. We'll discover how class inheritance can save us time when creating applications and how we can use object-oriented techniques to make data components that can look after themselves. We'll be doing this by creating a fully featured data storage application you could use to run a business.

Manage errors with exceptions

In Chapter 9, when we were looking at JSON, we discovered that JSON uses exceptions to signal when things go wrong. An exception is an object that describes something bad that has just happened. A piece of JavaScript can raise or throw an exception to interrupt a running program. Now is the time to find out what this means and discover the part that exceptions play in creating reliable applications.

If you remember, JSON (JavaScript Object Notation) is a standard for encoding the contents of JavaScript variables into text so that they can be stored or transferred to another machine. We used JSON to convert the Tiny Contacts store into a string so that it could be stored using local storage in the browser. The JSON object provides methods called stringify and parse that can move JavaScript objects to and from text strings.

```
var test = {};
test.name = "Rob Miles";
test.age = 21;
var JSONstring = JSON.stringify(test);
```

The statements above create a JavaScript object called test, which contains name and age properties. The contents of this object are then converted into a string called JSONstring by the stringify method.

```
{"name":"Rob", "age":21}
```

This is the string that would be stored in JSONstring. This string can be converted back into a JavaScript object by using the JSON parse method:

```
var test = JSON.parse(jsonString);
```

Breaking JSON

The `stringify` and `parse` methods will fail if they are given invalid inputs. They fail by *raising* or *throwing* an exception. Let's investigate what this means and how programs can be made to handle this failure. Use your browser to open the example application in the **Ch10 Advanced JavaScript\Ch10-01 JSON Validator** examples folder.

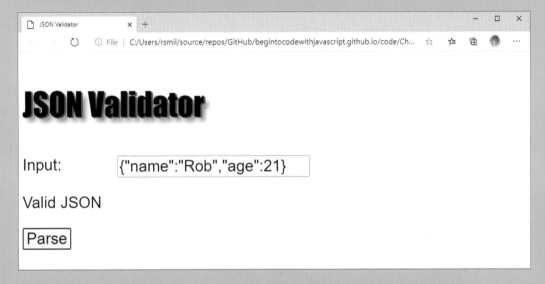

This application tests strings of text to find out if they contain valid JSON. It works by handing exceptions thrown by the JSON `parse` method. When the **Parse** button is pressed, the application reads the string from the input and displays whether the string contains valid JSON. Look back through Chapter 9 to find some valid JSON to use to test it. Try it with a few strings to prove that it works.

Now press F12 to open the Developer View and select the **Console** tab so that we can investigate the application. The JSON `parse` method fails by throwing an exception. Let's see what that means. Type in the following statement, which attempts to parse a string with the dangerous sounding contents `kaboom`. Press Enter to see what happens.

```
> JSON.parse("kaboom");
```

The JSON `parse` method is not able to make sense of kaboom, and it indicates this by *throwing an exception*. We have not included code to catch the exception, so the JavaScript console displays an error message in red:

```
> JSON.parse("kaboom");
Uncaught SyntaxError: Unexpected token k in JSON at position 0
    at JSON.parse (<anonymous>)
    at <anonymous>:1:6
```

We are not used to JavaScript programs complaining in the event of an error in the program code. If our program combines values incorrectly, JavaScript will use the values Not a Number (NaN), `undefined`, or `overflow` to indicate that something has gone wrong. Our program must test for these values to decide whether an action has worked properly.

The error created by `parse` is called an *exception*. It denotes the fact that the requested action can't be performed. If the exception is not caught, the sequence of execution will end. Statements that might throw an exception can be placed inside a `try` block of code. The `try` block is followed by a `catch` block, which contains statements to be performed if an exception is thrown. This is called a `try-catch` construction. Let's type one in. Enter the code below, remembering to press Enter at the end of every line.

```
> try {
    JSON.parse("kaboom");
} catch {
    console.log("bad json");
}
```

When you press Enter after the closing curly bracket of the `catch` block, the JavaScript code runs. The `parse` method will fail and throw an exception, but this time the exception is thrown inside a `try` block, and the associated `catch` clause will run and log a message on the console:

```
> try {
    JSON.parse("kaboom");
} catch {
    console.log("bad json");
}
bad json
```

Enter the same construction replacing the word kaboom with some valid JSON, such as {}. Note that this time, the `bad json` message is not displayed because `parse` doesn't throw an exception if the JSON string is valid.

Catching exceptions

The JSON validator above uses the `try-catch` construction to display an appropriate message.

```
function doValidate(){
    var inputElement = document.getElementById("inputString");
    var outputElement = document.getElementById("outputResult");

    var inputText = inputElement.value;
    try {                                              Start of the try block
        var result = JSON.parse(inputText);            Code that might cause an exception
        outputElement.innerText = "Valid JSON";        Statement that is only performed if
    }                                                     no exception is caused
    catch {                                            Start of the catch block
        outputElement.innerText = "Invalid JSON";      Code that is obeyed if the
    }                                                     exception is caused
}
```

The `doValidate` function is called when the **Parse** button is pressed in the JSON validator web page. If the user types in valid JSON, the `JSON.parse` method doesn't throw an exception, and none of the statements in the `catch` block are performed. Instead, execution goes straight to the end of the method. However, if the `JSON.parse` method can't parse the string that was typed in, the exception is generated and execution transfers immediately to the block of code under the `catch` keyword.

The `try` block can contain many statements. However, this might make it hard for you to work out which statement caused the exception.

CODE ANALYSIS

Exception handling

You might have some questions about how exceptions are handled.

Question: How does the exception stop the display of the Valid JSON message?

```
var result = JSON.parse(inputText);
outputElement.innerText = "Valid JSON";
```

Answer: The statements in `doValidate` that parse the input JSON and display the message are shown above. When the `parse` method throws an exception, the normal execution of this sequence of code is interrupted and program execution moves to the `catch` part of the `try-catch` construction. `Valid JSON` is not displayed because when `parse` throws an exception, execution does not get that far.

If no exception is thrown, the code in the `try` block is completed and execution then skips the statements in the `catch` block.

Question: How can a program get hold of the exception object?

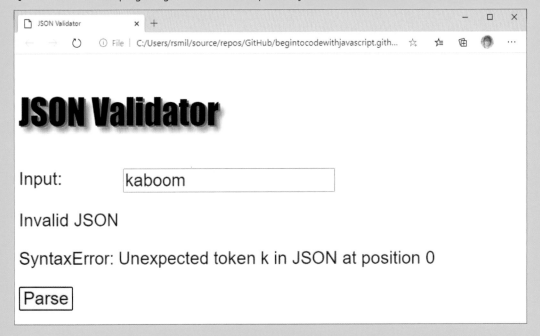

Answer: The first version of the JSON Validator program ignored the error object produced by the `JSON.parse` function. However, we can add the display of the error message by picking up the error object as a parameter to the `catch` construction:

```
catch (error) {                                          Catch with error parameter
    var errorElement = document.getElementById("outputError");
    errorElement.innerText = error;                      Display the error
    outputElement.innerText = "Invalid JSON";
}
```

This is the code that runs in the `catch` part of the `try-catch` construction. It displays the error value (which is highlighted) on an element in the HTML to give the display above. You can find this version of the validator application in the example files in the **Ch10 Advanced JavaScript\Ch10-02 JSON Validator Error** folder.

Question: Can I throw my own exceptions?

Answer: Yes, you can. The `throw` statement is followed by the value that is being thrown to describe the error.

```
throw "something bad happened";
```

Question: What happens when an exception is thrown?

Answer: Throwing an exception stops the sequence of execution. Any statements following the `throw` statement are not performed.

```
throw "something bad happened";
console.log("This message is never printed");
```

In the code sample above, the second statement, which logs a message on the console, is never performed because when the `throw` is performed, the execution of this sequence of instructions is ended.

Question: Is it possible to return to a sequence of execution after an exception has been thrown?

Answer: No. Throwing an exception ends the running of a sequence of statements.

Question: Is it possible for the JSON `stringify` method to throw an exception?

Answer: Yes. It turns out that there are some JavaScript objects that can't be saved into a string of text. Let's see if we can make one. Go back to the Developer Console in the browser and start by making an empty object called `infiniteLoop`. Type the statement below and press Enter.

```
> var infiniteLoop = {}
```

Creating variables always returns an undefined result, so you should see the `undefined` message.

```
> var infiniteLoop = {}
<- undefined
```

Now we are going to add a property to the object that contains a reference that refers to the object itself. Type in the following statement and press Enter.

```
> infiniteLoop.loopRef = infiniteLoop
```

When you press Enter, the JavaScript console adds a new property to the infiniteLoop variable that contains a reference to the infiniteLoop variable. In other words, this variable now contains a reference to itself.

```
> infiniteLoop.loopRef = infiniteLoop
<- {loopRef: {…}}
```

Now, let's try and stringify the value in infiniteLoop. Type the following and press Enter:

```
> JSON.stringify(infiniteLoop)
```

When you press Enter the stringify method tries to save the contents of infiniteLoop. It does this by working through each of the properties inside the value and saving each one in turn. It finds the loopRef property, so it follows that reference to save that value. The reference leads to the infiniteLoop variable, so with stringify, this save process would go on forever, rather like a reflection between two parallel mirrors. Fortunately, the people who created the stringify method are aware of the problem and have added a test for what is called a "circular" reference. If you try to stringify an object that contains a reference to itself, you will get an error.

```
> JSON.stringify(infiniteLoop)
Uncaught TypeError: Converting circular structure to JSON
    --> starting at object with constructor 'Object'
    --- property 'loopRef' closes the circle
    at JSON.stringify (<anonymous>)
    at <anonymous>:1:6
```

Exceptions and errors

Now that we know how to throw and catch exceptions, we can consider how we can use them in our applications. However, before we do that, I want to talk about the two types of fault that can occur in a program:

1. Things that shouldn't happen

2. Things that **really** shouldn't happen.

Things that shouldn't happen include users typing in numbers that are out of range (perhaps an age value of -99) and network connections failing. These are bad things that we expect. Things that **really** shouldn't happen include faults in functions and methods that are used by our applications.

The starting point for the discussion of exceptions was the way that the `JSON.parse` method throws an exception if it is used to parse a string that does not contain valid JSON (for example, "kaboom"). This should never happen in the Tiny Contacts program. The only way that this could happen is if the browser storage is corrupted in some way. Is this really a problem? I would say yes, and I've added code to my Tiny Contacts application to deal with this.

```javascript
const STORE_LOAD_OK = 0;
const STORE_EMPTY = 1;
const STORE_INVALID = 2;                         Constant values for the status codes

function loadDataStore() {

    // get the data from local storage
    var dataString = localStorage.getItem(storeName);

    // if there is no data make an empty store
    if (dataString == null) {
        dataStore = [];
        return STORE_EMPTY;                       Return a status code
    }

    // read the stored contacts
    try {
        dataStore = JSON.parse(dataString);
    }
    catch {
        // if the parse fails make an empty store
        dataStore = [];
        return STORE_INVALID;                     Return a status code
    }

    return STORE_LOAD_OK;                          Return a success code
}
```

The code above is a modified version of the `loadDataStore` function from the Tiny Contacts application in the example programs in the folder **Ch10 Advanced JavaScript\Ch10-03 Tiny Contacts Secure**. The call of the `JSON.parse` method is now enclosed in a `try` block, and the `catch` block creates an empty contact store if the `parse` method fails with an exception. The first version of `loadDataStore` returned the Boolean value `true` if it worked and `false` if it failed. There are three possible ways that this version of `loadDataStore` can complete:

1. The data is not present in local storage because this is the first time the application has been used.

2. The data loaded from local storage is not valid JSON. (This will cause an exception in `parse`.)

3. The data was found and loaded successfully.

The function returns one of three status values to indicate which of these possible outcomes happened when `loadDataStore` was called. Programmers can then test this value to determine what happened when the contacts store was loaded.

```
const STORE_LOAD_OK = 0;
const STORE_EMPTY = 1;
const STORE_INVALID = 2;                            Constant values for the status codes
```

These values have been declared using the keyword `const`. This means that their value cannot be changed by the program when it runs. This is sensible because they are being used to indicate status values. The return values from `loadDataStore` are used by the function `doStartTinyData`. If the store is empty or invalid, an alert is displayed for the user.

```
function doStartTinyData(storeNameToUse) {
    storeName = storeNameToUse;

    var loadResult = loadDataStore();           Try to load the contact store

    switch(loadResult){
        case STORE_LOAD_OK:              If the store loaded OK we don't do anything
            break;
        case STORE_EMPTY:                If the store was empty we make a new one
            alert("Empty store created");
            saveDataStore();
            break;
        case STORE_INVALID:              If the store was corrupted, we make a new one
            alert("Store invalid. Empty store created");
            saveDataStore();
            break;
    }
}
```

It is very important that once we have created some error-handling code, we also create a way of testing it. In this case, I created a new application that breaks the storage. You can see it in **Figure 10-1** and find the application itself in the folder **Ch10 Advanced JavaScript\Ch10-04 Store Breaker** in the examples. You can use this application to "break" the data storage for the Tiny Contacts application.

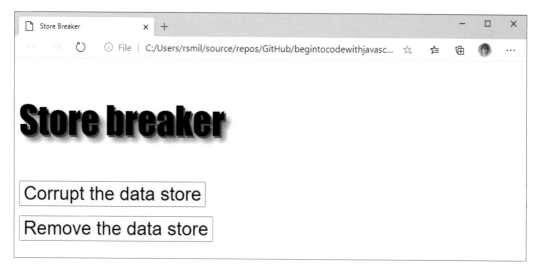

Figure 10-1   Store breaker

```
<!DOCTYPE html>
<html lang="en">

<head>
  <title>Store Breaker</title>
  <link rel="stylesheet" href="styles.css">
  <script src="breakstore.js"></script>
</head>

  <p class="menuHeading"> Store breaker</p>

  <p>
    <button class="menuButton" onclick="doBreakStore()">Corrupt the data store</button>
  </p>
  <p>
    <button class="menuButton" onclick="doEmptyStore()">Remove the data store</button>
  </p>
</body>
</html>
```

This is the HTML for the store breaker application. It contains two buttons. One button is pressed to corrupt the data store. It stores the string kaboom in the data store, which will cause JSON.parse to fail. The second button is pressed to remove the data store completely. These allow us to test the two possible errors.

```javascript
const storeName = "TinyContactsStore";            // Name of the store in local storage
function doBreakStore() {                          // Called to break the JSON storage
   var reply = confirm("Click OK to corrupt the data store");   // Show a confirm dialog
   if (reply) {                                    // If the user confirms perform the action
      localStorage.setItem(storeName, "kaboom");   // Save an invalid store name
   }
}

function doEmptyStore() {                           // Called to empty local storage
   var reply = confirm("Click OK to remove the data store");
   if (reply) {
      localStorage.removeItem(storeName);           // Remove the local storage item
   }
}
```

These functions use a feature of JavaScript that we haven't seen before. The confirm function allows a user to confirm an action. It pops up a message box containing the prompt string and offers the user a chance to either confirm the action or cancel. If the user confirms the action by clicking the **OK** button, as shown in **Figure 10-2**, the confirm function returns the value true.

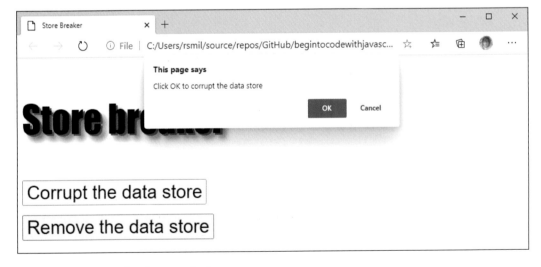

Figure 10-2   The confirm function display

Class design

From what we've learned up to now, we can regard a Java object as a container. We've
seen that a program can add properties to an object so that it can assemble related
items. We explored this by creating an object-based application that stores contact
details. Object properties were added by the program one at a time, building up a
complete set of contact information by adding name, address, and phone number
properties to an "empty" object. This works well for small applications, but sometimes
you want to map out your class design, rather than building it up as the program runs.
And, as we shall see, using classes to design objects also brings benefits by reducing
the amount of code that we write.

Fashion Shop application

Your lawyer client is very happy with her Time Tracker application. She's been showing
it to her friends, and they've been very impressed—particularly a friend who runs a
fashion shop and has been looking for an application to help her manage her stock.
She sells a range of clothing items and needs help tracking inventory. She's keen to
get your help, and she's offering discounted prices or even free clothing in exchange.
Free fashion sounds like an interesting idea, so you sit down with your new client and
talk about what she needs.

She tells you that stock arrives from suppliers, and she enters the details in her stock
book. For each different item that she sells, she stores a page of data in the book. She
updates the stock level in the book when stock arrives from her suppliers and when
she sells something. She shows you two of the pages from her book.

Figure 10-3 shows us what Imogen does when she works with the stock data. We can use this as the basis of our program specification. As usual, we draw some designs showing how the program will be used. There will be more than one design because this program will be spread across several "pages." For each page, we will need to also write a story that describes how the page will be used. This will also allow us to work through the feature provided by that page to make sure that we know exactly what the program should do. "User stories" are an important part of software design. You can find out more about them at *https://www.mountaingoatsoftware.com/agile/user-stories*.

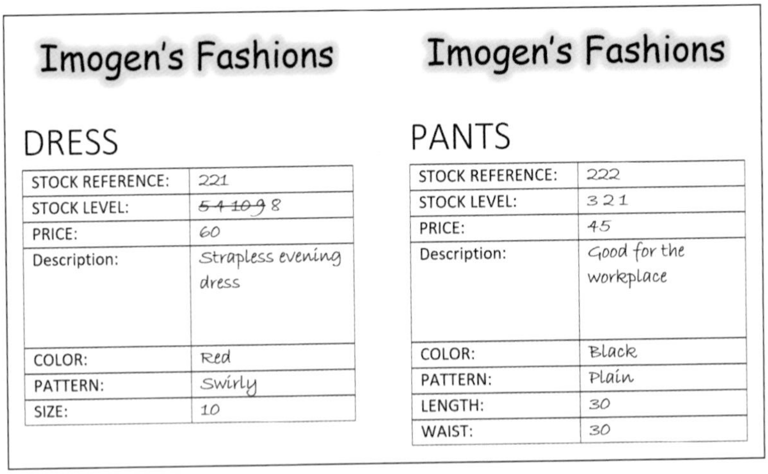

Imogen's Fashions	
DRESS	
STOCK REFERENCE:	221
STOCK LEVEL:	5 4 10 9 8
PRICE:	60
Description:	Strapless evening dress
COLOR:	Red
PATTERN:	Swirly
SIZE:	10

Imogen's Fashions	
PANTS	
STOCK REFERENCE:	222
STOCK LEVEL:	3 2 1
PRICE:	45
Description:	Good for the workplace
COLOR:	Black
PATTERN:	Plain
LENGTH:	30
WAIST:	30

Figure 10-3   Fashion shop stock items

Figure 10-4 shows the main menu of the program. Imogen can click the buttons to select pages to add dresses, pants, skirts, and tops to her stock. She can select an update page to edit any existing stock items to change their description or stock levels. She can also obtain a list of all her stock items by pressing the **List** button.

Figure 10-4   Fashion shop main menu

Figure 10-5 shows what Imogen would see when she presses the **Dress** button on the main menu to add a dress to stock. When she clicks **Save** on this page, the program will assign a stock number to the item and save it.

Imogen's Fashions

Add dress

Price:	60
Stock Level:	8
Description:	Strapless evening dress
Color:	Red
Pattern:	Swirly
Size:	10
Save item	Save
Cancel add	Cancel

Figure 10-5   Fashion shop add item

When a new item is added to the store, the program displays an alert, as shown in **Figure 10-6**. This gives the stock number, which was assigned to the new item.

Imogen's Fashions

This page says
dress 221 added

OK

Figure 10-6   Add complete

The **Update** stock item button on the main menu starts a search for a given stock number that is to be updated. **Figure 10-7** shows the search page. When the **Find** button is clicked, the program will search for a stock item with the given id value and display the item for editing.

Figure 10-7 Update Stock

The final button on the main menu shown in Figure 10-4 is the **List** button. Imogen will press this to generate a list of stock items that she can look through. Each item has an **Update** button that she can click (see **Figure 10-8**) to open the update page for that item.

Figure 10-8 Stock List

Imogen thinks this will be a good start for the application; you agree a price in stylish clothing and start working on the program. The first thing that you need to do is decide how the different stock items are going to be stored.

MAKE SOMETHING HAPPEN

Manage Imogen's Fashions

The application in the sample folder **Ch10 Advanced JavaScript\Ch10-05 Fashion Shop** implements a working fashion shop store. It creates a set of test data that you can view. You can also create your own fashion items, store them, and then search for them by their stock reference. You should spend some time adding and editing stock items to get a feel for how it is used. Then we can start working out how each part works.

Store stock data

We could store information for a particular stock item in a JavaScript object by creating an empty object and then adding properties to it:

```
myDress = {}
myDress.stockRef=221;
myDress.stockLevel=8;
myDress.price=60;
myDress.description="Strapless evening dress";
myDress.color="Red";
myDress.pattern="Swirly";
myDress.size=10;
```

Create an empty object
Add a stockRef property

The statements above create an object called myDress that contains all the data for the dress in Figure 10-3. However, there is a much easier way of creating objects that contain properties. We can create a class that tells JavaScript how to make a Dress object and what the object contains:

```
class Dress{
    constructor(stockRef, stockLevel, price, description, color, pattern, size){
        this.stockRef = stockRef;
        this.stockLevel = stockLevel;
        this.price = price;
        this.description = description;
        this.color = color;
        this.pattern = pattern;
        this.size = size;
    }
}
```

The JavaScript above doesn't store any data. Instead, it tells JavaScript the properties that are stored inside a Dress object and how to construct one. The constructor method is called to create an instance of the Dress class. Now we can create a new Dress much more easily:

```
myDress=new Dress(221,8,60,"Strapless evening dress","red","swirly",10);
```

The new keyword tells JavaScript to find the specified class and run the constructor method in that class to create a new instance of the class. When the constructor method runs, it copies the parameter values into properties in the newly created object. The keyword `this`, which you can see in the constructor method above, means "a reference to the object that this method is running inside."

property of the object
parameter to the function

```
this.price=price;
```

The confusing-looking statement above takes the price value that was supplied as an argument to the constructor and assigns it into a newly created `price` property on the object that is being created.

```
yourDress=new Dress(221,2,50,"Elegant party dress","blue","plain",12);
herDress=new Dress(222,5,65,"Floaty summer dress","green","floral",10);
```

If the word `this` is confusing, consider the two statements above. They create two `Dress` instances. Each time the constructor in the `Dress` class runs, it must set up a different object. In the first call of the constructor to set up the `yourDress` the keyword, `this` represents a reference to the `yourDress` object. In the second call of the constructor to set up `herDress`, the keyword `this` represents "a reference to the `herDress` object."

CODE ANALYSIS

Objects and constructors

Question: What happens if I create a class that doesn't contain a constructor?

> **Answer:** If you don't add a constructor method, JavaScript will create one for you that is empty.

Question: What happens if I omit some arguments from the call of a constructor?

> **Answer:** If you omit the arguments to a call of a JavaScript function or method, the values of those parameters are set to `undefined`.

```
shortDress = new Dress(221,0,50);
```

This statement would create a `Dress` with the stock reference (221), stock level (0), and price (50), but the description, color, pattern, and size properties would be set to the value `undefined`.

Question: What is the difference between a function and a method?

    Answer: A method is exactly like a function, but it is declared within a class. The constructor for a class is the first method that we have created. Later in this section, we will discover how we can add methods to classes to make objects that can provide services for our programs. A function is declared outside of any class.

Question: I still don't understand `this`. What does it mean?

    Answer: To understand what `this` does, it is a good idea to remember the problem it is solving. When a constructor method runs it must write property values in the object that it is setting up. The constructor for the `Dress` object needs to set the values of stock reference, stock level, price, and so on. JavaScript provides the keyword `this` to represent that reference.

Object-oriented design

It would make sense to create a class to hold each kind of data we wish to store. Programmers call this object-oriented programming. The idea is that elements in a solution are represented by software "objects." The first step in creating an application is to identify these objects.

In the English language, words that identify things are called nouns. When trying to work out what classes a system should contain, it's a good idea to look through the description of a system and find all the nouns. As an example, consider the following description of a fast-food delivery application.

"The customer will select a dish from the menu and add it to his order."

I've identified four nouns in this description, each of which will map to a specific class in the application. If I were working for the fast-food delivery company, I would next ask them what data they stored about customers, dishes, menus, and orders.

> **PROGRAMMER'S POINT**
> ## Don't write any code before you have completed your data design
>
> For a commercial project, you would spend a lot of time on the design of the classes in your system before you wrote a single line of code. This is because design mistakes are much easier to fix at the beginning of the project, rather than after code has been written.
>
> In the case of our fast-food management example above, we would want to make sure that the customer class holds all the information required to make the business work. We would do this by creating "paper" versions of the classes and then working through all the usage

scenarios (creating an order, cooking an order, and delivering an order) to make sure that all the data the application needs is being captured.

If the application must store a customer telephone number so that the delivery driver can call for directions if needed, it is best to discover this at the beginning of the project, rather than after the entire user interface has been created.

We will write code and discuss it as we go along because we are learning about data design and JavaScript programming. However, if I were creating a professional solution, I'd spend a lot of time away from JavaScript working out the design before I created any classes.

When we talk to our fashion shop customer, she'll talk about the dresses, pants, hats, tops, and other items that she wants the application to manage. Each of these could be objects in the application and can be represented by a class. Each class will contain the properties that describe that item of clothing. Let's start by considering just the information for dresses and pants and create some classes for these objects. We already have a class for Dress, so let's make one for Pants.

```
class Pants{
    constructor(stockRef, stockLevel, price,
                description, color, pattern, length, waist){
        this.stockRef = stockRef;
        this.stockLevel = stockLevel;
        this.price=price;
        this.description=description;
        this.color = color;
        this.pattern = pattern;
        this.length = length;
        this.waist = waist;

    }
}
```

The code above defines a Pants class. It contains a constructor method to set up the contents of that class. Our program can now create instances of these classes:

```
myDress=new Dress(221,8,60,"Strapless evening dress","red","swirly",10);
myPants=new Pants(222,1,45,"Good for the workplace","black","plain",30,30);
```

When I wrote this sample code, I found myself using a lot of block-copy commands in the editor when I created the constructor. This is not necessarily a good thing.

Creating superclasses and subclasses

JavaScript classes support a mechanism called *inheritance*. This is another aspect of object-oriented design. Inheritance lets us base one class on an existing superclass. This is called extending the superclass. We can greatly simplify the design of our classes for the Fashion Shop program by creating a superclass, which we can call `StockItem`.

The `StockItem` class will store all the attributes common to all the data items in the shop. These are the stock reference, price, color, and stock level. The `Dress` and `Pants` classes will extend the `StockItem` class and add the properties particular to dresses and pants. **Figure 10-9** shows the arrangement of the classes we're creating. In software design terms, this is called a class diagram.

The class diagram shows the relationship between classes in a system. Figure 10-9 shows that both `Pants` and `Dress` are subclasses of the `StockItem` class (meaning they are based on that class). We could also say that the `StockItem` class is the superclass of `Dress` and `Pants`.

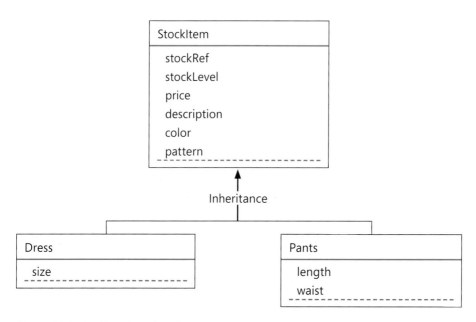

Figure 10-9 Fashion shop class diagram

In real life, inheritance means stuff that you get from people who are older than you. In JavaScript terms, inheritance means the attributes a subclass gets from its superclass. Some programmers call the superclass the parent class and the subclass the child class.

The key to understanding inheritance is to focus on the problem it is solving. We're working with a collection of related data items. The related items have some properties in common. We want to implement the shared properties in a superclass and then use this superclass as the basis of subclasses that will hold data specific to their item type. That way, we only need to implement the common properties once, and any faults in the implementation of those properties need only be fixed once.

Working in this way has another advantage. If the fashion shop owner decides that she would find it useful to be able to store the manufacturer of the items she's selling, we can add a manufacturer attribute to the `StockItem` class, and all the subclasses will inherit that attribute, too. This will be easier than adding the attribute to each class.

Abstraction using objects

Another way to think of this is to consider what we are doing as abstraction. We first encountered abstraction in Chapter 9 in the section "Use a data schema," where we created a design for all data stores rather than building individual ones. We have seen abstraction means "stepping back" from the problem and taking a more general view. In our conversations with the fashion shop owner, we would like to talk in general terms about the things she would like to do with the stock in her shop. She will want to add stock items, sell stock items, find out what stock items she has, and so on. We can talk to her about her stock in abstract terms and then later go back to fill in the specific details about each type of stock and give them appropriate behaviors.

Programmers use abstraction a lot. They talk about things like stock items, customers, and orders without considering specific details. Later, they can go back and "fill in the details" and decide what particular kinds of stock items, customers, and orders with which the application will work. We'll create different kinds of stock items in our Fashion Shop program. The StockItem class will contain the fundamental properties for all the stock, and the subclasses will represent more specific items.

The diagram in Figure 10-9 is called a class hierarchy. It shows the superclass at the top and subclasses below. When you travel down a class hierarchy, you should find that you move from the abstract toward the more concrete. The least abstract classes are Pants and Dress because these represent actual physical objects in our application.

CODE ANALYSIS

Understanding inheritance

Here are some questions about object-oriented design and inheritance. Try to come up with your own answers before reading the answers I've provided.

Question: Why is the superclass called "super"?

> **Answer:** This is a good question and one that has confused me for a long time. The word "super" usually implies something better or more powerful. A "superhero" has special powers that ordinary people do not. However, in the case of a superclass, this doesn't seem to be the case. The superclass has fewer powers (fewer properties) than the subclass that extends it.
>
> I think the word "super" makes sense if you consider it as something that classes descend from. The super object is above the sub object, just like superscript text is above subscript text. The object is the superclass because it is above everything else.

Question: Which is most abstract, a superclass or a subclass?

> **Answer:** If you can work out the answer to this question, you can start to consider yourself an "object-oriented ninja." Remember that we use abstraction as a way of "stepping back" from the elements in a system. We'll say "receipt" rather than "cash receipt" or "StockItem" rather than "Pants."

Question: Can you extend a subclass?

Answer: Yes, you can extend a subclass. We could create a Jeans class that extended the Pants class and contained a style property that could be "skinny," "high waist," "bootcut," or "flared." In JavaScript, there is no limit to how many times you can extend classes, although I try to keep my class diagrams fairly shallow, with no more than two or three subclasses.

Question: Why is the pattern property not in the StockItem class?

Answer: Most impressive. Well spotted. The pattern property is in both the Dress and Pants classes. It might seem sensible to move the property into the StockItem class with the color, stockLevel, and price attributes.

The reason I haven't done this is that I think that the fashion shop might sell some stock items that have no pattern—for example, items of jewelry. I want to avoid a class having data properties that aren't relevant to that item type, so I've put pattern values into the Dress and the Pants class instead.

I'm not particularly happy with this because ideally, a property should appear only in one class, but in real-world design, you come across these issues quite often. One possible way to resolve the issue would be to create a subclass called PatternedStock that is the superclass for Dress and Pants. However, I think that would be too confusing.

Question: Will our system ever create a StockItem object?

Answer: JavaScript will allow the creation of a StockItem object (an instance of the StockItem class), but it's unlikely that we would ever actually create a StockItem on its own.

Some programming languages, such as C++, Java, and C#, allow you to specify that a class definition is abstract, which stops a program from making instances of that class. In these languages, an abstract class exists solely as the superclass for subclasses. However, JavaScript does not provide this feature.

Question: The owner of the fashion shop thinks that one day she might like to keep track of which customer has bought which item of stock. This will allow her to look at their past purchases and make recommendations for future purchases. Here are three ways to do this. Which would make the most sense?

1. Extend the StockItem class to make a Customer subclass that contains the customer details because customers buy stock.

2. Add customer details to each StockItem.

3. Create a new Customer class that contains a list of the StockItems that the customer has bought.

Answer: Option 1 is a bad idea because a class hierarchy should hold items that are in the same "family." In other words, they should all be different versions of the same fundamental type. We can see that there is some association between a Customer and a StockItem, but making a Customer a subclass of StockItem is a bad idea because they're different kinds of objects. The StockItem holds attributes such as price and stockLevel, which are meaningless when applied to a Customer.

Option 2 is a bad idea because several customers might buy the same `StockItem`. The customer details cannot be stored inside the `StockItem`.

Option 3, adding a new `Customer` class, is the best way to do this. Remember that because objects in JavaScript are managed by references, the list of items in the `Customer` class (the items the customer has bought) will just be a list of references, not copies of `StockItem` information.

Store data in a class hierarchy

Now that we've decided using inheritance is a good idea, we need to consider how to make it work with our classes.

```
class StockItem{
    constructor(stockRef, stockLevel, price, description, color){
        this.stockRef = stockRef;
        this.price=price;
        this.description=description;
        this.stockLevel = stockLevel;
        this.color = color;
    }
}
```

This is the `StockItem` class file. It contains a constructor method to set up a `StockItem` instance. The `StockItem` class will be the superclass of all the objects that the fashion shop will be selling. We can create a `Dress` class that is a subclass of the `StockItem` class to hold information about dresses that the fashion shop will be selling.

```
class BrokenDress extends StockItem{
    constructor(stockRef, stockLevel, price, description, color, pattern, size){
        this.pattern = pattern;
        this.size = size;
    }
}
```

The `BrokenDress` class extends the `StockItem` class. It only contains the properties that are specific dresses. However, we have a problem if we try to use the `BrokenDress` class:

```
myDress=new BrokenDress(221,8,60,"Strapless evening dress","red","swirly",10);
```

The statement above tries to create an instance of the `BrokenDress` class. This statement will fail with an error:

Uncaught ReferenceError: Must call super constructor in derived class before accessing 'this' or returning from derived constructor at new BrokenDress

JavaScript is telling us that to create a `BrokenDress`, our constructor must first create a `StockItem`. The constructor in the `BrokenDress` class that we have created doesn't do this, so this class is broken (hence the name). To fix it, we need to make a `Dress` class that contains a constructor that first constructs the super object. JavaScript provides the `super` keyword, which can be used in a constructor to call the constructor in the superclass. The constructor method for the `Dress` class calls the constructor method in the `StockItem` class by means of the `super` keyword.

```
class Dress extends StockItem{
    constructor(stockRef, stockLevel, price, color, pattern, size){
        super(stockRef,stockLevel, price, color);———— Call the constructor in the superclass
        this.pattern = pattern;
        this.size = size;
    }
}
```

 MAKE SOMETHING HAPPEN

Investigate using super to create instances

The example application in the folder **Ch10 Advanced JavaScript\Ch10-06 Fashion Shop Classes** contains the `StockItem`, `BrokenDress`, and `Dress` classes that you can experiment with. You can use the Developer View to debug the process of creating a `Dress` by placing a breakpoint at the first statement of the `Dress` constructor and then stepping through the JavaScript as the `super` keyword is used to call the constructor in the `StockItem`.

Add a method to give an object a behavior

Things that are part of a class are called the members of the class. We know how to create properties which are members of a class. Now we are going to find out how to add method members. Adding a method member to a class allows it to do things for our program. At the moment, the classes we have created don't contain any methods. A useful method might be one that allows a `Dress` to provide us with a string describing its contents. We can use this to produce the text to be displayed for the Stock List menu item.

```
class Dress extends StockItem{

    constructor(stockRef, stockLevel, price, description, color, pattern, size){
        super(stockRef,stockLevel, price, description, color);
        this.pattern = pattern;
        this.size = size;
    }

    getDescription(){
        var result = "Ref:" + this.stockRef +
            " Price:" + this.price +
            " Stock:" + this.stockLevel +
            " Description:" + this.description +
            " Color:" + this.color +
            " Pattern:" + this.pattern +
            " Size:" + this.size ;
        return result;
    }
}
```

getDescription **method**

Assemble a string containing a description

Return the string

The `Dress` class above contains a method called `getDescription` that can be called to get a description of the contents of the object. Note that the method uses the `this` reference to access the properties of the object that is being described. A program can use this method to get a string that describes a particular dress.

```
myDress=new Dress(221,8,60,"Strapless evening dress","red","swirly",10);
console.log(myDress.getDescription());
```

The first statement above creates a dress object called `myDress`. The second statement uses the `getDescription` method on the `myDress` object to display a description of the dress. It would display the following:

```
Ref:221 Price:60 Stock:8 Description:Strapless evening dress Color:red
Pattern:swirly Size:10
```

The Fashion Shop application will use the `getDescription` method to build an HTML element to be displayed in a stock list.

Investigate the `getDescription` method

The example application in the **Ch10 Advanced JavaScript \Ch10-07 Fashion Shop Methods** folder contains the `StockItem`, `Dress`, and `Pants` classes that you can experiment with. You can use the Developer View to create `Dress` and `Pants` instances and call the `getDescription` method to view their contents.

Objects and polymorphism

The next thing I want to talk about has the most impressive name in the entire book. The word polymorphism comes from the Greek language and means "the condition of occurring in multiple forms." In software engineering, it means regarding an object in terms of what it can do rather than what it is.

A great thing about the `getDescription` method is that other parts of the Fashion Shop application don't need to know how the `Dress` and `Pants` classes store their data or even what data is stored inside them. A part of the program that needs to produce a description of a `Dress` doesn't have to pull out the various properties from a `Dress` instance; it just has to call the `getDescription` method to get a string that describes that particular dress. What's more, this part of the program doesn't need to care whether it is dealing with dresses or pants, it can just view these items as "things I can use `getDescription` to get a description of."

Polymorphism means thinking about objects in terms of what they can do, rather than what they are, and allowing each object to perform a particular action in a way specific to that object. A given object can be viewed in many ways, depending on what you want to do with it. Different parts of the Fashion Shop will view objects in terms of abilities such as "get a description string," "set a discount," "save," and "load." Each of these abilities can be provided by methods inside the object with a characteristic name, which can then be used by the rest of the system to perform that action. Part of an object-based design process involves identifying the behaviors required of objects and specifying them as methods.

Overriding methods in subclasses

A fundamental principle of object-oriented design is that a given object contains all the behaviors for that particular object. In this respect the `getDescription` method in the `Dress` class is not good. The first four items that are used to build the description string are not held in the `Dress` class. Instead, they are held in the `StockItem` superclass.

```
getDescription(){
    var result = "Ref:" + this.stockRef +
        " Price:" + this.price +
        " Stock:" + this.stockLevel +
        " Description:" + this.description +
        " Color:" + this.color +
        " Pattern:" + this.pattern +
        " Size:" + this.size ;
    return result;
    }
}
```

	value is from the StockItem class
	value is from the StockItem class
	value is from the StockItem class
	value is from the StockItem class
	value is from the StockItem class

If we added a new property to the StockItem class, we would have to also change the getDescription method in the Dress class to display the new property. If StockItem had many subclasses, we would have to change every one. What we would like to do is make the StockItem class responsible for delivering the description of what it contains, and then use that description in the Dress class. It turns out that we can do this by creating a getDescription method in the StockItem class and then overriding the getDescription method in subclasses of StockItem.

```
class StockItem{
    getDescription(){
        var result = "Ref:" + this.stockRef +
            " Price:" + this.price +
            " Stock:" + this.stockLevel +
            " Description:" + this.description +
            " Color:" + this.color;
        return result;
        }
}


class Dress extends StockItem{
    getDescription(){
        var result =   super.getDescription() +
            " Pattern:" + this.pattern +
            " Size:" + this.size ;
        return result;
        }
}
```

Override the getDescription method in the superclass

Call getDescription from the superclass

Both StockItem and Dress contain a getDescription method. We say that the getDescription method in the Dress class overrides the getDescription method in the StockItem class. A description of a Dress must include a description of the contents of the super object of Dress, so the JavaScript super keyword is used to invoke the getDescription method in the StockItem object. Within a method in a class the word super is a reference to the super object (the one above the object in the class hierarchy).

Understanding super

The example application in the folder **Ch10 Advanced JavaScript \Ch10-08 Dress Shop Override Methods** contains the StockItem, Dress, and Pants classes that work in exactly the same way as the previous example. But these versions use overridden versions of the getDescription method. You can use the debugger to explore how the overridden method is called. However, you might also have some questions.

Question: How does the super reference work?

Answer: When a program is running JavaScript keeps a lump of data about each class that is being used. One of the items of information that JavaScript stores is the superclass of each class. When JavaScript sees the keyword super in a statement it looks in the definition of the class the method is part of to find the superclass. It then finds the specified method in the superclass and runs it.

Question: What would happen if you tried to use super in a class at the top of a hierarchy?

Answer: This would cause an error because JavaScript would not find a super method.

Question: Can you override a function in a JavaScript program?

Answer: No. A function is not part of an object. You can only override a method, which is part of an object.

Static class members

You will have noticed that the demonstration Fashion Shop app contains a lot of test data. This is generated by the data objects themselves. The data and methods to create test dresses are not part of any Dress instance. Instead, they are part of the Dress class itself. JavaScript lets us do this by creating properties and methods, which are static. The word "static" in this context means "always there," rather than unchanging. We don't need to use new to create an instance of the Dress class to get hold of the static members of the class. These members exist as soon as the JavaScript class is loaded by the browser.

```
static colors = ["red", "blue", "green", "yellow"];        ──── Static array of colors
static patterns = ['plain', 'striped', 'spotted', 'swirly'];── Static array of patterns
static sizes = [8, 10, 12, 14];                            ──── Static array of sizes
                                                               Static function to get test data
static getTestItems(dest) {                         ──── Make sure we don't repeat stock numbers
    var stockNo = StockItem.getLargestStockRef(dest) + 1;
    for (let color of Dress.colors) {        ────────────── Work through the colors
        for (let pattern of Dress.patterns) {──────────── Work through the patterns
            for (let size of Dress.sizes) {──────────── Work through the sizes
                let price = StockItem.getRandomInt(10, 200);── Get a random price
                let stock = StockItem.getRandomInt(0, 15);──── Get a random stock level
                let description = color + " " + pattern + " dress";
                dest[dest.length] =                   ──── Build a description string
                new Dress(stockNo, stock, price, description, color, pattern, size);
                stockNo = stockNo + 1;────────────────── Advance the stock number
            }
        }
    }
}
                                                ──── Create a new Dress and store it
```

The method getTestItems above works through arrays of colors, patterns, and sizes to create a large number of dress stock items, which it adds to an array supplied as a parameter. The getTestItems method is static, so it can be called without the program needing to make an instance of the Dress class. The data arrays that are used by the getTestItems method are also defined as static. The getTestItems method also uses the static method getRandomInt, which is declared in the StockItem class. The getRandomInt method is used to obtain random prices and stock levels for the dresses that are created. It is based on the function that we created to make a random dice. The getLargestStockRef method is used to search the fashion store to find the highest stock number in it. This ensures that the function doesn't create any stock items with the same stock number as existing ones.

The static members of a class are marked with the static keyword. Static class members are accessed via the class identifier so the above method can be used as follows to create an array full of Dress values:

```
demo = []
Dress.getTestItems(demo);
```

Understanding `static`

The example application in the folder **Ch10 Advanced JavaScript \Ch10-09 Fashion Shop Static Members** contains `Dress` and `Pants` classes that contain static `getTestItems` method that create large amounts of data that can be used to test our system. However, you might also have some questions.

Question: Does `static` mean that a class member cannot be changed?

> **Answer:** No. The `static` keyword affects where a class member is stored, not what you can do with it. `Static` marks members of a class that are part of a class, not an instance of the class. If you want to make a variable that cannot be changed you can declare it as `const`.

Question: Can you give me an example of a good use for static members of a class?

> **Answer:** Static members are things that you want to store for the entire class. Suppose that you wanted to set a maximum price for all the dresses that the fashion shop sells. This could be used to help detect when someone mistypes a price value. This value should be stored in a static member of the class since it does not need to be stored with every dress. If we need to change the maximum price of a dress, we can just update the static value and the maximum price for all the dresses will be changed.
>
> You make a method member of a class static when you want to use the method without creating an instance of the class. The JavaScript Math class contains lots of static methods to perform mathematical functions. These are declared as static so that we don't have to create an instance of the `Math` class to be able to use them.

Question: Where does the stock ref number come from when we create a new stock item?

> **Answer:** Each item of stock has a stock reference number. This number identifies a stock item in the same way that a given credit card number identifies a credit card. Imogen will enter the stock reference number to find an item she wants to edit. It is very important that each stock item has a unique stock reference number. The `getLargestStockRef` method searches through all the items and returns the largest stock reference that it has found. The program then adds 1 to this value to get the next stock number to be used.

```
static getLargestStockRef(items) {
    if (items.length == 0) {          If there are no items return 0
        return 0;
    }

    var largest = items[0].stockRef;   Start with the first stock reference number
```

```
    for (const item of items) {———————————————  Search through the stock items
        if (item.stockRef > largest) {————— If the item has a larger stock reference, save it
            largest = item.stockRef;
        }
    }

    return largest;————————————————————————————  Return the largest stock number
}
```

Data storage

We have one last problem to solve before we can build the finished solution. We need a way of saving the dress shop data. The Tiny Contacts application that we created in Chapter 9 used JSON to encode the contact objects into text that was then stored as strings in browser local storage. We can do something similar, but the use of a class hierarchy makes it a little bit trickier. To understand why, consider what happens when we convert a dress value to a string using the JSON.stringify method.

```
{"stockRef":1,"stockLevel":"11","price":"85",
"description":"red plain dress","color":"red","pattern":"plain","size":"8"}
```

The text above is a JSON string that describes a dress. It contains all the properties in a Dress instance, including those in the StockItem object superclass. When we load this object back into our program we want to be able to use it as a Dress object. Unfortunately, there is nothing in the JSON string that tells a program reading it that this is a stored Dress value.

Add type information to JSON

The way to fix this is to add an extra property to our data that gives the type of the data. We can do this in the constructor for the class:

```
constructor(stockRef, stockLevel, price, description, color, pattern, size) {
    super(stockRef, stockLevel, price, description, color);
    this.type = "dress";————————————————————  Add a type property to the dress
    this.pattern = pattern;
    this.size = size;
}
```

This is the modified `Dress` constructor. We can modify the constructor for the other types of clothing so that they create an appropriate `type` property. For example, the `Pants` constructor must set a `type` value of `"pants"` and so on.

Use the stored type property

```
{"stockRef":1,"stockLevel":"11","price":"85","type":"dress",
"description":"red plain dress","color":"red","pattern":"plain","size":"8"}
```

The JSON above describes a dress that contains a `type` property. I've highlighted the type information in yellow. What we need now is a way of creating a `Dress` instance from this JSON source string. I created a member function in the `StockItem` class to do this. The function is called `JSONparse`. It takes in a string of JSON and returns an object of the type specified by the `type` value in JSON. It uses a `switch` construction to decide what type of object to create.

```
static JSONparse(text) {                        Static method to read a stock object
    var rawObject = JSON.parse(text);           Create a raw object from the JSON string
    var result = null;                          Create an empty result

    switch (rawObject.type) {                   Decide which type of object is being loaded
        case "dress":
            result = new Dress();               Make an empty Dress object
            break;
        case "pants":
            result = new Pants();               Make an empty Pants object
            break;
    }
    Object.assign(result, rawObject);           Copy the properties from the object into the result
    return result;
}
```

The `JSONparse` method also uses a method that we have not seen before. It is called `Object.assign`, and you can see it used in the last but one statement in the method. The `Object.assign` function copies all the data properties from one object to another. The program uses this to take all the data properties from the JSON object that we read and copy them into the empty object that we have just created. The first argument to the `assign` function is the destination object for the copy. This is the newly created object of the required type. The second argument to the `assign` function is the `rawObject` that was loaded from JSON. This contains all the data properties.

Load and save

The example application in the **Ch10 Advanced JavaScript \ Ch10-10 Fashion Shop No Test Data** folder is a version of the Fashion Shop that doesn't generate test data when first started. You can create and store stock items and they will be persisted when the browser is closed. It uses local storage in exactly the same way as the Tiny Contacts program, but it creates an array of JSON strings to store the data.

Question: The object that we loaded from the JSON object contains all the data properties that the program needs. Why do we have to copy it into another object?

> **Answer:** This is because a Dress instance contains function members as well as data members. The system needs to be able to ask a Dress instance to do things like getDescription. An object created from JSON will not have these methods. So we need to create an "empty" Dress instance that contains the required methods and then add the data from the object that we have read from JSON.

Question: Why has the JSONparse method been made `static`?

> **Answer:** The JSONparse method is called to read stock items from storage. It has to be `static` because when the program is first started there are no stock items loaded.

Question: Do you need a copy of the JSONparse method in every stock class (for example Dress and Pants)?

> **Answer:** No. The nice thing about this is that a single copy of the JSONparse method in the StockItem class will load data for any of the classes because it just copies what has been saved. However, you do need to make sure that the `switch` statement in the JSONparse method is kept up to date. If you add a new type of stock (perhaps hats), you would have to add a `case` for that type to the switch.

Build a user interface

We now have all the behaviors that we need to make the Fashion Shop application. We can put all the different kinds of data in objects which can be saved and loaded. Our class-based design means that data properties shared by all the different objects are only stored in one place. The only thing missing is the user interface element. We need a menu system for the application along with views of the different types of data.

Make stock items display themselves

We have already built HTML documents that look very similar to parts of the Fashion Shop application. When we created the Tiny Contacts application, we created schema objects to describe the display elements that were needed. We can use the same approach to design HTML elements for each of the data classes in the Fashion Shop. If you're not sure how we used schemas to design an HTML document, take a look in the "Use a data schema" section in Chapter 9.

```
static StockItemSchema = [
    { id: "price", prompt: "Price", type: "input" },
    { id: "stockLevel", prompt: "Stock Level", type: "input" },
    { id: "description", prompt: "Description", type: "textarea", rows: 5, cols: 40 },
    { id: "color", prompt: "Color", type: "input" }];
```

The code above shows the display schema for the StockItem class. This is the same schema design as we used for the Tiny Contacts application. There is an entry for each item to be displayed. The item gives the id of the property, the prompt to be displayed, and the type of the input. Three of the items are single-line inputs, and one is a text area. If you take a look at Figure 10-5 from earlier in this chapter, you will see how this schema defines the display of the top four values to be entered.

```
static buildElementsFromSchema(HTMLdisplay, dataSchema) {
    // work through each of the items in the schema
    for (let item of dataSchema) {                          ──── Work through the schema
        // make an element for that item
        let itemElement = StockItem.makeElement(item);      ──── Create the display element
        // add the element to the container
        HTMLdisplay.appendChild(itemElement);               ──── Add the element to the page
    }
}
```

The buildElementsFromSchema method works through the elements in a schema and uses a function called makeElement to create each element from the schema informa-tion and add it to an HTML element. It is the same mechanism that was used to create the display of the Tiny Contacts application.

```
getHTML(containerElementId) {
    StockItem.buildElementsFromSchema(containerElementId, StockItem.StockItemSchema);
}
```

The StockItem class contains a method called getHTML that calls buildElements FromSchema with the parameters required to build the part of a display needed to edit a StockItem. Now that we know how to build the display for a StockItem, we can consider how to build the display for a Dress.

```
static DressSchema = [{ id: "pattern", prompt: "Pattern", type: "input" },
{ id: "size", prompt: "Size", type: "input" }];                    Schema for the Dress display
                                                Function to add the property elements to an HTML document
getHTML(containerElementId) {
    super.getHTML(containerElementId);                    Add the elements from the parent object
    StockItem.buildElementsFromSchema(containerElementId, Dress.DressSchema);
}
                                                                Add the elements from the Dress
```

The code above is the code that builds the display for the dress. The getHTML method uses a schema that defines just the extra elements that need to be added to the HTML document for the dress. It calls the getHTML function of its super object (which is the StockItem) to get the HTML for that object and then adds its own elements on the end.

 CODE ANALYSIS

Creating HTML

A great programming language is one where you can create code that you are proud of. I'm quite proud of this HTML-generating code. It is easy to use and easy to extend. We can add more stock types and easily express what each stock type contains. However, you might have some questions about it.

Question: What does this code do again?

> **Answer:** Good question. Remember that our data design has given us some classes that hold all the different data properties in a stock item. We have used inheritance to create a superclass called StockItem that holds all the properties shared by all the stock items (such as the price and the number of items in stock). Then we've created subclasses of StockItem that hold data specific to that type of item (such as the length and waist properties of Pants).
>
> If we want the user to interact with these properties, we will need to create HTML (labels and input elements) in the HTML document displayed by the browser. We could do this by hand, but it would be tedious. When we made the Tiny Contacts application, we created a schema object that defined the properties to be displayed and then wrote a method that that worked through the schema making HTML elements to edit each item. Think of a schema as a "shopping list" of items to be displayed.
>
> The process described above takes the same approach as we used for Tiny Contacts and adds a schema to each type of stock item. It uses the super keyword so that the display builder (the getHTML method) in Dress can call the getHTML method in the StockItem class. It is necessarily complicated, but if you stare at it hard enough, it does make sense. And if you understand it, you can call yourself a "class hierarchy ninja."

Question: What would I need to do if I wanted to add a new data property to the StockItem class?

Answer: This is a situation in which this approach would pay off. If Imogen decides that she wants the system to record some new data in the StockItem class, we could add a new item to the StockItem schema. The display elements produced would be added to the edit displays of all the stock items because they are all subclasses of StockItem.

Start the application

This application uses four variables that are shared between all the functions:

```
var mainPage;   // HTML element that contains the user interface
var dataStore;  // Array of stock items
var storeName;  // name of save data in local storage
var activeItem; // currently active stock item (for entry and edit)
```

When the Fashion Shop starts, these variables must be set up. The body element of the HTML document containing the application contains an onload attribute that specifies the function to be called when the page is loaded. This function starts the Fashion Shop running. The function is called doStartFashionShop.

```
<body onload="doStartFashionShop('mainPage','fashionShop')" class="mainPage">
```

The function doStartFashionShop is very similar to the function doStartTinyContacts that we created in Chapter 9 to start the Tiny Contacts application. This function needs to load the stock data from the browser and set up the other shared variables.

```
function doStartFashionShop(mainPageId, storeNameToUse) {

    mainPage = document.getElementById(mainPageId);     Set mainPage to refer to
                                                        the page container

    storeName = storeNameToUse;                         Set the name of the local storage string

    loadDataStore();                                    Load the stock data

    doShowMainMenu();                                   Show the main menu
}
```

The last statement in doStartFashionShop displays the user menu. Lets take a look at how that works.

Create user menus

The user interacts with our program by pressing buttons on the screen that select the various menu options. If you look back to Figure 10-4, you can see the main menu for the display. Each of the program options is selected by pressing a button, and when the button is pressed, the application calls the function for that option.

```
function doShowMainMenu() {
    openPage("Main Menu");

    showMenu(
        [{ desc: "Add Dress", label: "Dress", func: "doAddDress()" },
        { desc: "Add Pants", label: "Pants", func: "doAddPants()" },
        { desc: "Add Skirt", label: "Skirt", func: "doAddSkirt()" },
        { desc: "Add Top", label: "Top", func: "doAddTop()" },
        { desc: "Update stock item", label: "Update", func: "doUpdateStock()" },
        { desc: "List stock items", label: "List", func: "doListFashionShop()" }]);
}
```

I'm using yet another schema to describe each menu option. The function showMenu works through the schema and builds the display. If you look back to Figure 10-4, you can map the application main menu onto the items in the schema above. The function openPage removes all the elements on the page and displays a heading.

Add a stock item

The menu calls an add function for each stock item. The doAddDress function looks like this:

```
function doAddDress() {
    addStock(Dress);
}
```

It calls the addStock function and does something we've not seen before. It uses the Dress class as an argument to the call of addStock. We do this so that we can have a single addStock function that can create any type of stock item.

```
function addStock(StockClass) {

    activeItem = new StockClass();                          Create a new item
```

```
    openPage("Add " + activeItem.type);                    ─────────    Display a new page

    activeItem.getHTML(mainPage);                           ─────────    Get the HTML for the new item

    showMenu(
        [{ desc: "Save item", label: "Save", func: "doSaveAdd()" },
         { desc: "Cancel add", label: "Cancel", func: "doShowMainMenu()" }]);
                                                            ─────────    Show a menu for the add page
    }
```

The addStock function makes a new item of the required class (the class is supplied as
a parameter). It then creates a new display page and fills it with the HTML generated
by the new item. At the end of the page, the function builds a menu containing Save
and Cancel buttons. The function handler for the Cancel button just displays the main
menu. The function for the Save button copies the inputs from the HTML elements
into a new copy of the stock item. This function has the name doSaveAdd. The job of
doSaveAdd is to copy the data from the HTML document into the currently active item.
This item is then stored in the data store.

```
    function doSaveAdd() {                                  ────  Load the data from the HTML into the new item
        activeItem.loadFromHTML();                          ────        Assign a stock number
        activeItem.stockRef = StockItem.getLargestStockRef(dataStore) + 1;
        dataStore[dataStore.length] = activeItem;           ────             Store the item
        alert(activeItem.type + " " + activeItem.stockRef + " added");
        saveDataStore();                                    ────        Save the data store
        doShowMainMenu();                                   ────        Display the main menu
    }
```

Exploring the Fashion Shop application

There is a lot to explore in the Fashion Shop and you can learn a lot by exploring it.
The application is heavily based on the Time Tracker application. I would strongly
advise you to spend some time going through the code. You can use the Developer View debugger to work through the code as it runs. The great thing about the
application is that it is very clear what the intent of each function is. For example, the
edit function, which we have not explored in this chapter, must find a stock item to
be edited, make that item the active item, and when the edit is completed, copy the
edited properties from the HTML document into the data store.

Note that we have not explored the function that provides a list of stock items. You
can use it, and you can look at the code that makes it work, but we will be investigating that function and adding some great features to it in the next chapter.

Expand the fashion shop

You can also learn a lot about programming by adding features to an existing application. Here are some things that you might like to do with the Fashion Shop application:

- Add a new type of clothing called `suit`. A suit has the properties jacket size, pant size, color, pattern, and style. You can do this by adding a new class that is a subclass of `StockItem`.

- Add a new property called `manufacturer`, which is to be stored for all the items in stock. You can do this by adding a new attribute to the `StockItem` class.

- Add some data validation to the application. At the moment the user can save stock item records that have missing data fields. Write a function that tests for empty fields and only allows a record to be saved if all the fields have been filled in.

- Create a totally new data storage application, which can store information for another business, perhaps a fishing tackle store. You should find this quite easy to do. You can use the Fashion Shop application as a great starting point.

What you have learned

In this chapter, you learned how JavaScript objects allow programs to store related items as properties of a single object and how to make programs that work with objects.

1. JavaScript programs can create and *throw* exception objects that describe an error that has been detected by the code. JavaScript statements that may throw exception objects can be enclosed in a try block as part of a `try-catch` construction. The `catch` element of the construction contains JavaScript code that only runs in the event of an exception being thrown. This construction allows a program to detect and deal with errors in a managed way.

2. A program should only raise an exception when something exceptional has occurred. Errors that are to be expected in the normal running of the program (such as invalid user input or network failures) should not be managed using exceptions.

3. A JavaScript class lets a programmer design the contents of an object by specifying data to be used in the class constructor method to set initial values of properties in the class.

4. A JavaScript class constructor method accepts parameters that can be used to initialize properties in a newly created class instance.

5. The JavaScript `new` keyword is used to create a new instance of a class by calling a constructor method in that class. Because missing method arguments to a JavaScript method call are replaced by the value `undefined` you can use a constructor call with no parameters to create an "empty" class instance that contains undefined values for all the properties.

6. A JavaScript class can contain methods that are members of the class. A member method can be called by code outside the class to allow an object to provide behaviors for that code.

7. Within a class method the reference `this` refers to the object within which the method is running.

8. JavaScript inheritance allows the creation of "super" or "parent" classes that can be extended to create "sub" or "child" classes. A subclass contains all the members of the parent. This allows attributes shared by a number of related classes to be stored in a single superclass.

9. A subclass can *override* methods in the superclass by providing their own implementations of the method. The keyword `super` allows a method in a subclass to call the superclass. The constructor of a subclass must contain a constructor method that makes use of the `super` mechanism to initialize the properties of the superclass.

10. A class can contain *static* data and method members which are stored as part of the class rather than being part of any instance of a class. A static method is a way that class can provide a behavior or data property that can be used without the need to create an instance of the enclosing class.

Here are some questions that you might like to ponder about what we have learned in this chapter:

What happens if a JavaScript program doesn't catch an exception that has been thrown?

If an exception is thrown in some JavaScript that is not part of a `try-catch` construction the exception will be caught by the browser and the execution sequence will end. If you have the Developer View open, you will see the exception displayed in the form of a red error message.

When should a JavaScript program throw an exception?

Exceptions should only be used in exceptional circumstances. Some JavaScript functions, for example `JSON.parse`, use exceptions to signal error conditions. You can also make your code generate exceptions. When you start work on a project you need to decide on all the possible error conditions and then decide how each should be handled. Exceptions are useful because they provide a way that a low-level failure can be quickly propagated to a higher-level error handler.

Must my JavaScript programs catch all exceptions?

No. For me, the biggest concern when I write a program is not that the program might fail. It is that the user might think that it has worked when it has not. If an application fails with an obvious error, the user will get upset. If an application "pretends" that it has worked and the user later finds out that they have lost all their data, they will get very upset. You should ensure that exceptions are logged and reported in a way that makes their error reports useful.

Do I have to use classes in my programs?

No. However, they can make some kinds of programs (particularly those that need to deal with different types of related data) easier to write.

Can a JavaScript class have multiple constructors?

No. Some programming languages have a mechanism called "overloading" where a class can contain multiple versions of a method that all share the same name but have different parameters. JavaScript does not support overloading, so a class can only contain a single constructor method. If you want to provide different ways to construct an object, you must write code in the constructor method to decide what the parameters to the function mean.

What is the difference between a method and a function?

A method is declared as part of a class, whereas a function is declared outside any class. Both can accept parameters and return a result.

Can the `this` reference be used as an argument to a function call?

Yes. Within a method, the `this` reference refers to the object that the method is running within. If an object wants to send another object a reference to itself, it can pass the value of `this` as a function argument. This is like me calling you on the phone and telling you my phone number.

Can I use the `this` reference inside a static method?

No. A static method is a member of the enclosing class and is not associated with an existing instance.

11
Creating applications

What you will learn

In this chapter, we are going to make some applications. We are going to discover how JavaScript programs can work with functions to control how data is processed and then move on to consider how JavaScript applications can fetch services from the Internet. Finally, we'll use the Node.js platform to create a JavaScript-powered web server of our own and build an application that can consume services from it. At the end of this chapter, you will know how web applications really work and how to build one of your own.

Data analysis

We are going to start off by performing some analysis for the Fashion Shop application that we created in Chapter 10. This will allow us to explore some advanced features of JavaScript functions and discover how easy it is to perform analysis of the contents of arrays of data. We are going start by considering how a JavaScript program can display a list of items.

Fashion Shop stock list

At the end of Chapter 10, we had created an application to manage the stock in a Fashion Shop. The shop contains a variety of different stock items, each of which is represented by an instance of a particular object. The entire stock is stored as an array of stock items. One of the features of the application lets the user see all the stock in the shop in one long list (**Figure 11-1**). Now we are going to explore how this works.

Figure 11-1   Fashion Shop stock list

The Fashion Shop application produces a stock list, as shown in Figure 11-1. Each stock item is displayed on a line of text. The item details on each line of the list are preceded by an **Update** button that can be pressed to update the stock details for that item. Let's look at how the stock list is produced. When the user presses the button to produce the stock list, the following JavaScript function runs:

```
function doListFashionShop() {
    createListPage("Stock List", dataStore);
}
```

The function doListFashionShop calls the function createListPage. The createListPage function is provided with two arguments. The first argument is the heading for the list. In this case, the heading is "Stock List." The second argument is the list of items to be displayed. In this case, the program is listing the entire contents of the data store. The function createListPage creates the list page and displays it. Let's have a look at how that works.

```
function createList(heading, items) {
    openPage(heading);                           Display the page with the requested heading
    for (let item of items) {                    Work through all the items in the list
        let itemPar = createListElement(item);   Create a list element for an item
        mainPage.appendChild(itemPar);           Append the list item to the main page
    }
}
```

The function createList works through all the list items and calls the function createListElement for each one. The list element that createListElement returns is then added to the mainPage. The mainPage variable is the HTML element in the document that the browser is displaying. It is how the Fashion Shop application displays data to the user. The final thing we need to look at is the createListElement function, so let's see how that works.

```
                                                 Create a function call for the button click event
function createListElement(item) {
    let resultPar = document.createElement("p");           Create an enclosing paragraph

    let openButton = document.createElement("button");     Create the Update button
    openButton.innerText = "Update";                       Set the Update button text to "Update"
    openButton.className = "itemButton";                   Set the style sheet for the button
    let editFunctionCall = "doUpdateItem('" + item.stockRef + "')";
    openButton.setAttribute("onclick", editFunctionCall);
    resultPar.appendChild(openButton);                     Add the button to the paragraph

    let detailsElement = document.createElement("p");      Create the details paragraph
    detailsElement.innerText = item.getDescription();
    detailsElement.className = "itemList";                 Set the style sheet for the description
    resultPar.appendChild(detailsElement);                Add the description to the paragraph

    return resultPar;                                      Return the created paragraph
}
                                                 Get the item description and add it to the details
                                                 Add the onclick event to the button
```

The output from this function is an element that is used to display the item in the HTML document for the Fashion Shop application.

```
<p><button class="itemButton" onclick="doUpdateItem('4')">Update</button>
<p class="itemList">Ref:4 Price:10 Stock:14 Description:red plain dress
                    Color:red Pattern:plain<ic:ccc> Size:14</p></p>
```

This is the HTML produced by `createListElement` for one of the stock items. The HTML includes a button that will call the `doUpdateItem` function when the button is clicked. The call of the `doUpdateItem` function is given an argument, which is the `stockRef` of the item being displayed. In the above HTML, the element with `stockRef` 4 is being displayed. The `doUpdateItem` function finds the requested element and displays it for update.

Fashion Shop data analysis

Imogen has found the Fashion Shop application very useful. She especially likes the stock list feature. Now she would like to add some more data analysis features:

- A list of items in sorted in order of the number in stock so that she can quickly discover which items are running low

- A list of items sorted in descending order of price so that she can identify expensive items that might be worth discounting

- A list of items sorted in order of "investment" (price times number of stock items) so that she can identify where she has spent the most money

- A list of just the items that have zero stock

- The total value of all her stock

You decide to implement this by adding a **Data Analysis** option to the main menu for the program, as shown in **Figure 11-2**.

When Imogen clicks the **Analysis** button, the application will display a list of analysis commands, as shown in **Figure 11-3**.

This is our first "submenu" in the application. We could have put all the data analysis functions on the same page as all the other functions, but I think it the program is easier to use if some of the less-popular functions are placed on a different menu. We can create the menus just by creating the schemas for each one as we did in Chapter 10 in the "Build a user interface" section. We can then go back and fill in the functions that are required. Imogen can approve our "empty" menus before we write the code that makes them work.

Main Menu	
Add Dress	Dress
Add Pants	Pants
Add Skirt	Skirt
Add Top	Top
Update stock item	Update
List stock items	List
Data analysis	Analysis

Figure 11-2   Fashion Shop data analysis

Data Analysis	
Order by stock level	Stock level
Order by price	Price
Order by investment	Investment
Zero stock items	Zero
Total stock value	Total
Return to main menu	Main menu

Figure 11-3   Fashion Shop Data Analysis menu

Work with array methods

The first three functions requested from Imogen involve sorting the stock data. The items in the Fashion Shop data storage are held in the order that they were added. To meet the first requirement, we want to sort the dataStore array in order of stock level. Sorting is something that a lot of programs need to do, so the JavaScript array type provides a sort method that we can use to sort the array. We just have to tell the sort method how to decide the order of elements during the sort.

We do this by providing a comparison function that compares two values and returns a result that indicates their order. If the result is negative, it means that the first value is "smaller" than the second. If the result is positive, it means that the first value is "larger" than the second. If the result is zero, it means that the two values are the same. We can generate a stock level comparison return value by subtracting one stock level from another.

```
function stockOrderCompare(a,b){
    return a.stockLevel-b.stockLevel;
}
```

The function `stockOrderCompare` takes in two parameters. It gets the stock level values from each item and then returns the result of subtracting one stock level from another. This comparison function can be provided as an argument to the call of the `sort` method to get the `dataStore` sorted in this order.

```
dataStore.sort(stockOrderCompare);
```

We don't need to know how the `sort` method sorts the `dataStore` any more than we need to know how JavaScript adds two numbers together. One thing that it is useful to know, however, is that the sorting process will not move any `StockItem` values around in memory. The datastore contains an array of *references*. We can change the order of the references without having to move anything in memory.

```
function stockOrderCompare(a, b) {
    return a.stockLevel - b.stockLevel;
}

function doListStockLevel() {
    dataStore.sort(stockOrderCompare);
    createList("Stock Level Order", dataStore);
}
```

This is the code that produces a list of stock item sorted by stock level. The function `doListStockLevel` above is called when Imogen selects the option to display the stock sorted in the order of stock level. It sorts the `dataStore` array and then uses the `createList` function to display the sorted list.

CODE ANALYSIS

Sorting stock items

The Fashion Shop application in the **Ch11 Creating Applications\Ch11-01 Fashion Shop Stock Sort** example folder contains the analysis feature that can be used to display a list of stock items that have been sorted by stock level. You might have some questions about how it works.

Question: What happens when we use the `stockItemCompare` function as an argument to the `sort` method?

Answer: A JavaScript function is an object, like lots of other things in JavaScript programs. Objects are managed by references, so the `sort` method receives a parameter, which is a reference to the `stockItemCompare` function.

Question: What happens if we try to use the `stockItemCompare` function on a list of objects that don't have `stockLevel` properties?

```
var names = ["fred", "jim", "ethel"];
names.sort(stockOrderCompare)
```

Answer: The JavaScript above shows how we would this. The first statement creates an array of strings, which is called `names`. The seconds statement tries to sort the names using `stockOrderCompare` as the comparison function. This will not work because the strings in the names array do not have a `stockLevel` property, but what would it do?

We can work out what would happen by considering what JavaScript does when things go wrong. If we try to access a nonexistent property in an object, JavaScript returns a value of `undefined`. This means that the `stockOrderCompare` function would be comparing two undefined values. The result of any calculation involving `undefined` is the Not a Number (NaN) value. This means that the comparison function returns NaN, which is ignored by the `sort` method, leaving the array unchanged.

Question: How would I sort an array of names?

Answer: We would have to create a comparison function that compares two strings and returns the required result. JavaScript expressions can be used to determine if one string is "greater than" (further down the alphabet) than another. We can make a `stringOrderCompare` function.

```
function stringOrderCompare(a,b) {
    if(a<b) return -1;           a less than b
    if(b<a) return 1;            b less than a
    return 0;                    Both strings the same
}
```

This function can be used to sort the name array we created earlier. The `stringOrderCompare` function is declared within the **Ch11 Creating Applications\ Ch11-01 Fashion Shop Stock Sort** example.

```
> names.sort(stringOrderCompare)
["ethel", "fred", "jim"]
```

Anonymous functions

We can control how `sort` behaves by changing the function that is used to perform the comparison, but it is rather unwieldly to have to create the function and then use it as an argument to the call of `sort`. JavaScript makes it easier to do this by allowing us to declare the comparison function directly in the arguments of the `sort` call:

```
dataStore.sort(function(a,b){
    return a.stockLevel-b.stockLevel;
});
```

This `sort` does the same job as the original one, but the comparison function is provided as an argument to the call of `sort`. This type of function declaration is called an *anonymous* function because it has no name. The function can't be called by any other code. It has the double advantage of making the program slightly smaller and also binding the comparison directly to the call of `sort`. With the above code, you don't have to go and find out what the `stockOrderCompare` function does. The application in the **Ch11 Creating Applications\Ch11-02 Fashion Shop Simple Function** example folder uses this simplified function format to control the `sort` behavior.

Arrow functions

Arrow functions are a way of making programs even faster to write. Rather than having to type `function` to create an anonymous function, you can express the function like this:

```
dataStore.sort((a,b) => { return a.stockLevel - b.stockLevel});
```

The parameters to the function are given before the arrow (=>), and the block of statements that make up the body of the function is given after the arrow. If your function contains only one statement, you can dispense with both the statement block and the return keyword to make a very short arrow function:

```
dataStore.sort((a,b) =>   a.stockLevel - b.stockLevel);
```

The statement above would sort the datastore in ascending order with the lowest stock levels first. What change do you think you would have to make to sort in descending order?

```
dataStore.sort((a,b) =>  b.stockLevel - a.stockLevel);
```

This turns out to be a very small change to the program. We just have to reverse the order of the subtraction, as shown in the statement above.

CODE ANALYSIS

Anonymous functions

Anonymous functions and arrow functions are very powerful JavaScript features, but they are also rather confusing when you first see them.

Question: Why is an anonymous function called "anonymous"?

Answer: Because it has no name. Up until now, all the functions and methods that we've created have been given names so that we can refer to them in other parts of the program. However, with an anonymous function, I just want to describe a particular behavior to be performed at one point in the program. I could give the behavior a name (as in stringOrderCompare) above, but it is much easier if I can just drop the JavaScript code directly into my application at the point where I want to use it. Programmers sometimes call anonymous functions *lambda* functions.

Question: Can I call an anonymous function from a different part of my application?

Answer: No. The only place that the code in an anonymous function can be used is the point when it is declared. It can't be accessed anywhere else because it has no name.

Question: Can an anonymous function call other functions?

Answer: If you wanted to, you could write an anonymous function containing many thousands of lines of code. However, I would not recommend this. I see anonymous functions as just offering a way of dropping a small piece of specific code into a program.

Question: Can I use an anonymous function as an argument to a function?

Answer: Yes, you can. In JavaScript, a function is an object like anything else and can be passed around a program like any other value. In fact, we have already done this. When we use sort, we pass it a function that is to be used to compare two values to be sorted.

Question: Is there any difference between an anonymous function created using the keyword function and one created using the arrow notation?

Answer: We have seen that there are two ways we can describe an anonymous function:

```
dataStore.sort(function(a,b){
    return a.stockLevel-b.stockLevel;
});
```

This version makes an anonymous function to perform the comparison in a sort operation. The anonymous function is supplied as an argument to the sort method.

```
dataStore.sort((a,b) => { return a.stockLevel - b.stockLevel});
```

This version uses an arrow function to perform the same task. For the task above, you can use `function` or `arrow` interchangeably. However, there are differences between how the two anonymous functions work. The most important one is the way that the keyword `this` works inside an anonymous function. We know about `this` because we've used it to access elements of an object from methods running inside the object. If you want to write an anonymous function that makes use of `this` to get hold of elements in an enclosing object, you must use the arrow function notation to create the anonymous function. When you use the word `function` to make an anonymous function, you create a new object that the function code runs inside. Code running inside this kind of anonymous function can only access elements declared inside that function body, which is not usually what you want.

However, code running in the body of an anonymous function created using the arrow notation picks up the value of `this` from the enclosing object, so the code can get hold of properties from the object. All this is rather complicated, so suffice it to say that if you had an anonymous function running inside a `Dress` object, and you wanted that function to be able to get hold of the `size` property of the dress, you should use arrow notation to create the anonymous function.

Sorting by price and value

Sorting in order of price (which is the second data analysis that Imogen wants) can be achieved by changing the comparison function to compare two stock items by their price properties:

```
function doListPrice() {
    dataStore.sort((a,b) =>  b.price - a.price);     ——————— Arrow function comparison
    createList("Price Order", dataStore);
}
```

The doListPrice function is a slightly modified version of the doListStockItem function. The final sorting command, which sorts by the amount invested in each type of stock, is slightly more complex because the comparison function needs to work out the total value of each stock item. This value will be the price of an item multiplied by its stock level.

```
function doListInvestment() {
    dataStore.sort((a,b) =>  (b.price * b.stockLevel) - (a.price * a.stockLevel));
    createList("Investment Order", dataStore);
}
```

The application in the **Ch11 Creating Applications\Ch11-02 Fashion Shop All Sorts** folder contains a version of the Fashion Shop application that implements the sorting behavior using arrow functions.

Use `filter` to get items with zero stock

The next thing that Imogen wants is a feature that lists all the stock items that have zero stock. We could create a for-loop that will work through the dataStore array and pick out all the items with a stockLevel value of 0. However, there is a much easier way to do this by using another method provided by the array object. We have seen that all arrays provide a sort method that can be used to sort their contents on the basis of a particular comparison function. Arrays also provide other useful methods, including one called filter that works through an array, applying a function that tests each element in the array. If the test evaluates to true, the array element is added to the result.

```
function doZeroStockItems() {
    var zeroStockList = dataStore.filter((a) => a.stockLevel==0);    Filter the stock
    createList("Zero stock items", zeroStockList);
}
```

I've written the test as an arrow function that accepts a stockItem (which is what is in the array) and returns true if the stockLevel property of the item is zero. The filter function returns a list that is then displayed by the createList function. As with stockLevel, the zeroStockList contains references to stock items, not the items themselves. The **Ch11 Creating Applications\Ch11-03 Fashion Shop Filter** example folder holds a version of the Fashion Shop application that will list the stock items with zero stock levels. We can use this technique to filter the list on any criteria that we like by simply changing the behavior of the selection function.

Use reduce to calculate the total value of the stock

The next feature that Imogen wants is the ability to calculate the total value of all her stock. We could create a `for-of` loop that works through the datastore array, but there is an easier way to do this by using the `reduce` method provided by arrays. The `reduce` method reduces the content of an array to a single value by performing a `reduce` function on each element in the array and adding up all the results. To make things clearer, I'll start with a named function before converting it into an arrow function.

```
function addValueToTotal(total,item){
    return total+(item.stockLevel*item.price);
}
```

The function `addValueToTotal` accepts the current total as the first parameter and a reference to a stock item as the second parameter. It calculates the value of the stock item, adds this to the total, and then returns the result. We can use the `reduce` method in the `dataStore` array to apply this function to every element in the stock list and work out the total value of the stock:

```
var total=dataStore.reduce(addValueToTotal, 0);
```

The first argument to the `reduce` method is the function that will be called to update the total. The second parameter is the initial total value, in this case, zero. We can convert the `addValueToTotal` function into an arrow function, in which case, the call of `reduce` looks like this:

```
var total = dataStore.reduce(
    (total, item) => total + (item.stockLevel * item.price),
    0);
```

The application in the **Ch11 Creating Applications\Ch11-04 Fashion Shop Total Value** example folder displays the total value of the stock. You can select **Total** from the **Data Analysis** menu, and the function displays an alert containing the total stock value. Note that because this program generates new test data each time it is started, you will find that the total value changes each time it is run.

Use map to discount all stock items

You give Imogen the completed version of the software and she is very happy with it—for a while. Then she comes back with another request. She would like to be able to apply a discount to all the items in stock. She would like to be able to drop all the prices by 5 percent. You could do this with a `for` loop that works through the array, but an array provides a function called `map` that will apply a given function to every element in the array. To apply a 5 percent discount, you can multiply the price by 0.95.

```
dataStore.map((item)=>item.price = item.price*0.95);
```

This single statement will do the job. The `map` method accepts a function that has a single parameter. The parameter is the item to be worked on. The statement above will drop the price of every item in stock by 5 percent. You can find this example program in the **Ch11 Creating Applications\Ch11-05 Fashion Shop Discount** folder.

MAKE SOMETHING HAPPEN

Create extra Fashion Shop functions

Now that you know how to use the `map`, `filter`, and `reduce` methods, you could add some other functions that Imogen might like. Note that for some of them, you might have to use more than one method to achieve the requested result.

- Add a command that removes a 5 percent discount. (Note that this does not mean that you would add 5 percent to all the prices; you will have to add more than that because the price has been discounted.)

- Add a command that reduces the price of all items that cost more than $50 by $5. In other words, a dress costing $20 would stay the same price, but a dress costing $60 would be reduced to $55.

- Add a command that displays the number of items in stock that are colored red.

Read the weather

In this section, we are going to discover how JavaScript programs can fetch and use data from the Internet. You can use this technique to fetch data from a huge range of sources. We are going to create an application that reads weather information from the OpenWeather service at *https://openweathermap.org*. It is free to create an account on the OpenWeather site and use it to make a limited number of weather requests each day. I've also created some "fixed" weather data on the GitHub site for this book that you can use to test your program if you don't want to register. The weather information is supplied as a JSON-encoded object that arrives in a string of text. The first thing we must investigate is how to fetch a string of text from a server on the Internet.

Fetch data from a server

Until now, all the actions performed by our JavaScript programs have completed very quickly. However, it can sometimes take a while for information to arrive from the Internet, and sometimes a network request can fail completely. A JavaScript application that uses a network connection will have to deal with slow responses and the possibility that a request might fail. A good way to do this is to make the fetch process *asynchronous*.

Asynchronous operation

There are two ways that I can go shopping. I can go to a shop, select what I want, pay for it, and take it home. My actions are *synchronized* with the shop because I must wait for the sales assistant to accept my payment and hand over the goods before the shopping is completed. Alternatively, I can email my shopping list to the shop and ask them to deliver my purchases. Now I can do other things, such as dig in the garden while I wait for my shopping to arrive. My actions are not synchronized with the shop, meaning they are *asynchronous*. If the shop takes a long time to deliver, it just means that I might have more time for gardening (which is actually not a win for me as it turns out—I'd rather stand in a shop than work in the garden). Up until now, when a JavaScript program has asked for something to be done, the action has been performed synchronously. For example, consider this statement.

```
descriptionPar = document.createElement("p");
```

This statement is from the Fashion Shop application. It calls the `createElement` method to create a new document element. When this statement is performed, the application waits for the `createElement` method to deliver a new document element in the same way that I wait in a shop for my shopping. The `createElement` method runs very quickly, so the application is not kept waiting long. However, a function that uses a network connection to fetch data from a distant server could take several seconds to complete. This would pause the application for several seconds. The user would not be able to click any buttons on the screen for that time because the browser only allows a JavaScript application to perform one action at once. If you've ever had the experience of a web page "locking up" when you try to use it, you will know how bad this feels.

JavaScript promise

To get around this problem, JavaScript introduces the idea of *promises*. A promise is an object that is associated with a task that a program wants to perform. JavaScript provides a method called `fetch`, which is used to fetch data from a server. However, the `fetch` function does not return the data; instead, it returns a promise to deliver the data at some point in the future.

```
var fetchPromise = fetch('https://www.begintocodewithjavascript.com/weather.html');
```

The statement above uses `fetch` to fetch the contents of the file at `'https://www.begintocodewithjavascript.com/weather.html'`. This call of `fetch` returns a promise object. The variable `fetchPromise` refers to this object. The fetch will start to happen asynchronously. You can think of this as the point in the process where I call the shop and ask them to deliver my shopping.

The `fetchPromise` object is a link between our application that requested the data and the asynchronous process fetching the data. We set a property on a promise object to identify a function to be called when the promise is kept. A promise object provides a method called `then`, which accepts a reference to the method to be called when the promise has been kept.

```
fetchPromise.then(doGotWeatherResponse);
```

The statement above tells `fetchPromise` to call the function `doGotWeatherResponse` when it has finished fetching. So now we need to find out what the `doGotWeather Response` function does.

```
function doGotWeatherResponse(response) {
    if (!response.ok) {                               Check to see if the request succeeded
        alert("fetch failed");                        Display an alert if the request failed
        return;
    }

    jsonPromise = response.json();          Get another promise to decode the JSON in the response
    jsonPromise.then(doGotWeatherObject);              Call doGotWeatherObject when
}                                                             the JSON is decoded
```

The parameter to a function called when a promise is kept is the result delivered by that promise. In the case of `fetch`, the parameter is a `response` object that describes what happened when it tried to fetch the data. It is possible that a network request can fail, so the first thing that the doGotWeatherResponse function does is check the ok property of the response. If this is false, an alert is displayed and the function ends.

If the response is ok, the doGotWeatherResponse function starts the process of getting the data. It uses a "promise-powered" process to obtain the JavaScript object from the JSON in the response.

Get JSON from the network

The json method provided by the response will get the text from the network and convert it from JSON into a JavaScript object. This might take some time. There might be a lot of data to be fetched and decoded, so it makes sense that this process is performed asynchronously, too. The then method of the JSON promise is used to nominate a method called doGotWeatherObject to be called when the weather object has been created from the network.

```
function doGotWeatherObject (weather) {
    let resultParagraph = document.getElementById('resultParagraph');
    resultParagraph.innerText = "Temp: "+ weather.main.temp;
}
```

The doGotWeatherObject function gets the temperature information from the weather object and displays it in a paragraph on the page.

```
{"coord":{"lon":-0.34,"lat":53.74},
 "weather":[{"id":804,"main":"Clouds","description":"overcast clouds","icon":"04d"}],
 "base":"stations",
 "main":{"temp":18.14,"feels_like":17.24,"temp_min":18,"temp_max":18.33,
        "pressure":1019,"humidity":82},
 "visibility":10000,"wind":{"speed":3.6,"deg":270},
 "clouds":{"all":98},"dt":1599639962,
 "sys":{"type":1,"id":1515,"country":"GB","sunrise":1599629093,"sunset":1599676358},
 "timezone":3600,"id":2645425,"name":"Hull","cod":200}
```

This is the JSON that describes the weather. You can see that the object contains a main property that contains a temp property that is the temperature value. Note that the temperature is delivered as a value in degrees Celsius, not Fahrenheit. The application in the **Ch11 Creating Applications\Ch11-06 Weather Display** example folder contains these functions and will display the weather information when the **FETCH** button (shown in **Figure 11-4**) is pressed.

Figure 11-4 Weather display

Use anonymous functions to simplify promises

The code we have just written will work perfectly well and shows how functions are bound to promises. However, it is also rather long-winded. It turns out that we can use anonymous functions to simplify the code a lot. We can express an anonymous function using the arrow notation. Take a look the "Arrow functions" section above if you want to refresh your understanding of how they work. In this code, we are going to use an arrow function to specify actions to be performed when a promise is fulfilled.

```
function doGetWeather(url) {
  fetch(url).then( response => {          Function that runs when the response is complete
    if(!response.ok){
      alert("fetch failed");
      return;
    }
    response.json().then( weather => {    Function that runs when JSON decoding is complete
      let resultParagraph = document.getElementById('resultParagraph');
      resultParagraph.innerText = "Temp: " + weather.main.temp;
    });
  });
}
```

The doGetWeather function accepts a parameter that gives the network address of the item to be loaded. The function has exactly the same logic as our previous implementation. However, the functions that are to run when the promises are fulfilled are now written as arrow functions that are given as parameters to then. You can find a weather application that uses this function in the **Ch11 Creating Applications\Ch11-07 Weather Arrow Functions** sample folder. You can use this code to read JSON objects from different locations by changing the URL string.

Get text from the network

If you just want to read the text from a website rather than the JSON, you can use the `text` method, which returns a promise to deliver text rather than a JavaScript object. You can see this in use in the application in the **Ch11 Creating Applications\Ch11-08 Weather Text** sample folder.

Handle errors in promises

In JavaScript, as in real life, it can sometimes be impossible to fulfil a promise. Perhaps the network is broken, or the text delivered by the server does not contain a valid JSON string. In these situations, the promise will not fulfill by calling the function nominated by `then`. Instead, a promise can call an error-handling function that has been nominated by a call to the `catch` method of a promise. The `catch` function is used in exactly the same way as the `then` function. It accepts a parameter that describes the error that has occurred.

```
function doGetWeather(url) {
  fetch(url).then( response => {
    if(!response.ok){
      alert("Fetch failed");
      return;
    }
    response.json().then( weather => {
      let resultParagraph = document.getElementById('resultParagraph');
      resultParagraph.innerText = "Temp: " + weather.main.temp;
    }).catch ( error => alert("Bad JSON: " + error)); // json error handler
  }).catch( error => alert("Bad fetch: " + error)); // fetch error handler
}
```

You can see the two catches in the `doGetWeather` function above. They display an alert that contains any error message that was produced when the promise failed.

Use `finally` to enable a button after a fetch

The weather application we have created makes a `fetch` request each time the **FETCH** button is clicked. This can lead to problems. One thing that users quite like to do is repeatedly click a button if they don't get a response within a second of their first click. In the weather application, this would cause lots of fetch requests. A well-written application would disable the **FETCH** button once it has been clicked to prevent this behavior. So let's make our application well-written. A JavaScript program can disable a button by adding a `disabled` attribute to the button:

```
let fetchButton = document.getElementById('fetchButton');
fetchButton.setAttribute("disabled","");
```

Find the button with the ID FetchButton
Disable the button

These two statements disable a button with the ID `fetchButton`. Once the fetch has completed, the program can enable the button. We could add code to the `then` and `catch` functions to enable the button, but as you know, I hate writing the same code twice. Instead, we can add a `finally` function to a promise that identifies code to run when the promise has completed, regardless of whether it succeeds. This would guarantee that the **FETCH** button is enabled once the `fetch` is complete.

```
.finally( message => {
  let fetchButton = document.getElementById('fetchButton');
  fetchButton.removeAttribute("disabled");
})
```

Find the button
Remove the disabled attribute

This is the code that I added to remove the `disabled` attribute from the **FETCH** button. You can find it in the sample application in the **Ch11 Creating Applications\ Ch11-09 Weather Finally** example folder.

CODE ANALYSIS

Investigating promises

The application in the **Ch11 Creating Applications\Ch11-10 Weather Error Handling** example folder uses the `doGetWeather` function above to display the temperature. It also contains two other buttons that activate two broken `fetch` behaviors. The first attempts to load the weather from a nonexistent network address, and the second loads a file that does not contain JSON data. You can use these to experiment with failed promises.

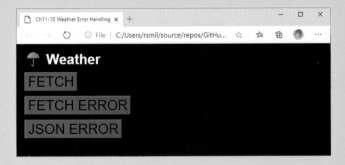

Question: What does a promise do again?

Answer: If this is confusing, think of the problem that it is trying to solve. Our program wants to get some information from the network that would take a long time to arrive. So rather than call a method that delivers the information, it calls a method that delivers a *promise* to perform the action. In other words, rather than saying, "Give me the data from the network," we say, "Give me a promise object that will be fulfilled when the data has been fetched from the network."

An application can attach functions to a promise object to be called when the promise is *fulfilled* (then) or *broken* (catch). Our program can then continue running without having to wait for the data to arrive. The actions required to deliver on the promise will be performed asynchronously, and at some point in the future, the promise will either be kept or broken, and one of the functions called.

Question: Can I have two promises active at the same time?

Answer: Yes, you can. If you click the **FETCH ERROR** button in the example above, you will notice that it takes several seconds for the error message to appear. While you are waiting for the error, you can click the **FETCH** and **JSON ERROR** buttons to perform their fetch behaviors.

Question: Can I write code of my own that implements promises?

Answer: Yes, you can. We will be doing this in the next chapter when we create a promise that is fulfilled when an image has been loaded into our game.

Question: Why do I need to create a catch behavior for the fetch promise? Can't I enclose the call of fetch in a try-catch construction to catch any errors that are thrown by fetch?

Answer: If you understand this question and the answer, you can consider yourself a "promise ninja." JavaScript code can throw an error object when things get tough. This is called an *exception*. We've seen that code working with JSON throws exceptions if it can't convert a string into a JavaScript object. Look in Chapter 10 in the section "Catching exceptions" to find out how this works. You might think that we could just put a call of fetch inside a try-catch construction in our application to pick up any errors when they occur.

```
try{
  fetch(url).then( response => {
  // rest of fetch code here
}
catch{
  // handler for errors during fetching
}
```

The code above shows what you might try to do. However, this would not work because the fetch function only starts the process of fetching network data. Once the process of fetching begins, the fetch function completes, and the application continues out of the enclosing try-catch construction. Errors that arise while getting the data from the server can't be handled by a try-catch around fetch because the program execution will have left the try-catch block long before the exception is raised.

Question: When would I use finally?

Answer: You use finally when you want to nominate a behavior that must be performed once the promise has ended (by being either fulfilled or broken). This might be to enable a button (which is what we have done) or to tidy up resources that were obtained when the promise started. It is a good idea to get into the habit of using finally, as it is guaranteed to run at the end of the promise, even if code in then or catch functions fail in ways you weren't expecting.

Node.js

Up until now, all the JavaScript applications that we have written have run inside the browser and used the HTML document to interact with the user. This is fine for creating client applications (meaning applications that fetch data and work with it), but it would be useful to be able to create JavaScript applications that could work as servers that provide data for client applications. In this section, we are going to discover how to use a platform called Node.js to create a server application written in JavaScript. Node.js was created by taking the JavaScript component out of a browser and making it into a freestanding application that can host JavaScript code.

 MAKE SOMETHING HAPPEN

Install and test Node.js

Before we can use Node.js, we need to install it on our machine. The application is free. There are versions for Windows PC, macOS, and Linux. Open your browser and go to *https://nodejs. org/en/download/.*

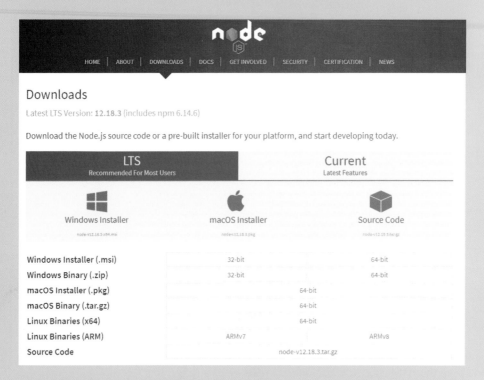

Downloads

Latest LTS Version: **12.18.3** (includes npm 6.14.6)

Download the Node.js source code or a pre-built installer for your platform, and start developing today.

	LTS Recommended For Most Users	Current Latest Features
	Windows Installer node-v12.18.3-x64.msi	macOS Installer node-v12.18.3.pkg	Source Code node-v12.18.3.tar.gz

Windows Installer (.msi)	32-bit	64-bit
Windows Binary (.zip)	32-bit	64-bit
macOS Installer (.pkg)	64-bit	
macOS Binary (.tar.gz)	64-bit	
Linux Binaries (x64)	64-bit	
Linux Binaries (ARM)	ARMv7	ARMv8
Source Code	node-v12.18.3.tar.gz	

Click the installer for your machine and go through the installation process. Once you have completed the installation, you can start to work with Node.js. The first thing you can do is test that the installation has worked correctly. We can do that by using the terminal in Visual Studio Code. Start Visual Studio Code, open the **View** menu, and select **Terminal**. The terminal window will open in the bottom right-hand corner of Visual Studio Code. You use this window to send commands to the operating system of your computer. I'm using a Windows PC, so my commands will be performed by Windows PowerShell. Enter the command **node** and press Enter.

The Node application starts and displays a command prompt. You should find this remarkably familiar. If you enter a JavaScript command, it will be obeyed in the same way as if you were using the console in the Developer View in your browser.

```
OUTPUT   TERMINAL   DEBUG CONSOLE   PROBLEMS 1     1: node

PS C:\Users\rsmil\source\repos\GitHub\begintocodewithjavascript.github.io> node
Welcome to Node.js v12.16.1.
Type ".help" for more information.
> console.debug("Hello from node.js");
Hello from node.js
undefined
>
```

388 **Chapter 11** Creating applications

You can exit from the Node.js command prompt by holding down the CTRL key and pressing D.

The Node.js application provides a way for a computer to run JavaScript applications. If you had entered the command `node myprog.js`, the command prompt would have executed the JavaScript program in the myprog.js file. Note that because this application is not running in a browser, it can't use an HTML document to communicate with the user. In other words, Node.js applications can't use buttons, paragraphs, and all the other elements because there is nowhere for them to be displayed. The job of Node.js applications is to host processes that provide services. It is perfectly possible that the weather service that we have just used is hosted by a Node.js application running on a server connected to the Internet.

Create a web server with Node.js

In Chapter 2 in the "HTML and the World Wide Web" section, we discovered that a web browser uses the HTTP protocol to fetch data from web servers. HTTP describes a way that one program (the browser) can ask for resources from another program (the server). A web server is an application that receives HTTP-formatted requests and generates responses.

Use the HTTP module

The Node.js platform is supplied with a module containing a JavaScript program that can respond to HTTP requests and act as a web server. A *module* is a package of JavaScript code that we want to use. We can include a module in our application by using the `require` function to load it. The module is then exposed as an object. The application using the module will then call methods on that object.

```
var http = require('http');
```

This statement above creates a variable called `http`, which refers to an HTTP instance. Now we can use the HTTP object to create a web server. We can do this by calling the `createServer` method:

```
var server = http.createServer((request, response) => {
  response.statusCode = 200;
  response.setHeader('Content-Type', 'text/plain');
  response.write('Hello from Simple Server');
  response.end();
});
```

Define the content type in the response header

Set the status code for the response

Send the content of the response

End the response and send it

The statement above uses the `createServer` method supplied by the `http` object to create a simple web server. The variable `server` is set to refer to the new server. The `createServer` method accepts a single argument, which is an arrow function that works on two parameters. This function provides the behavior of the server. It will be called each time a client makes a request of the server. The first parameter to the function describes the request that has been received. The second parameter will hold the response that is to be produced. Our server behavior is implemented by an arrow function that accepts the parameters `request` and `response`. The function above ignores the contents of the request and just prepares a response that is a text message `'Hello from Simple Server'`. Now that we have our server object, we can make it listen for incoming requests.

```
server.listen(8080);
```

The `listen` method starts the server listening for incoming requests. The `listen` method is supplied with an argument specifying the *port* that the server will listen on. Each computer on the Internet can expose a set of numbered ports that other computers can connect to. When a program connects to a machine, it specifies a port that it wants to use. Port number 80 has been set aside for HTTP access, and browsers will use this port unless told otherwise. Our server will listen on port 8080.

CODE ANALYSIS

Using a server

You can find this sample server application in the examples for this chapter. We will not be using this application from the browser; we will start the server running from within Visual Studio code and then view the page that it generates with a browser. Start by opening the Visual Studio Code application and then open **simpleServer.js** in the **Ch11 Creating Applications\Ch11-11 HTML Server** example folder, as shown below:

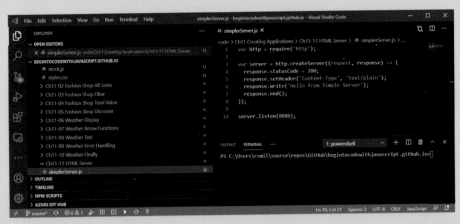

To start the server, you need to run the program in **simpleServer.js**. Make sure that this file is selected in the file browser as shown above. Open the **Run** menu and select the **Start Debugging** option. There are several different ways that Visual Studio Code can run your application, so you will be asked to select the environment you want to use:

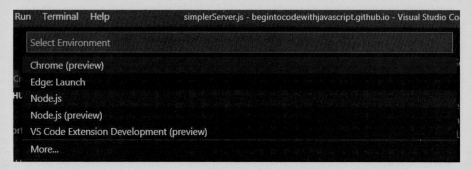

Click the **Node.js** option, and the server will start. Now you can open your browser and connect to this server. Because the server is running on your machine, you can use the Internet address *localhost*. You need to add the port number that you are using to this address, so enter the address *localhost:8080* address into the browser and press Enter to open the site.

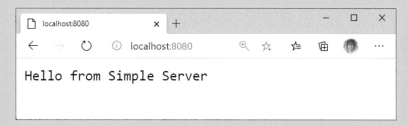

When you do this, you will see the message from the function that is running inside the server. You might have some questions about what you have just done:

Question: Would this server work on the Internet?

    Answer: Yes. You are running both the server (the Node.js program) and the client (the browser) on your PC. However, you could run the server on one machine and access it from the browser on another. If the server machine were on the Internet, it would be possible for distant machines to access the server. One thing to bear in mind, however, is that modern operating systems include a *firewall* component to manage their network connections. The firewall limits the network services that one machine exposes to another in case malicious programs try to take advantage of too much connectivity. If you want to create a server and allow people access to it, you can use Node.js to do this, but you would have to configure the firewall on the host machine and also take steps to ensure that you provided the services in a secure way.

Question: Does the server program run forever?

Answer: Yes. The call to the `listen` method will never return. You can use Visual Studio Code to stop the program by clicking the red square box stop button on the right-hand side of the program controls.

Question: How is the response message from the server constructed?

Answer: The server creates a response object that is sent back to the client. The response tells the client if the server could satisfy the request and contains the data that was requested. The server application performs four statements to create and send the response that is received by the browser:

```
response.statusCode = 200;
```

The first statement sets the status code of the response. A status code of 200 tells the browser that the page was found correctly.

```
response.setHeader('Content-Type', 'text/plain');
```

The second statement adds an item to the response header by using the `setHeader` method. A response header can contain items to help the browser deal with the incoming response. Each item is provided as a name-value pair. This statement adds a `Content-Type` value that tells the browser that this response contains plain text. We could use different types to return things like audio files and images.

```
response.write('Hello from Simple Server');
```

The `write` method writes the content of the page being returned. This server always sends the same text: `Hello from Simple Server`. It could, instead, send a very large amount of data.

```
response.end();
```

The `end` method tells the server that it can now send the response and the content back to the browser client.

Routing in HTML

In the "Fetching web pages" section in Chapter 2, we saw that the URL expressing the location of a web page contains a *host* element (the Internet address of the server) and a *path* element (the path on the host to the item that the client wants to read). The simple server above returns the same text for any path that you use to read from the host. In other words, the URLs *http://localhost:8080/index.html* and *http://localhost:8080/otherpage.html* both return the message `Hello from Simple Server`, as would any other path. The first web server used the path component of a URL to identify the file that the server should open and send to the client. We can improve our simple web server to allow it to respond differently to different paths.

```
var http = require('http');                              Use the http object
var url = require('url');                                Use the url object

function sendResponse(response, text){                   Send a response to the browser
  response.statusCode = 200;
  response.setHeader('Content-Type', 'text/plain');
  response.write(text);
  response.end();
}

var server = http.createServer((request, response) => {

  var parsedUrl = url.parse(request.url);                Parse the incoming response URL
  var path = parsedUrl.pathname;                         Get the page path from the parsed URL

  switch (path) {                                        Switch on the path

    case "/index.html":                                  Send the response for index.html
      sendResponse(response, "hello from index.html");
      break;

    case "/otherpage.html":                              Send the response for otherpage.html
      sendResponse(response, "hello from otherpage.html");
      break;

    default:                                             Send the response for any other path
      response.statusCode = 404;
      response.setHeader('Content-Type', 'text/plain');
      response.write('Page ' + path + ' not found');
      response.end();
      break;
  }
}
```

```
});

server.listen(8080);
```

The code above implements a server that recognizes two paths: `index.html` and `otherpage.html`. If the client tries to access any other path, the sever responds with a "page not found" message. Note that the "page not found" message has a status code of 404 to represent this. The program parses the `url` property of the request parameter to extract the path that was requested in the URL. This path is then used to control a `switch` construction that selects the response to be sent. You can find this example server in the example folder. This server program could be expanded to serve a number of different pages.

CODE ANALYSIS

Using multiple paths

You can find the multiple page server in the **Ch11 Creating Applications\Ch11-12 Multi page server** example folder. Start Visual Studio Code and from the examples folder, open **multiPageServer.js**. Ensure that the **multiPageServer.js** file is selected in the file browser. Now click **Run -> Start Debugging** to start the application. Select the **node.js** environment when prompted by Visual Studio Code. Now open your browser and navigate to: *http://localhost:8080/index.html*.

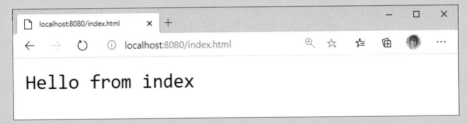

The browser will show the text for this URL. Now change the address to *http://localhost:8080/otherpage.html* and reload the page.

The browser will now display the response for the other page. Finally, you can try a missing page. Change the address to *http://localhost:8080/missingpage.html* and reload.

If a given path is not recognized, the `default` element in the `switch` is performed. This displays the "page not found" message. You might have some questions about this code:

Question: What does the `sendResponse` function do?

> **Answer:** I hate writing the same code twice. The `sendResponse` function sends a string as a response to a web request. It saves me from writing the same code to respond to the two different URL paths.

Question: How does the server get the path to the resource that the client has requested?

> **Answer:** The URL is the entire address sent by the browser to the server to request a particular web page. The path part of a URL describes the location of a resource on the server. For example, the server might receive the URL *http://robmiles.com/index.html*. The path in this URL is */index.html*. The URL that was given to the web request is provided as the `url` property of the `response` parameter to the method called by `createServer`. The method called by `createServer` must extract the path from this URL so that the server can decide what to send back to the browser. The server does this by using the URL module that was loaded at the start of the program.

```
var url = require('url');
```

The URL module provides methods that an application can use to work on URL strings. One of the methods that is provided is called `parse`. The word "parse" means "look through something and extract meaning from it." The `parse` method accepts a URL string as an argument.

```
var parsedUrl = url.parse(request.url);
```

The `parse` method creates an object that exposes different parts of the URL as properties. The statement above creates a parsed URL object (called `parsedUrl`). I use `parse` because I am lazy and don't want to have to write JavaScript that extracts the path from the URL string.

```
var path = parsedUrl.pathname;
```

Once we have a parsed version of the URL (called `parsedUrl`), we can extract data from the properties in this object. The `pathname` property of a parsed object gives the path that the user entered. The statement above gets the path name from the parsed URL and sets the variable `path` to this name. We are going to use `parse` again later in this chapter to extract other information from the URL.

Question: What would I need to do if I wanted to add extra "pages" to my server?

Answer: The present version of the server only recognizes the /index.html and /otherpage.html pages. If you want to add other pages such as /aboutpage.html, you just have to add another case to the switch:

```
case "/aboutpage.html":
  sendResponse(response, "hello from aboutpage.html");
  break;
```

The example program in the **Ch11 Creating Applications\Ch11-13 Three page server** folder serves three pages.

Question: Can I serve HTML pages using this server?

Answer: Yes, you can. However, you need to change the content type from *text/plain* to *text/html* so that the browser knows how to process the response.

```
response.setHeader('Content-Type', 'text/html');
```

The example program in the **Ch11 Creating Applications\Ch11-14 HTML server** folder serves an index page that is HTML.

Question: Is this how you build servers?

Answer: You could build server like this, but it would be hard work. Your server would also have to serve out the image and style sheet files along with the HTML files. I just want to show you how this works so that you can understand how servers work. The Express framework (which we will see later) provides a much quicker way of creating a JavaScript application that will act as a server. However, it uses the same fundamental principles that we have been using.

Use query to add data to a client request

A client can use different path values to select locations on a website, but it would also be useful for the client to be able to send additional data to the server. We can do this by adding a *query* string to the URL that is sent by the client to the server. You will often see query strings in your browser when you navigate e-commerce sites. A query string starts with a question mark (?) and is then followed by one or more name-value pairs that are separated by the ampersand (&) character:

```
http://localhost:8080/index.htm?no1=2&no2=3
```

The URL above contains two query values: no1 (set to the value 2) and no2 (set to the value 3). These query values are sent to the server in the URL string. We could create a server that accepted these values and returned their sum. The server could use the parse method from the url module to extract the query values.

```
var parsedUrl = url.parse(request.url,true);
```

We used the url.parse method in the previous section when we needed to extract the resource path from the incoming URL. The call of parse is different in that I've added the parameter true to the call, which tells the parse method to parse the query string in the URL.

```
var queries = parsedUrl.query;
```

Once I've done this, I can extract the value of the two queries from the parsedUr, as shown above. Now my addition program can convert these two query strings into numbers and perform the required calculation:

```
var no1 = Number(queries.no1);
var no2 = Number(queries.no2);

var result= no1 + no2;
```

The query values are always sent as strings of text. Our application uses the `Number` function to convert the query values into numbers. It then calculates their sum. The listing below is the complete source of an "addition" service, which accepts a query containing two numbers and returns their sum.

```javascript
var http = require('http');
var url = require('url');

var server = http.createServer((request, response) => {

    var parsedUrl = url.parse(request.url,true);
    var queries = parsedUrl.query;

    var no1 = Number(queries.no1);
    var no2 = Number(queries.no2);

    var result= no1 + no2;

    response.writeHead(200, { 'Content-Type': 'text/plain' });
    response.write(String(result));
    response.end();

});

server.listen(8080);
```

The addition service that we created above does not produce a web page as a result. It returns a string that contains the result of adding two query values together. This kind of service is called a *web service*. It uses HTTP to transfer messages, but the messages do not contain HTML documents. A more complex web service could return an object described by a string of JSON. We've already used one web service, the weather service from *openweather.org*. Now we know how to create our own web services using JavaScript and Node.js to host them. A Node.js application could also use the file system module `fs` to open files held on the server and send them as responses.

CODE ANALYSIS

Investigate the addition server

You can find the addition server in the **Ch11 Creating Applications\Ch11-15 Addition Server** example folder. Start Visual Studio Code and open **additionServer.js** in the example folder. Ensure that the file **additionServer.js** is selected in the file browser. Now use **Run -> Start Debugging** to start the application. Select the **node.js** environment when prompted by Visual Studio Code. Now open your browser and navigate to *http://localhost:8080/index.html?no1=2&no2=3*.

The server program will work out the result of the calculation (2+3) and return the result. Try changing the values of no1 and no2 and reload the page. The page will update with the new result.

Question: What happens if I don't supply the query values?

> **Answer:** Try it. Just load the *http://localhost:8080/index.html* URL and leave off the query.

> Accessing a missing property of an object (in other words, trying to get the properties no1 and no2 from a query that does not contain them) will produce the JavaScript value Undefined. Any calculations involving the value Undefined will produce the result Not a number, which when converted to a string, is displayed as NaN.

Question: Can I call the addition service by using fetch in a JavaScript program running in a web page?

> **Answer:** That is a fantastic question, and the answer is yes. This is how most web pages work. We've already written an application that used fetch to get information from the weather server. We could write another application that used fetch to call the addition service to perform a calculation.

```
var url = "http://localhost:8080/docalc.html?no1=2&no2=3";
```

Node.js   **399**

The JavaScript statement above creates a URL that could be used to call an addition service at *docalc.html*.

```
fetch(url).then(response => {
    response.text().then(result => {
        let resultParagraph = document.getElementById('resultParagraph');
        resultParagraph.innerText = "Result: " + result;
    }).catch(error => alert("Bad text: " + error)); // text error handler
}).catch(error => alert("Bad fetch: " + error)); // fetch error handler
```

This is the JavaScript that performs the `fetch` to get the result from the service. The service responds with text that is used to set the value of the `resultParagraph` element on the web page. This code is very similar to the code that was used to read the weather from *openweather.org*.

You can find this example code at **Ch11 Creating Applications\Ch11-16 Addition Application**. Stop the present server running and navigate to the file additionApplication.js in this folder. Use Visual Studio Code to run this program using Node.js and then navigate to *http://localhost:8080/index.html* in your browser. Click the "Add 2 + 3" button. This will run the `fetch` above, which will then be displayed on the page.

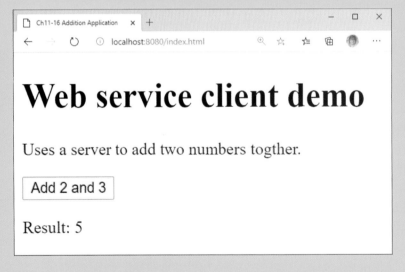

This is a big moment. Almost all this book has been leading up to this point. You now know how web applications work. The HTML document describes the page, and the JavaScript in the page can do things. If the JavaScript wants to get data from a server, it creates a request and sends it to the server, which decodes the request, generates the result, and sends it back. You should spend some time taking a long hard look at the web page, the server, and the client code until you understand what each part does.

Node package manager

You could use the modules from Node.js to create a complete application server. However, you would have to write a lot of code to decode the requests and build the responses. The good news is that someone has already built a system for creating servers. The system is called Express, and it provides what is called *scaffolding*, which you can use to construct an application that is powered by HTML pages and web services.

The even better news is that there is also a way of using prebuilt code like Express. It is called *node package manager* or npm. The npm program is provided with the Node.js installation. You use the npm program to fetch and install prebuilt modules that you can then add into your server programs using the `require` function that we have seen before. Each application has a configuration file called a `manifest` that identifies the packages that are to be used by the application. This is all especially useful and extremely powerful, but it is all built on the foundations that you have learned in this chapter. You will create arrow functions that give the behaviors of your server, and you will use promises to ensure that none of your functions block the execution of your program. You can find out how to build your first Express application at *http://expressjs.com/en/starter/hello-world.html*.

Deploying a Node.js server

The Node.js services that we have created so far have run on our local computer. You would not normally make your computer visible to the Internet so that other people can use your services. Instead, you would host your JavaScript program on an external server. You don't need to own a server machine. Instead, you can run your JavaScript application as a *service* in the cloud. You can get started with this for free by creating an Azure account and then using the App Service Extension for Visual Studio Code to configure and deploy the service that you have created. You can find out more at *https://azure.microsoft.com/en-us/develop/nodejs/*.

What you have learned

In this chapter, you learned how JavaScript code can be embedded directly in a program as anonymous functions and how the arrow notation makes this easier. You also discovered how programs can interact with the network and how the JavaScript promise mechanism allows the applications to contain asynchronous execution.

Finally, you have investigated the Node.js platform that allows JavaScript programs to run on a computer and provide services for JavaScript client applications running in a browser.

1. JavaScript arrays provide a `sort` behavior that will sort their content. We used this to sort the Fashion Shop stock list in order of stock level. The order of a sort is determined by a comparison function that is supplied to the `sort` behavior. The `comparison` function accepts two parameters, which are array elements. It compares the elements in some way and returns a value that is negative, zero, or positive, depending on the order in which they are to be sorted. The `comparison` function can be supplied as a named function or as an *anonymous* function directly as an argument.

2. An anonymous function can be expressed using an *arrow notation* in which the parameter list and body of the function are separated by an arrow operator (=>). If the body of the arrow function is a single statement, it does not need to be enclosed in a block, and if the single statement returns a value, the return keyword can be omitted.

3. JavaScript arrays provide a `filter` behavior. We used `filter` to create a list of Fashion Shop stock items with zero stock. The `filter` behavior returns another array containing selected elements. The behavior of the `filter` is determined by a `filter` function that is supplied to the `filter` behavior. The `filter` function accepts a single parameter and returns `true` if the value of that parameter means that it should be included in the filtered results.

4. JavaScript arrays provide a `reduce` behavior, which can convert an array into a single value. We used `reduce` to calculate the total value of all the stock in the Fashion Shop. The `reduce` behavior is provided with a function that accepts two parameters: the current total and a reference to an element in the array. The function calculates the new total by adding the value for the given element (in our case, the price of the element multiplied by the number in stock) to the total. The `reduce` behavior on an array is also provided with a starting value (which is usually 0) for the total.

5. JavaScript arrays provide a `map` behavior that applies a given function to every element in the array. We used this to apply a sale discount to the price of every item for sale in the Fashion Shop. The `map` behavior is provided with a function that accepts a single parameter—the element to be updated.

6. A JavaScript application running inside a web browser can consume the contents of a web service that is located at a particular address on the Internet. The web service can provide the data in the form of a JSON object, which can be decoded by the client application and displayed to the user. We used this create an application that read weather information from a server at *openweather.org*.

7. Some JavaScript operations, such as the `fetch` function that reads a message from a network, can take a noticeable time to complete. It is important that time-consuming operations such as `fetch` do not cause an active application to pause in a noticeable way. If a button-click handler in a web page takes a long time to complete, the web page would appear to have "locked up," and the user would not be able to interact with it. JavaScript allows long-running operations (such as fetching from a network) to be performed asynchronously.

8. The JavaScript promise mechanism allows a programmer to invoke operations that will be performed asynchronously. A promise exposes a `then` property that can be used to specify JavaScript code that will be performed when the asynchronous behavior "promised" to the calling application has completed. A promise also exposes a `catch` property that specifies code to be performed if the asynchronous operation fails.

9. JavaScript promise operations can be chained together. This allows an action that processes data delivered by a promise to return a promise to produce the processed data. We used this to allow an asynchronous JSON decoder to run directly after a `fetch` operation has completed.

10. A JavaScript promise exposes a `finally` property that can be used to specify code that will be run whether the promise is "kept" (the operation completed successfully) or "broken" (the operation could not be completed). We used the `finally` property to run code that enabled a button in the HTML document.

11. The Node.js framework allows a computer to run JavaScript programs without opening HTML files in the browser. The Node application contains a JavaScript runtime environment that will run JavaScript code. Code running inside Node.js cannot interact with the user via an HTML document (because there is no document), but it can provide JavaScript powered services for other applications. Node.js can be downloaded and installed for free on most computing platforms. (It is an open-source application.)

12. You can run Node (the program that implements the Node.js framework) from the command line. Node can provide a console like that in the browser Developer View, or it can open files containing JavaScript code and run them. You can run Node from the command prompt within Visual Studio Code.

13. The Node.js framework is supplied with a number of modules. The `require` function is used in an application to load a module and make it available for use in a program. One such module is the `http` module, which can be used to create web servers and clients.

14. The `http` module in Node.js can be used to create a server. The server will run on a computer and accept HyperText Transport Protocol (HTTP)–formatted messages that will request services from that computer. Clients making requests of the server will use a *uniform resource locator* (URL) to specify the network address of the server, the port number (if the port is not port 80), and the path to the resource on the server. The local server that we used for the demonstration code has this address: *http://localhost:8080/index.html*.

15. The `http.createServer` method used to create a server is called with a single argument, which is the *service function* for that server. The service function takes two parameters: the request and the response. The request parameter contains a description of the request received from the browser, and the response parameter is an object that can be used to build the response.

16. The `http.listen` method is called with a parameter of the port number that the sever is to listen on. The `listen` method will call the service function each time a remote client makes a request of the server. The `listen` method will never stop running; it will repeatedly respond to requests. Our first server ignored the content of the request parameter and sent a simple text response. This response was sent each time a browser client navigated to the server.

17. A response contains a status code (which is 200 for success), a header (which is content type information), and the response text (which is the data that the server is sending to the client).

18. The `service` function can parse the request and obtain the path component of the URL that was specified by the client. The `service` function can then serve up different responses for different paths.

19. A URL can also contain query data which is made up of name-value pairs which can be used by the server function to determine the response that is to be provided. We created an addition server that used a query data string containing values for two numbers to be added together. Query data is one way that a client can communicate with a server.

20. A JavaScript program running inside a browser can use the `fetch` function to interact via query data with services provided by a server.

21. A single Node.js application can both serve up HTML pages for a browser and respond to queries. This is the basis by which many web applications work.

22. The Node package manager provides a way for prewritten JavaScript frameworks to be incorporated into applications. The Express framework provides the "scaffolding" that can be used to create JavaScript-powered applications that run from a server.

Here are some questions that you might like to ponder about what we have learned in this chapter:

What is an anonymous function?

An anonymous function is one that has no name. That's probably not a useful answer, though. If you want to call a function by name, you can create it with a name. If you just want some code to give to another part of your application, you can just pass the code itself over. The sort method for an array needs to be given a behavior that tells it how to put items in order. We could pass the sort method the name of a function to call. Alternatively, we can provide the code itself in the form of an anonymous function.

Can I reuse code in an anonymous function?

No. Code in an anonymous function exists in one place in the code and is used from there. If you want to use a behavior in different parts of your program, you can make a named function and then call it by name every time you want to use it in your code.

Are there any performance advantages to using anonymous functions?

No. All that happens is that the JavaScript system places the code that implements the function in particular place in memory and then uses that address to call it. An anonymous function is called in exactly the same way as any other when the program actually runs.

Are there any performance advantages to using arrow functions to denote anonymous functions?

No. The arrow function was created to make it easier for programmers, not to make the program itself run more quickly.

Is there such a thing as an anonymous method?

No. A method will always have a name because it is named element in an object.

What does it mean if a function returns a promise?

A promise is an object that represents a statement of intent. At some point in the future, the code that implements the promise will run and either work (the promise is fulfilled, and the function specified by `then` is called) or fail (the promise is broken, and the function specified by `catch` is called). The code to implement the promise will run asynchronously, allowing the code that requested the action to continue running.

Can a promise have multiple `then` behaviors?

Yes, it can. You use the `then` method to tell a promise what to do when the promise is fulfilled. You can call `then` multiple times on a given promise. Each call of `then` can specify code to run when the promise is fulfilled. When the promise is fulfilled, the `then` functions will be called in the order that they were assigned.

Can multiple promises be active at one time?

Yes, they can. As an example, a program might fire off several successive calls to `fetch` to obtain multiple resources from the network. Note that because each call is asynchronous, the program has no idea which of the promises will be fulfilled first. It might be that the most-recent `fetch` returns its result first. It is the job of the program that requested the promises to synchronize the responses.

What happens if a promise is never kept?

If a promise is never kept, the `then`, `catch`, and `finally` functions will never be called by the promise.

What is the difference between a request and a response in a web server implementation using HTTP?

The request describes what is being asked for by the browser. It is a lump of data that describes the HTTP request. The request contains the URL entered so that the server can determine the path to the resource to be returned. The URL may also contain query items. The response object is used to build the response from the server. The response contains the status code for the response (`200` means "worked okay"), header information, and the data to be sent back. The job of the server function is to use the request information to work out what is required and then put that information into a response to be sent back to the client.

How many query items can a URL contain?

A URL can contain many query items and each item can be quite long. If you look at the URL in the browser of an e-commerce site such as Amazon, you will see that the address can contain many query items. These are used by the server to maintain a session with the browser connection.

Can a Node.js application display graphics for the user?

Not directly. The Node.js platform will run JavaScript applications, but it does not maintain an HTML document for the application to communicate with the user. However, a web application running on a machine can be sent HTML documents by an application running under Node.js. The final example application, **Ch11 Creating Applications\Ch11-16 Addition Application**, does this.

Can an HTML server application create a "session" with a web client?

HTTP is described as *stateless*. Each request made by a web client is "atomic." Once it has completed, the server forgets about it. If you want to create a "session" with a server, the application must provide data to the server program to identify the session it is part of. One way to do this is for code in the browser to use query string values to identify the session.

12
Creating games

What you will learn

Writing games is great fun. Unlike applications created to solve a specific problem, games are not always tied to a formal specification and don't need to do anything useful. They only need to be fun to play. Games are a great place to experiment with your software. You can write code just to see what happens when it runs and see whether the result is interesting. Everyone should write at least one computer game in their lives. In this chapter, you'll start creating games. You'll learn how to make a complete game and finish with a framework you can use to create more games of your own design. Along the way you'll discover how to use the HTML Canvas and learn more about the asynchronous loading of resources.

Use the HTML Canvas

In this section, we'll get started with the HTML canvas element. We'll create some shapes and display them. Up until now the browser has determined the final position of every element on the screen. We have used Hyper Text Markup Language (HTML) and Cascading Style Sheets (CSS) to express preferences about layout, style, and color, but these are only general instructions. This is as it should be. It makes it possible for a page designer to create content without having to worry about the specifics of the output device. However, some displays must be drawn with pixel-level precision. The HTML Canvas is provided to allow programs to do this. The canvas is an area of the display, within which a program can precisely draw items.

```
<canvas id="canvas" width="800" height="600">
  This browser does not support a canvas.
</canvas>
```

The HTML above shows how we create a canvas element in an HTML document. It works in the same way as the audio element that we saw in Chapter 2 in the "Adding sound to the egg timer" section. In the same way that not all browsers can support audio, not all browsers can support the canvas element. If the canvas element is not supported (meaning the browser does not know what to do when it sees the word canvas) the HTML enclosed in the element is displayed. However, if the browser understands the word canvas it will ignore the text in the element so that the message does not appear. All modern browsers provide canvas support, but it is still important to make sure that your pages do sensible things when running on ones that don't.

 MAKE SOMETHING HAPPEN

Draw on a canvas

The best way to understand how a canvas works is to draw something on it. Open the browser and go to the **Ch12 Creating Games\Ch12-01 Empty Canvas** example page. An empty canvas is displayed as a white area on the screen underneath the heading. Press F12 to open the Developer View of the web page and select the **Console** tab so that we can enter some JavaScript statements and draw on the canvas.

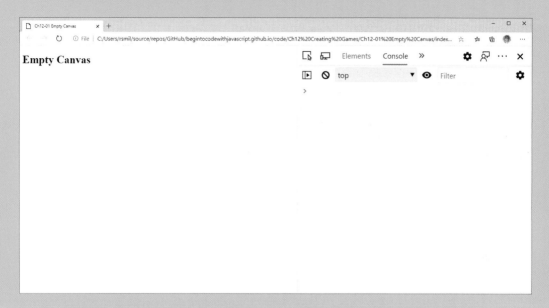

The initial color of a canvas is white, so the canvas in the figure above just looks like an empty area of the page. Now we need to write some JavaScript to draw items on the canvas. We know that JavaScript programs interact with an HTML document by obtaining a reference to an element in the document and then interacting with that element. The first thing we need to do is get a reference to the canvas element by using the document.getElementById method. Enter the statement below and press Enter.

```
> var myCanvas = document.getElementById("canvas");
```

When you press Enter, a variable called myCanvas is created and made to refer to the canvas element. This process does not return a value, so the JavaScript console displays undefined.

```
> var myCanvas = document.getElementById("canvas");
<- undefined
```

You might think that we could now call methods on the myCanvas reference to draw things on the canvas in the HTML document. However, this is not how it works. A canvas provides a drawing *context* that is used to perform drawing operations. We want to use the 2D drawing context, so we have to ask the canvas for it. Enter the statement below and press Enter:

```
> var myContext = myCanvas.getContext('2d');
```

When you press Enter, a variable called myContext is created that refers to the 2D graphics context of the canvas. This process does not return a value, so the JavaScript console displays undefined.

```
> var myContext = myCanvas.getContext('2d');
<- undefined
```

The context object can be used for all further graphics operations. It exposes many methods for drawing on the canvas. One way to draw is to define a *path* and then ask the context to draw the path. Enter the following statement to begin a path:

```
> myContext.beginPath();
```

A path contains move and draw operations. You can add many of these operations to the path. We are going to start the path by moving to the origin. The moveTo method accepts two parameters. The first is the "x coordinate" or distance across the screen of a pixel position. The second parameter is the "y coordinate" or distance down the screen. The position (0,0) is known as the *origin* of the graphics coordinates. Let's move the path position to the origin. Enter the following statement to move the path position to (0,0).

```
> myContext.moveTo(0,0)
```

Moving doesn't draw anything on the canvas. To draw a line, we use the lineTo method, which also accepts x and y coordinates as parameters. Enter the following statement to draw a line to the position (800,600).

```
> myContext.lineTo(800,600);
```

We have told JavaScript to draw a line, but the line has not appeared on the screen yet. This is because the context saves all the move and draw operations until the stroke method is called. Enter the following statement to draw the line on the canvas:

```
> myContext.stroke();
```

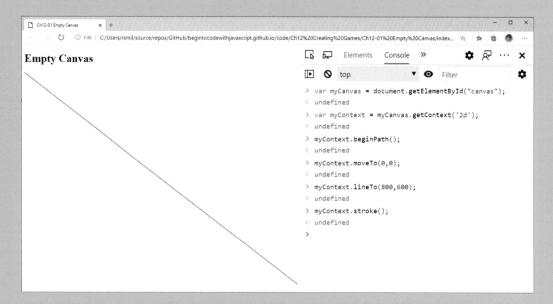

When you enter the `stroke` method, you should see a diagonal line drawn down the entire canvas. This is because the canvas has been defined as being 800 pixels wide and 600 pixels high.

Canvas coordinates

You might have been surprised by the line that has just been drawn. You might have expected the line to start at the bottom-left corner, rather than the top. This is because placing the origin in the top-left corner is standard practice when drawing graphics on a computer. The important thing to remember is that the origin, which is the point with the coordinate (0,0), is the top-left corner of the display. Increasing the value of x moves you toward the right of the screen, and increasing the value of y will move you down the screen, as shown in **Figure 12-1**. If you draw outside the range of the canvas dimensions—for example, if we tried to draw something at location (1000,1000)—this would not be displayed, but it would not cause an error in the program. I've chosen a canvas size of 800 pixels wide and 600 pixels high because this results in a reasonable game display on most devices.

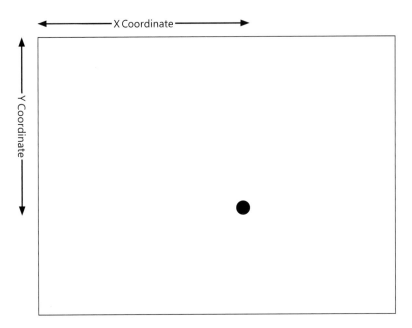

Figure 12-1 Canvas coordinates

Computer art

We can use JavaScript graphics to create some nice-looking images. The program below draws 100 colored lines and 100 colored dots. The program uses functions that create random colors and positions on the display area.

```
<!DOCTYPE html>
<html>

<head>
   <title>Ch12-02 Art Maker</title>
</head>

<body onload="doDrawArt()">                    Call doDrawArt when the page is loaded
<canvas id="canvas" width="800" height="600">   Set the canvas width to
   This browser does not support a canvas.      800 wide and 600 high
</canvas>

   <script>
```

```
var canvasWidth = 800;                                          Global variable giving canvas width
var canvasHeight = 600;                                         Global variable giving canvas height
var context;                                                    Canvas drawing context

function getRandomInt(min, max) {              Gets a random integer in the specified range
  var range = max - min + 1;
  var result = Math.floor(Math.random() * (range)) + min;
  return result;
}
                                                               List of color names
colors = ['red', 'green', 'blue', 'yellow', 'cyan', 'magenta', 'grey',
  'silver','lightgreen','orange', 'purple', 'gold', 'lightblue'];

function getRandomColor() {                    Pick a random color name from the list
  return colors[getRandomInt(0, colors.length)];
}

function drawDot(x, y, radius, style){         Draw a dot of a particular size and style
  context.beginPath();
  context.arc(x, y, radius, 0, 2 * Math.PI);                    Draw a circle
  context.fillStyle=style;                             Set the fill style to the color
  context.fill();                                              Fill in the dot
}

function drawRandomDot(){                                       Draw a random dot
  var radius = getRandomInt(5, 100);                            Pick a random dot radius
  var x = getRandomInt(radius, canvasWidth-radius);             Pick random x
  var y = getRandomInt(radius, canvasHeight-radius);            Pick random y
  var color = getRandomColor();                                 Pick random color
  drawDot(x,y,radius,color);                                    Draw the dot
}

function drawLine(startX, startY, endX, endY, style, linewidth) {    Draw a line
  context.beginPath();                                          Start the path
  context.moveTo(startX, startY);                      Move to the start of the line
  context.lineTo(endX, endY);                                   Draw the line
  context.strokeStyle = style;                               Set the line style
  context.lineWidth = linewidth;                           Set the line thickness
  context.stroke();                                            Draw the line
}

function drawRandomLine() {                                     Draw a random line
  var startX = getRandomInt(0, canvasWidth);                    Pick line start x
```

```
      var startY = getRandomInt(0, canvasHeight);         Pick line start y
      var endX = getRandomInt(0, canvasWidth);             Pick line end x
      var endY =.getRandomInt(0, canvasHeight);            Pick line end y
      var color = getRandomColor();                        Pick random line color
      var thickness = getRandomInt(1,6);                   Pick random line thickness
      drawLine( startX, startY, endX, endY, color, thickness);   Draw a random line
    }


    function doDrawArt() {
      var canvas = document.getElementById("canvas");      Get the drawing canvas
      if (canvas.getContext) {
        // We have a canvas to work with
        context = canvas.getContext('2d');                 Set the draw canvas to 2d
        for (let i = 0; i < 100; i = i + 1) {              Repeat 100 times
          drawRandomDot();                                 Draw a random dot
          drawRandomLine();                                Draw a random line
        }
      }
    }
  </script>
</body>
</html>
```

The computer art program can produce some rather nice-looking images, as you can see in **Figure 12-2**. You can find it in the example **Ch12 Creating Games\Ch12-02 Art Maker** folder. Each time you run the program, it will generate a different image because the positions of each item are determined randomly.

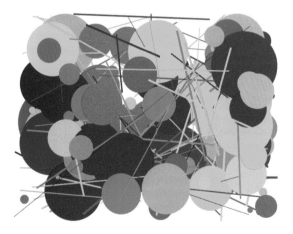

Figure 12-2   Computer art

Random artwork

As you can see in Figure 12-2, the program above can produce some vaguely artistic-looking images. However, you may have some questions about the code.

Question: Where do the `context`, `canvasWidth`, and `canvasHeight` values come from?

> **Answer:** These variables are *global*. They are not declared in any function, so they can be shared by all of them. I've decided that it makes the program easier to write if these values are shared by all the functions in the program. The value of `context` (the context to be used for all the drawing operations) is set at the start of the `doDrawArt` function.

Question: How does the program draw a round dot?

> **Answer:** There is no way of drawing a round dot on an HTML canvas. Instead, the program draws a circle and fills it in. The `arc` drawing method accepts a coordinate that gives the center of the arc, a radius, and two angles in radians. It then draws an arc between the two angles. If the initial angle is 0 and the second is 2*Pi (which is the radian equivalent of 360 degrees), the result is a circle.

```
context.arc(x, y, radius, 0, 2 * Math.PI);
```

> You can use this method to draw interesting curves by only drawing part of the circle. This will also provide a very good workout of your trigonometry skills.

Question: Why does the program subtract the radius value from the random dot positions?

```
var radius = getRandomInt(5, 100);
var x = getRandomInt(radius, canvasWidth-radius);
var y = getRandomInt(radius, canvasHeight-radius);
```

> **Answer:** Above, you can see the statements that pick a random position to draw a round dot. The radius of a dot is between the values 5 and 100. When the dot is drawn, I don't want it to "go off" the picture. This is an artistic decision—JavaScript will happily draw items that don't all fit on the screen. The `getRandomInt` function picks a random number between start and end values. By making sure that the start position is never less than the radius of the dot or greater than the canvas size subtracted from the radius, I can make sure that my dots never go off the screen. If your artistic judgment is different from mine, you are welcome to change this code.

Question: Does the drawing have to be on a white background?

Answer: No. A program can use the `fillRect` drawing function to draw a filled rectangle to change the canvas to any desired color:

```
context.fillStyle = "blue";
context.fillRect(0, 0, canvasWidth, canvasHeight);
```

The statements above would fil the entire canvas with blue.

Question: Can I create my own colors?

Answer: Yes. The art program above uses fixed color names such as "red," but you can also create a color by calling the `rgb` function with three arguments giving the intensities of red, blue, and green in the color:

```
rgb(255,0,0)
```

The intensity values can range from 0 to 255. The above call of `rgb` would produce the value bright red.

```
function getRandomColor() {
  var r = getRandomInt(0,255);
  var g = getRandomInt(0,255);
  var b = getRandomInt(0,255);
  return "rgb("+r+","+g+","+b+")";
}
```

This version of `getRandomColor` produces a completely random color by choosing random values for red, green, and blue and then creating an `rgb` result that makes that color. You can find it in the **Ch12 Creating Games\Ch12-03 Random Color Art Maker** example folder. You might like to compare the results of the two programs to see which you prefer.

 MAKE SOMETHING HAPPEN

Make some of your own art

You can have a lot of fun with the art program above to make some really interesting images. Here are a few ideas that you might like to explore:

• You could create a program that displays a different pattern every now and then.

- You could use the time of day and the current weather conditions to determine what colors to use in the pattern and create a display that changes throughout the day (perhaps with bright primary colors in the morning and mellower and darker colors in the evening).

- If the weather is warm, the colors could have a red tinge, and if it's colder, you could create colors with more blues.

Draw images on a canvas

In Chapter 2, in the "Add images to web pages" section, we saw that an HTML document can use `img` elements to display images. The images were stored in files on the server alongside the HTML documents. The browser loads the image files and displays them. We are going to use images for the objects in our game. Our game must load the images and can then draw them on the canvas.

Image file types

There are several different formats for storing pictures on computers. There are two popular formats that you might want to use:

- **PNG**—The PNG format is lossless, meaning it always stores an exact version of the image. PNG files can also have transparent regions, which is important when you want to draw one image on top of another. Files containing PNG images have a `.png` file name extension.

- **JPEG**—The JPEG format is lossy, meaning the image is compressed in a way that makes it much smaller but at the expense of precise detail. Files containing JPEG images have the file name extension `.jpg` or `.jpeg`. I tend to use the shorter extension (`.jpg`) to name my JPEG files, but you can use either. Just make sure that the name of the file matches the reference in the web page.

The games you create should use JPEG images for the large backgrounds and PNG images for smaller objects drawn on top of them. If you have no usable pictures of your own, you can use the ones I've provided with the sample files for this chapter, but your games will work best if you use your own pictures.

If you need to convert images into the PNG format, you can load an image using the Microsoft Paint program and then save it in this format. With Paint, you can also scale and crop images if you want to reduce the number of pixels in the image. Mac owners can use the Preview image editor, and if you are using a Unix-powered PC, you can use the Gimp program, which is freely available for most machines. You can download Gimp here: *https://www.gimp.org*.

Figure 12-3 shows my picture of the cheese we'll be using in the game that we will create. In the game, the player will control the cheese and use it to catch crackers around the screen. You can use another picture if you wish. In fact, I strongly advise that you do.

Figure 12-3   Cheese

Load and draw an image

The JavaScript to create and draw an image looks very easy to write:

```
var image = new Image();
image.src = "cheese.png";
context.drawImage(image,0,0);
```

Create a new image object
Set the src property to the location of the image
Draw the image on the screen

The statements above are all completely correct. They create a new `Image`, tell the image that the path to the image resource is the URL *cheese.png*, and then draw the image on the canvas context at the top-left corner of the screen (coordinate 0,0). Unfortunately, these statements will not work. This is because loading images is like fetching everything else from the network. It takes a while to complete. The image starts to load when the `src` attribute is set, but the JavaScript code above draws the image before it has loaded. This means that the cheese would not be displayed. Loading an image is performed *asynchronously*. We first saw asynchronous operation in Chapter 11 in the "Fetch data from a server" section. In that section, we used the `fetch` function to get weather data from a server.

We can get a notification that an image has been loaded by connecting a function to the onload property exposed by the image. When the image has been fetched, it calls this function. This is called an *event*, and the function connected to the event is called an *event handler*. Connecting an event handler to an event is called *binding* the handler to the event. We could bind an event handler function that draws the image as soon as it has arrived:

```
var image = new Image();
image.src = "cheese.png";
image.onload = () => context.drawImage(image, 0, 0) ;
```

These statements would draw the cheese as soon as it was loaded. The last statement binds an arrow function to the onload event so that the image is drawn when it has been loaded. You can find a program that draws cheese in this way in the **Ch12 Creating Games\Ch12-04 Image Load Event** folder in the example programs. We can also bind an event handler to the onerror event that an image will generate if the image cannot be loaded.

```
image.onerror = () => alert("image not loaded");
```

This statement binds an arrow function to the onerror event. The arrow function displays an image not loaded alert. You can find a program that produces this error alert in the **Ch12 Creating Games\ Ch12-05 Image Load Fail** example programs folder.

Create an image loading promise

A JavaScript program can use an event to detect when a single image is loaded, but our game will need to load several images for the different elements in the game. We need to draw cheese, crackers, tomatoes, and a tablecloth background. It would be hard work to bind event handlers to all the onload events for all these images in turn. However, it turns out that JavaScript has a very neat way of managing multiple asynchronous operations that is based around the JavaScript Promise object.

When we used the fetch function in Chapter 11 in the "Fetch data from a server" section, we discovered that the fetch function returns a Promise object. Our program bound handlers to the then and catch events exposed by a Promise. The first thing we need to do is create a function that generates a Promise for the image loading process.

```
function getImageLoadPromise(url) {
    return new Promise((kept, broken) => {                    Controller function for the promise
        var image = new Image();                                    Create the new Image
        image.src = url;                                            Set the url of the image
        image.onload = () => kept(image);        Connect the onload event to the kept parameter
        image.onerror = () => broken(new Error('Could not load' + url));
    });                                        Connect the onerror event to the broken parameter
}
```

The `getImageLoadPromise` function is given the URL of the image resource and returns an `Image` object containing that resource. The constructor for a new `Promise` object is given a function that accepts two parameters. This is the controller function for the promise. The controller function above is an arrow function that accepts two parameters that specify event handlers to be called when the promise has been kept (the image was loaded) or broken (the image could not be loaded). The controller function creates the new image, sets the `src` property to the `url`, and then connects the `onload` event in the new image to the `kept` function in the promise and the `onerror` event in the new image to the `broken` function in the promise. You might need to take some time getting your head around this, so it might be helpful if we look at how a `Promise` is used:

```
var imagePromise = getImageLoadPromise("images/cheese.png");           Get the promise
imagePromise.then((image) => context.drawImage(image, 0, 0));          Bind to then
imagePromise.catch((error) => alert(error));                           Bind to catch
```

This code uses `getImagePromise` to get a promise and then uses the `then` part to trigger drawing the image and the `catch` part to trigger displaying an alert. You can find a program that uses this promise in the **Ch12 Creating Games\Ch12-06 Promise Image Load** in the example programs folder.

Use `Promise.all` to handle multiple promises

Now that we can create promises to handle image loading, we can use a very powerful JavaScript feature called `Promise.all` to manage image loading. `Promise.all` lets a program wait for a number of promises to complete. All our program has to do is assemble a list of promises and give them to a call of `Promise.all`. The `Promise.all` method delivers a single promise that is fulfilled when all the promises have been fulfilled.

```
function getImages(imageUrls){

    var promiseList = [];                                    Make an empty promise list
```

```
    for (url of imageUrls){                            Work through the list of image URLs
        promiseList[promiseList.length]=getImageLoadPromise(url);
    }                                                  Create a load promise and add it to the list
                                                       Work through the images returned by the promises
    Promise.all(promiseList).then( (images)=> {
        var x = 0;                                     Set x draw coordinate to 0
        var y = 0;                                     Set y draw coordinate to 0
        for(image of images){                          Work through the images returned by the promises
            context.drawImage(image,x,y);              Draw the image
            x = x + image.width;                       Move x across by the width of the image
            y = y + image.height;                      Move y down by the height of the image
        }
    })
}
```

The `getImages` function creates a list of promises by calling the `getImageLoadPromise`
function for each of the image URLs it has been asked to load. It then calls `Promise.all`
and passes it this list. When all the promises in the list have been fulfilled, the `then` part
of `Promise.all` is called, which works through the images that were returned and draws
them down the canvas. The `getImages` function is called with a list of image paths:

```
var imageNames = ["cheese.png", "tomato.png", "cracker.png", "background.png"];
getImages(imageNames);
```

Figure 12-4 shows the result produced for each of the images in the game that have
been loaded from the image files.

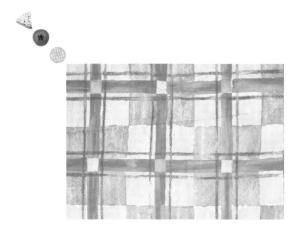

Figure 12-4   Game images that have been loaded and displayed

Use async to "wait" for promise results

The `getImages` function that we have created draws the images on the screen when they have all been loaded. However, the game program will not want to do this. Once the images are ready, the game application will want to start running and display the images as the game runs. Ideally, we would just like the program to be able to "wait" for the result from a call of the `getImages` method.

It turns out that there is a way of doing this, but it doesn't involve waiting. Instead, it involves `await`. To understand how `await` works, we must first go back to why we are doing all this. The problem we are solving is in two parts:

1. Some things (for example fetching images) take a while to perform.

2. Our programs are not allowed to stand and wait for things to be performed.

JavaScript solves this problem by letting us create a `Promise` object that describes the intent of the action. We attach code to the `then` part of the `Promise`, which will run when the promise is kept. Setting up a promise doesn't take very long so our program does not spend time waiting. But using `then` is a bit clumsy in this situation. We don't want to do something when the images have arrived; we just want to move on to the next part of the game.

JavaScript provides a way of "wrapping" up a `Promise`, which makes things easier. It uses the keywords `async` and `await`. Firstly, any function that contains an `await` must be marked as `async`. This tells JavaScript to change the way that the function is called to make the `await` possible. Then the function can use the `await` keyword to wait for the results of promises. We could make an asynchronous version of `getImages` as follows:

```
async function getImages(imageUrls){          Asynchronous function to get all the images

    var promiseList = [];                     Empty list of promises
    for (url of imageUrls){                   Work through the image URLs
        promiseList[promiseList.length]=getImageLoadPromise(url);
    }                                         Get an image load promise for each
                                              URL and add it to the list

    var result = await Promise.all(promiseList);  Wait for all the promises to be fulfilled
    return result;                            Return the list of images
}
```

I've highlighted the `await` and `async` keywords in the listing above. When a program reaches a statement that awaits a promise, the JavaScript execution of the function containing the statement is suspended until the promise is fulfilled. The `getImages` function now awaits the result of the call of the `Promise.all` function. When the promise is fulfilled, the function is resumed.

We don't need to know how this magic works, we just have to marvel at how much easier it makes it for a program to wait for asynchronous actions to complete. The only hard thing to remember about this is that calls of `async` functions must always be made using `await`. In other words, any calls to this version of `getImages` must `await` it. This is the complete code of the method that draws the images using `await`:

```
async function doLoadImage() {                          Called when the HTML document is loaded

    var canvas = document.getElementById("canvas");       Get the canvas from the document

    if (canvas.getContext) {                              Check for a graphics context

        context = canvas.getContext('2d');               Get the "2d" graphics context
                                                          Image name array
        var imageNames = ["cheese.png", "tomato.png", "cracker.png", "background.png"];
        var images = await getImages(imageNames);         Get the images

        var x = 0;                                        Work through the images and display them
        var y = 0;
        for (let image of images){
            context.drawImage(image,x,y);
            x = x + image.width;
            y = y + image.height;
        }
    }
    else {
        alert("Graphics not supported");
    }
}
```

Promise.all and async/await

You can find the async/await version of the image loading program in the **Ch12 Creating Games\Ch12-08 Promise Await Load** in the example files folder. It displays the images just like the earlier versions. However, the code to fetch and use the images is much simpler because it looks like sequential code. You may have some questions about all this:

Question: How does the Promise object work?

Answer: I don't know the details. I know that an operating system (Windows 10, macOS, or Linux) can be used to control the starting and stopping of different parts of active programs called *threads*. Also, I know that different parts of the JavaScript environment run on different threads that are managed by the browser, but beyond that, I don't know how they are run. I just know how to use promises, which is good enough for me. After all, I don't really know how the engine in my car works, but I'm very happy to drive it.

Question: What happens if one of the promises in a Promise.all fails?

Answer: Promise.all is given a list of promises. If one of these can't be kept (perhaps an image resource can't be found), the catch behavior will be called. I've left this out of my example above to keep things smaller. The catch behavior is given the error message from the first promise that failed.

Question: Could a program await the result of the fetch function we used in Chapter 11 to fetch network data?

Answer: Yes, it could, and in some situations, it makes using fetch much easier.

Question: Does using await cause the browser user interface to lock up?

Answer: Good question. We use Promise and await to prevent functions in our program taking a long time to complete and causing the browser user interface to lock up. When a JavaScript function runs in response to a button click on an HTML page, the browser will not accept any further user input until the function finishes. Using a Promise will make a function complete quickly because it does not have to wait for the promise to be fulfilled; it just has to start the promise. You might think that if you use await in a function that function is stopped until the Promise is fulfilled. However, this is not what happens. Instead, JavaScript converts the code following the async into the body of a "then" event handler, creates a Promise, and then runs it. Both Promise and await work in the same way.

Question: What happens if an awaited Promise cannot be fulfilled.

Answer: We can add a catch element to a Promise to nominate JavaScript to run if the Promise cannot be fulfilled. A program can catch errors in awaited promises by enclosing the await in a try-catch construction.

Animate images

The drawImage function is given x and y values that specify where the image is to be drawn.

```
context.drawImage(cheese,x,y);
```

The statement above would draw the Image referred to by cheese on the canvas. The values in the variables x and y specify where in the canvas the image above would be drawn. We can make an image appear to move by repeatedly drawing the image at slightly different positions. This is how all games work. To perform the game animation, we need a regular source of update events. In Chapter 3 in the "Create a ticking clock" section, we used the setInterval function to repeatedly call a function at regular intervals and make our clock tick. We could use this to trigger game display updates, but this would not be a very good idea because it would result in the game display flickering.

If the browser redraws the screen while our game is halfway through updating the positions of objects on the screen, the player would see the display appear to flicker. To avoid flickering, we need to synchronize the game updates with screen updates from the browser. Fortunately, there is a way to do this. The browser maintains a window object, which contains methods that we can use in our applications. One of these is the requestAnimationFrame method. This method accepts a single parameter, which specifies a function to call the next time the browser is updating the display.

```
window.requestAnimationFrame(gameUpdate);
```

The statement above asks the browser to call the `gameUpdate` method the next time the browser is updating the display. The game can then redraw the canvas as part of this process.

```
function gameUpdate(timeStamp) {
    context.fillStyle = "cornflowerblue";          Set the fill color to cornflowerblue
    context.fillRect(0, 0, canvasWidth, canvasHeight);   Draw a blue rectangle that clears
                                                                            the canvas

    context.drawImage(cheese, x, y);               Draw the cheese on the canvas
    x = x + 1;                                     Update the value of x
    y = y + 1;                                     Update the value of y
    window.requestAnimationFrame(gameUpdate);      Request the next call of the
                                                                  animation frame
}
```

This is a `gameUpdate` function that will draw the cheese image moving down the screen. The screen is cleared before each redraw. After each draw, the values of the x and y positions of the cheese are increased by 1, which will move the cheese draw position.

 MAKE SOMETHING HAPPEN

Move an image

We can investigate the way that games make objects appear to move by opening the example page in the **Ch12 Creating Games\Ch12-09 Moving Cheese** folder. If you open this page, you should find that the cheese moves majestically down the screen for a while and then disappears off the bottom.

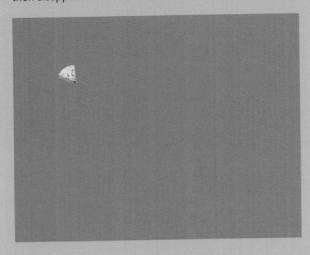

Most browsers update the display 60 times a second. The screen is 600 pixels high, and the cheese is moved down the screen one pixel each time it is updated. This means that after around 10 seconds, the cheese will vanish off the bottom of the screen. If you want to make the cheese appear to move more quickly, you can increase the amount you add to the position. The amount you change the position of an item on the screen gives you the speed of that item. See if you can change the program to make the cheese move twice as fast down the screen. These are the two statements that you need to look for:

```
x = x + 1;
y = y + 1;
```

By changing the values to 2, you can double the speed. You can find my faster version in the **Ch12 Creating Games\Ch12-10 Speedy Cheese** example folder.

Control gameplay

Now that we know how to make things move around the screen, the next thing we need is a way that a player can control them. We are going to use the keyboard to steer the cheese with the arrow keys. When the user presses an arrow key, we want the cheese to move in the corresponding direction. To make this work, we are going to create an event listener that runs when the player presses a key on the keyboard.

Window events

We have already used the `requestAnimationFrame` function to ask the `window` object to tell our game when it is time to redraw the screen. Now we are going to ask the `window` object to bind a function to events generated by the keyboard. The `addEventListener` provided by the `window` object lets a program connect a JavaScript function to a particular event. The events are specified by name, and there are many events. We can start by investigating how events work. We are going to use the `keydown` event.

```
function doKeyboardReader() {

    var resultParagraph = document.getElementById("result");        Get a reference to the paragraph
                                                                     that will display key values

    window.addEventListener("keydown", (event) => {                 Listen for key down messages
```

```
        resultParagraph.innerText="Key Down: " + event.code;
    });
}
```

Display the code property of the event

The function above adds an arrow function to the `keydown` event. The function is supplied with an `event` parameter. It displays the `code` attribute of the event in a paragraph in the document.

CODE ANALYSIS

Keyboard events

You can find the keyboard event handler code in the **Ch12 Creating Games\Ch12-11 Keyboard Events** example folder. Use the browser to open this page and investigate what it does.

Above, you can see the display that is produced when I pressed the A key on the keyboard. Try some other keys, including nonprinting ones such as Shift and Control. Also, try holding down the Shift key and pressing letters.

Question: Why does it not display the character produced by that key on the keyboard?

    Answer: The code values that are captured by this event are more concerned with the actual key rather than the character that is sent to a program when a key is pressed. Each key has a name (the A key is called "KeyA"), including the Shift keys. This event even distinguishes between left and right Shift keys, calling them "ShiftLeft" and "ShiftRight." This is very useful for our game.

Question: Can a program detect when a key is released?

Answer: Yes. A program can bind to an event called keyup, which is triggered when a key is released.

Question: Does this code detect all keypresses on the computer?

Answer: No. The key events only fire when the browser is the active application. If the user selects another application, the keyboard events will no longer happen.

Question: Can a single event have multiple listeners?

Answer: Yes. The window will call each of the functions bound to a particular event in turn.

Control object position with a keyboard

We can now use the keyboard to control the draw position of the cheese, making it possible for the player to steer the cheese around the screen:

```
window.addEventListener("keydown", (event) => {
    switch(event.code){
        case 'ArrowLeft':
            x = x - 1;                   Decrease x to move to the left
            break;
        case 'ArrowRight':
            x = x + 1;                   Increase x to move to the right
            break;
        case 'ArrowUp':
            y = y - 1;                   Decrease y to move up
            break;
        case 'ArrowDown':
            y = y + 1;                   Increase y to move down
            break;
    }
});
```

The code above binds an event listener to the keydown event and then uses key values to control the x and y positions of the cheese. When the cheese is drawn at its new position, it will appear to move under the control of the player.

Cheese steering

You can find the cheese steering code in the **Ch12 Creating Games\Ch12-12 Keypress Cheese Control example folder**. Use the browser to open this page and investigate what it does.

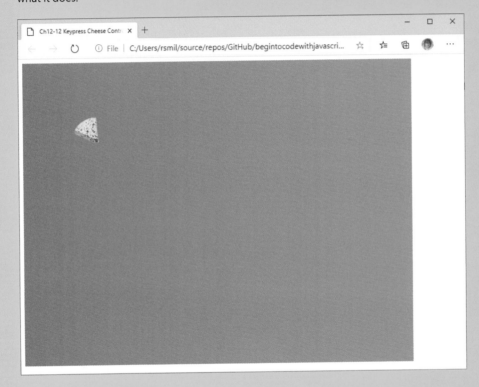

You can press the arrow keys to move the cheese around the screen. Each time you press an arrow key, the cheese moves one pixel in that direction.

Question: How does the cheese appear to move?

> **Answer:** Remember that the canvas is being redrawn 60 times a second. Keyboard events will happen in-between redraws and update the x and y positions of the cheese so that the cheese appears to move.

Question: Why does the value of y increase as the cheese moves down the screen?

> **Answer:** This is because the *origin* of the coordinates (the point with the coordinate 0,0) is the top-left-corner. This means that increasing the value of y will move the cheese down the screen.

Question: What happens if I move the cheese off the screen.

Answer: Quick answer: You can't see it anymore. Longer answer: You can think of the canvas as a view onto a larger area. If you move the drawing position out of the visible area, you will not be able to see the object, but you can make it visible again by moving it back into view.

Question: Why does the cheese start to move continuously if I hold down an arrow key?

Answer: This is because keys on the keyboard will auto-repeat if held down. This causes repeated calls to the event handler, causing the cheese to move continuously. This is not a very good way to get continuous movement. In the next section, we will discover a better way.

Question: How would I make the cheese move more quickly?

Answer: To increase the speed of the cheese, you can add or subtract a value greater than 1 from the position each time the key is pressed.

Use keydown and keyup events

The previous example showed the principle of controlling an object with a keyboard, but it was not very user friendly. We don't want the user to have to press the key each time they want to move the cheese a small amount. It would be much better if the cheese would move while a key was held down and stop when the key was released. We can do this by detecting both keydown and keyup events and using them to control the speed of the cheese.

```
var cheeseX = 0;
var cheeseY = 0;
var cheeseSpeed = 5;
var cheeseXSpeed = 0;
var cheeseYSpeed = 0;
```

Cheese X position	
Cheese Y position	
Overall speed of the cheese	
Current X speed of the cheese	
Current Y speed of the cheese	

These variables control the speed and position of the cheese in our game. The speed and position values are used in the function gameUpdate, which updates the cheese position and then draws it.

```
function gameUpdate(timeStamp) {
    context.fillStyle = "cornflowerblue";
    context.fillRect(0, 0, canvasWidth, canvasHeight);          Clear the canvas

    cheeseX = cheeseX + cheeseXSpeed;                           Update the X position
    cheeseY = cheeseY + cheeseYSpeed;                           Update the Y position

    context.drawImage(cheese, cheeseX, cheeseY);                Draw the cheese
    window.requestAnimationFrame(gameUpdate);                   Connect to the next draw operation
}
```

Each time this function is called, it will clear the screen, update the position of the cheese, and then draw the cheese at the new position. If the speed values are zero, the cheese will not move with each redraw.

```
window.addEventListener("keydown", (event) => {
    switch(event.code){
        case 'ArrowLeft':
            cheeseXSpeed = -cheeseSpeed;
            break;
        case 'ArrowRight':
            cheeseXSpeed = cheeseSpeed;
            break;
        case 'ArrowUp':
            cheeseYSpeed = -cheeseSpeed;
            break;
        case 'ArrowDown':
            cheeseYSpeed = cheeseSpeed;
            break;
    }
});
```

This event hander starts the cheese moving when the user presses a key. It doesn't move the cheese on the screen; instead, it sets the speed value of the cheese so that it will move in the selected direction the next time the update method is called. If the cheese is to move backward or upward, the speed for that direction will be negative. Because the position of the cheese is being updated repeatedly by the gameUpdate function, this will mean that the cheese will start to move as soon as the key is pressed down.

```
window.addEventListener("keyup", (event) => {
    switch(event.code){
        case 'ArrowLeft':
            cheeseXSpeed=0;
            break;
        case 'ArrowRight':
            cheeseXSpeed=0;
            break;
        case 'ArrowUp':
            cheeseYSpeed=0;
            break;
        case 'ArrowDown':
            cheeseYSpeed=0;
            break;
    }
});
```

This is the event handler that causes the cheese to stop moving when the player releases a key. It sets the speed value for the particular direction to zero.

 WHAT COULD GO WRONG

Losing focus

You can find this cheese steering code in the example program **Ch12 Creating Games\Ch12-13 Steerable Cheese**. If you open the page in this folder with a browser, you will find that you can control the cheese movement very well. If you hold down two arrows you can even make the cheese move diagonally. However, the code does have a problem. If you start the cheese moving and then select another window on your desktop the cheese doesn't stop when you release the movement key. This is because a modern windowed operating system like Windows 10, macOS, or Linux has the idea of *focus*.

At any given instant, the events from the keyboard and mouse are sent to the currently selected window, which is called the one that has *focus*. As soon as you select another application, the browser moving our cheese around loses focus and keyboard events are no longer sent to it. This means that there is no keyup message to stop the cheese moving, which causes it to keep moving and eventually vanish off the canvas.

We can fix this by binding a handler to a window event that is fired when the application loses focus. This is called the blur event. When this event fires, the game must stop the movement of the cheese.

```
window.addEventListener("blur", (event) => {
    cheeseXSpeed = 0;
    cheeseYSpeed = 0;
});
```

The code above shows how we would do this. When the window loses focus, it now sets the speed values for the cheese to 0, causing it to stop moving. The application in the **Ch12 Creating Games\Ch12-14 Steerable Cheese with focus** example folder uses this event handler to stop the cheese moving when browser loses focus. If you repeat the experiment you performed with the earlier version, you will find that the cheese stops moving as soon as you select a different window from the browser.

Create game objects

The game we are making is called "Cracker Chase." The player will control the cheese, with the aim of capturing as many crackers as possible while avoiding the deadly killer tomatoes. The game will display four different items on the screen:

1. The tablecloth background—This contains an image that is the background of the game.

2. Cheese—The player will steer the cheese around the screen trying to capture crackers and avoid the killer tomatoes.

3. Crackers—The player will try to capture crackers by touching them with the cheese.

4. Killer tomato—The tomatoes will chase the cheese. If a tomato catches the cheese, the game ends.

Game sprites

Each of these screen objects is called a *sprite*. A sprite has an image drawn on the screen, a position on the screen, and a set of behaviors. Each sprite will do the following things:

1. Initialize itself when the game is loaded.

2. Draw itself on the screen.

3. Update itself. Each sprite will have a characteristic behavior.

4. Reset itself between games. When we start a new game, we must reset the state of each sprite.

Sprites might have other behaviors, but these are the fundamental things that a sprite must do. We can put these behaviors into a class:

```
class Sprite {

    constructor(game, url) {                              Sprite constructor
        this.game = game;                       Store the game the sprite is part of
        this.url = url;                         Store the path to the sprite image
    }

    reset(){                                        Rest the sprite for a new game
        this.x=0;
        this.y=0;
    }

    getInitializePromise() {                    Get a promise to perform initialization
        return new Promise((resolve, reject) => {
            this.image = new Image();
            this.image.src = this.url;
            this.image.onload = () => {
                this.reset();                   Reset the sprite when the image has loaded
                resolve(true);                      Resolve the load promise
            }
            this.image.onerror = () => reject(new Error('Could not load' + this.url));
        });
    }

    update(){                                           Update the sprite
    }

    draw() {                                            Draw the sprite
        this.game.context.drawImage(this.image, this.x, this.y);
    }
}
```

Sprite superclass

The code above defines the superclass for all the sprites in the game. You may have some questions about it.

Question: What is the game parameter used for in the initializer?

> **Answer:** When the game creates a new sprite, it must tell the sprite which game it is part of because some sprites will need to use information stored in the game object. For example, if a cracker is "captured," the score value in the game will need to be updated. The sprite constructor makes a copy of the game reference so that it can interact with the game when it needs to.
>
> Programmers say that the sprite class and the game class will be tightly coupled. Changes to the code in the CrackerChaseGame class might affect the behavior of sprites in the game. If the programmer of the CrackerChaseGame class changes the name of the variable that stores the score from score to gameScore, the Update method in the Cracker class will fail when a cracker is captured.
>
> I think about coupling in the same way I think about global variables. Global variables are an easy way to allow several functions to share application data. However, when I write the code, I have to make sure that none of my functions change the value of a global variable in a way that the other functions weren't expecting. A mistake I make in one function might cause another to fail.
>
> Coupling classes together makes it easier for them to cooperate, but it also means that changes to one class might break behaviors in the other class. When I decide to use global variables or couple two classes together, I'm always aware that I'm balancing convenience (easier and quicker to write) against risk (slightly more vulnerable to mistakes).

Question: Why is the update method empty?

> **Answer:** You can think of the Sprite class as a *template* for subclasses. Some of the game elements will need methods to implement update and reset behaviors. The cheese sprite will need an update method that moves it around the screen. The cheese class will be a subclass of Sprite and add its own version of this method.

Question: How is the getInitializePromise method used?

> **Answer:** The game will create a list that contains all the sprites in it. Once all the sprites have been created, the game will then create a list of initialise promises from the sprites that it will feed into a call of Promise.all. In other words, the promise behavior that we used to load individual images in the previous section has been moved into the Sprite class.

The Sprite class doesn't do much, but it can be used to manage the background image for this game. The game will take place on a "tablecloth" background. We can think of this as a sprite that fills the screen. We can now make our first version of the game object that contains a game loop that just displays the background sprite.

The game object

The `CrackerChaseGame` object holds all the game data, including a list of all the sprites that the game will use. It also holds methods that will enable the gameplay.

```
class CrackerChaseGame {

    gameUpdate(timeStamp) {                                          Method to update the game

        for (let sprite of this.sprites) {                          Update all the sprites
            sprite.update();
        }

        for (let sprite of this.sprites) {                          Draw all the sprites
            sprite.draw();
        }
                                                                    Request the next update
        window.requestAnimationFrame(this.gameUpdate.bind(this));
    }

    gameReset() {                                                   Reset all the sprites
        for (let sprite of this.sprites) {
            sprite.reset();
        }
    }

    constructor() {
                                                                    Get a reference to the game canvas
        this.canvas = document.getElementById("canvas");
        this.context = canvas.getContext('2d');                     Get the graphic context for this canvas

        this.canvasWidth = canvas.width;                            Store the canvas width
        this.canvasHeight = canvas.height;                          Store the canvas height

        this.sprites = [];                                          Create an empty sprite list
                                                                    Create a background sprite
        this.background = new Sprite(this, 'images/background.png');
        this.sprites[this.sprites.length] = this.background;
    }                                                               Add the background sprite to the
                                                                    sprite list
    async gameInitialize() {                                        Method to load all the sprite images
        var promiseList = [];                                       Make a promise list
```

```
        for (let sprite of this.sprites) {                Work through the sprites in the game
            promiseList[promiseList.length] = sprite.getInitialisePromise();
        }

        await Promise.all(promiseList);                    Wait for the sprites to finish loading
    }

    gameStart() {                                          Start the game running
        this.gameReset();                                  Reset the game
        window.requestAnimationFrame(this.gameUpdate.bind(this));
    }                                                      Start the game animation running
}
```

CODE ANALYSIS

The CrackerChaseGame class

The code above defines the class that will implement our game. You might have some questions about it.

Question: How does the game pass a reference to itself to the sprite constructor?

Answer: We know that when a method in a class is called, the this keyword represents a reference the object within which the method is running. In a method which is part of the CrackerChaseGame class the keyword this represents a reference to the CrackerGameClass instance. We can pass the value of this into other parts of the game that need it:

```
this.background = new Sprite(this, 'images/background.png');
```

The code above makes a new Sprite instance and sets the value of the game argument to this so that the sprite now knows which game it is part of.

Question: Why does the game call the draw method on the sprite to draw it? Can't the game just draw the image held inside the sprite?

Answer: This is a very important question, and it comes down to responsibility. Should the sprite be responsible for drawing on the screen, or should the game do the drawing? I think drawing should be the sprite's job because it gives the developer a lot more flexibility.

For instance, adding smoke trails to some of the sprites in this game by drawing "smoke" images behind the sprite would be much easier to do if I could just add the code into the "smoky" sprites rather than the game having to work out which sprites needed smoke trails and draw them differently.

Question: Does this mean that when the game runs, the entire screen will be redrawn each time, even if nothing on the screen has changed?

Answer: Yes. You might think that this is wasteful of computer power, but this is how most games work. It is much easier to draw everything from scratch than it is to keep track of changes to the display and only redraw parts that have changed.

Starting the game

Now that we have our game class, we can start the game running. Below is the body of the HTML document for the game. It contains a canvas, and the `<body>` element has an `onload` attribute that calls the JavaScript function `doGame` when the page is loaded.

```html
<body onload="doGame()">
  <canvas id="canvas" width="800" height="600">
    This browser does not support a canvas.
  </canvas>
</body>
```

```javascript
async function doGame() {
    var activeGame = new CrackerChaseGame();
    await activeGame.gameInitialize();
    activeGame.gameStart();
}
```

Below, you can see the `gameStart` method. The first statement calls the `gameReset` method to reset the game and make it ready to play. The second statement calls `window.requestAnimationFrame` to connect the `gameUpdate` method to the next screen animation event. We need to have a detailed look at the code here because it tells us some important things about the `this` reference.

```javascript
gameStart() {
    this.gameReset();                                         Reset the game
    window.requestAnimationFrame(this.gameUpdate.bind(this));
}                                                             Start the animation running
```

Investigating this

We started using the this reference when we created the stock storage objects in the Fashion Shop application in Chapter 10. We discovered that in a method inside a class the keyword this means "a reference to the object that this method is running inside." If this seems confusing, consider the sequence of statements that are being performed. The function doGame contains the following statement to start the game running:

```
activeGame.gameStart();
```

The statement means "follow the reference activeGame to an object and call the gameStart method on that object." The JavaScript system finds the object and calls the gameStart method in it. Just before it runs the code in gameStart, the JavaScript system sets the keyword this to refer to the same object as activeGame. The gameStart method contains the statement:

```
this.gameReset();
```

The statement follows the this reference (which is referring to the activeGame object) and then calls the method gameReset on that object. So everything works as it should, and the correct game object is reset and ready for play. The reference this.gameUpdate refers to the game update method that we want to have called to update our game. So you might think that we can just pass the method reference into the window.requestAnimationFrame method as a parameter.

```
window.requestAnimationFrame(this.gameUpdate);
```

The problem is that the code above does not work because the gameUpdate method will not be called from a reference to the activeGame object. It is called by the JavaScript window object when it is time to redraw the display. In other words, the this reference inside gameUpdate will refer to the wrong thing when the function runs. We can fix this by explicitly binding the this reference in the call of gameUpdate to a reference to the active game object:

```
window.requestAnimationFrame(this.gameUpdate.bind(this));
```

The bind part of the call above is highlighted. It explicitly says to JavaScript "When you call the gameUpdate function, make the value of this in the gameUpdate the same as the value of this in the gameReset function." You might find this confusing. I certainly did. It helps to remember just who is calling the gameUpdate function. It is not called via a reference to a game object; it is called from within the window object. The result is that it can't have a this reference to the active game at the point it runs. So we need to explicitly bind in a value of this for the method to use. If you run the example program in the **Ch12 Creating Games\Ch12-15 Background Display** folder, you will see the background displayed.

Add a cheese sprite

The player sprite will be a piece of cheese that is steered around the screen. We've seen how a game can respond to keyboard events; now we'll create a player sprite and get the game to control it. The Cheese class below implements the player object in our game.

```
class Cheese extends Sprite {
    constructor(game, url) {
        super(game,url);

        this.width = game.canvasWidth / 15;
        this.height = game.canvasWidth / 15;

        this.speed = 5;
        this.xSpeed = 0;
        this.ySpeed = 0;

        window.addEventListener("keydown", (event) => {
            switch(event.code){
                case 'ArrowLeft':
                    this.xSpeed = -this.speed;
                    break;
                case 'ArrowRight':
                    this.xSpeed = this.speed;
                    break;
                case 'ArrowUp':
                    this.ySpeed = -this.speed;
                    break;
                case 'ArrowDown':
                    this.ySpeed = this.speed;
                    break;
            }
        });
```

```
        window.addEventListener("keyup", (event) => {
            switch(event.code){
                case 'ArrowLeft':
                    this.xSpeed = 0;
                    break;
                case 'ArrowRight':
                    this.xSpeed = 0;
                    break;
                case 'ArrowUp':
                    this.ySpeed = 0;
                    break;
                case 'ArrowDown':
                    this.ySpeed = 0;
                    break;
            }
        });
    }

    update(){
        super.update();

        this.x = this.x + this.xSpeed;
        this.y = this.y + this.ySpeed;

        if(this.x<0) this.x=0;
        if(this.x + this.width > this.game.canvasWidth){
            this.x = this.game.canvasWidth - this.width;
        }

        if(this.y<0) this.y=0;
        if(this.y + this.height > this.game.canvasHeight){
            this.y = this.game.canvasHeight - this.height;
        }
    }

    draw() {
        this.game.context.drawImage(this.image, this.x, this.y, this.width, this.height);
    }
}
```

Player sprite

The code above defines the Cheese sprite. You can find it in the **Ch12 Creating Games\ Ch12-16 Background and Cheese** sample code folder. Use your browser to open the web page there.

You can use your cursor to move the cheese around the canvas. Note what happens when your cheese reaches the edge of the canvas. You might have some questions about this.

Question: Why does the Cheese object have width and height properties?

> **Answer:** Unless you specify otherwise, an image is drawn with the size of the original resource. The playfield image is 800 pixels wide and 600 pixels high and fits the canvas perfectly. However, I want to be able to control the size of the cheese sprite so that I can vary the game play. If we find out during testing that the players would like a larger cheese, I want to make this as easy as possible. Use this code to change the size of the cheese to one-fifteenth of the screen width:

```
this.width = game.canvasWidth / 15;
this.height = game.canvasWidth / 15;
```

> At the moment this is done, the drawImage function can draw an image in a particular width, so the Cheese class *overrides* the draw method in the parent Sprite class.

```
draw() {
    this.game.context.drawImage(this.image, this.x, this.y, this.width, this.height);
}
```

> This also makes it possible for the game to change the size of the cheese during the game.

Question: How does the program stop the cheese from moving off the screen?

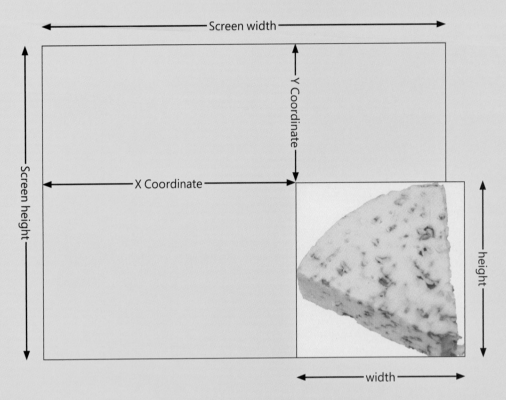

Answer: If you try to steer the cheese off the screen with the arrow keys, you will find that you can't. The image above shows how this works. The game knows the position of the cheese and the width and height of the canvas. If the x position plus the width of the cheese is greater than the width of the screen (as it is in the image above), the update method for the cheese will put the cheese back on the right edge:

```
if(this.x + this.width > this.game.canvasWidth){
    this.x = this.game.canvasWidth - this.width;
}
```

The cheese update method also makes sure that the cheese cannot be moved off the other edges of the canvas. The game also uses the width and height properties to place the cheese in the middle of the canvas at the start of the game.

```
reset() {
    this.x = (this.game.canvasWidth - this.width) / 2.0;
    this.y = (this.game.canvasHeight - this.height) / 2.0;
}
```

Add a Cracker sprite

Moving the cheese around the screen is fun for a while, but we need to add some targets for the player. The targets are crackers the player must capture with the cheese. When a cracker is captured, the game score is increased, and the cracker moves to another random position on the screen. The Cracker sprite is a subclass of the Sprite class:

```
class Cracker extends Sprite {

    constructor(game, url) {
        super(game, url);

        this.width = game.canvasWidth / 20;
        this.height = game.canvasWidth / 20;
    }

    getRandomInt(min, max) {
        var range = max - min + 1;
        var result = Math.floor(Math.random() * (range)) + min;
        return result;
    }

    reset() {
        this.x = this.getRandomInt(0, this.game.canvasWidth-this.width)
        this.y = this.getRandomInt(0, this.game.canvasWidth-this.height)
    }

    draw() {
        this.game.context.drawImage(this.image, this.x, this.y, this.width, this.height);
    }
}
```

The Cracker class is very small because it gets most of its behavior from its superclass, the Sprite class. The constructor sets the width of a cracker to a 20th of the screen size. The reset method for the cracker picks a random location on the canvas. It uses the same random number function that we used to position dots in the art program. We can add a Cracker to our game by creating it and then adding it to the list of sprites in the game:

```
this.sprites = [];

this.background = new Sprite(this, 'images/background.png');
this.sprites[this.sprites.length] = this.background;

this.cracker = new Cracker(this, 'images/cracker.png');
this.sprites[this.sprites.length] = this.cracker;

this.cheese = new Cheese(this, 'images/cheese.png');
this.sprites[this.sprites.length] = this.cheese;
```

The sample in the **Ch12 Creating Games\Ch12-17 Cheese and Cracker** folder shows how this works. See **Figure 12-5**.

Figure 12-5   Cheese and cracker

Add lots of crackers

We would like to have 30 crackers in the game for the player to chase after. It turns out that this is very easy to do. We can use a loop to create crackers and add them to the sprite list.

```
for (let i = 0; i < 30; i = i + 1) {
    this.sprites[this.sprites.length] = new Cracker(this, 'images/cracker.png');
}
```

Figure 12-6 shows the game now. If we want to have even more crackers, we just need to change the limit of the range in the for loop that creates them. The sample in the **Ch12 Creating Games\Ch12-18 Cheese and Crackers** folder contains this code. If you run the sample, you will see a screen full of crackers that a player can move the cheese over.

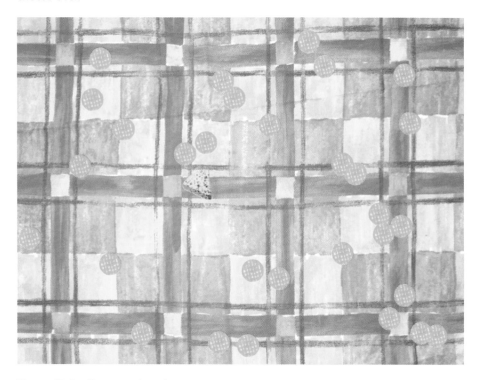

Figure 12-6 Cheese and crackers

Catch the crackers

The game now has lots of crackers and a piece of cheese that can chase them. But nothing happens when the cheese "catches" a cracker. We need to add a behavior to the Cracker that detects when the cracker has been "caught" by the cheese. A cracker is caught by the cheese when the cheese moves "on top" of it. The game can detect when this happens by testing whether rectangles enclosing the two sprites intersect.

Figure 12-7 shows the cheese in the process of catching a cracker. The rectangles around the cheese and cracker images are called bounding boxes. When one bounding box moves "inside" another, we say that the two are intersecting. When the cracker updates, it will test to see whether it intersects with the cheese. The cheese is intersecting with the cracker because the right and bottom edges are "inside" the cheese.

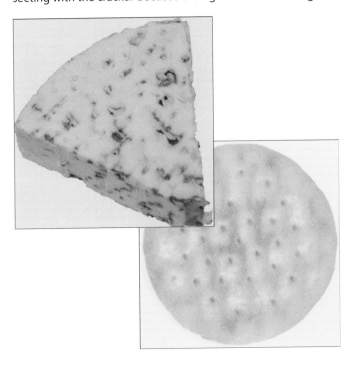

Figure 12-7   Intersecting sprites

Figure 12-8 shows how the test will work. In this figure, the two sprites are not intersecting because the right edge of the cheese is to the left of the left edge of the cracker. In other words, the cheese is too far to the left to intersect with the cracker. This would also be true if the cheese were above, below, or to the right of the cracker.

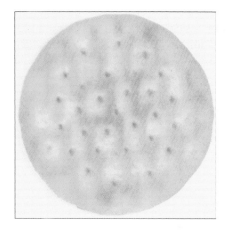

Figure 12-8 Nonintersecting sprites

We can create a method that tests for these four situations. If any of them are true, the rectangles do not intersect.

```
intersectsWith(sprite) {
    if ((this.x + this.width) < sprite.x) return false;
    if ((this.y + this.height) < sprite.y) return false;
    if (this.x > (sprite.x + sprite.width)) return false;
    if (this.y > (sprite.y + sprite.width)) return false;
    return true;
}
```

The method can be added to the Sprite class. The method returns true if the sprite intersects with a particular target. We add this method to the Sprite class so that all sprites can use it. Now we can add an update method to the Cracker class that checks to see whether the cracker intersects with the cheese:

```
update() {
    if (this.intersectsWith(this.game.cheese)) {
        this.reset();
    }
}
```

When the cheese moves over a cracker, it is reset to a different position in the screen. The sample in the **Ch12 Creating Games\Ch12-19 Eating Crackers** folder contains this code. If you run the sample, you will see a screen full of crackers that a player can move the cheese over. When the cheese is moved over a cracker, the cracker disappears and is redrawn somewhere else on the screen.

Add sound

At the moment our game is silent, which is a bit boring. We could improve the cracker class so that it plays a sound when it is eaten. We've made JavaScript programs that play sound in the past. We added a sound element to the egg timer in Chapter 2. Our game can make sound by using an Audio object:

```
constructor(game, imageUrl, audioURL) {          Constructor now accepts audio URL
    super(game, imageUrl);

    this.audioURL = audioURL;                    Store the URL for the sound resource
    this.audio = new Audio();                    Set the src of the Audio item to the resource
    this.audio.src = this.audioURL;              Create a new Audio item

    this.width = game.canvasWidth / 20;
    this.height = game.canvasWidth / 20;
}
```

The constructor for the Cracker class now accepts an additional parameter giving the URL that specifies the location of the sound resource. When the Cracker constructor runs, it creates an Audio object for the sound effect and then sets the src property of the new Audio object to the sound resource location.

```
this.cracker = new Cracker(this, 'images/cracker.png', 'sounds/burp.wav');
```

When the cracker is created, the constructor is given a path to the sound file to be used. The update method can now play the sound whenever the cheese "eats" a cracker:

```
update() {
    if (this.intersectsWith(this.game.cheese)) {
        this.reset();
        this.audio.play();                              Play the sound effect
    }
}
```

You can find the noisy version of the game in the **Ch12 Creating Games\Ch12-20 Eating with sound** example folder. If you want to create your own sound effects, you can use the program Audacity to capture and edit sounds. It is a free download from *http://www.audacityteam.org/* and is available for most types of computers.

Adding scores

Keeping score is another great way to motivate the player of a game. In Cracker Chase, the player will increase their score by 10 each time they eat a cracker.

```
update() {
    if (this.intersectsWith(this.game.cheese)) {
        this.game.score = this.game.score + 10;         Increase the score
        this.reset();
        this.audio.play();                              Play the sound effect
    }
}
```

The Cracker update method above adds 10 to the score in the game each time a cracker is eaten. The score value is held in the CrackerChaseGame class and is drawn each time the screen is updated:

```
gameUpdate(timeStamp) {

    for (let sprite of this.sprites) {
        sprite.update();
    }
```

```
    for (let sprite of this.sprites) {
        sprite.draw();
    }

    this.context.font = "40px Arial";————————— Set the font and size for the score display
    this.context.fillStyle = "red";————————————— Set the color for the score display
    this.context.fillText("Score: " + this.score, 10, 40);———————— Draw the score

    window.requestAnimationFrame(this.gameUpdate.bind(this));
}
```

We draw the score on the canvas using a set of methods from the canvas context that we've not seen before. The fillText method draws filled text on the screen. The fillStyle method lets us set the color of the text, and we can set the text size and style by assigning a value to the font property of the context.

Figure 12-9 shows how the score is displayed. You can find the scoring version of the game in the **Ch12 Creating Games\Ch12-21 Eating with scores** example folder.

Figure 12-9   Score display

Bad collision detection

There are some problems with using bounding boxes to detect collisions. The image above shows that the cheese and the cracker are not colliding, but the game will think that they are. This should not be too much of a problem for our game. It makes it easier for the player, as they don't always have to move the cheese right over the cracker to score a point. However, the player might have grounds for complaint if the game decides they have been caught by a killer tomato because of this issue. There are a few ways to solve this problem:

- When the bounding boxes intersect (as they do above), we could check the intersecting rectangle (the part where the two bounding boxes overlap) to see if they have any pixels in common. Doing so provides very precise collision detection, but it will slow down the game.

- We could make the bounding boxes slightly smaller so that they don't overlap as much.

- We could detect collisions using distance rather than intersection, which works well if the sprites are mostly round.

- The final solution is the one I like best. I could make all the game images rectangular, so the sprites fill their bounding boxes, and the player always sees when they have collided with something.

Add a killer tomato

Currently, the game is not much of a game. There is no jeopardy for the player. When you make a game, you set up something that the player is trying to achieve. Then you add some elements that will make this difficult for them. In the case of the game Cracker Chase, I want to add "killer tomatoes" that will relentlessly hunt down the player. As the game progresses, I want the player to be chased by increasing numbers of tomatoes until the game becomes all about survival. The tomatoes will be interesting because I'll give them "artificial intelligence" and physics.

Add "artificial intelligence" to a sprite

Artificial intelligence sounds difficult to achieve, but in the case of this game, it is actually very simple. At its heart, artificial intelligence in a game simply means making a program that would behave like a person in that situation. If you were chasing me, you'd do this by moving toward me. The direction you would move would depend on my position relative to you. If I were to your left, you'd move left, and so on. We can put the same behavior into our killer tomato sprite:

```
if(this.game.cheese.x > this.x){
    this.xSpeed = this.xSpeed + this.acceleration;
}
else {
    this.xSpeed = this.xSpeed - this.acceleration;
}

if(this.game.cheese.y > this.y){
    this.ySpeed = this.ySpeed + this.acceleration;
}
else {
    this.ySpeed = this.ySpeed - this.acceleration;
}
```

This condition shows how we can make an intelligent killer tomato. It compares the x positions of the cheese and the tomato. If the cheese is to the right of the tomato, the x speed of the tomato is increased to make it move to the right. If the cheese is to the left of the tomato, it will accelerate in the other direction. The code above then repeats the process for the vertical positions of the two sprites. The result is a tomato that will move intelligently toward the cheese. We could instead make a "cowardly" tomato that runs away from the player by making the acceleration negative so that the tomato accelerates in the opposite direction of the cheese. This would be useful for games where the player has to chase down targets.

PROGRAMMER'S POINT

Making game elements "intelligent" makes games much more interesting

Artificial intelligence (AI) is the field of computing that aims to make software that can do things that normally require human intelligence. Making a "killer tomato" that always chases the cheese is not necessarily creating AI, but it is a great way to make gameplay more interesting for the player. It gets especially interesting if you have a number of different objects with different "intelligent" behaviors for the player to deal with.

Add physics to a sprite

Each time the game updates, it can update the position of the objects on the screen. The amount that each object moves each time the game updates is the speed of the object. When the player is moving, the cheese's position is updated by the value 5. In other words, when the player is holding down a movement key, the position of the cheese in that direction is being changed by 5. The updates occur 60 times per second because this is the rate at which the game loop runs. In other words, the cheese would move 300 pixels (60*5) in a single second. We can increase the speed of the cheese by adding a larger value to the position each time it is updated. If we used a speed value of 10, we'd find that the cheese would move twice as fast.

Acceleration is the amount that the speed value is changing. The statements below update the xSpeed of the tomato by the acceleration and then apply this speed to the position of the tomato.

```
this.xSpeed = this.xSpeed + this.acceleration;
this.x = this.x + this.xSpeed;
```

The initial speed of the tomato is set to zero, so each time the tomato is updated, the speed (and hence the distance it moves) will increase. If we do this in conjunction with "artificial intelligence," we get a tomato that will move rapidly toward the player.

Add friction to a sprite

If we just allowed the tomato to accelerate continuously, we'd find that the tomato would just get faster and faster, and the game would become unplayable. The statement below adds some "friction" to slow down the tomato. The friction value is less than 1, so each time we multiply the speed by the friction, it will be reduced, which will cause the tomato to slow down over time.

```
this.xSpeed = this.xSpeed * this.friction;
```

The friction and acceleration values are set in the constructor for the Tomato sprite:

```
constructor(game, imageUrl) {
    super(game, imageUrl);

    this.width = game.canvasWidth / 12;
    this.height = game.canvasWidth / 12;
    this.acceleration = 0.1;
    this.friction = 0.99;
}
```

After some experimentation, I came up with the acceleration value of 0.1 and a friction value of 0.99. If I want a sprite that chases me more quickly, I can increase the acceleration. If I want the sprite to slow down more quickly, I can increase the friction. You can have a lot of fun playing with these values. You can create sprites that drift slowly toward the player and, by making the acceleration negative, you can make them run away from the player. You can have some fun avoiding the killer tomato with the game example in the **Ch12 Creating Games\Ch12-22 Killer tomato** folder.

PROGRAMMER'S POINT

When you write a game, you can always cheat

When you're writing a game, you should always start with the simplest, fastest way of getting an effect to work and then improve it if necessary.

The "physics" that I'm using are not really an accurate simulation of physical objects. The way that I've implemented friction is not very realistic, but it works and gives the player a good experience. I find it interesting that six or seven lines of JavaScript can make something that behaves in such a believable way. The Cracker Chase game uses very simple collision detection, a form of artificial intelligence, and physics, but it is still fun to play. It really feels as if the tomatoes are chasing you. Making the physics model completely accurate would take a lot of extra work and would add very little to the gameplay.

Create timed sprites

It's important that a game be progressive. If the game started with lots of killer tomatoes, the player would not last very long and would not enjoy the experience. I'd like the first tomato to appear after five seconds and a new tomato to appear every 10 seconds after that. We can do this by giving each tomato an "entry delay" value when we construct it:

```
for (let tomatoCount = 0; tomatoCount < 5; tomatoCount = tomatoCount + 1) {
    let entryDelay = 300 + (tomatoCount * 600);
    this.sprites[this.sprites.length] =
        new Tomato(this, 'images/tomato.png', entryDelay);
}
```

This code uses a loop to create 5 tomato sprites with delay values starting at 300 and going up in steps of 600. The constructor in the Tomato class stores the value of entryDelay for that tomato.

```
constructor(game, imageUrl, entryDelay) {
    super(game, imageUrl);

    this.entryDelay = entryDelay;               Store the entry delay in the sprite

    this.width = game.canvasWidth / 12;
    this.height = game.canvasWidth / 12;
    this.acceleration = 0.1 ;                   Give each sprite a different acceleration
    this.friction = 0.99;
}
```

The `entryDelay` value is used to delay the entry of the sprite:

```
update() {

    this.entryCount = this.entryCount + 1;

    if (this.entryCount < this.entryDelay) {
        return;
    }

    .. the rest of the update method goes here
}
```

The `update` method is called 60 times per second. The first tomato has an entry delay of 300, which means that it will arrive at 300/60 seconds, which is 5 seconds after the game starts. The next tomato will appear 10 seconds after that, and so on, up until the last one. When I played the game with 5 tomatoes chasing me, I noticed that the gameplay was not very thrilling because all the sprites merged into one another, making them very easy to avoid. This is because they were all accelerating at the same rate. To fix this, I used the entry delay to calculate a change to the acceleration. This means that the later sprites accelerate more quickly and don't bunch together.

```
this.acceleration = 0.1 + entryDelay / 10000;
```
Give each sprite a different acceleration

The example program in the **Ch12 Creating Games\Ch12-22 Killer tomatoes** folder shows how this works. It can get rather frantic after a few tomatoes have turned up and are chasing you.

Complete the game

We now have a program that provides some gameplay. Now we need to turn this into a proper game. To do so, we need to add a start screen, provide a way that the player can start the game, detect and manage the end of the game, and then add a high score because it adds a lot to the gameplay.

Add a start screen

A start screen is where the player will—you guessed it—start the game. When the game is complete, the game returns to the start screen. **Figure 12-10** shows the start screen for this game.

Figure 12-10   Start screen

The drawStartScreen method draws the start screen. It uses a helper function called displayMessage that centers text on the screen.

```
drawStartScreen(){
    this.background.draw();
    this.context.font = "50px Arial";
    this.displayMessage("Cracker Chase",70);
    this.context.font = "40px Arial";
    this.displayMessage("High score: " + this.topScore, 110);
    this.displayMessage('Welcome to Cracker Chase', 240);
    this.displayMessage('Steer the cheese to capture the crackers', 280);
    this.displayMessage('BEWARE THE KILLER TOMATOES',320);
    this.displayMessage('Arrow keys to move', 470);
    this.displayMessage('Press G to play', 520);
}
```

We saw the screen drawing methods earlier when we added code to the update method that drew the score on the screen. The displayMessage method also uses the measureText method to get the width of the text so that it can be centered on the screen. It draws the text twice. The first time, the text is drawn in black, and then the text is drawn again in red. The second time the text is drawn, it is moved slightly to make it appear that the black text is a shadow.

```
displayMessage(text, yPos){
    var textSize = this.context.measureText(text);      Measure the size of the text message
    var x = (this.canvasWidth-textSize.width)/2.0;      Calculate an offset to center the text
    this.context.fillStyle = "black";                   Set the text to black
    this.context.fillText(text, x, yPos);               Draw the text background
    this.context.fillStyle = "red";                     Set the text to red
    this.context.fillText(text, x+2, yPos+2);           Draw the text slightly offset
}
```

PROGRAMMER'S POINT

Don't worry about making the graphics hardware work for you

You might think it's rather extravagant to draw all the text on the screen twice just to get a shadow effect. However, modern graphics hardware is perfectly capable of many thousands of drawing operations per second. I've been known to draw text 20 times just to get a nicely blurred shadow effect behind it. If you think something might look good, my advice is to try it and only worry about performance if the game seems to run very slowly after you've done it.

Start the game running

The start screen in Figure 12-10 tells the player to press the G key to start the game. So now we need to add the code to make this happen.

```
gameStart() {
    this.drawStartScreen();                                    Draw the start screen
    window.addEventListener("keydown", (event) => {            Bind to the keyboard
        switch (event.code) {
            case 'KeyG':
                if(!this.gameRunning){                         If the game is not running
                    this.gameRun();                            Run the game
                }
                break;
            default:
        }
    });
}
```

The `gameStart` method is called when the user starts the game. It calls `drawStartScreen` to draw the start screen and then binds an arrow function to the `keydown` event. The arrow function checks for the `'KeyG'` key and calls the `gameRun` method if the `gameRunning` property of the game is `false`.

```
gameRun() {
    this.gameReset();
    this.gameRunning = true;                                   Set game running to true
    window.requestAnimationFrame(this.gameUpdate.bind(this));
}
```

The `gameRun` method runs the game, sets `gameRunning` to `true`, and then triggers the first animation frame in the game. When the game is running, the `gameUpdate` method updates the sprites and then checks to see if any of them have ended the game. If the game is over, it displays the start screen and the final game score:

```
for (let sprite of this.sprites) {
    sprite.update();
}
```

```
if (!this.gameRunning) {
    this.drawStartScreen();
    this.displayMessage("Your score: " + this.score, 150);
    return;
}
```

If one of the sprites has ended the game, we display the start screen

Detect the game end

We've seen that the game has two states, which are managed by the gameRunning property. This property is set to true when the game is running and false when the start screen is displayed. Now we need to create the code that manages the gameRunning value. The game ends when the player collides with a killer tomato, which is detected in the update method for the tomato sprite:

```
update() {
    // update the tomato here
    if (this.intersectsWith(this.game.cheese)) {
        this.game.gameEnd();
    }
}
```

The test in the update method for the Tomato sprite checks to see if this tomato intersects the cheese. If it does gameEnd method is called to end the game.

```
gameEnd() {
    this.gameRunning = false;
    if(this.score > this.highScore){
        this.highScore = this.score;
    }
}
```

Stop the game from running
Update the high score

The gameEnd method sets gameRunning to false. It also updates the highScore value. If the current score is greater than the highest score so far, it is updated to the new high score. The value of the high score is displayed on the start screen of the game.

Always make a playable game

Something else I noticed while judging game development competitions was that some teams would produce a brilliant piece of gameplay but not attach it to a game. You'd start playing the game and find that it never actually ended. You should make sure that your game is a complete game from the very start. The game should have a beginning, middle, and end. As you have seen in this section, it's easy to do this, but when people start making a game, they seem to leave it to the last minute to create the game start screen and the game ending code, so that what they produce is not a game. Instead, it is more of a technical demo, which is not quite the same thing. Making your game into a proper game right from the start also makes it much easier for people to try it and then give you feedback.

You can find the completed game in the **Ch12 Creating Games\Ch12-24 Complete Crackerchase** folder. It's fun to play for short bursts, particularly if there are a few of you trying to beat the high score. My highest score so far is 740, but then I never was any good at playing video games.

 MAKE SOMETHING HAPPEN

Build your own game

The Cracker Chase game can be used as the basis of any sprite-based game you might like to create. You can change the artwork, create new types of enemies, make the game two-player, or add extra sound effects. When I said at the start of this book that programming is the most creative thing you can learn to do, this is the kind of thing I was talking about. You can create a game called "Closet Frenzy" where you are chased around by coat hangers while you search for a matching sock. You could create "Walrus Space Rescue," where you must steer an interplanetary walrus through an asteroid minefield. Anything you can think up, you can build. However, one word of caution. Don't have too many ideas. I've seen lots of game development teams get upset because they can't get all their ideas to work at once. It is much more sensible to get something simple working and then add things to it later.

Now that you know how a game works, you can take a look at some game engines, which do a lot of the hard work for you. The Phasor game engine is a great place to start, with many example games you can use as starting points. You can find it at *https://phaser.io*. If you want to create multiplayer games, you should take a look at Socket.io, which you can use to create a game that is hosted on a Node.js server and can be played by people all over the world. You can find it at *https://socket.io/*.

What you have learned

1. An HTML document can contain a canvas element within which items can be drawn at arbitrary positions.

2. JavaScript can draw Image objects on a canvas at a particular position and of a particular size.

3. JavaScript images are loaded asynchronously. The `onload` event will fire when an image is loaded. This can be used to create a `Promise` object to manage a load.

4. A number of simultaneous promises can be placed in a list and resolved with a single call of `Promise`, all of which generates a promise that returns when all the promises in the list have been fulfilled.

5. An asynchronous JavaScript function (one which has been declared with `async`) can use the `await` keyword to await the result of a promise. The asynchronous function is suspended while the result of the promise is awaited. Suspended functions do not block browser execution.

6. Animation in a game is achieved by repeated redrawing of the game screen. The `window.requestAnimationFrame` method allows a game to bind a function call to the screen redraw event in the browser.

7. A game can bind to window events including `keyup` and `keydown` events that produce events specifying which keyboard key has been pressed or released. Keyboard events do not necessarily indicate that a printable character has been entered. There are events for Shift and Control keys, which all have characteristic names.

8. It is also possible to bind to an event that indicates that the user has moved their window "focus" to another window—at which point, a game should stop updating.

9. The display of a game can be made up of sprites. A sprite is an object that has an associated image, position, and perhaps other properties such as speed and acceleration.

10. A class hierarchy containing a Sprite superclass and game object subclasses is a good way to manage the objects in a game. A class can also be used for the game itself. The game class contains a list which holds all the sprites as well as properties that indicate the state of the game.

11. The `this` reference to be used in a function body can be bound to a specific reference by adding bind information to the call of the function. This technique is especially useful when functions are to be called by external frameworks (such as the browser window object) and you want to set the context of the function call to be an object in your application.

12. Sprites in a game can be given simple physics and "artificial intelligence" that allows them to interact with the player and make the game much more interesting.

Hopefully, you've also taken a few ideas of your own and used them to create some more games.

Here are some points to ponder about game development:

What does `await` do?

`Await` is a way of allowing a function to return "early" if code in the function must perform an operation that will take a long time. To understand how this works, imagine if I had the power to make copies of myself. When I went shopping, I could select all the items I wanted to buy, make a duplicate Rob, and then send him to pay for the items and bring them home. I could go home and get on with something more interesting. At some point in the future, "duplicate Rob" would turn up with my shopping.

The `await` keyword works in exactly the same way. When execution reaches an `await` statement, a new process is created, which will wait for the awaited promise to be fulfilled. In the meantime, execution returns from the function containing the `await`. When the awaited promise is fulfilled, the process then moves on to the statement in the function after the awaited one. This continues until the process reaches the end of the function, at which point the process is destroyed.

Functions that contain awaited operations are called "asynchronous." We don't know when they will finish executing. With a normal function, we know that when the function returns it has performed all the statements in the function. However, an asynchronous function will return before any awaited actions have finished. In other words, completion of the function is not synchronized with the call. For this reason, we need to mark functions that contain `await` as `async`.

Can a function contain multiple `await`s?

Yes, it can. Each awaited statement is awaited in turn as the function is performed.

Must a function that is called asynchronously always perform an awaited action?

No. Sometimes when a function runs, it might decide that the awaited action cannot be performed, so it can return without awaiting anything. However, marking a function as `async` makes it slightly less efficient to call, so you should only mark a function as `async` if it contains `await`.

Can an anonymous function contain `await`**s?**

Yes, it can. However, the declaration of the anonymous function must be preceded by the `async` keyword to mark the anonymous function as asynchronous.

Can you draw any HTML element on a canvas?

No. An HTML document brings together a collection of HTML elements. However, when an object is drawn on a canvas all that happens is that a particular path or image is rendered onto that canvas. The commands to set the format of drawing actions (for example select a font or fill style to be used) look very similar to attributes that you might add to an HTML element. However, these commands just control the drawing operation, not the properties of an object in the canvas.

Can a page contain multiple HTML canvases?

Yes. A JavaScript program could hold several context references that can be used to draw on different canvases.

Will the browser slow down if I draw a lot on the canvas?

Yes, it will slow down eventually. However, modern browsers are very good at drawing graphics, so you will have to draw something very complicated for this to be noticeable.

How would I create an attract mode for my game?

Many games have an "attract mode" screen as well, which displays some gameplay. Currently, our game just has two states that are managed by the Boolean `gameRunning` property. We could use an integer to hold a range of states, including "attract mode." We could make an "AI player" who moved the cheese around the screen in a random way and then just run the game with the random player at the controls. We could add an "attract mode" behavior to the tomatoes so that they were aiming for a point some distance from the player, to make the game last longer in demo mode.

How could I make the gameplay the same each time the game is played?

The game uses the JavaScript random number generator to produce the position of the crackers, which means each time the game runs, the crackers are in a different position. We could replace this with a random number generator that always produced the same sequence of numbers, or we could add a table of fixed positions that could be used to place the crackers. This would mean that the crackers would be drawn and would respawn in the same sequence each time the game was played. A determined player could learn the pattern and use this to get a high score.

Is the author of the game always the best person at playing it?

Most definitely not. I'm often surprised how other people can be much better than me at playing games I've created. Sometimes, they even try to help me with hints and tips about things to do in the game to get a higher score.

Index

Symbols

* (asterisk) character, 52, 101

\ (backslash) character, 120, 141

` (backtick) character, 119, 141, 143

= (equals) character, 47, 107

+ (plus) operator, 111, 119, 120

; (semicolon) character, 76

{ } (curly braces), 161, 173, 288, 296, 319

[ ] (square brackets), 189, 288, 296, 319

" (double quote) character, 119, 141, 143

' (single quote) character, 119, 141, 143

A

`<a>` tag, 41–42

about this book, xv–xvii

abstraction, 305, 344–345

acceleration values, 458

`activeGame` object, 442

`addEventListener` method, 429

adding machine program, 122, 124–126

addition service, 398, 399–400

`addStock` function, 361–362

`alert` function, 12, 52, 213

`alertInputText` ID, 46

aligning text, 71, 88

alternative text, 39

analyzing data, 370–371

Andreessen, Marc, 28

animating images, 427–429

anonymous functions

    `awaits` contained in, 468

    code analysis of, 375–376

    explanation of, 374, 402, 405

    simplifying promises using, 383

`appendChild` method, 200

applets, 5

applications

    adding machine, 122, 124–126

    data-processing, 96–97

    digital dice, 222–232, 236

    egg timer, 52–56

    fashion shop, 335–363, 368–379

    ice cream sales, 242–269

    multiplication table, 196–203

    pizza calculator, 127–131

    ride selector, 161–172, 178–196

drawing

    on canvas, 410–413, 419–425, 468

    computer-generated, 414–419, 440

`drawStartScreen` method, 462, 463

E

egg timer program, 52–56

    functions used in, 52

    investigation exercise, 53–54

    sound added to, 55

Eich, Brendan, 5

elements, 37, 46, 58, 246

Elements window, 8

`else` keyword, 159, 160, 174

`<em>` tag, 30, 60

`em` units, 70, 88, 90

emojis, meanings of, 33

empty objects, 288, 300, 316

encapsulation, 234

`end` method, 392

end tags, 32

`entryDelay` value, 459–460

equality operator, 151, 152, 153, 174

equals (=) character, 47, 107

error handling

    adding to applications, 227–232

    JavaScript promises and, 384

errors

    exceptions and, 330–334, 363

    finding in advance, 228–233

    floating-point values and, 114–115

    importance of managing, 335

    logic, 109–110

    spelling, 110

    testing for, 110, 126

    See also bugs; faults

escape sequences, 120, 141, 143

event handlers, 421

events

    attributes of, 87

    definition of, 421

    keyboard, 430–435

    window, 429–430

exceptions

    catching, 327

    errors and, 330–334, 363, 386

    explanation of, 299, 324, 364–365

    handling of, 327–330

    JSON use of, 299, 324, 325–326

Express system, 401

expressions

    Boolean, 149–150

    evaluated by JavaScript, 100–102, 111

    operators and operands in, 100, 110, 141

    processing data with, 100

<input> tag, 44–45, 244, 278, 318

input paragraphs, 254–257, 258

input validation, 175

installing

    Git program, 14

    Node.js program, 387–389

    Visual Studio Code program, 15–16

Internet of Things (IoT), 97

Internet vs. World Wide Web, 59

isNaN function, 230

J

Java programming language, 5, 346

JavaScript

    Boolean thinking in, 146–157

    data processing in, 99, 100, 104

    evaluating expressions with, 100–102

    examples of talking to, 10–12

    exceptions thrown by, 324, 364–365

    functions and statements in, 43

    HTML and, 45–50, 58, 199–201

    identifiers in, 108–109

    local storage, 292–295

    origins and intention of, 5

    programming languages and, 4–5, 6, 23

    prototype example, 279–280

    tools for working with, 13

    variables in, 46, 58, 105–108

    web browsers and, 6

JPEG file format, 419

JSON (JavaScript Object Notation), 295–299

    adding type info to, 355–356

    class hierarchy and, 355

    code analysis of using, 299

    encoding object data with, 295–298, 317

    example of working with, 296–297

    exceptions thrown by, 299, 324, 325–326

    fetched data and, 382

    validator web page, 327

JSONparse method, 356, 357

K

keyboard events, 430–435

    code analysis, 430–431, 432–433

    gameUpdate function, 433–435

    object position control, 431, 432–433

keydown event, 429–430, 433, 463

keyup event, 431, 433

keywords, 24

L

label element, 244, 255

lambda functions, 375

layouts

    fixed-width, 268–269

    paragraph, 34

    styles vs., 81

length property, 271

objects, 288, 316–317

    abstraction using, 344–345

    class creation and, 339–340

    constructors and, 340–341

    creating, 288–291, 339

    empty, 288, 300, 316

    example of using, 291–292

    JSON for encoding data in, 295–298

    polymorphism and, 350

    position control for, 431

    promise, 381–382, 424, 426

    properties of, 50–51, 300, 316–317

    references to, 49, 60, 290–291, 299, 317

    schema for building, 308

    storing data in, 288, 292–293, 295

`<ol>` element, 164

`onclick` attribute, 43, 225, 236

`onerror` event, 421

`oninput` function, 313–314, 315

`onload` event, 74, 77, 253, 421, 441

`onmouseout` event, 67

`onmouseover` event, 66, 86

`openPage` function, 361

OpenWeather service, 379, 398

operands, 100, 110, 141, 142

operators, 100, 110, 141, 142

    comparison, 150–152

    logical, 154–157

    numeric, 111

ordered lists, 164

overlapping elements, 37

overriding methods, 350–352

P

`<p>` tag, 34

paragraphs

    creating input, 254–257, 258

    laying out text in, 34

parameters

    arguments and, 216–217

    functions with multiple, 218

    as values, 217

`parse` method

    JSON strings and, 297, 299, 317, 325–326

    URL strings and, 395–396, 397

party games, 137–140

paths

    defining and drawing, 412

    in URL structure, 29, 393

    using multiple, 394–396

Petzold, Charles, 104

Phasor game engine, 465

physics of games, 457–458, 459

pixels, 39, 78, 88, 90

pizza calculator, 127–129

playback control, 56, 140

player sprite, 445–446

plus (+) operator, 111, 119, 120

PNG file format, 419

polymorphism, 350

`pos` variable, 284, 285

`<pre>` tag, 35–36

preformatted text, 35–36, 59

Preview image editor, 419

`print` function, 12

problem solving, 311

programming languages, 4–5, 6

    compiled, 23

    determining the "best," 5

    scripting, 23, 102

programs

    audio added to, 55

    bugs vs. faults in, 67

    comments added to, 131–133, 141

    data processing in, 98–99

    error handling for, 227–232

    good specifications for, 134

    interpreting, 102

    user interface for, 162, 163–165

    variables in, 105–108

    See also applications

`Promise.all` method, 422–423, 426

promises, 381–387, 405–406

    controller function for, 422

    explanation of, 381–382, 386, 403, 405

    `finally` function in, 385

    handling errors in, 384

    image loading, 421–425

    importance of understanding, 427

    investigating, 385–387

    JSON delivery process, 382

    managing multiple, 422–423, 426

    simplifying with anonymous functions, 383

    text delivery process, 384

    waiting for results of, 424–425, 426

properties

    attributes vs., 60

    explanation of, 300

    object, 50–51, 300, 316–317

property accessors, 300–304

    explanation of, 300, 305, 319

    investigation of, 301–303

property identifiers, 303

`propertyName` variable, 304

proportional fonts, 36

prototypes

    HTML, 277–278

    JavaScript, 279–280

    style sheet, 278–279

pseudocode, 249

`px` unit, 78, 88, 90

Q

query strings, 397–398, 404, 406

quote character, double (") and single ('), 119, 141, 143

R

random artwork, 417–418

random function, 116, 117, 118

random numbers, 116–118, 137–139, 222–226, 469

Raspberry Pi computers, xviii

real numbers

    floating-point numbers and, 114–116

    whole numbers vs., 112–113, 141, 142

recursion, 212

reduce method, 378, 402

refDemo variable, 290–291

references

    as arguments, 219–220

    array of, 372

    game, 440

    object, 49, 60, 290–291, 299, 317

    property accessors and, 319

    stored in JSON strings, 299

relational operators, 152

removeChild method, 201, 204

removeItem function, 295

repeating code, 343

repositories, 17–19

requestAnimationFrame method, 427, 429

requests, HTTP, 406

require function, 389, 401, 403

resetFind function, 314

resource information, xix

responses

    contents of, 404

    JavaScript commands and, 10–12

    requests vs., 406

result variable, 125

return keyword, 222

rgb function, 418

ride selector program, 161–172

    code added to, 165–168

    example of modifying, 178–181

    fixing faults in, 181–183

    switch construction in, 168–170, 171

    user interface for, 162, 163–165

rollover style, 87

running games, 463–464

S

salesItems element, 259–260

sans-serif fonts, 68, 70

saving files, 20

scaffolding, 401

schemas, 304–308

    data storage created from, 309

    designing for applications, 304–305

    HTML built from, 305–308, 358–359

    objects built from, 308

scope of variables, 234–235

scores

    adding to games, 453–454, 464

    displaying in programs, 270

`<script>` element, 43, 58

scripting languages, 23, 102

searching. *See* finding

selectors

    color highlighting using, 86–87

    style sheets using, 80

semicolon (;) character, 76

`sendResponse` function, 395

serif fonts, 68, 70

servers

    code analysis of using, 390–392

    deploying Node.js, 401

    process of building, 396

    See also web servers

service function, 404

`setAttribute` method, 187

`setInterval` function, 74, 77, 88, 427

`setItem` method, 294, 295

`setTimeout` function, 52, 54, 57, 58

`setup` element, `for` loop, 191

shadow effect, 164–165, 462

side effects, 136, 137

single quote (') character, 119, 141, 143

slide shows, 57

software. *See* programs

solving problems, 311

`sort` method, 371–373, 374

sorting data, 371–373, 376–377, 402

sound

    adding, 55, 140, 452–453

    playback control, 56, 140

source code, 13

source code highlighting, 24

source code management (SCM) software, 14

Source Control dialog, 18

`<span>` element, 84–85, 88, 90

specifications, 134

spelling errors, 110

sprites, 436–438, 443–452, 456–460

    AI added to, 456–457

    cheese, 443–444

    cracker, 447–452

    friction added to, 458

    killer tomato, 456–458

    physics of, 457–458, 459

    player, 445–446

    superclass for, 438

    timed, 459–460

square brackets [ ], 189, 288, 296, 319

`src` attribute, 39, 55, 57, 420

start and end tags, 32

start screen for games, 461–462, 463

`startsWith` method, 312, 314, 317

superclasses

    class hierarchy and, 345

    game sprites and, 438

    inheritance mechanism and, 343–344

    `super` keyword and, 348, 352

`switch` construction, 168–171

    explanation of using, 168–170

    missing breaks in, 171

    path for controlling, 394

symbols, HTML display of, 32–33, 58

synchronized actions, 380

T

TCP/IP protocol, 29

temperature conversion program, 130–131

template, subclass, 438

`test` element, `for` loop, 191

testing

    error, 110, 126

    Node.js, 388

text

    aligning, 71, 88

    alternative, 39

    arrays of, 265

    combining numbers and, 120–121

    converting into numbers, 122–123

    delimiters for, 119

    displaying, 49–50, 462

    emphasizing in HTML, 30

    encoding with JSON, 295–299

    escape sequences for, 120

    fonts selected for, 68–71

    getting from networks, 384

    heading creation, 35

    indicating with quotes, 10

    margins around, 77–79

    paragraph layout, 34

    preformatted, 35–36, 59

    as property accessors, 300–304

    shadow effect, 164–165, 462

    styling, 64, 71

`text` method, 384

`textarea` element, 278, 318

`textContent` property, 49, 50–51

Theme Park Ride Selector. *See* ride selector program

`then` method, 381, 382, 384, 386, 403, 405–406

`this` keyword, 340, 341, 364, 365, 376, 440, 442–443

threads, 426

`throw` statement, 329

ticking clock program, 72–77

    code analysis, 75

    creating, 74–75

    time display, 72–73

timed sprites, 459–460

`timeString` variable, 73

Tiny Contacts application. *See* contacts app

toFixed method, 130

Torvalds, Linus, 14, 24

total variable, 135, 136

totalizer program, 133–137

trim function, 314, 317

true keyword, 146, 147–148

try block, 326, 327, 328

try-catch construction, 326, 327, 328, 363, 386–387

Twitter information, xix

two-dimensional arrays, 272

type attribute, 44

type property, 356

U

<ul> element, 164

undefined value, 106, 107, 141, 142

unordered lists, 188

update element, for loop, 191

update method, 434, 438, 451, 453, 460, 464

URLs (uniform resource locators)

    parse method and, 395–396, 397

    query strings added to, 397–398, 406

    structure of, 28–29, 59, 393

user interface

    designing for customers, 162, 252–254

    examples of building, 163–165, 252–264, 357–359

    improving for contacts app, 309–316

    input paragraph creation, 254–257

users

    reading input from, 44–45

    receiving ideas from, 310, 316

    written stories for, 336

V

validator site, 38, 327

value attribute, 44

values

    Boolean, 146–149, 173, 174

    floating-point, 114–115

    functions returning, 222–226

    NaN, 11, 125, 141, 142, 148, 230, 231

    parameters as, 217

    query, 397

    undefined, 106, 107, 141, 142

var keyword, 48, 72, 75–76, 205, 235, 238

variables

    control, 191

    creating, 48, 72, 75–76, 193, 236, 239

    function of, 46, 105, 141

    global, 134–136, 142, 143, 235, 417

    local, 135, 233–236

    scope of, 234–235

    working with, 106–108

video walkthroughs, xviii

Visual Studio Code program, 13, 25

    App Service Extension, 401

    cloning repositories with, 18–19

color styles added in, 65

editing files with, 19, 20–22

finding files in, 21

font selector in, 69

installing, 15–16

keywords in, 24

Node.js test in, 388

server run in, 390–391

Visual Studio suite, 25

W

weather application, 379–385

web browsers

badly formatted HTML in, 37–38

JavaScript used in, 6

local storage managed by, 293, 318

web pages, 28

building from code, 196–201

fetching with URLs, 28–29

ideas for creating, 57

images added to, 38–40

viewing code on, 6–9, 273

web servers

creating with Node.js, 389–400

deploying Node.js, 401

JavaScript and, 23

web services, 398, 402

websites, 28

while loop, 201–202, 204

whole numbers, 112–113, 141, 142

window events, 429–430

window object, 427, 429

World Wide Web (WWW)

HTML and, 28

Internet vs., 59

World Wide Web Consortium (W3C), 28

write method, 392

Plug into learning at

MicrosoftPressStore.com

The Microsoft Press Store by Pearson offers:

- Free U.S. shipping

- Buy an eBook, get three formats – Includes PDF, EPUB, and MOBI to use with your computer, tablet, and mobile devices

- Print & eBook Best Value Packs

- eBook Deal of the Week – Save up to 50% on featured title

- Newsletter – Be the first to hear about new releases, announcements, special offers, and more

- Register your book – Find companion files, errata, and product updates, plus receive a special coupon* to save on your next purchase

 Pearson